DIAN

DIANE KEATON

Artist and Icon

by DEBORAH C. MITCHELL

McFarland & Company, Inc., Publishers
Jefferson, North Carolina, and London

Library of Congress Cataloguing-in-Publication Data

Mitchell, Deborah C., 1951–
Diane Keaton : artist and icon / by Deborah C. Mitchell.
p.   cm.
Includes bibliographical references and index.
ISBN 0-7864-1082-5 (softcover : 50# alkaline paper) ∞
1. Keaton, Diane.   2. Motion picture actors and actresses—
United States—Biography.   I. Title.
PN2287.K44M56   2001   791.43'028'092—dc21 [B]   2001034247

British Library cataloguing data are available

Cover photograph ©2001 Dewey Nicks/Corbis Outline

Manufactured in the United States of America

*McFarland & Company, Inc., Publishers
Box 611, Jefferson, North Carolina 28640
www.mcfarlandpub.com*

To Lou Giannetti, who taught me new ways of seeing
And to Leo Hogan, whose courage changed my life

Acknowledgments

First, I would like to thank Diane Keaton for being so gracious in talking with me about her films and her career. As one of America's most gifted actresses, she has entertained me and inspired me. In part, this project grew out of my appreciation for her talent and continuing dedication to honest work. I would like to acknowledge her agent and staff—Jeff Field, Laura Citrano, and Elena Ritchie—for their help in setting up the interview sessions. I am also grateful to Woody Allen for taking the time to respond to my questions about his friend and favorite muse.

I owe a huge debt of gratitude to several people at Case Western Reserve University: Park Goist, Christa Carvajal, and Gladys Haddad, who urged me onward and upward with their wise counsel and thoughtful suggestions; my friends Bill Doan and Suzanne Prestien, who encouraged me every step of the way; and, most especially, my mentor, Lou Giannetti, without whose vision and guidance this work would not have been possible.

I would like to thank the following people at Westminster College for their advice and support in this project: James Perkins, Monika Becker, Peggy Cox, Richard Sprow, David Barner, Dorita Bolger, Dean John Deegan, faculty development officer Fritz Horn and so many other thoughtful friends and colleagues who took such an avid interest in my progress. I am grateful to Bill McTaggart for finding several rare articles on Diane Keaton and her photography and to Amy Williams for editing my bibliography.

My deepest thanks goes to my family, especially my mother and my son, Rennie, who took care of me and kept me sane.

I would like to acknowledge the following individuals and institutions for their help in finding publicity photographs and for allowing me to use copyrighted material: Mary Corliss and Jennifer Tobias, Museum of Modern Art, Film Stills Archive; James Monaco, "Looking for Diane Keaton" (© 1977); Stig Bjorkman, *Woody Allen on Woody Allen* (© 1993, Grove/Atlantic, Inc., reprinted by permission); Marcelle Clements, "On the Keaton Track" (© 1993); Guy Flatley, "The Applause You Hear Is for Diane Keaton" (© 1974, *Los Angeles Times,* reprinted by permission); Jack Mathews, "Insecure About Her Insecurity" (© 1995, *Los Angeles Times,* reprinted by permission); Judy Klemesrud, "Diane Keaton: From Mr. Allen to 'Mr. Goodbar'" (© 1977, *New York Times,* reprinted by permission); "Hide and Seek with Diane Keaton" (© 1985 by Dominick Dunne, originally published in *Vanity Fair,* reprinted by permission of William Morris Agency, Inc., on behalf of the author); Larry Worth, "Diane: 50 and Loving It" (© 1996, *New York Post,* reprinted by permission); Annette Insdorf, "Play It Again, Woody" (© 1993); Maureen Dowd, "The Old Pals Act" (© 1993, *The Guardian,* reprinted by permission); "The Life and Lurves of Diane Keaton" (by Ben Fong-Torres from *Rolling Stone,* June 30, 1977, by Straight Arrow Publishers, Inc., 1977, all rights reserved, reprinted by permission); "Woody Allen: The Rolling Stone Interview" (by Anthony DeCurtis from *Rolling Stone,* September 16, 1993, by Straight Arrow Publishers Company, L.P. 1993, all rights reserved, reprinted by permission); John Skow, "Love, Death and La-De-Dah" (© 1977, *Time,* used by permission); Richard Schickel, "Dysfunctioning Just Fine" (© 1995, *Time,* used with permission); Janine Dallas Steffan, "Star Watcher" (© 1997, Seattle Times Company, used with permission); Natalie Gittelson, "The Faces of Diane Keaton" (reprinted with permission of *McCall's Magazine,* copyright © 1978 by Gruner & Jahr USA Publishing); Molly Haskell, "People Are Talking About ... Venus Substitutes" (originally published in *Vogue,* January 1988, reprinted by permission of Georges Borchardt, Inc., for the author); Hal Hinson, "'The Good Mother' and the Far Better Keaton" (© 1988, *The Washington Post*); Sharon Waxman, "Role Reversal: Women Become More of a Force in Film" (© 1997, *The Washington Post*).

Finally, I would like to thank all of the writers who, over the years, have provided invaluable insights into Diane Keaton, the artist and the icon.

Deborah Mitchell
Poland, Ohio

Table of Contents

Introduction:
The Keaton Persona

I've always thought she was born to be a movie star.
  —Woody Allen (*Rolling Stone*, June 30, 1977)

Diane Keaton doesn't act like a movie star. Woody Allen was referring to her talent, not her ego. Australian director Gillian Armstrong, who worked with her on *Mrs. Soffel* (1984), once said that with Keaton "there's none of that sort of star business about being late or not turning up or staying out all night, or any of those things. She is absolutely dedicated and hardworking" (qtd. in Dunne 38). In fact, Keaton has no entourage, no fancy cars. She rejects preferential treatment accorded to the rich and famous. She waits in line for restaurant tables and theater seats—like everybody else. She prefers to live in the margins of Hollywood rather than its limelight, spending time with her family and friends rather than Tinseltown's glitterati. Her interviews and public appearances are rare, and, from the beginning, she has refused to discuss her intimate relationships or much of her private life. After three decades in the business, Keaton remains about as elusive as the Grail.

For that, she is often called the Garbo of her generation. Her behavior, however, has nothing to do with wanting to be alone. It has everything to do with her attitude toward fame. She has repeatedly said: "Too much celebrity is a dangerous territory.... You have to go away from it to have any semblance of reasonableness in your life" (qtd. in Mathews, "Secure" 3).

Yet Diane Keaton is a star. She won an Oscar for Woody Allen's revisionist romantic comedy, *Annie Hall* (1977). She is equally adept at drama, winning critical praise for her performances in *Looking for Mr. Goodbar* (1977), *Interiors* (1978), *Shoot the Moon* (1982), *Mrs. Soffel* (1984), and *The Good Mother* (1988). She received Academy Award nominations for *Reds* (1981) and *Marvin's Room* (1996). Keaton is now a successful producer and director as well as a serious photographer with four books to her credit. By all accounts, she has made it in a highly competitive industry obsessed with youth and given to relegating its female stars of a certain age to its outer galaxies. No small feat. But to hear Keaton tell it, "I've never considered myself an outstandingly popular actress. Let's face it, I never became a superstar" (qtd. in Worth 23). This proclivity to downplay her success and shy away from fame is a Keaton trademark.

Like her friend and mentor, Woody Allen, Keaton resists the seduction of stardom and its trappings by focusing on her work. Once when a fan asked her to autograph a photograph of her and Woody standing in a field of grass, Keaton signed her name in the grass, the signature barely perceptible to the casual observer (Pearlman 1E). While actions like this inspire film critics and journalists to comment on her lack of vanity and ego, it is also Keaton's way of shifting attention from her star status to the work itself. She considers the process as important as, if not more important than, the product.

Keaton often defines herself in terms of work. In 1997, when Oprah Winfrey expressed her awe at Keaton's success as a first-time feature film director, Keaton responded: "Directing is just about work. You put in the time and effort, and you prepare. I'm not a genius director, but I *can* work. Work hard, figure it out, and do your homework." For the past three decades, she has been one of Hollywood's most productive stars, often aligning herself with friends and colleagues who share her dynamic, tireless enthusiasm for learning and trying and doing. Woody Allen and Steve Martin are two such friends who, like Keaton, thrive on moving from one creative project to the next, whether it's acting, directing, producing, or writing.

Critics also regularly compare her to Katharine Hepburn, one of Keaton's favorite actresses, in part because both are firmly rooted in the American work ethic. When Keaton graced the cover of the June 30, 1977, issue of *Rolling Stone*, which included her first major interview,

the headline read: "Diane Keaton, the Next Hepburn." Both women have star images that are intelligent and feisty, honest and private, vulnerable and neurotic, independent and eccentric. In her 1987 profile of Keaton, Lynn Hirschberg noted that "like Hepburn, Keaton is strong-willed and curious and quite definite in her views" (41). Both actresses are adept at playing comedy as well as drama. They frequently placed their careers above their personal lives and won the respect of their peers through hard work, discipline, and perseverance.

There are obvious differences, however, not the least of which is Keaton's humility, a trait not usually associated with Hepburn. And while the older icon, with her Bryn Mawr accent and aristocratic air, hobnobbed with the rich and famous in many of her screen roles, Keaton seldom ventures beyond the middle class, enacting characters for whom nothing comes easily, least of all happiness. With regard to professionalism, though, Keaton found a kindred spirit in her predecessor and remarked: "I'd like a life like Katharine Hepburn's in terms of work. She matured. She made the changes" (qtd. in Gilliatt 38).

Several other characteristics of the Keaton persona appear consistently in her interviews and profiles over the last thirty years. Most writers, for example, mention the duality of Keaton's personality: shy, sensitive, and self-effacing on one hand; ambitious, exacting, and highly opinionated on the other. Charming with an edge, Keaton herself has admitted that while extremely private, she craves attention and approval from others. Many of her film characters exhibit this same two-sided personality. Her star image resolves these contradictory traits of toughness and vulnerability, traits that are difficult to reconcile for many people sitting in the audience. This, in part, accounts for her mass appeal. As film critic Molly Haskell once said, "The truly great stars combine contradictory characteristics" (A&E's *Biography*).

In addition, terms like "humble," "honest," "sexy," "neurotic," "artistic," "American," "modern," and "highly intelligent" are frequently used to describe the star. The emphasis is usually on "sexy" and "intelligent," suggesting that intelligence and sex appeal are not mutually exclusive. One writer ventured to say: "If sex appeal were two minutes, Diane Keaton would be an hour. That's partly because of the manner in which she combines a saucy bohemian brilliance with an almost disabling vulnerability" (Robbins 156). But while Keaton's star image is highly feminine, attractive to men, women respond to her spunk. Woody Allen has said that men have a tendency to want to protect her (Linet 11). Yet Keaton doesn't seem to need that protection. Keaton has never married and has managed a successful, diverse career as well as a fulfilling personal life that includes her role as a single parent.

Many of the characters she plays are often described in the same terms as the star herself, which is possibly one reason why the public tends to confuse Keaton herself with her on-screen roles. Some actors, Keaton included, manage to retain certain core elements of their own personalities while playing a variety of roles. For example, with few exceptions, Keaton brings her own sense of style, or fashion, to the characters she plays. In the 80s, one writer remarked: "In real life she looks exactly the way she does as Louise Bryant, Annie Hall, and Mary Wilke in *Manhattan*" (Buck 107). Unlike personality stars, who essentially play themselves in film after film, Keaton and other interpreters of material enact characters similar to, but not exactly like, themselves. Joseph Boggs and Dennis Petrie explain in *The Art of Watching Films*:

> Interpreters and commentators play characters closely resembling themselves in personality and physical appearance, and they interpret these parts dramatically without wholly losing their own identity. Although they may slightly alter themselves to fit the role, they do not attempt to radically change their individual personality traits, physical characteristics, or voice qualities. They choose instead to color or interpret the role by filtering it through their own best qualities, modifying it to fit their own inherent abilities. The end result is an effective compromise between actor and role, between the real and the assumed identity [280].

These core characteristics may give unity and lend a sense of consistency to the star image, lead an audience to expect certain behavior from a star and even think that they know the "real" person. Sometimes a star's publicly constructed image dovetails so well with his or her film performances that the on-screen and off-screen images get blurred. Tom Hanks, for example, comes across as a charming, likable, regular guy in so many interviews, profiles, and film roles that audiences would have a tough time accepting him as a villain. The predisposition of some stars to play the same types of roles, often within the same genre, also contributes to this sense of consistency. James Cagney's tough-guy image was developed by playing one gangster after another.

Repetition breeds familiarity, and the result can be confusing for audiences and interviewers alike. In the mid-seventies, for example, after Keaton had won an Oscar for her portrayal of the charming but inarticulate *Annie Hall*, several interviewers seemed genuinely surprised that she could finish a sentence. When one reporter asked her what she would like people to know about her, she replied: "One thing only. That I can complete a sentence. They always say I never can" (qtd. in L'Ecuyer, "Diane Keaton" 38). In truth, Keaton did sound a lot like her *Annie Hall* character in the early interviews, especially throughout the seventies. Profiles of her reveal a stammering, scatterbrained, somewhat naive young woman who used *Annie Hall*–isms like "la-de-dah" and "isn't that something." But a friend once revealed: "She's very incisive and articulate when she decides to be" (qtd. in Gittelson 28).

The dither-speak was Keaton's way of avoiding probing, personal questions. Today, she is more direct. She simply refuses to answer questions that invade her private world, and refuses to apologize for it. When pressed, she will explain herself: "I do not approve of people talking about their private lives.... If you do that, what do you have that's private?" (qtd. in Friedman NC27). In interviews, her voice is deep, rich, self-assured, and, in conversation, her thoughts come out clear, concise. Occasionally, when she is nervous or unprepared, she still tends to get a bit unfocused in her speech.

Like Hepburn, Keaton has matured over the years. She has made the changes; consistency of core characteristics does not necessarily mean that the individual never grows. A star's image is rarely static. The complex set of visual representations that make up the star's image, also known as the star's iconography, can change and develop from film to film, from interview to interview, privileging certain traits over others at any given point in the star's career, all the while retaining those core characteristics. In short, the star is like a work in progress, evolving over time. Keaton's career has had its peaks and valleys, but her enduring star status is due, in part, to her willingness to move in new directions, take risks, experiment, and yet stay true to herself.

Though we can never know the real or private person behind the public persona, we can construct a portrait of the star by pulling together information from many different sources. As noted film scholar Richard Dyer argues:

The star phenomenon consists of everything that is publicly available about stars.

A film star's image is not just his or her films, but the promotion of those films and of the star through pin-ups, public appearances, studio hand-outs and so on, as well as interviews, biographies and coverage in the press of the star's doings and "private" life [*Heavenly Bodies* 2–3].

Reactions to Keaton from interviewers and critics have helped to shape the star's public image over the years. Most of the comments fall in line with Penelope Gilliatt's of *New Yorker* magazine who called her "one of the most comedically pure and brainy actresses in our midst" (38). Seldom is heard a disparaging word from man or woman regarding Diane Keaton. Patrick Pacheco, who has interviewed her, explains her consistently good press: "To the media, which regard actors as little more than meat puppets, a beautiful woman who's also brainy causes the same sort of awe as a talking dog" (103). Most commentators tend to emphasize this beguiling combination of beauty and brains and charm, but they also mention another characteristic in the Keaton iconography: her unwavering commitment to family and its importance in her life. She once told *Vanity Fair*: "Time is precious. Important. You don't want to miss any moment you have with your family. I don't. All my casual, fun time is spent with them" (qtd. in Collins 96). The phrasing may change from interview to interview, but the sentiment remains the same. Ask her today what matters most to her, and the answer is not fame, fortune, or star status. It is still family. "Family is the key to everything," she says. "It is the foundation of your life" (personal interview).

Keaton gravitates to family dramas in her film and television work. Dyer once noted that "stars matter because they act out aspects of life that matter to us; and performers get to be stars when what they act out matters to enough people" (*Heavenly Bodies* 19). Keaton fits Dyer's description of a star since what she acts out is relevant to so many people. The subjects she is interested in tend to be universal, as evidenced by this statement: "I've always been totally attracted to films about family and missed moments and the depths of people's inability to communicate with each other even though they love each other" (personal interview).

The comment immediately brings to mind some of her past roles in *The Godfather* trilogy, *Looking for Mr. Goodbar* (1977), *Interiors* (1978), *Shoot the Moon* (1982), *Mrs. Soffel* (1984), *Crimes of the Heart* (1986), *The Good Mother* (1988), *Marvin's Room* (1996), *The Only Thrill* (1998), *The Other Sister* (1999), *Hanging Up* (2000), or television features she's directed or starred in like *The Girl with the Crazy Brother* (1990), *Wildflower* (1991), and *Northern Lights* (1997) for the Disney Channel. All deal with complex family relationships. As Kay Corleone in the *Godfather* saga, for example, she enacts the "other," the WASP outsider, often the only voice of sanity in a high-profile crime family. She has played a mother (of ever increasingly older children) in almost half of the films she has made to date. The interplay between siblings, especially sisters, also fascinates Keaton. Some of her memorable characters are sisters, or close friends, in female ensemble films like *Interiors*, *Crimes of the Heart*, *The Lemon Sisters* (1990), *Marvin's Room*, *First Wives Club* (1996), and *Hanging Up*.

Many of her comedies, like *Play It Again, Sam* (1972), *Baby Boom* (1987), *Father of the Bride* (1991), *Father of the Bride II* (1995), and *First Wives Club*, spin laughs around family relationships and situations. Even the first feature film Keaton directed, *Unstrung Heroes* (1995), is about a family's ultimate ability to reach out to each other after a tragic loss. She once likened the job of director to that of a parent but was quick to make the distinction between the family-like atmosphere on a movie set and the real thing:

A movie set does not become like your family. They're impermanent, not lasting. And that's the frustrating thing about it. You have these close, seemingly intimate relationships, and they aren't at all. Because they don't go through any of the trials that real intimacy has. It's all heightened and it's a kind of a false family situation and I just don't trust those things [qtd. in Hirschberg 44].

Keaton considers herself "lucky" to be an interpreter of material, whether acting or directing, and to have the opportunity to choose material that she is interested in (personal interview). She puts family themes at the top of this list, and, in interview after interview, she credits her own family's support and encouragement as instrumental to her success. If her life has not followed a traditional path, she seems quite comfortable with it, philosophical even. Her mantra has become "no one gets everything."

Richard Dyer has pointed out that star images have histories, and this analysis is an attempt to reconstruct the star history of Diane Keaton. Dyer's *Stars* (1979) and *Heavenly Bodies: Film Stars and Society* (1986) aided in my understanding of how star images can be studied and analyzed while Louis Giannetti's *Understanding Movies* (1999) provided a methodology for analyzing the thematic and stylistic characteristics of Keaton's films. To date, there has been no book-length critical study of her work, either in front of or behind the camera. Only two short biographies exist: Susan Munshower's *The Diane Keaton Scrapbook* (1979) and Jonathan Moor's *Diane Keaton: The Story of the Real Annie Hall* (1989). These deal mainly with Keaton's personal life. Though both are now dated, these sources have been helpful in establishing a chronology of events in Keaton's life.

Several biographies of Woody Allen and Warren Beatty have also helped shed some light on Keaton's star image and film work since she has been so closely linked with these two men both person-ally and professionally: Eric Lax's *Woody Allen* (1991); Stig Bjorkman's *Woody Allen on Woody Allen* (1993); Julian Fox's *Woody: Movies from Manhattan* (1996); Tim Carroll's *Woody and his Women* (1993); Nancy Pogel's *Woody Allen* (1987); Susan Munshower's *Warren Beatty: His Life, His Loves, His Work* (1983); David Thompson's *Warren Beatty and Desert Eyes: A Life and a Story* (1987); and John Parker's *Warren Beatty: The Last Great Lover of Hollywood* (1994).

The magazine and newspaper arti-cles written about Keaton and her activ-ities; the few in-depth profile pieces and interviews she has granted over the past thirty years; the even fewer guest appear-ances she has made on talk shows like *Oprah Winfrey* and *Larry King Live*; and the reviews of her film, television, and photography work have provided invalu-able glimpses into the Keaton persona and rich insights into her work. Many of the same stories, anecdotes, and bio-graphical details have been passed down from decade to decade, appearing in both articles and books and lending a consis-tency to Keaton's star image. I am grate-ful, too, for Woody Allen's observations on Keaton and her work. I hope that my own analyses of the feature films and tele-vision movies that she has acted in and directed, commentaries on her published articles and photography books, and in-terviews with the star herself will add to this growing body of information. Taken together, these sources help tell the story of one of America's most gifted and in-triguing women—a star who has evolved from Woody Allen's Galatea to a respected actress and director in her own right.

The chapters move chronologically, beginning with Keaton's early years. The primary focus is on her career spanning the 1970s, 1980s, and 1990s. Each chap-ter begins with a brief overview of the significant events and influences in Kea-ton's life during a particular period. The second part of the chapter is a thematic and stylistic analysis of Keaton's feature films, television movies, and photography collections. I have included discussions of Keaton's own photography and edited collections because her life-long love of the camera and visual images led to her interest in directing and greatly influenced her directorial style. The film analyses in-clude an examination of themes as well as technical elements such as cinematogra-phy, mise-en-scène, movement, editing, sound, acting, costumes, sets, and narra-tive structure.

The portrait that emerges in the con-cluding chapter is of an increasingly self-confident, persistent, productive star, more willing than ever to take chances and branch out in new directions. After hav-ing said, for example, that she would never direct herself in a film, she has done it in *Hanging Up*, costarring Meg Ryan, Lisa Kudrow, and Walter Matthau. She shows no signs of slowing down. In fact, Keaton is more active today than at any time in her career. In the last half of the 1990s alone, she made seven films. Sev-eral new projects are currently in prog-ress. Her maturing star image and her durability make Keaton an interesting barometer of the movement of women in the Hollywood film industry and a role model for the next generation of female stars.

CHAPTER 1

1946–1970

The Early Years

Family is the key to everything.
—Diane Keaton (personal interview, 1998)

By all accounts, Keaton's childhood was a happy one and her creative talents recognizable from an early age. She was born Diane Hall in Los Angeles on Saturday, January 5, 1946, the first official year of the Baby Boom generation. Her father was Jack Hall, a civil engineer who became a successful real estate broker later in life. Her mother, Dorothy (Keaton) Hall, is an artist, photographer, and former Mrs. Los Angeles. Diane has a brother, Randy, and two sisters, Robin and Dorrie. She describes herself as the "overblown personality" in the family (qtd. in Collins 97), and sister Dorrie's oft quoted comment seems to confirm Keaton's assessment: "Everything she did was always big. Her laugh was big. She walked like a truck driver. She exaggerated everything" (qtd. in Kroll, "Thoroughly Modern Diane" 56).

Keaton's parents remember that she was always entertainment-oriented. Singing was her first love. Keaton frequently tells the story about going out into her backyard and "singing to the moon" when she was about five years old: "It was like

plugging into a great big battery" (qtd. in Skow 71). It was also a way of getting attention from her parents. "They were always thrilled whenever I would do any of this kind of thing, and it always seemed to be the only thing I could do" (qtd. in Munshower, *Scrapbook* 16). Keaton put on little skits for the family and later wrote and organized her own neighborhood productions with parts for all her siblings. Dorothy Hall has said, "We never watched television because they were so much better" (qtd. in Kroll, "Thoroughly Modern Diane" 56). Another much repeated anecdote goes that the family captured Keaton acting out the part of Clyde in her version of Bonnie and Clyde on 8-mm film. When Keaton and Warren Beatty (who played the character of Clyde in Arthur Penn's 1967 film) became a couple, Keaton's parents showed him the home movie, which he enjoyed so much that he insisted on watching it over and over again.

When Keaton was ten, the Halls moved from Los Angeles to Santa Ana in Orange County where she lived out a fairly normal childhood, vacationing at the beach and camping with the family. School was another story. Though she desperately wanted to be popular, she was too self-conscious and insecure about her looks and her body, traits that come up time and again not only in interviews but in many of the characters that she has played. She saw herself as the ugly duckling of the family. In an April 1993 article for *Mirabella* magazine, Keaton wrote:

> When I was a girl, around twelve, I knew something was wrong. I wasn't pretty. Being the first of four children, I couldn't understand why all the attractive genes had been passed on to my younger sisters, Robin and Dorrie. I didn't like my nose, so I slept with a bobby pin stuck on top, hoping the bulb would squeeze itself into a straight line. I'd spend hours at my mom's bathroom mirror practicing a special smile, convinced it would hide my flaws. I actually pried my eyes open as wide as possible, determined to make them grow bigger [53].

Keaton spent most of her high school years trying to fit in. Looking back, Keaton said:

> I feel so sad for myself, so embarrassed, remembering what I was like. I smiled my way through high school. My main concern was being popular.... I never learned to *think*. Once I played Blanche in *A Streetcar Named Desire*, and do you know something? I had no idea—no idea—what that play was about [qtd. in Munshower, *Scrapbook* 16].

She once lamented: "I just wish I had a little more sophistication and a better education" (qtd. in Fong-Torres 75).

At the time, however, Keaton had little interest in academic subjects, and, instead, found her niche in the drama club, where she excelled and where her talent brought her the attention she craved. Friend Leslie Morgan recalled that Keaton had "a great sense of style" and "overwhelming charisma" which was evident when she sang "Mata Hari" in *Little Mary*

Sunshine (qtd. in Gittelson 32). Keaton was surprised by the audience's, as well as her father's, appreciative reaction. She told interviewer Nancy Collins: "I felt a tremendous closeness to him regarding performing. My father was extraordinary, like a light, when he would come backstage. I had his attention in, yeah, oh boy, a big way" (qtd. in Collins 96).

Jack Hall, who died in 1990 of an inoperable brain tumor at the age of 68, had worked for the cities of Los Angeles and Santa Ana after receiving a civil engineering degree from the University of Southern California. He later founded Hall and Foreman, Inc., which became one of the most successful engineering companies in Southern California. His illness prompted Keaton's move back to California after many years of living in New York. It was her turn to support the man who had supported her career choices, influenced her fashion sensibilities, and encouraged her strong sense of independence. His own independent spirit derived from his mother, Mary, or Grammy Hall, immortalized in Woody Allen's *Annie Hall*.

In the few extended interviews that Keaton has done over the years, she often mentions Grammy Hall as a guiding force in her life. Always told with great affection, Keaton's stories about her paternal grandmother reveal a tough, spirited individual with a great sense of humor; a reverence for work, family, and honesty; and a fierce skepticism about the rewards of heaven—all characteristics that have been attributed to the Keaton persona at one time or another. Grammy Hall, who appears in Keaton's documentary *Heaven*, never really understood why her granddaughter became successful. Keaton once explained, "She understood what it meant in terms of money. But she really didn't understand what I had that was so special" (qtd. in L'Ecuyer 40).

It was Dorothy Hall, an artist and photographer, who cultivated her daughter's interest in the visual. From an early age, Keaton was drawn to pictures and images, which she still collects today, often incorporating them into artistic collages or big notebooks which serve as reference material for the way she frames a shot or composes the elements in a scene when directing. Taking photographs or collecting them is also Keaton's way of documenting the important events and people in her life and of holding onto memories, the overriding theme of *Unstrung Heroes*, her feature film directorial debut.

Keaton has published four collections of photography: *Reservations*, *Still Life*, *Mr. Salesman*, and *Local News*. She has had her own exhibits and sometimes curates shows for her friends in the art world. This personal interest in photography even folds into some of Keaton's on-screen characters who can be caught making memories by snapping pictures. In *Annie Hall* (1977), for example, Annie is an amateur photographer, the walls of her apartment decorated simply with her work. When she and Alvy (Woody Allen) plan to make a lobster dinner, the lobsters escape, sending the squeamish Alvy into shrieks of panic and glee. Annie runs to get her camera, and in a single click captures forever one of their happiest times together.

Keaton's visual flair also extends to the clothes she wears and the way she decorates her homes. References are usually made in profiles to her "artistic" way of dressing and her art gallery–like taste in decor. She likes open spaces, clean lines, and lots of white, broken only by her framed photographs, artwork, and spare furniture. She has said, "I like to be soothed by the atmosphere of a room.... I don't like clutter.... My brain is cluttered enough" (qtd. in Garis, sec: Features). Most of the feature pieces on Keaton begin with a description of how she *looks* and what she is wearing. Her layered ensembles that cover most of her body have been the talk of the fashion world for years, beginning with *Annie*

Hall. Director Woody Allen permitted Keaton to wear her own off-beat creations in the film, and they spread like wildfire in the popular culture. Curator of the Metropolitan Museum of Art's Costume Institute Richard Martin ventured to say: "Annie Hall is the model for how we dress in the last quarter of the 20th Century" ("Style Setters" 236).

Influenced and supported by her family, Keaton performed in summer stock after she graduated from high school in 1963. That fall, she enrolled at Santa Ana College where she spent one semester before transferring to Orange Coast College. Her drama coach there, Lucien Scott, encouraged her to quit after only two semesters, to study with Sanford Meisner in New York. Keaton's family was behind the move. In 1965, they drove her across country to Meisner's Neighborhood Playhouse School of the Theater, a brownstone on 54th Street off First Avenue, where Keaton had received a scholarship. She told the *New York Post*: "I felt a lot of security behind me. Don't think I'd have dared to come otherwise" (qtd. in Champlin, "Attention" 36).

From Meisner, Keaton learned that "acting is living truthfully under imaginary circumstances" (Silverberg 9). His live-in-the-moment approach forces actors to listen, pay attention to each other instead of thinking about their next line, so that they can respond truthfully to what others give them. Keaton explains:

> I need help from the people around me. I respond to what I'm given because that's the sort of work that I was raised on with Sanford Meisner being my teacher. It all comes from them, and I respond to what people give me. So if somebody's not with me in a scene, I kind of like fall apart. I don't fly on my own very well. I come from, you know, a spontaneous moment really and how I'm connecting with my partner [personal interview].

Sanford Meisner was a shy, unassuming man whose famous students included

Gregory Peck, Joanne Woodward, Grace Kelly, and Robert Duvall. Directors Sidney Lumet and Sydney Pollack and playwright David Mamet also studied with him. Meisner, born in 1905 in Brooklyn, started out as an actor. He was a member of the 1930s Group Theater which patterned itself after the Moscow Art Theater and Konstantin Stanislavsky's method-acting approach. He became the director of the Neighborhood Playhouse from 1936 to 1959 and again from 1964 into the '80s.

Meisner came to believe that acting is instinctive and behavioral. Rather than live a role internally, as in method acting, he felt that an actor should live in the present and work off of other actors. "Act Before You Think" was one of his mottoes. He also taught his students that by thinking of their fellow actors as more important than themselves, by looking outside rather than within, they could free themselves to react in a truthful, honest way.

Though Meisner focused on teaching, he acted and directed periodically. In the late '50s he went to work for 20th Century–Fox, directing its new-talent division and performing when he had the chance. He eventually went back to New York to direct at the Neighborhood Playhouse again, but he never gave up acting. Meisner played a patient on the television drama *E.R.* shortly before his death in 1997. As Keaton reveals, he was both adored and feared by his students who carry on his work (personal interview).

While studying with Meisner, Keaton sang with friend Guy Gillette and his brother, Pip, in their rock band called the Roadrunners. She took art classes, studied dance with Martha Graham, and befriended other young, upcoming actors—like Al Pacino. What she didn't do, however, was hang out or love in, though the social scene in New York during the mid to late sixties was in full frenzy. She found that she simply wasn't a night per-

son. "I sort of go flat," she admitted (qtd. in Morice 78).

Throughout the 1960s, Keaton focused on her work, feeling fairly disconnected from the social revolution around her. She spent two years with Meisner, and, after graduating from the Neighborhood Playhouse, she did summer theater in Woodstock, including a production of *Oh! What a Lovely War!* For several months afterwards, she tried out for one role after another, usually striking out. She returned home to California, discouraged. It was Grammy Hall who convinced her to go back to New York and try again. Four months later, Keaton landed a role in *Hair*, billed as Broadway's American Tribal Love Rock Musical.

The audition was traumatic, and, at first, she thought she had been rejected again. The producers said her resumé and photos were bad. She got as far as the elevator before one of the producers found her and told her to stay. She doesn't know why they decided to keep her, but even at that point in her career, Keaton exhibited signs of the "impostor syndrome," a feeling that when something good happens, it couldn't possibly be because she deserved it.

She explains: "In some ways, you think you deserve your success because it did happen to you.... But, on the other hand, you're totally insecure, like you're afraid you're going to get caught and found out who you really are" (qtd. in Mathews, "Secure" 3). Around this time, she also took her mother's maiden name since there was a Diane Hall already registered with the Screen Actors Guild.

In April 1968, *Hair* opened at New York's Biltmore Theatre with Diane Keaton in the chorus. She quickly graduated to understudy for lead Lynn Kellogg, and when Kellogg left the play, Keaton was offered the role—provided she trim down and spruce up her appearance. She took the advice and went on a special diet. "It's one of those weird ones," she explained, "placenta of unborn lamb. A shot every day. The 'Hair' people paid for half of it and I paid the other half—$35 a week— and I lost a lot of weight and never gained it back" (qtd. in Gage 9).

But Keaton, known to wear footless tights while swimming, had definite opinions about her body, and she became famous for being the only cast member who did *not* take off her clothes at the end of the first act. The nudity was not mandatory, but cast members who disrobed received an extra $50. Keaton passed on the money. In one Paramount press release, Keaton explained: "I suppose I could get over being self-conscious if I thought it was important enough. But sometimes I really wonder about the necessity of it, whether it's really needed or called for."

While Keaton found the nudity in *Hair* meaningless, she overcame her shyness and disrobed for *Looking for Mr. Goodbar* (1977), in which she plays Terry Dunn whose credo—one man's too many, one hundred's not enough—invites tragic consequences. It was integral to the plot. Keaton has not done another nude scene since. In fact, many of her film characters convey the same sense of awkwardness and self-consciousness that Keaton expresses about her own body. Her layers of clothing are as complex as her persona. Blouses are buttoned all the way up to the collar. Little skin is ever revealed. Keaton is quick to point out, however, that she's not prudish. She just likes to be clothed. "I'm not comfortable unless I have a lot of clothes on," she said in one article (qtd. in Garis, sec: Features). In several interviews she good-naturedly admits that during *Hair* she did get a kick out of looking at everyone else running around naked.

The cast of *Hair* became the media darlings of the moment. Their photos appeared everywhere. Television talk shows courted them. Keaton hated the hype, but she liked the energy on stage. She especially enjoyed singing songs like "Good

Morning Starshine" and "Easy to Be Hard." But organized and disciplined in her own work, she took exception to the show's overall hypocrisy and lack of professionalism. She never knew what would happen on a given night. All the peace and love on stage masked fierce competition between cast members and political maneuvering behind the scenes for attention and publicity, she told *Rolling Stone* (Fong-Torres 75). Keaton stayed with *Hair* for nine months.

It is ironic that someone who felt isolated from the social and political upheavals around her should wind up starring in such an overtly political, anti-war play, and that someone so self-conscious about her body should appear in a production remembered chiefly for its nudity. That Keaton was able to assess the reality of the situation yet find some joy and value in the experience may suggest that even at this early period in her career she could separate the personal from the professional. In written and televised interviews, Keaton has said that the work itself is all-important to her, the thing on which she focuses. Fellow actors and directors often comment on the fact that she can distance herself from the swirling chaos around her and concentrate on the task at hand, and the one thing that she *has* consistently given herself credit for is her ability to work hard.

Also, at this point, Keaton began to display certain contradictory traits. Already we can see the dichotomy between her toughness and vulnerability. She continued to "put herself out there" despite her insecurities, but she stopped short of following the crowd by her refusal to strip, willingly participate in the media hype, or get involved in backstage politics. By her own admission, she never considered herself a member of the "tribe," as the cast of *Hair* was often called.

Part of what makes Keaton's star image distinctive is her strong will and centeredness, which comes, in part, from her family support. Keaton's parents taught her to think for herself—a useful lesson given the mob mentality of the late sixties. She is not a follower, nor is she easily impressed. Woody Allen once said that Keaton's "mind is never clouded by popular opinion, the need to score points" (qtd. in Skow 72). Her image has come to embody a free-thinking, independent spirit. It was this quality that first captivated Woody Allen.

Keaton and Allen's meeting has become the stuff of Hollywood legend. He was already a "name" in stand-up comedy, as well as film. Allen had written and starred in *What's New, Pussycat?* (1965), written, dubbed, and starred in *What's Up, Tiger Lily?* (1966), starred in *Casino Royale* (1967), penned the play on which *Don't Drink the Water* (1969) was based, and directed and starred in *Take the Money and Run* (1969). He had married comedienne Louise Lasser on Groundhog Day, 1966. Keaton herself was becoming a name in certain circles, but taken together their names became something bigger than either one of them individually. Though they seldom work together today and Keaton has since built a reputation and career on her own merit, they maintain a close friendship. During Allen's difficult breakup with Mia Farrow, it was Keaton who stood by him and, at the last minute, stepped into the role he had created originally for Farrow in *Manhattan Murder Mystery*.

After thirty years, it's still hard to find an interview with either star that doesn't mention the other's name. Many articles focus on Allen's influence on Keaton, crediting him with guiding and shaping her career; however, Woody Allen rarely fails to acknowledge Keaton's influence on *him*. He once said:

> I've made contributions to her life ... but not nearly as profound contributions as she's made to mine. I never have a good

understanding of people; she has an uncanny understanding of people—when they are vulnerable, when they are covering up, when they are hostile [qtd. in Kroll, "Thoroughly Modern Diane" 57].

He insists that from the beginning, Diane Keaton was always very much her own person:

> When I first met her, as young as she was she would never hesitate to express her likes and dislikes, no matter how against the grain they may have been. If she liked something unpopular, she liked it with no defensiveness; that was just it. And if she didn't, you could tell her all day long that, say, these plays of Shakespeare are masterpieces, and if she didn't like them, she just didn't care. She had utter, total conviction in her own taste—and her own taste was superb. She knows who the good actresses and actors are, and what the good plays are, and what the good paintings are, and who's funny and who's not. There's just some unclouded instinct in her that's never been messed up by peer pressure. She was a supporter of, I think, the best instincts of mine [qtd. in Lax, *Biography* 244].

Who knows why two people click? They did, and, in the popular imagination, their names will be forever linked. Allen says, "We have very good chemistry and know how to play off each other—just lucky chemistry" (personal interview). Keaton describes their chemistry as a "mysterious, strange thing" (personal interview). Jack Kroll called it "a meeting of two high-tension nervous systems" ("Thoroughly Modern Diane" 57).

In 1968, Allen had written a play called *Play It Again, Sam*, a tribute to Humphrey Bogart and *Casablanca*, one of his favorite films. It was about a nerdish film critic, Allan Felix, who has no success whatsoever with women because he's always trying to emulate the suave Bogart—and failing miserably. He gets a little help from his best friend's wife, Linda Christie (played by Keaton), and the ghost of Bogie. In a spin on *Casa-*

blanca's final airport scene, he sends Linda off with her husband, tells Bogie that the "secret's not being you, it's being me," and walks off into the mist alone.

About 50 actresses auditioned for the part of Linda. Keaton was one of them. Lucien Scott, her drama coach at Orange Coast College, actually got her the audition since another of his former students, Joe Hardy, was directing the play. Allen and producer David Merrick had already heard that Sandy Meisner considered Keaton "just the best actress around" (qtd. in Kroll, "Thoroughly Modern Diane" 57). Though she was nervous, she impressed Allen and Hardy enough that they called her back. Keaton remembers that Woody had to come up on stage and audition with her: "He was as scared as I was ... which I found very appealing" (qtd. in Fong-Torres 74). Allen explains: "I was scared because—first of all, I had never acted in my life. I was strictly a nightclub comic. And then, when we called her back we were worried that she'd be too tall.... So we got onstage together ... and we measured back to back.... We were just about the same height, and so that was it" (qtd. in Fong-Torres 74).

Allen says that Keaton was different from the rest. Instead of acting, he felt like they were conversing with each other. According to Keaton, Allen likes performances to be as natural as possible. "The thing I remember about Woody is that he always wanted people to behave and look sort of like they did in real life.... He always liked the idea of overlapping and loosening up the dialogue" (personal interview). Of Keaton's acting style, Allen told Eric Lax, "Diane is strictly behavioral. She can make anything funny. Diane can tell you about going to the corner to buy the papers and you'll laugh because there's something behaviorally funny about her" (qtd. in Lax, *Biography* 309). Keaton got the part.

Allen's comments about Keaton are particularly helpful in understanding her

developing star image. He was taken with her immediately. In several interviews, he mentions Keaton's famous sense of fashion, which some women copied, some considered eccentric, and others found simply bizarre. Allen, however, appreciated her artistic style right from the beginning, during rehearsals of *Play It Again, Sam*: "She'd come in every day with an absolutely spectacularly imaginative combination of clothes. They were just great.... A football jersey and a skirt ... and combat boots and, you know, *oven mittens*," he said (qtd. in Fong-Torres 74). Later, in *Annie Hall*, when he encouraged Keaton to wear whatever she wanted for the role of Annie, he helped usher in a fashion craze. Her baggy chinos, big shirts buttoned to the neck, men's vests, floppy ties tucked in at the belt, and bowler hats became for many women of that era the *ensemble de rigueur*.

Allen also appreciated Keaton's comedic talents—and still does. He and Keaton and Tony Roberts (who played Keaton's husband Dick Christie), spent a lot of time together when they were doing the play. Allen once told *Time*:

> Tony and I couldn't stop laughing at Diane. It was nothing you could quote later; she couldn't tell a joke if her life depended on it. Tony tried to figure it out one time, what it is she does. He says she has this uncanny ability to project you back into an infantile atmosphere, and you are suddenly a little kid again. There is something utterly guileless about her. She's a natural [qtd. in Skow 71].

Even today, Allen maintains: "She's the funniest human I ever met" (personal interview).

He found her comic timing impeccable, her naiveté charming, and her self-deprecation endearing. In a sense, Allen and Roberts became Keaton's public relations team, promoting her, pointing up her talent and charm in a way that she could never and would never do for herself.

For example, Allen's following quote reads like passage out of a press release:

> She's incredibly intelligent and complex.... She sings beautifully, she can act dramatically well, and comically well, she paints, she draws, she does collages, she photographs. She is gifted graphically and she has an unfailing ear for acting [qtd. in Mathews, "Secure" 3].

Allen's anecdotes and references to Keaton's intelligence served as a counterpoint and balance to the gum-cracking babe-in-the-woods that viewers frequently saw sitting opposite Johnny Carson on the *Tonight Show*. She says she went on talk shows back then because she got to sing a number or two, but when it came to talking, she often got scared, giggled, and said anything that popped into her head (Gage 14). She would later say, "In the '70s I was more of a chatterbox. I used to have this feeling that if people asked me a question, I had an obligation to tell them everything. I don't approve of that anymore" (qtd. in L'Ecuyer, "Diane Keaton" 37).

Carson got a lot of mileage out of Keaton's daffy remarks, but her friends didn't recognize the Diane Keaton they knew. Allen once tried to explain Keaton's paradoxical persona this way:

> You'd never know it from just a quick meeting with her—or the quality she projects—but Keaton is a genuine intellectual.... When you meet her she is a gangly, sometimes awkward, sweet kind of actress, and you tend to think of the other actresses you meet who are obsessed with the part and agents and parties and she's not that way at all. She is very responsive to books and ideas. If she reads Camus or Dostoevski, it doesn't just wash over her. She gets very, very involved with ideas and knows what they're saying and how it affects her life, and life in general. Her personality belies that completely, and that's the most curious thing about her [qtd. in Fong-Torres 74].

Allen's observation is particularly important since intelligence is one of the key aspects of Keaton's star image today. He recently likened her to "a kid in school who for two days whines about how lousy she did on a test and ends up getting 100. That's Diane in a nutshell," he said (qtd. in Mathews, "Secure" 3). Comments like these drew attention to what others could not see because Keaton was too shy, and perhaps too insecure, to discuss the likes of Dostoevski in public.

In Allen, Keaton found a kindred spirit. She worked hard to educate herself and make up for what she had missed academically. Allen had done the same thing. In Jack Kroll's 1978 feature on Allen for *Newsweek*, the comedian admits that the heaviest reading he had ever picked up was a comic book until he started dating. He began reading the great classic and contemporary works of literature so that he could keep up his end of the conversation (62). He preferred sports over academics. He, too, gravitated toward the entertainment field early in life, writing gags for stand-up and television comedians like Sid Ceasar and Garry Moore—while still in his teens. Allen also took up music and taught himself to play the clarinet and saxophone. He still plays the clarinet every Monday night at Michael's in Manhattan. Once he began educating himself, Allen never looked back.

Eleven years her senior and by now well-read himself, Allen introduced Keaton to his world of literature, music, and film. She learned a great deal from him, and, in 1990 paid him this tribute:

> He changed my life completely.... If I hadn't met Woody, I don't think I would have been where I am now. I probably would have been an actress, but I don't know if people would have found something special in me. He took the time to find it. I mean, it was very unusual, what he did. I think everything came my way because of him [qtd. in Garis, sec: Features].

As recently as 1997, Keaton again gave a nod to her mentor: "He's always been behind me. He's always said, 'Yes, you can.' And that's just a huge help, because it's very easy for people to say, 'Well, I don't think so' and 'Probably not.' He believed that I could do it. So I did" (qtd. in Sumner, "Keaton Keeps on Blooming" C1). These statements help explain Keaton's steadfast loyalty and unwavering friendship toward Allen.

They became a couple sometime during the run of *Play It Again, Sam* which opened at the Broadhurst Theater on 13 February 1969. A *New York Times* article dated 28 May 1972 says that they had been dating ever since her audition. In 1982, Allen told Jack Kroll that though they were both attracted to each other, neither could make the first move. Outside of rehearsal they were too scared to talk to each other, but Allen screwed up his courage to ask her out when the play opened in Washington, D.C.

Tim Carroll in *Woody and His Women* suggests that Allen's initial reluctance to jump into a relationship with Keaton might have had something to do with his still being married to his second wife, Louise Lasser, from whom he was amicably estranged. Nevertheless, the reportage has Keaton and Allen living together in his Fifth Avenue apartment shortly after the Washington run. The arrangement lasted for about a year before Keaton found her own place nearby, on East 68th Street.

Allen insists that they lived together for the duration of the play, which closed in March of 1970, but they maintained a romantic relationship off and on "for a while." He told Eric Lax that he was "one of the first important relationships in her life," but that they eventually "grew apart.... She became a sophisticated woman and developed a million needs and plans, and I had my own plans—a number that coincided and a number that didn't. We parted amicably" (qtd. in Lax,

Biography 243–44). He still calls her his "lucky charm," and she is the first to screen his work whenever she is in town.

Keaton has never discussed the details of their private relationship. She once said to an interviewer who asked about Woody: "I don't like to talk about people in my life that are in the public eye—except in a professional way." She did, however, say that she thought Allen was a remarkable person.

> There's nobody like him. He's unique and gifted, an artist. And he's the best kind of artist because when he works, it's about work—it's not about deal-making, it's not about glamour, it's not about fame, it's not about awards, it's not about money. It's about making this movie, and then on he goes to the next movie [qtd. in Demaris 5].

In short, theirs is a mutual admiration society and a mutually beneficial relationship. Keaton helped develop Allen's visual instincts, showed him the beauty in old faces, gave him a greater sensitivity toward women—and she made him laugh. Allen, in turn, saw something in Keaton that others didn't, and possibly never would because, as she claims, she was always "just a little off" or "too eccentric." She explains:

> I think that Woody appreciated me, which I hadn't run into quite that way from anybody else. You know, I was around town in New York, and I was auditioning and frequently I didn't get the part. I think Woody just, he got a kick out of me. I don't know why. Maybe it's because I enjoyed his sense of humor or maybe it was because I was around for so long while we were making that play that he got used to me. He got to know me. Or, maybe it was just getting used to somebody as opposed to getting to know them. If you're around long enough, usually people will, you know, they're stuck with you. They start to like you [personal interview].

A modest assessment, but there's truth in it. Allen and Tony Roberts did like

Keaton and enjoyed her company during the run of *Play It Again, Sam*. Allen says that some nights they barely made it through a performance because something she did or said would send them into fits of laughter. He would have to sit still for a moment to compose himself. Keaton agreed: "If Woody blew a line, he just went up.... He couldn't continue the scene. Tony and I could mess up a line and go on, but not Woody. And then you started laughing. The discipline some nights was really bad" (qtd. in Lax, *Biography* 245). Keaton received a Tony nomination for Best Supporting Actress in 1969 for her performance as Linda Christie. And one story goes that Jack Benny came backstage one night predicting, "Woody, that girl is going to be gigantic!"

Critics and audiences alike credited Allen for Keaton's success. She was perceived as his Galatea. He fed her intellect, introduced her to psychoanalysis, and extolled her hidden virtues to the public. He created a safe environment, away from the shark-infested waters of Hollywood, for a shy, insecure actress and showcased her comedic talents in the stage version of *Play It Again, Sam* and in the seven films they eventually made together. He cultivated her natural talent and encouraged her sense of style. He gave her, as he did with all his actors, plenty of flexibility and room to experiment. He respected her opinions. He raised her to the status of an American icon in *Annie Hall*, the embodiment of the confused, modern woman trying to strike a balance

between her need for independence and her desire for a meaningful relationship. As Marcelle Clements writes: "Woody Allen made Diane Keaton's kookiness work in his movies. He showed us how endearing it could be, how lovable and sexy. And that, paradoxically, liberated Keaton to go on to other parts where she was anything but kooky" (104).

In *Celebrity and Power: Fame in Contemporary Culture*, P. David Marshall argues that if a "type is replicable by other performers, then the inherent value of the emerging screen star is limited" (99). Anything that can be mass produced loses its value. So it is with star images. Hollywood has a tendency to discover a prototype that works, usually financially, and clone it *ad nauseam*. Marilyn Monroe was soon followed by Jane Mansfield and Mamie Van Doren, Arnold Schwarzenegger by Steven Seagal and Jean-Claude Van Damme. Keaton's star image has been difficult to duplicate. Taken individually, certain elements of Keaton's emerging star image, or persona, could apply to any young, upcoming star at that time. She certainly wasn't the only intelligent or neurotic actress around. She also embodied traits of her predecessors, like Katharine Hepburn's feisty, independent spirit and Carole Lombard's zaniness. But, taken in total, the elements of Keaton's star image were developing into a complex paradox, something quite distinctive, and soon would catch the imagination of film audiences as she made the leap from the stage to the screen.

CHAPTER 2

1970–1976

The Road to Fame

> *If in some way I've contributed to bringing Diane to the attention of the public, it satisfies me more than anything else I've done in films.*
> —Woody Allen (*People*, Dec. 26, 1978)

In the early seventies, Diane Keaton was building a reputation as a versatile performer. She made a number of films that introduced her comedic as well as dramatic talents: *Lovers and Other Strangers* (1970); *The Godfather* (1972); *Play It Again, Sam* (1972); *Sleeper* (1973); *The Godfather: Part II* (1974); *Love and Death* (1975); *I Will, I Will ... for Now* (1976); and *Harry and Walter Go to New York* (1976). Three of these films are among Woody Allen's finest early comedies. *The Godfather,* parts one and two, consistently top lists of America's greatest films. Keaton received a great deal of media exposure by starring in these five films alone, and critics were quick to recognize her multi-faceted persona. One reviewer wrote: "In the studio era she would have thrived on a steady diet of several comedies, romances and three-hankie dramas a year opposite the top stars of her day" (A. Thompson, "Diane Keaton" L1). Another writer noted that Keaton had a face that slipped easily between tragedy and farce:

"Her eyelids slope down, her nose up; her mouth swings both ways" (McWilliams, "Wonder Women" E1).

When she wasn't working in films, Keaton appeared on television shows like *Love, American Style; Mannix; The FBI;* and *Night Gallery.* She probably got more exposure, more attention, and more money, however, for a series of Hour-After-Hour deodorant commercials that she didn't even like doing. Keaton received $6,000 for *The Godfather,* $21,500 for the movie version of *Play It Again Sam,* and $25,000 for the deodorant commercials. When she finally refused to make any more, Susan Sarandon replaced her as the "daisy-fresh" Hour-After-Hour housewife.

In the meantime, Keaton pursued a singing career. She had always envisioned herself a chanteuse, not an actress. In addition to the acting, art, and dance classes that occupied her free time, she took voice lessons and booked engagements in Greenwich Village cabarets like Reno

Sweeney's and Brothers and Sisters. Here's how one captivated reviewer described Keaton's on-stage presence:

> All eyes are riveted on a stunning girl who has suddenly slipped into the spotlight and now stands timidly peeping out into the darkness. She's all spiffed up like a boy-about-town, with blue velvet pants, pin-stripe jacket, and a jazzy polka-dot tie. But her face seems frozen in fright. She's dressed like a boy, but you can't help noticing she's a girl. Her hair is silken red, her skin smooth and creamy, and her figure—even in those just-a-buddy duds— is full where it should be full and frail where it should be frail. Her voice, too— when at last she sweetly glides into "Goody, Goody"—is choir-girl pure. And her manner afterward, as she floats on a sea of boisterous applause, is flushed and bubbly, like that of a child whose birthday has finally come [Flatley, "Applause" 25].

Another reviewer compared Keaton to Carole Lombard and Jean Arthur because of her "combination of soft femininity and tomboy brattiness," more evident on stage than in her films (Natale 24). Still another who saw her show at Reno Sweeney's commented on her appeal to both genders:

> She has a man-pleasing talent for making you feel she is looking at you and talking to you and feeling nice things about you while she sings. Yet she is so charming that the woman [sic] in the audience respond to her [Iachetta 64].

Television audiences could usually catch her act on talk shows like Merv Griffin and Johnny Carson when he was in New York. She once said: "I sing on all of them. That's why I do them" (qtd. in Guarino 17). Because of her performances on these shows, Keaton gained a wider audience base. This, in part, explains why her appeal has never been confined to her own generation. She spoke to Merv and Johnny's generation, for example, with her renditions of old pop tunes like "You Made Me Love You."

From the early days of her career, Keaton had something that fascinated the press—a quality that translated to many of her on-screen characters. Film critic Eleanor Ringel summed it up as "open-hearted likability" and innocence: "not innocence as in ignorant or youthful, but innocence as in hopeful and uncorrupted" ("On Film" L2). Woody Allen would capture this quality and immortalize Keaton's singing talents in Annie Hall (1977) and later in Radio Days (1987). In Annie Hall, he uses Annie's two numbers to illustrate the character's metamorphosis. In the first scene, a long shot shows Annie, a slim figure almost lost amid the noisy nightclub crowd, tentatively bleating out the words to "It Had to Be You." No one is listening. Toward the end of the film, a self-assured Annie sits on a stool, alone on the stage. The camera slowly zooms in to a close up as she confidently sings "Seems Like Old Times." We—and her on-screen audience—are locked on her face and her voice until the burst of applause at the end of the song.

In Radio Days, Allen's nostalgic tribute to music in the 1940s, Keaton has a small cameo role as a big band singer, Monica Charles. Keaton, in fact, has a singing scene in several of her films, including Reds (1981), Shoot the Moon (1982), Mrs. Soffel (1984), Crimes of the Heart (1986), The Lemon Sisters (1990), First Wives Club (1996), and Disney's made-for-television movie, Northern Lights (1997). It seems clear that she has never abandoned her first love.

Keaton has often commented that her twenties were marked with paralyzing fear on the one hand, intense ambition on the other. Curiosity and a desire to learn saved her. Rather than retreat to familiar territory, she took risks. With one brief return to the theater, starring as the teacher in Israel Horovitz's Off–Broadway comedy The Primary English Class, Keaton decided to focus exclusively on films. Though her reviews in the play were glowing, it was the last time she would appear live on stage. Today, neither Broadway's late working hours nor New York's cold weather appeals to her, so she resides in California, near her family and the film industry. She prefers the fragmentary process of movie-making which requires intense concentration for short periods of time rather than the long, sustained performances required of theater actors. As she puts it: "I like the pieces as opposed to a big, long-distance haul" (qtd. in Hirschberg 44). Once Keaton left the stage, she never returned.

There is a line in *Annie Hall* where Alvy Singer says to Annie: "A relationship is like a shark. It has to constantly move forward or it dies." Keaton has handled her career with a similar philosophy. She steers it in one direction, forward, and leaves no doubt as to who is in charge. One anonymous industry source said that Keaton clearly understands the business of movie-making and knows how to handle even the toughest studio executives: "She's very smart, sharklike, when it comes to that. She's highly sensitive to other people's strengths and weaknesses and can play them very well. She can be really tough" (qtd. in Pacheco 51). In the early seventies, however, glimpses of this tough, no-nonsense businesswoman were few, either in the press coverage on the star or in her on-screen characterizations.

Lovers and Other Strangers

After *Play It Again, Sam* closed on Broadway on May 14, 1970, Keaton won a small part in Cy Howard's *Lovers and Other Strangers*. The film, based on Renee Taylor and Joseph Bologna's play, captures the sexual angst of an age as it explores differences in attitude between men and women toward love, sex, family, and marriage. The sixties had shaken and popped the cork on naive, traditional

definitions of romantic relationships. Women came out of the kitchen; gays came out of the closet. Sex became political. Marriage became only one of many options. Dazed and confused, the seventies were left groping with the task of redefining, and reinventing, its notions of love. Keaton's debut film reflects the prevailing mood of doubt and disillusionment. In one scene, a divorcing son tries to explain to his father what went wrong with his marriage: "We're strangers, Pop." His father replies, "We're all strangers. We become deeper strangers. That's all there is."

The all-star cast of *Lovers and Other Strangers* includes Gig Young, Bea Arthur, Richard Castellano, Harry Guardino, Bonnie Bedelia, Anne Jackson, Cloris Leachman, Anne Meara, Michael Brandon, and Bob Dishy. They play members and extended members of an Italian-American clan in various stages of marriage. Beatrice (Bea Arthur) and Frank (Richard Castellano) head up the Vecchio family whose youngest son gets married while their oldest son's marriage falls apart. Beatrice and Frank have no illusions about marriage, but divorce is out of the question. They've stayed together by finding things in common—like food—which gives them something to talk about. And they've got plenty of advice for everyone, especially eldest son, Richie: "Don't look for happiness, Richie. It will only make you miserable." Beatrice blames the Ecumenical Council for most of life's problems. In one scene she tells Frank, "Once you start monkeying around with who's a saint and who isn't, it makes the young people crazy."

Keaton makes her appearance about one-third of the way through the film. She plays Joan, the WASP daughter-in-law, who has had enough of marriage. It hasn't lived up to her romantic expectations. We first see her enter a door in the center of the frame as she arrives late to Mike and Susan's wedding reception. Tall and slender in her mauve knit mini dress, the camera follows her as she makes her way across the room to the family table. With her long, straight reddish-blond hair, fringed with thick bangs, she stands out from the crowd. She looks like a Barbie doll at an Italian wedding. Sandwiched between Richie's parents at the table, Joan begins to answer their probing questions. It seems Richie ignored her birthday request. All she wanted was a book about Spain. She tells an incredulous Beatrice and Frank: "When you give a book about a romantic place, it's like saying that all your days should be as romantic as Spain, surrounded by a cover of happiness."

Though Keaton's part is small, her character is important because Joan coalesces all of the naive, unrealistic expectations young people often bring to marriage. She has one major scene with Bea Arthur. As Joan and Beatrice linger around an abandoned wedding table, Joan tries to articulate her sense of loss:

> Ever since I was 15, I loved Richie from afar. We had so much fun together. We both loved the beach. We were always kissing and hugging. Everyone said how great we looked on the dance floor. I really thought we'd get married and live happily ever after. But I guess we just weren't that lucky. I knew it was the real thing because I loved everything about him. I loved the way he moved. Sometimes I'd just spend hours and hours and watch him move around. And ... you're going to think I'm crazy, but I loved the way his hair smelled like raisins. And when he kissed me—I never told him this. The best part about being in his arms was that I could get a good whiff of his hair. Well ... I don't know if it's me or Richie that's changed, but it's just no big deal anymore—to feel him or smell him.

Keaton's delivery is sweetly sincere. With her melodious voice and facility for making absurd dialogue sound natural, Keaton humorously captures that moment in marriage when *ennui* sets in. This pivotal scene is intercut with Frank and Richie's conversation on the terrace, juxtaposing the often opposing points of view that men and women have toward marriage. At the end of the day, however, as Beatrice and Frank compare notes after the reception, Beatrice reduces the problem to one sentence: "Richie's hair stopped smelling like raisins."

The Godfather and *The Godfather: Part II*

In *The Godfather* films, Keaton plays the outsider in a different kind of Italian family. Based on Mario Puzo's best-selling novel and directed by Francis Ford Coppola, the Mafioso saga is about "a king with three sons" whose attempts to keep his youngest son out of the family "business" go tragically awry (Coppola, *A Look Back*). When Coppola saw Keaton in *Lovers and Other Strangers*, he asked her to audition for the part of Kay Adams, WASP girlfriend of youngest son, Michael Corleone (Al Pacino). She was one of the first actors signed, along with Robert Duvall (Tom Hagen) on February 15, 1971. According to Harlan Lebo's *The Godfather Legacy*, an excellent behind-the-scenes look at the making of *The Godfather* trilogy, Coppola wanted the twenty-five-year-old actress for the role precisely because of her offbeat personality. He thought she could bring a little "eccentricity" to an otherwise straight, rather bland, but essential character (54).

In truth, Coppola probably hired Keaton because she *looked* right for the part, and she came with the right price tag, $6,000. Coppola had little budget to spare for big-name actors. She also had the right mix of physical and psychological qualities to play Kay, which Coppola saw immediately in her screen tests with Pacino. Seated at a table in medium two-shot, they look like polar opposites. She is the girl next door: open, fresh-faced, and fair. He is the heir to a Mafia throne:

evasive and brooding. In a childlike and utterly guileless voice, she asks: "Michael, why are all these people bothering your father on a day like this?" As he carefully responds to her question, she performs the dance of innocent flirtation—smiling adoringly at him, looking away in flushed pleasure. She is "the other," the antithesis of the dark Corleones.

The role of Kay is small but important because it is through her eyes that the audience sees the corruption behind the family's romantic veneer. As a Corleone, she must be the obedient, submissive wife. The character is also the barometer of her husband's evil, which taints everything around him—and his radius is wide. Like Shakespeare's Richard III, he is "so far in blood that sin will pluck on sin" (4.2.154). Kay's adoration slowly turns to horror and disgust. Pacino has said: "I really enjoyed being with [Diane]. I had the most fun with her. She believed very much in the movie, and I thought played the role beautifully" (Coppola, *A Look Back*).

Keaton, however, never thought she was right for the part. In a Paramount press release she remarked: "I never thought of myself as right to play Kay, this nice, intelligent girl with a very proper New England background. I thought I'd be just a bit too—crazy." Coppola's wife, Eleanor, got a kick out of watching Diane's transformation into Kay Adams. Keaton would "arrive on the set in her 'big boots and kooky clothes' and emerge 'all flattened and straightened into Kay Corleone" (qtd. in Lebo 81). But Keaton has always maintained that she felt "strange" in *The Godfather* and voiced strong opinions about her character: "I had no interest in that woman. I thought she was such a dip. She was so willing to go along with all of it. She was such a nice WASP" (qtd. in Morice 80). It took Keaton years before she even watched the film. Whenever the subject comes up, her stock comment is "Pacino was great.

Robert De Niro was great. I was background music."

From the moment Kay appears on-screen, however, she becomes the focal point of the scene. She is so obviously the outsider at an Italian wedding reception. Her clothing and demeanor set her apart from other guests who seem to blend together with their dark complexions and more muted finery. Wearing a long, red dress with a white sailor collar, pearls, and wide-brimmed hat, Kay arrives arm in arm with Michael, dressed in his marine uniform. He escorts her through the gates of the family compound, bordered by high stone walls. Then, in a symbolic gesture, he takes her hand as they make their way through the crowd, drawing her into his world. The gesture is repeated later in the scene. Michael grabs her hand and pulls her into the family picture as Kay simpers: "No, Michael, not me." Against her better judgment, she follows him. With a click of the camera shutter, she becomes a part of the family fabric—forever.

Kay enters Michael's world only half reluctantly. As she and Michael sit at a table slightly apart from the rest of the crowd, an over-the-shoulder shot captures her smoking and staring intently at Luca Brasi, the "scary guy" by the door who is talking to himself. Coppola establishes early on that Kay is observant and highly intelligent. She watches everything and everyone around her with an almost morbid fascination. As Michael introduces her to his brother, Tom Hagen, Kay is quick to ask why they have different last names if they're brothers. Trying to avoid her probing questions about the family "business," Michael gives her a brief explanation and patronizingly changes the subject: "Do you like your lasagna?"

Kay seems compelled to pry the dark family secrets from her lover though she fears the answers. Michael hedges again, but she won't let him off the hook as she

The Godfather (Paramount, 1972). Though Al Pacino received an Academy Award nomination for Best Supporting Actor for his portrayal of Michael, Don Corleone's favorite son and successor to the Mafia throne, he had a tough time winning the role. Paramount studio executives did not believe that Pacino was right for the part. It took Coppola, producer Al Ruddy, and endless screen tests to convince them. One of those tests was with Diane Keaton who plays Michael's compliant armpiece, Kay Adams. In this still, Michael reads about the hit on his father in the *Daily News* as Kay watches his reaction, all too aware that the incident will pull the man she loves into the "life" forever. Production designer Dean Tavoularis' authentic sets and costumes, including details like the Janiro-Zavala fight, as well as the actors' naturalistic acting styles, give this scene an eerie believability.

begs him to tell her how Luca Brasi and his father got singer Johnny Fontaine out of his contract with a famous band leader. The camera lingers on Kay's reaction as Michael explains that his father made the band leader "an offer he couldn't refuse." While Luca Brasi held a gun to the man's head, Don Corleone threatened the band leader that either his brains or his signature would be on the contract. As Michael finishes the story, Kay notes the reluctant pride in his voice as he talks about his father. She watches the way he can't look her in the eye as he says, "That's my fam-ily, Kay, not me." In close-up, we see her lift her chin ever so slightly, her face reflecting full awareness and recognition of the family business. Kay knows what kind of life is in store for her, yet she *chooses* to believe Michael. As Keaton says, Kay goes along with it all.

The phone booth scene becomes a metaphor for Kay's place in the family. Michael and Kay are walking along a New York street one evening after seeing *The Bells of St. Mary's*. They pass a newsstand. It is Kay who notices the headline in the paper. Michael's father, Don Corleone, has been gunned down. Michael runs to the nearest phone booth to call home and closes the door on her for the first time. The camera is at eye-level. Michael is in the left foreground, the telephone in the right foreground. Between him and the phone, in mid-plane, we see only Kay's eyes looking into the phone booth. With the glass and the mesh wire between her and Michael, she cannot hear what he is saying. She can only watch helplessly. She is literally out in the cold. Kay has no voice in this family.

In fact, Kay is shut out several times in the film. Knowing he plans to execute the men who shot his father, Michael sees Kay for the last time over dinner at her New York apartment and closes the door on their relationship. These are people with little to say to each other. He won't reveal his plans; she's too numb to say anything except "When will I see you again?" He doesn't know. He doesn't want her involved and tells her to go back to New Hampshire. "I'll call you at your parents' house." As in many of these early scenes, Kay wears red, the color of passion, as well as danger. This time her dress is the shade of the wine in the glass before her. It falls carelessly off one shoulder, and, as Michael gets up to leave, he moves around behind her as she stares into her wine glass. Kissing her head and moving his hand along her bare shoulder, he walks out. They both realize that he has been drawn into the intricate web of vendetta.

More than a year lapses before we see Kay again. In another bit of subtle irony, she is on the playground with her elementary school class when Michael pulls up to the curb, the quintessential stranger in the black sedan. She knows nothing about his life in Sicily, or that he has been home for over a year. She knows nothing about Apollonia, his Sicilian wife, or how Apollonia became another death statistic in the Mafia crossfire. Dressed completely in black, a harder-edged Michael begins a different kind of courtship ritual with Kay, using words like candy to entice her into his car. Leaving the children behind, she walks with Michael toward the camera as he tells her that he is now working for his father who has "been sick."

> KAY: But you're not like him, Michael. I thought you weren't going to become a man like your father. That's what you told me.
> MICHAEL: My father's no different from any other powerful man. Any man who is responsible for other people ... like a Senator or President.
> KAY: You know how naive you sound?
> MICHAEL: Why?
> KAY: Senators and Presidents don't have men killed.
> MICHAEL: Oh, who's being naive, Kay.

That sweet, child-like, melodious voice that marks the vulnerable side of Keaton's paradoxical persona works well in this scene as Kay allows herself to be drawn in by Michael's honeyed words and assurances. She whimpers and cajoles, but she is ultimately lost in his promise that the Corleone family will be legitimate within five years. He says "trust me" and "that's all I can tell you about my business." (Note the possessive pronoun here.) Kay breaks down and begins to cry, asking why he came after all this time. He came for her, he explains, because he "needs" her. And Michael does need Kay. He has lost one breeder and must find another. He never uses the word "love" here until he has to. Instead he says: "I'll do anything you ask. Anything to make up for what was lost—because that's important, Kay. Because what's important is that we have each other, that we have a life together. That we have children—our children." Only after Kay refuses to look at him does he say: "I need you ... and I love you." It's a last ditch effort to get her into his car. Unlike the school children she leaves behind on the playground who are taught never to get into a car with strangers, Kay gets into the black sedan with a man she barely knows—and seals her fate.

The final scene of the film brings Kay and Michael's relationship full circle when Connie Corleone runs into the house accusing her brother Michael of killing her husband. She turns to Kay: "That's your husband. Read the papers." But by this time, Kay's curiosity and spirit have been snuffed out by her ruthless husband. When she meekly asks, "Is it true," Michael explodes, slamming his fist on his desk and yelling, "Enough! Don't ask me about my business." She looks down. He regains his composure and says, "All right. This one time. I'll let you ask me about my affairs." Kay must receive permission now to even ask a question, and Michael, no longer just evasive, has learned how to lie. He sends his wife away with a lie and a hug. We see her walk through three doorways and begin to fix them a drink.

Keaton doesn't give herself enough credit for her beautifully subtle performance in *The Godfather*. The film marks the first evidence of her ability to reflect several conflicting emotions simultaneously. The final shot of her face as she turns to look back at Michael in his study will go down as one of the most memorable moments in film history. Keaton is able to convey all of the fear and hopelessness of the betrayed and entrapped as Kay watches her husband become the new don, like his father before him. His men ritualistically kiss his hand and then close the door to their world, denying even her vision.

By the time Keaton made *Godfather II*, she had several films to her credit, including *Play It Again, Sam* and *Sleeper* with Woody Allen. She had matured to the point where she was no longer afraid of everybody on the set. In a 1974 interview, she explained:

On the first one, I felt so inconsequential and all I could do was be very friendly and very nice and very scared. Jeeze, every time I'd run into Marlon Brando on the set my face would turn red and I'd start laughing and laughing. I was so *high school*. So totally into self-loathing [qtd. in Flatley, "Applause" 71].

That insecurity proved useful in her portrayal of Kay in the first film, but the character is a much stronger presence in the *Godfather* sequel.

For the first half of *The Godfather II*, set in Nevada, Kay remains in the background of most shots. She has abandoned her red ensembles for cool blues and beiges. Kay looks like all the rest of the Mafia wives; however, she is ill at ease in her role. At her son's first communion party, she awkwardly poses with Senator Geary for a staged photo. In a bid for respectability, Michael has donated an undisclosed amount to a Nevada college. As she and Michael dance, we discover that she is once again pregnant. Michael asks: "Does it feel like a boy?" She dutifully replies, "Yes it does, Michael" and then reminds him of his promise to her seven years ago: that the Corleone family would be legitimate in five years. She chooses again to believe him—until a machine gun almost kills them in their own bedroom later that night. In the aftermath, she sits stonily on the sofa holding her daughter, refusing to look at her husband. When she does return his gaze, her look is filled with accusation. He turns away.

When a Senate committee convenes to investigate Michael's business dealings, Kay sits behind and to the left of her husband, always in the shot. Though she has no part in the hearings, Kay takes it all in. She listens to the committee's accusations and watches her husband as he denies them. At times, Kay looks down, ashamed and embarrassed, or looks away, deep in her own thoughts. Keaton's ability to project several emotions at once, evident also in this scene, subtly shifts our attention from what Michael has done to what she might do.

The Godfather: Part II (Paramount, 1974). As Mafia wife Kay Corleone, Keaton often appears to the sides of the frame or in the background, suggesting her place as outsider in this family. During the Senate's investigative hearings for Michael's mob activities, we frequently see her in the shot—seated behind her husband, looking embarrassed and uncomfortable or lost in her own thoughts.

Like many women during the forties and fifties, when these two films take place, Kay finds herself trapped in a society reestablishing its patriarchy after the war. With all the vigor of the newly converted, this society often punished women for testing its boundaries rather than placing their happiness in the protective custody of the opposite sex. The Mafia subculture, with its even more rigid patriarchy, offers no chance of personal freedom—yet Kay willingly walks into this world. Tapping into these conflicting levels of behavior, Keaton saves the character from stereotype and reveals the soul of an embittered, disillusioned woman waking up to the reality of her situation in life.

In the confrontation scene, Kay tells Michael that she and the children are leaving him. Neither his assurances that he will change nor his shouting work this time as Kay finds her voice: "You say you love me, and then you talk about allowing me to leave. You've become blind, Michael." He's also become deaf. He doesn't want to hear it when she tells him: "At this moment I feel no love for you at all. I never thought that would ever happen, but it has." When Kay realizes that he will never let her take *his* children, that he will use all of his power to stop her, she reveals her own dark secret: she aborted their last child, a son.

It wasn't a miscarriage. It was an abortion. An abortion, Michael, just like our marriage is an abortion. Something that's unholy. Evil. I didn't want your son, Michael. I wouldn't bring another one of your sons into this world. It was an abortion, Michael. It was a son—a son, and I had it killed because this must all end. I know now that it's over. I knew it then. There would be no way, Michael, no way you could ever forgive me, not with this Sicilian thing that's been going on for 2,000 years!

For once, Michael is visibly shaken with rage. He silences her, but it takes an act of physical violence this time, a fierce slap which sends her reeling backward onto a sofa. Kay's revelation, however, buys her own freedom at the price of her children's. In one of the final scenes, Kay sneaks back to see them, but Michael shows up before she can leave. As she stands in the doorway, stone walls on either side of her, he silently looks her up and down and then once again closes the door on her.

Keaton has definite opinions about these films and the Mafia in general. She calls them cautionary tales "in that you should just stay away from the Mafia. It's horrible" (personal interview). She recently told another interviewer that when her parents saw *Godfather II* in Los Angeles, the audience applauded when Michael slapped Kay in the confrontation scene. She defensively explained: "He was a horrible character.... I say to hell with those people who applauded. My parents were with me" (qtd. in Denerstein, "At 51" D6). Though "brilliant films," Keaton feels that *The Godfather* movies paint such a romantic picture of the mob that people fell in love with the characters. On the other hand, it is the raw, gritty, violent *GoodFellas* (1990), directed by Martin Scorsese, that she feels is "the politically correct" depiction of the Mafia. "And it is also a great movie," she adds (personal interview).

Play It Again, Sam

Keaton recently told Betsy Pickle of the *Star Tribune* that of all the films she has made over the years, those with Woody Allen mean the most to her. "Nobody comes close to Woody in my life, professionally" (qtd. in Pickle E1). By the time they made Herbert Ross' 1972 screen version of Allen's stage hit (*Play It Again, Sam*) Keaton and Allen were living apart, but they were still very good friends and saw each other on a regular basis. Keaton claims that she appears in the film version only because of Woody's influence. "I mean, I'm sure that Herb Ross and the studio wouldn't have cast me unless Woody said, 'I want her'" (personal interview).

Keaton felt comfortable working with Allen in *Play It Again, Sam*, a change from her experience on *The Godfather* which came out earlier in the year. She moved back into familiar territory surrounded by familiar faces. Allen restored her confidence, and Keaton no longer felt like background music. Allen, likewise, felt comfortable working with her. Their mutual affection and admiration for each other translated to a natural ease in their on-camera relationships. He played the nerdy, misunderstood underdog; she played his vulnerable, highstrung sidekick. Audiences rooted for them.

Ross captured their engaging, neurotic interplay as Keaton and Allen reprised their stage characters: Linda Christie and Allan Felix, two lonely, insecure people out of sync with an increasingly cold, impersonal world. Linda, a model, operates as little more than an armpiece for her husband Dick (Tony Roberts), a workaholic who can't sever the umbilical cord to his office. Shot in the days before cellular technology, Dick forwards phone numbers to his secretary at his every stop. When Linda and Dick stop at Allan's apartment to comfort him after his wife Nancy (Susan Anspach) leaves him, Dick heads for the phone. Linda stands, arms crossed, in a doorway and quips: "There's a phone booth on the corner. Want me to run down and get the number? We'll be passing it." Later that night as they are lying in bed, Linda tells Dick that all this talk about divorce upsets her. He's lying there with one arm around her and the other holding a phone to his ear. He interrupts his business conversation long enough to look over at her and say, "You are so insecure."

Linda and Allan are the outsiders in this world. Linda's first line in the film, for example, sets her apart from her husband as she greets Allan: "You poor thing." Her empathy is just what Allan needs. She, on the other hand, needs some attention. He has been emasculated by his ex-wife; she has been ignored by her husband. He needs to feel like a man; she needs to feel like a woman. They are also drawn together by common interests. They both gulp aspirin, see an analyst, get migraines and cold sores, and love apple juice with Darvon. Dick tells them: "You two should get married and move into a hospital."

Allan, a total failure with women, retreats into a fantasy world of movies where men know just what to do with a dame. Nancy calls him one of "life's great watchers." His entire apartment is filled with posters and memorabilia from films, especially starring his hero and confidant in matters of the heart, Humphrey Bogart. Bogart's face is often reflected along with Allan's in the film's many mirror shots as Allan desperately tries to imitate the smooth Bogie—often with disastrous results. In the opening of the film, we see Allan sitting in a darkened theater watching the final scene in *Casablanca*, his mouth slightly agape, as Ross cuts back and forth between the suave Bogart and the nerdish Allan. But it's a dejected Allan who emerges from the theater into the daylight: "Who am I kidding?" he asks. "I'm not like that. I never will be." He fails miserably with the string of women Linda and Dick try to fix him up with, including Sharon, star of *Gang Bang*, and Jennifer the nymphomaniac.

As Linda, Keaton exhibits that open-hearted, child-like likability and innocence that have become part of her on-screen persona. She wears little makeup. Her hair is parted in the middle in a shoulder-length bob. Her clothes are soft and feminine: lots of white blouses, short or long flowing skirts, bowler hats, and tailored plaid suits with ties. In one scene, Allan imagines himself sitting in front of a roaring fire with Linda. She's wearing a black, fairly low-cut, evening dress—a rarity for a Keaton character, unless we remember that this is Allan's fantasy.

Linda is so sweet that when Sharon asks her if the hyper-tense Allen is "on something," Linda makes excuses for him: "Well, he's been under some strain lately." Only she appreciates Allan's "complex" personality and sees him for the "bright and funny and romantic" guy he really is. She becomes his confidante, and, as they spend more and more time together, we see them on the phone as they discuss possible soul mates for Allan. Thematically reminiscent of *Casablanca*'s Paris flashback sequence, a series of connected scenes show Linda and Allan growing closer. They stroll through art galleries, sharing a "mystical attraction" for van Gogh who cut off his ear for the woman he loved. They walk along the beach while Dick conducts a business meeting at their vacation cottage. Allan remembers her birthday with a plastic skunk while Dick "pencils" her in for dinner and dismisses her when she interrupts his financial reports. It's Allan who dances with Linda at the night club, not Dick. They sit in the park, isolated amid rows of empty benches bounded by trees, happily planning dinner together while Dick flies to Cleveland on business.

Things begin to heat up in Allan's kitchen. Linda and Allan stand in the door frame in profile, locked on each other. Linda asks a question that reflects on one of the central themes of *Casablanca*'s love story: "Do you think it's possible to love

Play It Again, Sam (Paramount, 1972). The suave, tough-guy image of Humphrey Bogart in John's Huston's *Across the Pacific* looms over Allan Felix's bed, dwarfing and overwhelming the couple in the bottom of the frame. The poster serves as a visual metaphor for Allan's obsession with being Bogie, an actor whose dashing, cynical-but-sensitive screen persona often had women falling at his feet. Short and klutzy, Allan finds that his attempts to emulate his idol repeatedly misfire, and one date after another ends in chaos and disaster. His friendship and eventual love affair with his best friend's wife, a neglected neurotic herself, saves him in the end. He tells Bogie: "I guess the secret's not being you. It's being me."

ments in Allan's ear. Linda begins to share her innermost secrets with Allan. She's not the type for a fling, she couldn't take the excitement, she's not glamorous enough, life has passed her by, she should be selling Fanny Farmer chocolates.

Allan, sitting very close to Linda at Bogie's urging, reassures her that she's beautiful. The camera slowly moves in to a tight closeup as Allan lunges at Linda, knocking over the lamp behind him in the process. Lying underneath him, Linda screams: "I'll pay for the lamp! Will you please take $10?" She bolts out the door only to return two minutes later, declaring her love for him, kissing him. "As Time Goes By" swells underneath the action.

Their affair gives them what they both need: confidence. A tilt down shot shows them lying in bed discussing their night of passion underneath a poster of Bogie in *Across the Pacific*. Neither can resolve the dilemma of Dick. Linda is guilt-ridden. Allan imagines a series of hilarious vignettes with an angry Dick out for revenge. Bogie finally advises Allan to do the right thing by a pal (as Rick Blaine does in *Casablanca*) and sacrifice the woman he loves.

two people at once? A wife happily married suddenly finds she loves another man. Not that she doesn't love her husband, just that she loves somebody else. Do you think that's possible?"

"Very possible," Allan replies. They move to the sofa sipping champagne when the phantom Bogie appears, sitting on the arm of the sofa, whispering encourage-

As *Play It Again, Sam* comes full circle, Linda and Allan and Dick all end up on the airport runway at night and play out the "hill of beans" scene from *Casablanca*. The fog rolls in. We see lights in the distance. A plane waits in the background. Linda is wearing a wide-brimmed hat, Allan a trenchcoat. The characters position themselves as the camera duplicates the scene from *Casablanca*. It's Linda who speaks first: "A wonderful thing has happened. I love Dick, and although someone as wonderful as you is very tempting, I can't imagine my life without him. He needs me, Allan." She has let him down gently, but Allan has waited his whole life to enact this scene and say these words:

> Inside of us we both know you belong with Dick. You're part of his work, the thing that keeps him going. If that plane leaves and you're not on it, then you'll regret it. Maybe not today. Maybe not tomorrow, but soon and for the rest of your life.

He sends Linda off with Dick as Bogie appears and tells him: "That was great. You really developed yourself a little style.... You don't need me anymore." Allan walks into the mist alone saying: "I guess the secret's not being you. It's being me."

The teaming of Keaton and Allen was so successful that they continued their partnership in the early seventies with two more films, *Sleeper* (1973) and *Love and Death* (1975). In the eyes of an appreciative public, they became inextricably linked both on-screen and off. Their similarities in attitude and behavior prompted Johnny Carson to quip: "I think she's Woody's sister" (qtd. in Lax, "Off the Screen" 43). Even today, they tend to agree on many subjects. In Stig Bjorkman's 1993 book entitled *Woody Allen on Woody Allen*, for example, Allen discusses the daydreaming theme in *Play It Again, Sam*.

> It has been said, that if I have any one big theme in my movies, it's got to do with the difference between reality and fantasy. It comes up very frequently in my films. I think what it boils down to, really, is that I hate reality. And, you know, unfortunately it's the only place where I can get a good steak dinner.... It appears in my work all the time. The sense of wanting to control reality, to be able to write a scenario for reality and make things come out the way you want it.... So in my films I just feel there's always a pervasive feeling of the greatness of idealized life or fantasy versus the unpleasantness of reality [qtd. in Bjorkman 50–51].

Keaton echoes these same sentiments about reality in one 1993 interview:

> You know, people are always extolling "truth" and "real life" and "truth is beauty." I don't think that.... You can't really come face to face with reality too frequently or for too long a time because it'll wipe you out. It's too brutal [qtd. in Decurtis 50].

In his follow-up film, *Sleeper*, Allen lifted himself and Keaton completely out of the realm of reality and into a 22nd century fantasy world.

Sleeper

Woody Allen directed Diane Keaton for the first time in his sci-fi farce, *Sleeper*. Known as an actor's director, he hires talented people and gives them plenty of room to work and do what they do best. This is probably why few actors turn down a chance to work with Allen. Edward Norton (*Primal Fear*, *Rounders*), for example, told talk show host Larry King once that he accepted a role in Allen's *Everybody Says I Love You* without even knowing it was a musical. With *Sleeper*, Allen provided the perfect vehicle for Keaton's offbeat persona. He encouraged her proclivity for slapstick and cultivated her natural comic timing, child-like naiveté, and intelligence—all evident but restrained in *Play It Again, Sam*.

In *Sleeper*, which Allen cowrote with Marshall Brickman, Keaton and Allen play a space-age odd couple. He is Miles

Monroe, a jazz musician and owner of the Happy Carrot Health Food Restaurant, who is accidentally cryogenically frozen in 1973 during a routine ulcer surgery. He wakes up 200 years later in a society where everything is programmed, even sex. Keaton plays Luna Schlosser, the spaced-out poet with a Ph.D. in oral sex. Through a series of high jinks, edited to the music of Woody Allen with the Preservation Hall Jazz Band and the New Orleans Funeral Ragtime Orchestra, Miles and Luna become part of an underground movement to topple "The Leader" of this controlled society.

Allen frequently confesses that every time he acts with Keaton he ends up being *her* straight man, and, in truth, he does give her some great lines in this film. Several key scenes illustrate Keaton's own gift for the gag. For example, Luna and Miles are both "in disguise" when they meet. On the lam from the police, who want to exterminate him before he contaminates the 22nd century natives, Miles shows up at Luna's door as a robotic butler she ordered to serve at her dinner party. She opens the door, dressed from head to toe in white with the exception of a bright green facial cleansing mask. She looks him up and down and says: "Oh, no. Is this the best they could offer? I had hoped for something with at least decent features. Oh well, I'll bring you in next week and have your head removed." After the party, she says to her friend Harold: "I think we should have had sex, but there weren't enough people."

Keaton's Luna is a throwback to those smart but daffy heroines of screwball comedy, like Carole Lombard in *My Man Godfrey* or Katharine Hepburn in *Bringing Up Baby*. Luna idolizes Rod McKuen, writes poetry about butterflies that turn into caterpillars, and flies into hysterics when told she has inverted the metamorphosis process. She lives in a state of blissful cluelessness with her sex orb, telescreen, and orgasmatron until

Miles, the alien, kidnaps her so that she can help him get to the Western District, the underground movement's headquarters.

Like most couples in the screwball genre, Luna and Miles take an instant dislike to one another until circumstances throw them together and they eventually discover that they're made for each other. In some cases, the heroine, after she gets over her initial aversion to the hero, becomes the aggressor in the relationship. In one scene, for example, Luna and Miles sit on a curved stairway reminiscent of a Busby Berkeley musical set, all white orbs and silver pillars. Miles puts a clarinet together as Luna asks: "Do you want to have sex with me?" He responds: "I don't think I'm up to a performance, but I'll rehearse with you if you like." Luna majored in cosmetic sexual technique and poetry. She knows she's beautiful, so Miles' reaction to her invitation baffles her: "How come you're not attracted to me? Men go crazy over me. I'm great physically." In what will become a refrain in many of Keaton's movies, Luna says: "You think I'm stupid." But Miles just needs a little romance and flowers.

Sleeper has held up well over the years, largely because the synergism between the two stars is as hilarious today as it was in 1973. Their affectionate squabbling and bickering, evident in the film's final scenes, is one of the hallmarks of their comedy routine. Disguised as doctors, Miles and Luna argue their way right into enemy territory and infiltrate The Leader's stronghold. But when they are mistaken for cloning experts, chaos reigns. It seems The Leader has had an accident, and all that remains of him is his nose, which they must clone as the other doctors look on. Luna addresses the gallery. "I believe this is going to be a very difficult croning job," she tells them. "Cloning, you idiot, not croning," Miles responds. After a "medical moment," Miles begins to babble about procedure

Sleeper (MGM/UA, 1973). Allen's slapstick sci-fi flick established Keaton and Allen as a great comedy duo. His formula for creating a heroine with a penchant for getting the hero in trouble and then reacting to her antics with his own one-liners, worked successfully in their early comedies as well as when they reteamed twenty years later in *Manhattan Murder Mystery*. Her behavioral comedy and his verbal comedy were a perfect mix. The chase is on in this shot as Miles Monroe (Allen) and Luna Schlosser (Keaton) try to outrun a group of irate doctors after their attempt to "crone" the Leader's nose fails miserably.

while Luna slaps down shoes, gloves, a tie, and other items of apparel onto the operating table. Miles explains, "We're going to clone The Leader directly into the suit." They play out a magic act, steal the nose, and the chase begins. The nose falls under a steam roller while Miles and Luna escape, still arguing over love and death.

Woody Allen once explained that he envisioned Keaton's role in *Sleeper* as "a Buster Keaton-like heroine, someone who is funny and who is always getting the hero into trouble. And she did that well" (qtd. in Bjorkman 68). Indeed, Diane's character is very like Annabelle in *The General*, Buster Keaton's masterpiece about a Confederate soldier, Johnny Gray, who almost singlehandedly outwits the

Union army and wins the respect of the woman he loves. Annabelle, in many ways, is a prototype of the early screwball heroines.

In one scene, Johnny puts Annabelle in charge of firing the engine of *The General* while he fends off the pursuing Union soldiers. She slowly sorts through the woodpile and throws one small log at a time into the furnace. Exasperated, Johnny starts to wring her neck and then kisses her instead. In *Sleeper*, we see Allen mimic the silent film star's moves when Luna, pressing the wrong buttons on a giant tape machine, gets them tangled in yards of reel tape. Allen's own character, Miles Monroe, is much like Buster Keaton's Johnny Gray. Both diminutive heroes win the day and the girl by demonstrating how the courage and ingenuity of one individual can sometimes make a difference in a flawed system. The reward for their valor? A kiss from the heroine.

Keaton admits today that what she enjoyed most about *Sleeper* was the physical comedy (personal interview). She cut her teeth on it with this film and incorporates elements of slapstick in several of her screen characters.

Love and Death

At the end of *Sleeper*, Miles tells Luna that political revolutions never work. He believes only in sex and death: "Two things that come once in my lifetime. But at least after death, you're not nauseous." Allen picks up these same themes in *Love and Death*, his parody of Russian literature and film set to the music of Sergey Prokofiev. The title itself plays on Leo Tolstoy's *War and Peace*, Fyodor Dostoevski's *Crime and Punishment*, and Ivan Turgenev's *Fathers and Sons*.

This time the reluctant hero, Boris Petrovich Dmitrivich Greshenko (Allen), finds himself in nineteenth century Russia, in the midst of the Napoleonic wars. But he's a lover, not a fighter. He asks one of his comrades: "Do you think there's any difference whether we live under the Czar or Napoleon? They're both crooks. The Czar's a little taller." Like Turgenev himself, Boris sides with the serfs. "The serfs should be running things. They're the only ones who know how to do anything." Boris's emancipated, pacifistic views bring him nothing but ridicule, even from his cousin, the beautiful Sonja (Keaton) who doesn't just get him into trouble here. She gets him shot.

Sonja is a cross between Anna Odintsov in *Fathers and Sons* and Luna in *Sleeper*. Toss in Natasha from *War and Peace*, Grushenka from *The Brothers Karamazov*, and Anna Karenina and you've got what Boris calls a "complex woman." Sonja puts it more precisely: "I guess you could say I'm half saint, half whore." Boris adores her brilliant mind. Like Anna Odintsov and Eugene Bazarov, she and Boris have "deep conversations"— but theirs amount to little more than pseudo-existential babble. In one scene, Sonja, a "fierce wrangler" like Madame Odintsov, tries to convince a doubtful Boris of the beauty of nature and the existence of God.

> SONJA: Boris, let me show you how absurd your position is. Let's say that there is no God and each man is free to do exactly as he chooses. What prevents you from murdering somebody?
> BORIS: Murder is immoral.
> SONJA: Immorality is subjective.
> BORIS: Yes, but subjectivity is objective.
> SONJA: Not in any rational scheme of perception.
> BORIS: Perception is irrational. It implies imminence.
> SONJA: But judgment of any system or a priori relation of phenomena exists in any rational or metaphysical or at least epistemological contradiction to an abstract and empirical concept such as being, or to be, or to occur in the thing itself, or of the thing itself.
> BORIS: I've said that many times.

Working so closely and often with Woody Allen, Keaton learned early on how to handle difficult dialogue and "talky" scripts. She rarely fluffs a line, according to sources who have watched her perform. Following the scene above, she pulls off a perfectly absurd piece of Russian literary description. The camera moves in to a close-up on Keaton's face, and, with her eyes wide and staring as if focused on another world, she says dreamily: "We should go back downstairs. By now the last golden streaks of the sunset are vanishing behind the western hills. Soon the dark blanket of night will settle over us all."

Like Luna in *Sleeper*, Sonja is totally self-absorbed when first we meet her. She tells Boris that she wants a man whose mind she can respect, whose spirituality and lustful appetite for passion equal her own. Oblivious to Boris' passionate feelings for her, she proclaims her love for his brother, Ivan, but ends up marrying a herring merchant. Her extramarital affairs make her the talk of the town, but the herring merchant conveniently dies cleaning his gun to defend her honor.

At a party, she runs into Boris, who is leaving for the front, and all she can talk about is Ivan and her own misery. The exchange between Sonja and Boris offers another example of Keaton and Allen's perfectly timed interplay and illustrates why audiences often find their characters irresistible. Boris brings out the humanity in Sonja, a selfish, spoiled child. Sonja brings out the romantic in Boris, a cowardly nebbish. Their characters may not end up happily ever after, but they bring out the best in each other for a while. Their conversation goes like this:

> SONJA: Boris, I'm so unhappy.... I've become a scandal. For the past weeks, I've visited Seretski in his room. And before Seretski, Alexi. And before Alexi, Alegorian. And before Alegorian, Asimov.
> BORIS: Wait!
> SONJA: I'm still on the A's.
> BORIS: How many lovers do you have?
> SONJA: In the midtown area?

With Allen, Keaton learned how to deliver the one-liners. As Sonja skips away obsessing about Ivan, she sends Boris off to war with this afterthought: "Dress warmly, Boris, and have a nice time." The dialogue, as Allen himself admits, is a series of jokes or witticisms reminiscent of Bob Hope and Bing Crosby's "road" pictures (Bjorkman 72).

Sonja finally consents to marry Boris only because she thinks he'll be killed in a duel. When Boris survives, she's stunned but eventually comes to love him. In a series of vignettes, we see Sonja shed her jewels and velvet gowns for peasant dresses. Like Luna, Sonja makes a trans-

formation and eventually becomes part of the revolution. She serves Boris bowls of sleet, plays music with him, and frolics in the woods. Their happiness together, always fragile at best, unravels when Sonja becomes obsessed with assassinating Napoleon. Their hilarious, inept attempts misfire. Boris still finds murder immoral. Neither he nor Sonja can pull the trigger. Someone else does, however, but Boris is blamed and shot before a firing squad.

Stylistically, *Love and Death* spoofs the Soviet montage, or thematic style of editing. Many of the Soviet filmmakers believed that the juxtaposition of shots created new meanings. In *Potemkin*, for example, Sergei Eisenstein created a metaphor of the 1905 workers' uprising by linking shots of three stone lions: one asleep, one alert, one ready to spring. Allen reverses the order in *Love and Death* after Boris spends a night of passion with Sonja. Another scene, reminiscent of Eisenstein's Odessa Steps sequence, depicts a soldier, glasses cracked, shot through the eye. Allen also parodies Ingmar Bergman's formalistic style in both *The Seventh Seal* and *Persona*. Like *The Seventh Seal*, *Love and Death* begins with clouds rolling across the sky, though the sky is a little bluer and the clouds a bit fluffier in Allen's film. *Love and Death* also ends with the dance of death, albeit a humorous rendition of Bergman's dark dance in *The Seventh Seal*. In an extreme long shot, we see Boris and Death, in a white sheet, dance among long rows of poplar trees by a beautiful lake sparkling in the sunlight.

Keaton's final scene in the film is a wonderful parody of Bergman's *Persona*, a complex story about a convalescing actress who essentially absorbs the persona of her nurse told through visual metaphors in which the two at times become one image. Sonja, now in mourning, counsels young cousin Natasha (Jessica Harper) on matters of the heart: "To love is to

Love and Death (MGM/UA, 1975). Keaton often plays beautiful, brainy women, and the combination has become part of her public persona. Allen cultivated this image by casting her in "talky" comedies like *Love and Death*, and Keaton quickly gained a reputation as an actress who could deliver difficult dialogue, sometimes with head-spinning speed. In one of her few period pieces, Keaton plays the promiscuous Sonja, who captivates Cousin Boris Grushenko with her intellectual wrangling. Boris says: "In addition to being one of the most beautiful women I had ever seen, she was one of the few people I could have deep conversations with." Sonja's brilliant plan to shoot Napoleon, however, misfires, and Boris ends up facing the firing squad.

suffer. Not to love is to suffer. To suffer is to suffer." Boris' ghost appears at the window and tells her that death is worse than the chicken at Tresky's restaurant. (In *Sleeper*, Miles says that death is like spending a weekend in Beverly Hills.) Sonja turns from the window. She is in profile on the left side of the frame.

"Life must go on. The last traces of the shimmering dusk are settling behind the quickly darkening evening. And it's only noon. Soon we shall be covered by wheat." Natasha moves into the center of the frame, facing full front, slightly behind Sonja's profile. Their facial features line up so that they become one.

NATASHA: Did you say ...
TOGETHER: Wheat?

Love and Death, shot in France and Hungary, mainly to keep expenses down, is one of the few films that Allen has made out of the country. Keaton remembers their experience in France:

Only three people spoke English, Woody, his secretary and myself. The rest spoke French. Woody speaks French too. We didn't have much to say, so we'd sit in a trailer and talk in between shots which took forever. And every day we would have the exact same meal in the hotel. Woody would have fish, and I would have chicken. No wine. The waiter thought we were two of the most eccentric people in town [qtd. in Carroll 161].

Allen told his biographer Eric Lax that after completion of *Love and Death*, he would never make another film outside of New York. Between *Sleeper*, shot in California and Colorado, and *Love and Death*, he had been away from home almost two years (Lax 282–83).

Working Without Woody

Keaton was gaining a reputation as a gifted comedienne, but she was becoming a "type" and she knew it. Furthermore, she was being referred to as Woody's sidekick. Keaton felt it was time to strike out on her own. In 1976, she teamed up with Elliott Gould in Norman Panama's forgettable romantic comedy *I Will, I Will ... for Now* and the badly written rip-off of George Roy Hill's *The Sting* called *Harry and Walter Go to New York*. In the first, she and Gould play a young divorced couple, Les and Katie Bingham, who find each other again by enrolling in a sex clinic. Keaton's reviews were fair, though few people saw the film. *Harry and Walter*, starring Elliott Gould and James Caan, was a boxoffice bomb, though Keaton again received good reviews. However, the film is significant for a couple of reasons. On a personal level, Keaton's female costars, Kathryn Grody and Carol Kane, became two of her closest friends. She would reunite with them and Elliott Gould in *The Lemon Sisters* (1990).

Second, and perhaps more important, *Harry and Walter* marks the emergence of that two-sided personality which characterizes many of Keaton's roles as well as Keaton herself. Her most inspired performances are those in which her independent spirit and refusal to accept defeat rise above her insecurities. Her characters often make a psychological journey that ends in a transformation, a realization of some new dimension of self, which adds another layer to the multi-layered individuals she plays. No matter which set of characteristics (the tough and confident or the vulnerable and insecure) dominates any given performance, the other set lies right beneath the surface, rising up to merge in pivotal scenes, giving her performances depth, complexity, and authenticity. Actor/director Ben Stiller, one of her biggest fans, once explained that Keaton has an "edge" that separates her from other female stars. In "She's the One," he writes: "She came up at a time when movies were taking more chances. She created a persona that was singular, strong, and smart and at the same time feminine, sexy, and really neurotic" (76). Keaton's characters prior to this point in her career tend to emphasize the vulnerable, sweet, and daffy characteristics.

In *Harry and Walter Go to New York*, the paradoxical persona that audiences have come to associate with Keaton surfaces in Miss Lissa Chestnut, a sassy newspaper editor who gets hooked up with a couple of knuckleheaded vaudevillians. Together they attempt to scam a scam artist who's planning a bank heist. Miss Chestnut, a turn-of-the-century Robin Hood, outwits him by robbing the bank first.

In one scene, Keaton looks like a disheveled Gibson Girl. A contradiction in appearance and behavior, she paces wildly back and forth across the room in her ladylike lace dress: arms waving, hair falling in her face. Stomp. Stomp. Stomp. She's addressing her band of inept assistants as to why they must get the money first.

> I will not allow that money to be used for loose women, for ruffled skirts, and for a princely way of life that should have been abolished centuries ago. Not while children cry out for milk in the streets below us. If that bank has to be robbed, then by God let it be robbed in the name of decency. Let that money be taken from

the exploiters and returned to the people who need it!

The more fired up she gets, the faster she talks. A note of hysteria creeps into her voice, as it rises an octave. The vulnerability bubbles underneath the anger, as if she's not quite sure of herself or her effect on the others. The scene is classic Keaton. Comedy or drama, no matter what the role, at some point a Keaton character will "snap." She will lash out and dress down an opponent—and she is one of the very few actresses who can pull off this kind of neurotic frustration with comic effect.

Elliott Gould once tried to describe Keaton's style of comedy to Gene Shalit:

> Diane Keaton is very intelligent and sensitive and sexy. The really funny thing about Diane is that here she is the girl from Orange County, California, from a Puritan-Methodist background, and yet she has this funny, abstract mind, some chemical in her that makes her original and funny. She's like an Amish groupie [qtd. in Shalit 12].

In truth, Keaton was fortunate enough to hook up with another original at a critical time in her career. Woody Allen encouraged a shy, insecure talent to trust her instincts and take risks. Keaton says, "Being around Woody was a wonderful thing for me. I found him charming and unusual—and even naive, in certain areas. I never met anyone quite like him and doubt if I ever will again" (qtd. in Linet 11–12). Their next film, *Annie Hall*, based on their own personal relationship, would bring the comedy team more fame than either was ready for.

CHAPTER 3

1977

The Price of Fame

I'm an actress, not a fad.
—Diane Keaton (*New York Daily News*, May 15, 1977)

Shortly after *Annie Hall* was released in April of 1977, Diane Keaton was sitting in a First Avenue coffee shop telling film critic Rex Reed that she had never been hampered by a high public profile. After all, she said, it wasn't like she was Farrah Fawcett-Majors, poster goddess of the moment. "I don't think I'll ever have her public image. I'm an actress, not a fad," she told Reed (qtd. in Reed 7). No sooner had Keaton claimed that she could walk down the street—just another face in the crowd—than it all changed. *Annie Hall* was an instant hit. People lined up two deep around New York City blocks to catch Woody Allen's latest comedy starring his favorite muse, Diane Keaton. *Time* magazine reported that *Annie Hall* "addicts" were "returning to theaters three and four times," reciting their favorite lines verbatim (Skow 70). Suddenly the world was filled with inarticulate women who copied Annie's la-de-da-isn't-that-something mannerisms and Chaplinesque costumes.

Life got complicated, confusing, and a little frightening for Keaton, especially when Richard Brooks' dark and gritty *Looking for Mr. Goodbar* was released that October. With her *tour de force* performance as Theresa Dunn, the quintessential madonna/whore, Keaton became the number one female box-office draw in the country. At a time in film history when strong female characters were virtually nonexistent, Keaton had landed two antithetical but unforgettable roles that distinguished her as a versatile actress who could deliver comedy or drama. *Annie Hall* and *Looking for Mr. Goodbar* catapulted Keaton into the kind of fame that few actors ever experience, and even fewer are prepared for. The media frenzy caught her off guard.

Keaton's reaction was to retreat. Rex Reed's suspicions that day in the coffee shop were well-founded: "Beneath the wafting tones of disorganized speech, I sense[d] a genuine fear of the naked exposure that accompanies stardom" (Reed 7). In 1996, Keaton admitted to Karen Thomas of *USA Today*: "It scared me. And I pulled back from it. I was afraid of it, and it killed my adventurous spirit" (qtd. in Thomas 1D). She granted only two major interviews: one for *Rolling Stone* and one for *Time*.

James Monaco took her fame-averse attitude to task in his article, "Looking for Diane Keaton," for *Take One*. His grievance stemmed from Keaton and Allen's behavior during the New York Film Festival's opening night, black-tie gala. When they walked in wearing their "*Annie* garb," about 500 guests turned to stare. Monaco wrote: "The room stopped. The seas parted. Keaton did a long slow take: 'Oh, Wow.' Then rolled her eyes, retreated quickly into a corner with the equally 'shy' Allen, and left two minutes later" (26). Monaco's points are well-taken:

> If you are already an actress and you want to convey the impression of seriousness about your craft rather than celebrity, you don't shoot for the covers of major *news*making magazines. And if you do feel you must permit this limited (and, it must be said, all the more effective) sort of exploitation, you don't show up at major industry parties dressed in costume from your last film. Especially when you know the place is half-filled with gossip columnists and journalists. And if by some accident of naiveté you find yourself in this parlous situation, you don't do shtick followed by grand exit; you hang around and talk to people and pretty soon they treat you like a person, not a star [26–27].

After acknowledging her considerable talent, he wrote: "If you really don't like publicity, you don't decide to become an actress; it goes with the territory" (26).

Arlene Rothberg, Keaton's manager at the time, didn't agree. She believed that when the hype and hoopla die down, the public moves on to the next sensation. Disinterest follows overexposure. Her client had talent. That was enough. Rothberg's strategy, however, resulted in Keaton's increased popularity and the public's desire to know more about her. As Richard Dyer points out in *Heavenly Bod-*ies: Film Stars and Society*, audiences are always searching for the real person behind the public persona (17).

Like most stars, Keaton has experienced the vicious cycle of celebrity: on top one day, down the next. She has found her own way to deal with it. Dominick Dunne once asked her if she liked being famous. Keaton replied: "It's more comfortable for me to deny it" (qtd. in Dunne 40). According to Richard deCordova in *Picture Personalities: The Emergence of the Star System in America*, "the star who shuns stardom is as much a type today as the blond bombshell, and one that meets with much less resistance from the public, since such a star gives the illusion of being a real individual outside of the system" (10). If so, Keaton is in good company. Meryl Streep, Dustin Hoffman, Jack Nicholson, Harrison Ford, Robert De Niro, Sean Connery and others have made downplaying their popularity an art form. Like Keaton, they resist being commodified. To deal with the overwhelming deference and attention accorded them by besotted fans and press, they immerse themselves in their craft and try to carve out some semblance of a private life.

Actors like Keaton, however, have a particularly rough time on the talk-show circuit, where a star's appearance before a film's release can boost the opening weekend box-office take. Many contemporary actors view these interview shows as akin to a minefield. While trying to stick to discussing safe topics like the film they are promoting, they end up sidestepping questions about their personal lives and relationships. They also walk a fine line between promoting their films and distancing themselves from their characters on the screen. It is a difficult feat since, as P. David Marshall argues, stars are the "simultaneous embodiment of media construction, audience construction, and the real, living and breathing human being" (xi). After the release of *Annie Hall*, this feat for Keaton would prove virtually impossible. It would be years before audiences and critics alike stopped talking about her in terms of her most famous character.

Annie Hall

In the aftermath of *Annie Hall*, Keaton had a difficult time widening what Marshall calls the "space between the film image and the supposed 'real' person" (108). She couldn't seem to separate herself from her alter ego on the screen. There were several reasons why. First, she shared a name with her character. Annie Hall was, in effect, Diane Hall, her real name. Even in the early days of film, stars often bore the same names as their characters (i.e., Mary Pickford in *The Courting of Mary*), thus blurring the line between character and star in the public's perception (deCordova 89).

Second, though both she and Woody Allen deny that the film is autobiographical, they admit that there are "elements of truth in it" (Klemesrud 13). However, Keaton's father, Jack Hall, once confessed: "It's 85% true—even to Dorothy and my mother!" (qtd. in Fong-Torres 75). Keaton, on the other hand, told the *New York Times*:

> We didn't meet on the tennis court; we met at an audition for Woody's play.... I have a Volkswagen, but I'm a slow driver, a cautious driver, too slow. I'm a nervous wreck when I meet a man, but I don't smoke marijuana at all. I have in the past, when I was in *Hair*.... My parents are not from Wisconsin, but Balboa Island, Calif., and they're nothing at all like the parents in the film.... I've never had spiders in my bathtub. Roaches, maybe. And I've never had an affair with a rock 'n' roller [qtd. in Klemesrud 13].

Allen added that their breakup was nothing like Annie and Alvy's. "She [Keaton] was not involved with anybody else and she wasn't running away to California" (qtd. in Fong-Torres 75).

While not directly contradicting Keaton or Allen, many accounts over the years have tended to play up the autobiographical elements. In one oft-quoted comment, Allen said: "In *Annie Hall* I was trying to give the audience the view of Diane that I had—the feeling that if they can see her as I see her they will love her" (qtd. in Kroll, "Thoroughly Modern Diane" 57). Keaton's *Time* interview focused on the similarities between the characters and the real stars, stating: "Though many of the facts have been changed, *Annie Hall* is a fair portrayal of their relationship" (Skow 71). In his biography of Allen, Eric Lax suggests that at least in one scene, the first scene actually shot for the film, Allen and Keaton were playing themselves as they squeamishly prepare a lobster dinner at Alvy's beach house. "Neither Woody nor Diane was acting. Their laughter was completely spontaneous, and it gives the scene a vitality that cannot be planned" (Lax, *Biography* 245).

Conflicting stories like these confused the issue as well as audiences. If the public was reading any of Keaton's press at the time, they knew she had more than a few things in common with Annie. Like her character, Keaton was an actress and a singer; she loved gum, photography, and cats; she lived in a white on white apartment decorated mainly with her own framed photographs; she had an Aunt Sadie and a Grammy Hall who loved money; she went to swap meets with family members who Woody considered "very American and very healthy"; she loved California; she was more visual than verbal; she wore funky clothes that Woody loved; and she had a Pygmalion-type relationship with him. It's no wonder audiences speculated about what else in the film might be true. Focusing on these shared experiences and common interests, the reportage built a tight homology between the character and the star.

Keaton's fashion sense, especially, received a lot of attention and solidified the

Annie Hall (MGM/UA, 1977). It was the look that launched a fashion craze: big shirts, baggy chinos, men's vests, floppy ties, and bowler hats. Young women everywhere copied Diane Keaton's layered ensemble, still in evidence today with only slight modifications. When Alvy says to Annie, "Hey, I like what you're wearing," he's echoing Allen's own sentiments. He encouraged Keaton to wear what she wanted in the film, despite the protests of the wardrobe department, because he liked her offbeat style. The shirts, buttoned to the collar, the derby hats, and the layers of clothing have become a Keaton trademark. The overall image suggests a complex, modern American woman, a paradox of self-doubt and self-assurance.

tell her. Otherwise she can choose for herself" (qtd. in Bjorkman 83–85). Whether, as one friend observed, Keaton inherited her father's sense of style or whether, as Keaton herself recently explained, her look was lifted from the streets of SoHo, she was not "in costume" in *Annie Hall*. She was wearing her own creations.

In popular imagination, *Annie Hall* became a bewildering kaleidoscope of fact and fiction. Many of Allen's films, in fact, reflect his tendency to blur the boundaries between what was and what might have been. In *Woody and His Women*, Tim Carroll recounts how Allen's second wife, Louise Lasser, claimed that *Interiors* was a thinly veiled portrait of her own family (188). *Deconstructing Harry*, one of Allen's most recent films, is about a man who incurs the wrath of friends and family when he writes a novel "loosely" based on their interrelationships. Allen often deals with this theme of reality versus fantasy in terms of how we remember the

connection between the on-screen persona and the public figure. When filming began, costumer Ruth Morley went to Woody and complained about Keaton's wardrobe choice. "Tell her not to wear that. She can't wear that. It's so crazy," she said. Allen replied: "Leave her. She's a genius. Let's just leave her alone, let her wear what she wants. If I really hate something, I'll

past—how much of it really happened and how much of it is fabricated. Thus, while Allen brought Keaton to the attention of an appreciative public, he forever linked her with her on-screen persona by folding in elements of her own life and their life together as he and his character, Alvy Singer, remember them. For Allen, and for most writers, everything is copy.

In interviews, Keaton not only *looked* but also *sounded* like Annie Hall, which almost every interviewer noted, especially in the seventies and eighties. Judy Klemesrud of the *New York Times*, for example, wrote:

> In person, Miss Keaton seems very much like the kooky comedy characters she has played in four Woody Allen films. There is a constant, uneasy smile on her face, and she speaks slowly, shyly and softly, and says "Gee" and "Sure" and "TURR-if-ic" and "Well, uh..." alot [sic], all the while nervously twisting the ends of her long hair [13].

Whether, as a friend had suggested, it was all an act or whether it was nervousness on Keaton's part or whether the public just *wanted* her to be a character they loved, it took two decades before reporters and colleagues began noting: "She's not at all like Annie Hall."

Keaton made *Annie Hall* at a critical juncture for women in American culture. The aftermath of the Vietnam War, the Watergate scandals, economic recession, soaring inflation, drug epidemic, corruption in big business, and escalating divorce rate rocked the country. The atmosphere reeked of angst, mistrust, fear, and insecurity. Bree Daniel (Jane Fonda) summed up the general attitude best in *Klute*: "Let it all hang out. Do it all, and fuck it."

In this ism-infected age, Keaton became not just a star but an icon. Annie Hall, and with her Diane Keaton, represented all of the uncertainty and ambition of the new breed of woman—the seventies woman. Jack Kroll wrote:

> Annie's throwaway verbal style and her thrown-together dress style became symbols of the free, friendly, graceful, puzzled young women who were busy creating identities out of the epic miscellany of material swirling in the American cultural centrifuge.... The meltdown of moral absolutes has opened the gate to ambiguity and ambivalence, and Keaton

has these in her bones ["Thoroughly Modern Diane" 55].

Annie, like the paradoxical Keaton herself—edgy, vulnerable, and ultimately uncompromising—became a role model for American women on the move. As Stephen J. Spignesi summed up the character in *The Woody Allen Companion*:

> Her mannish wardrobe became trendy, and her nervousness and trepidation about romantic relationships coalesced the fears of a postsixties generation that was slowly awakening to the fact that there was no such thing as "free love" and that relationships came with a price, even if that price was only heartbreak and loss [114].

The seventies did not inspire many romantic comedies, so it is no surprise that the one of note reflects the neurosis of an entire society. Woody Allen's revisionist valentine to his former love explores the darker side of relationships, the ones that come with excess baggage and a disclaimer: enter at your own risk. It reveals the dysfunctional elements, the empty feelings left when relationships don't work out. Audiences everywhere identified with the subject matter and the characters, much to the surprise of Allen. He told Charles Champlin: "It's a very, very New York movie. It couldn't have been less universal to audiences in Australia or Italy or Idaho or Utah, but it turned out to have a universality nevertheless" (qtd. in "Attention" 36).

As Julian Fox points out in *Woody: Movies from Manhattan, Annie Hall* got off to a shaky start, in the tradition of other Oscar-winning films. (*Casablanca* and *It Happened One Night* immediately come to mind.) It was initially titled *Anhedonia*, which means the inability to experience pleasure or enjoy life. Originally a pastiche of scenes about the life and times and observations of a comic (Allen) interwoven with a murder mystery, the film had no real central theme. However, editor Ralph Rosenblum quickly noted that it was the love story between Alvy and Annie that persistently emerged as some of the best material and held the film together.

When Allen saw that, he eliminated the murder mystery and focused on the romantic relationship (Fox 86–91). Though Alvy begins and ends the film with jokes, they are thoughtful and reflective, acting almost as metaphors for his life and his relationship with Annie. In short, what started out as another Woody Allen comedy routine riddled with one-liners interrupted by bits of plot became a stylistic masterpiece with a message for the times. Furthermore, what started out as a subsidiary character for Keaton became a starring role and an Academy Award-winning performance. Keaton also won the Golden Globe, the National Society of Film Critics Award, the New York Film Critics Circle Award, the British Academy of Film Award, and the National Board of Review Award for Best Actress.

As with other films in Allen's oeuvre, *Annie Hall* is about love and death—specifically, the death of love. The film opens as Alvy Singer (Allen) breaks the fourth wall of the screen by talking directly to the audience as if to an analyst, which, of course, immediately pulls the audience into the story. We become his confidants as he tells us about his courtship, affair, and breakup with Annie not in chronological order but in a series of flashbacks linked only by memories that trigger other memories. As Alvy keeps "sifting the pieces of the relationship" through his mind trying to figure out where the "screw-up" came, the entire film becomes a post-mortem of this relationship, but, as often happens in real life, we never fully understand what went wrong. Like Alvy, we must draw our own conclusions based on selective memory and subjective analysis.

Alvy and Annie's first meeting is like a fidgety *pas de deux*. Annie, an insecure,

would-be chanteuse from Chippewa Falls, Wisconsin, is a bit intimidated by the urbane, native New Yorker, Alvy. She starts to speak, stops, shakes her head, looks down, and, with one hand on her hip, says: "Oh, well, la-de-da ... what a jerk, Annie." She comes off as flaky, nervous, and scattered, yet her baggy, layered, mannish clothing is as complicated as she is. The ensembles, clownish at first, seem to shout: "Pay attention to my mind, not my body." There's more to Annie than meets the eye. She does not seem contrived or cartoonish. In this scene, Allen uses a realistic editing style—long sequences, lengthy takes, and few cuts—to allow Keaton the luxury of a sustained performance and enable her to reveal this character in all her complexity. Allen gives us, and Alvy, time to know Annie.

After their tennis match, she invites Alvy up to her apartment where the courtship dance continues as Annie talks about her family and her photography. Annie covers her face with her hands, backs up while she's talking, and giggles when she's nervous. The mannerisms in these two scenes alone captured the public's imagination, especially that of impressionable young women who copied Annie's style of dress and speech, and entered the Keaton lexicon to be duplicated or modified in many of her future films.

As Annie and Alvy drink wine on her balcony, she tries to hold her own with his pseudo-intellectual babble about art and photography. Neither Annie nor Alvy understands what Alvy is saying. Allen uses comic subtitles to depict the contradictions that often exist between what we say and what we actually think. While Alvy expounds on aesthetic criteria for judging photography as an art form, he's really wondering what Annie looks like naked. For Annie, photography is simply "instinctive," but she's really afraid she isn't smart enough for him. Like Luna in *Sleeper*, Annie's refrain throughout the film is "You don't think I'm smart enough to be serious about." But Annie is smart; her problem is that she doesn't take herself seriously. Ironically, Alvy helps her see just how intelligent she is, pushes her to take risks, and eventually she leaves him behind.

Their relationship becomes, as Keaton and others have suggested, a Pygmalion story. "Here's this person who has a lot of raw something going for her, and she's taken under the wing by this guy," Keaton explains. "She kind of outgrows him and goes on and lives her life" (personal interview). An example of art imitating life, Alvy does guide and encourage Annie to improve herself. He becomes her teacher, in the tradition of romantic comedy heroes. He introduces her to his beloved city (always visible behind them in the balcony scene) and his upper East Side sensibilities.

Allen keeps the focus of the film on this relationship, the characters and the dialogue. There are no elaborate sets. The simple interiors do not call attention to themselves. In one scene, for example, Annie calls Alvy over to her apartment in the middle of the night to kill a spider in her bathroom. When he emerges, she is curled up in the corner of her bed, crying, with only the bare walls behind her. Alvy moves in beside her on the right. Nothing distracts the viewer from their conversation and reconciliation. Eventually, however, Luna's prophecy at the end of *Sleeper* comes to pass for Alvy and Annie: "Meaningful relationships between men and women don't last. That was proven by science. You see, there's a chemical in our bodies that makes it so that we all get on each other's nerves sooner or later."

Allen's sophisticated camera work and sense of composition point up the differences between men and women and give us a double perspective: what is and what ought to be. He uses the split screen technique to contrast Alvy's and Annie's families, their psychiatric sessions, and their attitudes toward sex and life in general—things that bind or fracture relationships. Their worlds comically collide in one scene, for example, as their mothers talk across a split screen which depicts two vastly different family meal scenarios. Alvy is Jewish and self-conscious about it. He grew up under a rollercoaster, a metaphor for the emotional rollercoaster he experienced as part of a bickering Jewish family. The WASPy Annie, as Alvy remarks, grew up in a "Norman Rockwell painting."

Allen also uses the split screen technique to illustrate their opposing views on sex. Allen shows Annie with her analyst on the left half of the frame and Alvy with his analyst on the right as they simultaneously discuss the frequency of their lovemaking. Three times a week is "constantly" to Annie and "hardly ever" to Alvy, who is obsessed with sex and wants to possess Annie's mind as well as her body. Allen often works with Gordon Willis, the master cinematographer responsible for the marvelous low-key lighting in the *Godfather* films. In one scene, Willis used a double exposure shot to show Annie's spirit leave her body and watch as she's making love to Alvy, suggesting not only how women can disengage during sex but also how Annie is reacting to Alvy's need to control.

The more psychoanalysis she experiences, the more education and sophistication she acquires, the more clearly she sees Alvy for what he is: isolationist and incapable of enjoying life. Like Alvy, Allen had been in analysis for years before he met Keaton and readily admits that he himself is anhedonic. And like Alvy, Allen is responsible for introducing Keaton to analysis which, over the years, has helped her rechannel her feelings of inadequacy into constructive behavior.

Annie ultimately develops an edge and acquires some self-confidence, but she trades one Pygmalion for another. Leaving New York and Alvy behind, she moves to California—where everybody wears white and "takes" meetings—with record producer Tony Lacy (Paul Simon). In *The Woody Allen Companion*, Spignesi calls Simon's role "a thinly disguised satirical depiction of Warren Beatty" (164) who initiated a romantic relationship with Keaton after he saw her work in both *Annie Hall* and *Looking for Mr. Goodbar*. Lacy, a smooth operator, offers Annie excitement and glamour, but, to Alvy, Los Angeles is a land of laugh tracks and bad sitcoms.

Allen's well-documented personal views on California mirror Alvy's. He frequently tells the story about talking to Keaton once over the phone and being amazed that she was getting ready to drive to the grocery store across the street (Skow 71). Alvy echoes Allen's sentiments as he, Annie, and friend Rob (Tony Roberts) arrive at one of Lacy's parties. "Don't tell me we're gonna have to walk from the car to the house," he says caustically. "My feet haven't hit pavement since I reached Los Angeles."

Though Annie eventually returns to New York, she never reconciles with Alvy except to reminisce one afternoon in a little coffee shop. The final scene is shot through the window of the café, their now empty table in the foreground. We see them take their farewells outside on the corner of West 63rd, under the One Way and Don't Walk signs. They walk off-frame in opposite directions. The street traffic continues and life goes on as we hear Annie's voiceover rendition of "Seems Like Old Times." A sense of loss replaces the usual happily-ever-after, making *Annie Hall*, surely, a romantic comedy for the times.

For Allen, it was a turning point. He calls *Annie Hall* the "first good woman's role I ever wrote" (qtd. in Bjorkman 87), and he has been writing for women ever since. He told the *Sacramento Bee* in 1998: "When I started going out with Diane, I started to write parts for her and started getting much better at writing parts for

women.... Since then, all my good parts have been for women" (qtd. in "Relationship" SC2). The comment illustrates Keaton's influence on Allen as an artist.

Reviews were universally positive for film, director, and star. Critics gushed. Terrance Rafferty of *The New Yorker*, who saw *Annie Hall* in Santa Cruz, California, wrote: "It was the film that drove me back to New York. Most of the people in the audience were transplanted New Yorkers, and it was like pouring water on people crawling through the desert" (qtd. in Fox 97). Janet Maslin, writing for *Newsweek*, said of Allen, "For the first time, he seems capable of inviting genuine identification from his viewers, of channeling his comic gifts into material of real substance, of exerting a palpable emotional tug" ("Woody's New Winner" 78). Andrew Sarris of *The Village Voice* wrote: "Any actress who can bring wit and humor to sex in an American movie has to be blessed with the most winning magic" ("Divine Diane" 49).

But while *Annie Hall* swept four Oscars at the Academy Awards—Best Picture, Best Director, Best Original Screenplay, and Best Actress—Allen was in New York, playing his clarinet in Michael's Pub, as he has done for years. He refuses to attend award ceremonies. He once said: "I cannot abide by the judgment of other people, because if you accept it when they say you deserve an award, then you have to accept it when they say you don't" (qtd. in Lax, *Biography* 281). Keaton did attend, however, dressed in a mid-calf striped skirt over slacks, topped with a suit jacket over a turtleneck sweater and scarf, and socks with black strappy sandals. Accepting her award, she thanked Woody and the Academy and gasped: "It's simply terrific. This is, um, something" (qtd. in Shales, "*Annie Hall*" B3).

Keaton's reactions to the public's proclivity to see her as Annie Hall have varied over the years, fluctuating from denial to acceptance. In 1996, she told Jay

Carr: "I'm not haunted by *Annie Hall*. I'm happy to be Annie Hall. If somebody wants to see me that way, it's fine by me" (qtd. in "Diane Keaton Rejoins the Club" N1). She echoed the same sentiment early in 1997 when she appeared on the *Oprah Winfrey Show* talking about her new movie, *Marvin's Room*, which won her an Academy Award nomination for Best Actress. When an audience member asked what her favorite role was, she replied, "I guess you would have to say *Annie Hall* because without *Annie Hall* I wouldn't be sitting here. *Annie Hall* is everything to me."

Though she has become philosophical about and grateful for the role that brought her fame, occasionally a note of exasperation and perhaps resentment creeps into a comment. She recently told *Newsday*:

> The expectation with me for *Annie Hall* was being *Annie Hall*.... It's like saying, "Don't carry on with your life, don't have other interesting things happen to you." Do I have to keep repeating that over and over? There's no way to sustain that, and why would I want to, really? [qtd. in "Fanfare: The Keaton Complex" 12].

To the *New York Post* she said: "I always hear a lot about *Annie Hall*, but no one ever, ever, ever mentions the others.... I feel like I never made them. I guess people just didn't like them, or me in them" (qtd. in Worth 23). People have mentioned her work in other films, and she has made other interesting things happen for her; however, one wonders whether Keaton would have been as closely identified with this particular character had *Looking for Mr. Goodbar* come out before *Annie Hall*.

Looking for Mr. Goodbar

After a string of successful comedies, Keaton decided to test her dramatic skills which audiences had only glimpsed in *The*

Godfather and *The Godfather: Part II*. Her next role changed the direction of her career for a long time. In the decade to follow, she would move from daffy screwball heroines to complex dramatic characters who reflected all of life's anxieties and ambiguities. Theresa Dunn in *Looking for Mr. Goodbar* was the first in a succession of troubled women Keaton played after *Annie Hall*. A twenty-something teacher of deaf children, Terry cruises singles bars at night in search of men and drugs. She discovers that there's never enough of either to make up for severe scoliosis as a child, a domineering father, a dysfunctional family that idolizes her beautiful sister, or an unrequited love affair with a mentally abusive married man. Terry was the polar opposite of Annie Hall, and every actress in Hollywood within age range coveted the role.

Writer/director Richard Brooks adapted his film noir treatment of *Looking for Mr. Goodbar* from Judith Rossner's bestselling novel. Rossner, in turn, based her dark, cautionary tale on an actual incident that occurred in the early seventies. Keaton had read the book and remembers: "I wanted to do it like everyone else, but for some reason he [Brooks] cast me, which remains an interesting choice on his part. I really don't know why. I guess I was hot at that time" (personal interview).

For Brooks, the choice wasn't that simple. Some 300 to 500 actresses vied for the role. (The numbers vary from story to story.) He kept coming back to Keaton, who also had a personal champion in Freddie Fields, the producer who made the movie deal with Paramount and had seen all of Keaton's films. However, Brooks wasn't convinced that she had the "range." He knew Keaton could play the teacher, but could she do the sex scenes? They met several times and finally, as Brooks explained to *Time* magazine,

> I was thinking, sitting there in my office with her, that she is not exactly what you

call a great beauty. Then it struck me that this is who this story is about: a nice-looking girl, a sexy girl, but not the best-looking girl in the class. Someone you would almost overlook [qtd. in Skow 72].

He made no attempt to coddle his newly-hired star. The role called for nude scenes. Lighting would be tricky. Some technician trying to get his camera focus right would run a tape measure from his lens to her "ass" while she lay there "like a piece of meat." Finally, Brooks told her that he would have to see her body in order to figure out how to photograph it. He told *Time*, "She just stared at me. She was shocked. And then, after a few moments, she said, 'O.K., Brooks'" (qtd. in Skow 77).

In another revealing interview, Brooks said that, at first, Keaton "withdrew" from doing the sex scenes: "So she went to her parents, separately. Her parents are no longer living together. She told me both gave their okay, when they were told the scenes were necessary and not dirty" (qtd. in Haun L7). The quote mentions, perhaps for the first time, that her parents weren't living together at the time—something Keaton herself never talked about.

Family support and music got Keaton through the difficult scenes. Brooks said: "We spent a good bit of money on the rights to some very unexpected pieces of music, and I stayed up nights trying to figure out what piece of music Diane would ask for next. But it was all worth it" (qtd. in Wunch, "Maverick" 18). Keaton still uses music to prepare for a scene. For the dark and depressing *Mrs. Soffel* (1984), she listened to Bette Midler's "The Wind Beneath My Wings." For her emotional scene with Meryl Streep in *Marvin's Room* (1996), she listened to Whitney Houston's "I Will Always Love You"—over and over again (*Larry King Live*).

Brooks was protective and paternal toward Keaton during the filming of these scenes. He used only a small crew—and kept them in line. Reportedly, when one technician joked that he didn't recognize Keaton with her clothes on, Brooks gave him a tongue-lashing he wouldn't forget. On the other hand, Brooks refused to use a double for any of the violent scenes. One in particular has Richard Gere's character (Tony) attack Terry with a switchblade. Brooks blocked out the scene but wouldn't let Keaton rehearse it, arguing: "When somebody starts beating hell out of her, she's going to react to it. And she did. He hit her, and she went after him like she was just shot out of a cannon. And fractured a rib" (qtd. in Haun L7).

Keaton eventually earned the director's respect, and Brooks was a man not easily impressed. An ex-sportswriter and NBC commentator, he moved to Los Angeles and began writing screenplays until World War II interrupted his budding career. He joined the Marine Corps but promptly returned after the war to pick up where he left off. In addition to screenplays, Brooks wrote several novels. *The Brick Foxhole* was adapted for the screen in 1947 and became *Crossfire*, a film about anti–Semitism starring Robert Young and Robert Mitchum. Brooks eventually became a director and worked with some of the biggest stars in the industry, including Humphrey Bogart in *Key Largo* (1948). He gained a reputation as one of Hollywood's good ol' boys—a man's man and a man's director—and dealt with hard-hitting, controversial material, like violence in American schools in *The Blackboard Jungle* (1955), greed and homosexuality in *Cat on a Hot Tin Roof* (1958). He also became known for successfully adapting literary material to film and won an Oscar for his *Elmer Gantry* (1960) screenplay, based on Sinclair Lewis' novel.

This tough, crusty director, who died in 1992 of congestive heart failure at the age of 79, told the *New York Sunday News* just before *Goodbar* was released in October of 1977:

We shot for 76 days, of which Diane shot 76 days.... She has tremendous range.... She's shy, but she's got stainless steel inside of her. She doesn't break very easily. She doesn't have a high opinion of herself, but she's got a lot of guts. And she's tough. She is tough internally [qtd. in Haun L7].

He would later say, "She has more artistic courage than anyone I know" (qtd. in Seagrave & Martin 107). Critics universally praised Keaton's artistry, calling her performance "electrifying," dazzling," "a *tour de force.*"

The film opens at night. Terry walks along a seedy street alone in her afterhours attire: flannel shirt, jacket, and jeans. Her hair is long and loose, swinging with the rhythm of her arms as they sway back and forth across her body. One hand holds a cigarette. She glances over her shoulder and smiles, unafraid in this part of town where headlights blur into flashing neon. A marquee announces Exotic Dancers in hot pink. Plaintive, fatalistic sax music builds to a driving disco beat as the streets and bars flood with the young and restless. A rapid succession of black and white shots—an arm, a leg, a cross dangling between a woman's breasts, a vacuous smile—suggests a world in which names don't matter. Expressions of pleasure quickly fade to emptiness and disillusionment.

During this sequence, we see Terry flash on screen for a moment and then vanish in the crowd until the final closeup shows her face in half light, half shadow. Brooks uses low key and high contrast lighting as well as mirrors throughout the film to depict the duality of Terry's personality: half madonna, half whore. Even her name suggests her double life, the saintly Theresa by day, the hipper Terry by night. This opening scene actually takes place three-quarters of the way through the story, but Brooks begins with it because it reflects the film noir tone: seductive, anxious, cynical, pessimistic.

The narrative bends back to the chronological start with a cut to Terry catching the subway to class. She's wearing a dress, her hair now pulled back and restrained with a clip. With her thick, brown-framed glasses, she looks like a librarian. In the classroom, her English professor reads aloud her personal essay about the last time she went to confession and the envious feelings she has toward her beautiful, older sister, Katharine (Tuesday Weld). But Terry, though intelligent and committed to completing her education as a teacher of deaf children, lusts after Professor Engle (Adam Feinstein). She daydreams about having an affair with him, and these girlish, romantic daydreams are so tightly interwoven into the film's narrative that it is difficult at times to distinguish the plot points from her imagination, one of the major criticisms of the film at the time. The lack of transitional cues, however, is meant to disorient and alert the audience. Terry is not a stable character. She often confuses reality and fantasy, and Brooks' technique deliberately blurs the distinction.

The exposition scenes, however, illustrate why Terry descends into self-destructive behavior. They show a sweet, vulnerable, insecure, painfully needy young woman whose traumatic bout with scoliosis and subsequent surgery have left her gulping aspirin and fending off verbal blows from her tyrannical father who yells: "You will never be Katharine!" The beautiful Katharine is a flaky stewardess who jumps from husband to husband like another flight assignment, barely taking time out for an abortion along the way. Terry's father (Richard Kiley), blinded by guilt and ignorance, bullies everyone except Katharine because she's "perfect." She has no physical flaws like Terry who we see in a series of macabre black and white flashbacks lying on a cot in a full body cast. Another miserable sister pops babies year after year because that's what is expected of her, while the beaten down

Mrs. Dunn fades to a ghostly, ineffectual presence. When Terry moves out of the house and into her sister's apartment building, Mama Dunn slides a Bible into Terry's book bag. The only thing that keeps this dysfunctional family together is the Catholic church. Divorce is sacrilege.

Keaton calls *Goodbar* a "case study." She explains that although the film was made at the peak of the women's movement and the sexual revolution, it is not a feminist statement.

> This was solidly based on just a plain old psychological dilemma of a girl who had low self esteem and was acting out in a way that she killed herself.... There was criticism about the movie that it [portrayed] just another female victim, but I didn't see it that way. I mean, my feeling was that this woman was really self destructive, and she couldn't handle it. She got herself into big danger by throwing herself around like that at bars and getting picked up and acting out in a kind of obsessive, compulsive way [personal interview].

Terry's affair with the married Professor Engle illustrates all of these characteristics. Her romantic daydreams become distorted by reality when she seduces him. When Engle inquires about her back pain, she unzips her dress and tells him, "I'd rather be seduced than comforted." Their sex is sordid. He is cruel; she is pathetic. After their "brief" first encounter, he looks at his watch and says, "I never had a virgin before." He rejects her Christmas gift, calling it "commercialized crap," and screams at her when she calls his house. But Terry obsessively persists in humiliating herself. When he calls, she drops everything to meet him. One night, after sex in his car, she asks: "I wonder why after we make love, we never talk or touch or anything?" He finally replies, "I just can't stand a woman's company right after I fucked her." But Terry blames herself when Engle breaks off their relation-

ship. "What happened?" she asks. "What did I do? Is my breath bad? Wrong toothpaste? Is my sex too straight? Tell me what you want." He shouts, "It's over!" and walks out the door with an inane "*Ciao*."

Terry's journey is a downward spiral. For a while she manages to separate her work with deaf children, which she clearly takes seriously, from her one-night stands. Scenes depicting her tender, compassionate commitment to her students are juxtaposed with her aggressive behavior with men. Keaton's own paradoxical character, vulnerable yet tough, surfaces in her portrayal of these alter-egos. Her face is a shifting landscape of thoughts and emotions in perfect sync with the delivery of a line. One moment she sweetly coos, "You've got a nice smile," and the next she snaps and tells Tony, a strungout Vietnam vet, "I choose. I decide who and when." Critic Jack Kroll noted: "She's innocent, perverse, vulnerable, vengeful, sad, funny, sexy, and sweet—not by turns but in a flashing prism of character that's constantly reflecting light, and darkness, from its different surfaces" (qtd. in *Current Biography* 30).

As the plot unfolds, Terry develops a hard edge, determined to play by her rules, which Engle discovers when he meets up with her one night in a club. His overtures are smugly rebuffed as Terry quips: "By parted lovers it is writ/Oh, darling, thou art still a shit—*Ciao*." In another scene, she angrily points out that she might be "alone, but not lonely" to the unctuous, insufferable social worker, James, who ingratiates himself into her family's life. Like the spider woman of film noir, she uses men for self-gratification. When a sympathetic bartender shares his problem—"One drink's too many; one-hundred's not enough," she responds, "I have the same problem with men."

As Terry's perverse lifestyle continues, less and less of the film takes place in daylight. Instead, we see Terry tightly framed in smoky bars, shot through red

Looking for Mr. Goodbar (Paramount, 1977). The cinematography and complex *mise-en-scène* beautifully capture the duality of Theresa/Terry Dunn's persona in Richard Brooks' adaptation of Judith Rossner's novel. By day, Theresa teaches deaf children, a job that proves useful and rewarding. In the brightly lit, uncluttered classrooms, Theresa has plenty of freedom to move and interact with the smiling children who respond to her warmth and compassion. She pulls her hair back, away from her face, and restrains it with a clip; she wears glasses but little or no make-up; and she dresses in shapeless, loose-fitting ensembles that never call attention to her figure—all evidence of how seriously she takes her work and all in direct contrast to the scene above. Brooks uses low-key lighting and smoke-filled bars to suggest the darker world of Terry Dunn. In this shot, with her hair swinging free, she is literally hemmed in from all sides by men. Trapped between their lustful stares and the booze on the bar, Terry has nowhere to go but down.

filters or in bed, naked, with some pick-up. She has more territorial space in her apartment, which is one large room sparsely furnished save for a bed, a couple of chairs, and a pornographic chime hanging in the center of the room. The two pictures on the wall are constant reminders of Terry's feelings of inadequacy. One is a beautiful photograph of her sister Katharine; the other is a hideous drawing of herself. In the sanctity of this space, Terry does drugs alone while roaches crawl over a sink full of dirty dishes. James's attempts to "save" her push Terry farther over the edge. When he

tells her he loves her, she says: "Don't love me. Just make love to me." Recognizing all of her own insecurities in him, she taunts him, laughing when he attempts to put on a rubber, which she promptly grabs and blows up like a balloon. "I've never seen one of these," Terry shrieks. "Is this supposed to protect you or me?" She has become as cruel as Professor Engle, her first lover.

Ironically, on her "last night cruising bars," Terry tries to avoid James and picks up the wrong man, a repressed homosexual ex-con who repeatedly stabs her while her strobe light flickers. Brooks moves the camera in close, from a tight eye-level to a direct overhead shot, forcing the audience emotionally into the scene. There's no way out for Terry or us until that final glimpse of her white face, her death mask, staring into the blackness. Brooks explained his interpretation of this final scene to the *New York Sunday News*: "I did not want a scene of such horror and blood and violence that the audience would just be riveted. I wanted, at the same time, people to feel, 'I can hardly *breathe*. I want to get *out*'" (qtd. in Haun L7).

The violent scenes and grueling filming schedule took their toll on Keaton. Like most actors who portray vivid, difficult characters, she couldn't always shake the doomed Terry Dunn when she went home, though she enjoyed the challenge of playing a character so different from herself and her previous roles. But while the critics heaped praises on her emotionally powerful performance, the moviegoing public had a difficult time accepting that difference. Woody Allen had made Keaton's neurotic insecurity charming and lovable. Brooks used it to explore the darkest part of the human soul. Fans resisted Keaton in the part and resisted the disturbing subject matter of the film perhaps even more. In short, Keaton experi-

enced what Mary Pickford went through when she tried to break away from her "Little Mary" or ingenue roles. The public did not line up at the box office.

The significance of both *Goodbar* and *Annie Hall*, however, in Keaton's artistic development cannot be overstated. *Annie Hall* established Keaton as one of the country's leading comediennes and accorded her a measure of fame stars seldom, if ever, achieve. Most of Keaton's popular success has been in comedies like *Baby Boom* (1987), the *Father of the Bride* films (1991 and 1995), and *First Wives Club* (1996). Although *Looking for Mr. Goodbar* was not as financially successful as *Annie Hall*, it did, in the minds of the critics and the film industry, establish Keaton as one of Hollywood's most versatile leading ladies, and not just Woody Allen's girlfriend. In 1991, Harvard's Hasty Pudding Club voted her Woman of the Year, presenting Keaton with a $1.69 Mr. Goodbar candy bar and a live lobster to commemorate her work in both 1977 films. Keaton would return to work with Woody in two more films, *Interiors* (1978) and *Manhattan* (1979) before moving on to work with the new man in her life, Warren Beatty, in *Reds* (1981).

CHAPTER 4

1978–1981

The Muse

You make every director you work with look good.
—Warren Beatty to Diane Keaton (Academy Awards, 1982)

For Warren Beatty and Woody Allen before him, Diane Keaton became The Muse. One reporter went so far as to label her "the most importantly overlooked collaborator in American movie history" ... since "two of her old boyfriends—Woody Allen and Warren Beatty—did the best work they will ever do as actor/directors in her company" ("Greek Goddess" G1). Both men have repeatedly acknowledged Keaton's influence on their professional and private lives, yet, in most interviews over the years, reporters have asked Keaton what she learned from them. She has been consistent in her reply: Allen taught her discipline and decisiveness while Beatty taught her to ask a lot of questions and "take a good idea when you hear it from someone else" (qtd. in "Greek Goddess" G1). During the late seventies, the lives of these three stars were inextricably linked. Keaton was seeing Warren but working with Woody. What Allen thought about that relationship, he kept to himself.

With *Looking for Mr. Goodbar*, Keaton's career had taken a more serious turn.

For the next decade, she seldom ventured out of dramatic roles that showcased her two-sided personality. She played a host of intelligent, ambitious, and edgy characters who were often foiled by their own doubts and insecurities. Many of them were artists, like herself, struggling with the desire to do more with their talents. Many were restless working women trying to juggle a job and a personal relationship. All, however, had one thing in common. They were representations of modern women dealing with contemporary issues and concerns.

In fact, it was in the late seventies that critics began referring to Keaton's "modern" style and American sensibilities, so much so that these characteristics have become part of her star image. Daphne Davis wrote in *Stars!*: "No actress ... represented the confused single woman who cannot live up to her personal vision of liberation better than Diane Keaton" (210). And Jack Mathews of *Newsday* called her "a master of the bewildered modern woman" ("Actors" B3). With her newly frizzed hair, natural makeup, and tailored clothing, Keaton projected the new woman of the seventies on the screen. Even today, her look, her voice, and her mannerisms are grounded in contemporary America. Woody Allen says Keaton is so American "she's like a female Huck Finn. Lanky, pretty, in love with the West and the desert" (personal interview).

In 1978, Keaton told Penelope Gilliatt: "I have a deep feeling for America. I'm definitely a product of this continent" (qtd. in Gilliatt 39). To date, she hasn't changed her mind and claims: "What I know is American themes and American family issues in this century," she says. "I don't think I'm good enough to do a movie about another time, too far away in the past, because I think you really have to be somebody well versed in that, and I'm not" (personal interview).

Keaton admits that there are many genres she's just not right for. She steers clear of action-adventure movies, for example, and doesn't do many period pieces or classics because, as she explains: "My speech pattern doesn't seem to fit them" (qtd. in S. Silverman 27). Keaton has attempted a dialect only twice in her thirty-year career. She managed to pull off an adequate Mississippi drawl for *Crimes of the Heart* (1986), Bruce Beresford's adaptation of Beth Henley's Pulitzer Prize–winning play set in the deep South, but failed in her attempt at a British accent for *Little Drummer Girl* (1984). Further limiting her choices are the scripts themselves. Keaton claims: "Most scripts aren't very well written. They aren't specifically unusual or precise; they're too general. I like nuances, strange tics" (qtd. in A. Thompson, "Diane Keaton" L1).

Keaton's next three roles exemplify her modern sensibilities and preference for nuance. All three of her characters are writers, artists wrestling with the creative muse, whose unhappiness exacts a toll on those closest to them. In *Interiors* (1978), she plays Renata, an "impotent" poet afraid of mortality, both for herself and her art. In *Manhattan* (1979), she plays the bitchy, neurotic pseudo-intellectual Mary Wilke who compromises her art by writing novelizations of pop movies. In *Reds* (1981), she enacts the real-life, tormented Louise Bryant who wanted desperately to escape the shadow of her husband, Jack Reed, and be accepted as an artist in her own right. Louise simply wasn't talented enough. Unlike previous characters Keaton had played, these women are not lovable, or even amusing. They are damaged and driven, self-absorbed and selfish. Keaton's performances in these roles led John Parker, Warren Beatty's biographer, to call her "the heroine of the neuroses of the late seventies" (238).

Interiors

Interiors was filmed, in part, on Long Island amid secrecy and speculation. Woody Allen, who had written the screenplay, was out of his element. This film was serious, a total departure for him, and he refused to give out any details about the project to the press so that if anything went wrong, he said, he could make changes before anyone learned of the mistakes (Flatley, "Woody Allen" C8). The director also refused to cast himself in the film because he was afraid audiences would take it as a cue to laugh. He knew the risks involved for a well-established comedian, but Allen was psychologically—and economically—ready for some radical changes. Now that he was financially secure, he was more afraid of repeating himself than gambling on something new.

To American critics like Jack Kroll, Stanley Kauffman, Richard Schickel and others, *Interiors* was a failure: too European and Bergmanesque. They rejected Allen's derivative technique, but admired his courage in attempting such a departure.

Nevertheless, the film made the "Top Ten" lists of many other leading critics and went on to receive five Academy Award nominations: Best Director (Allen), Best Actress (Geraldine Page), Best Supporting Actress (Maureen Stapleton), Original Screenplay (Allen), and Art Direction (Mel Bourne and Daniel Robert). *Interiors* lost in all categories but Geraldine Page won a British Academy Award for Best Supporting Actress while Maureen Stapleton picked up the Los Angeles Film Critics Award and the New York Film Critics Award for Best Supporting Actress.

Keaton received mixed reviews. One reviewer said that "when she tries for more complexity, she goes flat" (Gittelson 252). But Pauline Kael wrote:

> Diane Keaton does something very courageous for a rising star. She appears here with the dead-looking hair of someone who's too distracted to do anything with it but get a permanent, and her skin looks dry and pasty. There's discontent right in the flesh.... This physical transformation is the key to Keaton's thoughtful performance [Kael, *For Keeps* 786].

Interiors is also a departure for Keaton in that it is the first of her "sister" films, ensemble pieces that explore the interrelationships between women, especially within family situations. Keaton says that the subject is "totally important to me.... I am one of three sisters, and I'm close to my sisters. The dynamic is always fascinating to me and something I identify with and feel strongly about" (personal interview). Allen himself expressed the same sentiments in a conversation with biographer Stig Bjorkman: "I love the relationship of women to women.... The relationship between sisters is also very interesting to me" (qtd. in Bjorkman 99–100). In *Interiors*, Allen uses the dynamic between the sisters, as well as their relationships with other family members, to examine what happens when we place art over human values.

Uncharacteristically, he makes no attempt to make us like these characters.

The film opens in absolute silence. No sound track detracts from the series of interior shots of an upscale beachfront house. Each room has been carefully, meticulously decorated in cool earth tones, reflecting an impeccable, refined, sophisticated eye for detail. Though beautifully balanced and composed, the house looks austere and empty. Nothing clutters the design—not even people. The rooms are devoid of life. They are form without content. In this family, image is everything.

The lack of movement throughout the film, especially in this opening sequence, suggests both a spiritual and psychological paralysis. The inhabitants of this house are unhappy, trapped people, as all of their "interiors" have been designed by the same force that created the rigid, ordered rooms: Eve (Geraldine Page), the matriarch of the family. In fact, the film has a dollhouse-like feel about it, and there are times when we find ourselves praying for a hand to reach down and pluck these people out of their misery.

When we do finally see movement, it is reflected in the glass of a framed print. A figure in a trench coat enters like a ghostly presence. Her footsteps on the polished wood floors make no sound. The camera eventually locks on to Joey (Mary Beth Hurt) and follows her up the stairs, along a row of floor-to-ceiling windows, where she joins her two sisters who are looking out onto the beach below. They do not speak. Instead, Allen cuts to Arthur (E. G. Marshall), the head of this dysfunctional family. Standing with his back to the camera, he looks out over an urban skyline from his posh corner office that his wife Eve has decorated. In voiceover narration, he begins to tell us the story of his life as Allen cuts back and forth between Arthur and his daughters, all looking out of windows. (The working title of the film was *Windows*. It was Keaton who suggested calling it *Interiors*.) Arthur begins:

> I had dropped out of law school when I met Eve. She was very beautiful. Very pale and cool in her black dress with never anything more than a single strand of pearls—and distant. Always poised and distant. By the time the girls were born, it was all so perfect, so ordered. Looking back, of course, it was rigid. The truth is, she created a world around us that we existed in. But everything had its place. There was always a kind of harmony. Great dignity. I will say it was like an ice palace. Then, suddenly, one day out of nowhere, an enormous abyss opened up beneath our feet, and I was staring into a face I didn't recognize.

With her hair parted severely in the middle and swept back tightly in a knot and her ice-gray suits perfectly coordinated, Eve, like her creations, is form without substance. She likes a church before it gets "cluttered up with people." She "worships" creative talent. When there is nothing left to decorate, she meddles in and obsesses over her children's lives. Her selfish, obsessive behavior, bouts of depression, and suicide attempts victimize every member of her family. Renata (Keaton), the eldest daughter, is successful and talented, but, like her mother, she needs a controlled environment in which to work. The beautiful Flyn (Kristin Griffith) is a second-rate actress who needs to be looked at or else she doesn't exist. She buries her mediocrity in cocaine. Joey "has all of the anguish and anxiety of an artist without the talent," as Renata's husband astutely observes. A disappointed Arthur says, "She was an extraordinary child" but has no direction. She's desperate to be good at something but has no creative gifts. When Arthur announces one morning at the breakfast table that he plans to leave Eve, their ordered world comes apart at the seams, releasing the rage locked inside each character.

In several interviews, Allen admits that Renata speaks for him in this film. In truth, it is no difficult exercise to substitute Allen for Renata, especially in the scene when Renata confesses her fear of death and her creative paralysis, her inability to write. She cries: "What am I striving to create? To what end? What purpose?" Allen himself was preoccupied with these issues and usually made his angst the butt of his own jokes. But there are no jokes to relieve the tension in *Interiors*. Sitting in a black chair, in medium close-up, Renata talks directly to the camera. Just as Alvy Singer in *Annie Hall* made the audience his analyst with this same technique, so Renata makes us her confidant, revealing the long-standing sibling rivalry between herself and Joey, her father's favorite.

When one critic suggested that Keaton expressed a good deal of bitterness in her role as Renata, Keaton replied: "Oh, that's easy.... Bitterness, anger, resentment—those emotions are second nature to me. That was a very easy part for me to play" (qtd. in Gittelson 252). The comment—and the performance—were surprising to audiences who had never seen the total submergence of that lovable, funny side of Keaton's persona on the screen. The sweet, girlish voice has been replaced with a dead monotone. There is no hint of animation, no spark, no fire. Keaton restrains her usually lively gestures so that the smallest hand movement seems to take the maximum effort. She minimizes her physical attractiveness, wearing no makeup and nondescript, tailored but rumpled costumes that suggest a woman who doesn't care about or can't be bothered with her appearance. Gone are Annie Hall's wide smile and playful costumes. Instead, as Kael says, Keaton registers "discontent right in the flesh" (*For Keeps* 786). Renata's energy has been sucked dry by her art.

Renata's poetry, published in the *New Yorker*, receives consistent critical praise, yet she is a tortured artist plagued by "feelings of futility" in her work and paralyzed by her fear of death and "the real implication of dying." Totally self-absorbed, she keeps everyone at arm's length. She has little sympathy for her husband Frederick (Richard Jordan), tormented by his own demons to be a great writer and his jealousy of Renata's success. He regularly drowns his self-doubt and self-loathing with alcohol. As Renata tells Flyn, Frederick takes "his rage out in these critical pieces under the guise of high standards." Disgusted with himself and tired of making love to a woman he feels inferior to, he attempts to rape Flyn—and fails.

Though Renata wants to "help, not hurt," she flings accusations at Frederick: "I'm tired of your problems and your competitiveness. I have my own problems.... Stay home and drink yourself into unconsciousness." But even this burst of anger is half-hearted. Renata is tired, and Keaton delivers these lines with the weariness of a woman who has heard the same argument one too many times. As she sits at the bottom of the stairs with a distraught Frederick, her shoulders are hunched with the burden of a family that is draining her creativity. In only one scene does she actually hold her daughter, a small inconvenience, for a brief moment. When her youngest sister Joey asks, "Why do you keep pushing me away," Renata responds: "The creative thing is very delicate. The creative process needs isolation." Finally, her father, Arthur (E. G. Marshall), who sends her checks each month to subsidize her creativity, tells her, "You seclude yourself in Connecticut acting out the part of the aloof artist." Indeed, Renata holds herself aloof. She would rather avoid conflict and confrontation. Allen usually shoots her against bare walls, standing apart from the other characters on the periphery of a room, smoking and observing events unfold. Renata is incapable of helping anyone, least of all herself. She is the most emotionally barren of all Keaton's characters,

bartering her humanity for the serenity in which to practice her art, even if the serenity is only an illusion.

Allen's spare dialogue in *Interiors* also contributed to Keaton's restrained performance. Audiences were used to her lively characterizations in Allen's talky scripts with overlapping dialogue. If he had it to do over again, Allen said he would have "loosened up some of the dialogue" in *Interiors* and made it "more colloquial and less literary" (qtd. in Bjorkman 117). It would have been a mistake. Here, the lack of dialogue, as with the lack of motion, works well since it suggests emotional and physical paralysis.

Eve has created a family of watchers, not doers. They spend a great deal of time looking at the world from windows, but they don't know how to live in it. To borrow a term from Tennyson, they are "lost to life and use." In one scene, empty and disillusioned, Renata stands looking out of a window onto the beach below as three little girls play in the surf. She symbolically spreads her fingers against the glass pane as if to reach for something in her past that will save her. In another scene, she is working in her study. She turns to the window and sees a tangled mass of tree branches. Allen cuts back and forth between the branches and Renata's reaction. She begins to hyperventilate. Frightened, she walks into Frederick's study and tells him: "I just experienced the strangest sensation. I had a clear vision where everything seemed so awful and predatory. I was here. The world was out there. I couldn't bring us together."

She experiences the same sensation while sitting on the beach watching the ocean. She begins to breathe in rhythm with the waves and covers her face in fear. Natural images distress her, just as they do Allen himself who says that nature is "marked by murderous and cannibalistic competition" (qtd. in Bjorkman 105). Eve has never taught her family how to live outside the ordered ice palace

Interiors (MGM/UA, 1978). Woody Allen's compositions in *Interiors* suggest his characters' spiritual paralysis. In this shot, for example, sisters Renata (Keaton), Joey (Marybeth Hurt), and Flyn (Kristin Griffith) occupy the same frame yet remain isolated, trapped in their interiors, as they gaze outward instead of at each other. Victims of their elegant but cool and controlling mother, they can barely function in the real world, so they watch from their ordered "ice palace." Keaton's Renata, the archetypal artist, deliberately distances herself from her family, often watching their behavior from the margins of the frame. She strikes the pose of aloof, misunderstood poet, sacrificing intimacy for an art she thinks will save her.

she created, and so when they are forced to face reality the ice cracks. The anger that seeps out almost destroys them.

Enter Pearl (Maureen Stapleton), Arthur's fiancée, whose bright clothing and simple, direct manner of speaking are in voluble contrast to the insufferable snobbery of his family. She tells fortunes, does card tricks, and collects African art. Her warmth and liveliness breathe life into the cold rooms, but her presence alone cannot save this family. It takes Eve's death to free them.

When Arthur and Pearl marry, the camera stays on the other characters, all in a row, watching from the sidelines. Unbeknownst to them, Eve has come to the beachhouse and watches the ceremony from the shadows. Only Joey notices her and finally articulates the devastating toll Eve has taken on her children:

You shouldn't be here. Not tonight.... I've cared for you, and you have disdain for me.... You worship talent. What happens to people who can't create? I feel such rage toward you. You're not just a sick woman. That would be too easy. The truth is there's been perverseness and willfulness of attitude in many of the things you've done. At the center of a sick psyche there is a sick spirit. But I love you. And we have no other choice but to forgive each other.

Unable to accept the reality of the situation or deal with her emotions, Eve walks into the ocean in her designer suit and heels. When Joey's attempts to save Eve fail, it is Pearl who revives a nearly-drowned Joey with mouth-to-mouth resuscitation, "the kiss of life" as Allen calls it (qtd. in Bjorkman 98).

The ending of *Interiors* is ambiguous at best. As Allen suggests, there is a hint of hope as Joey and Renata hug, and we see Joey actually writing about their lives. However, Allen brings the film full circle when, in a Bergmanesque composition, the three sisters stand together at the window, looking at the ocean. Joey says: "The water's so calm." Renata replies: "Yes, it's very peaceful." The implication is that Eve has at last found peace in death, but her influence on her daughters will probably live on. As Keaton explains:

Interiors is a film about the kind of people who are artists and the kind of miserable life they have and the legacy that they leave. I don't think it was a very positive view of the artist. I think that it was saying in a certain sense they are not very human, and in comes this Maureen Stapleton character who is all life and kind of brassy and tasteless, yet she's the one who is the most successful in life—able to love, able to enjoy it, able to give love and also receive it. Human values.... I really think those concerns are very important. I really think that people romanticize art much more than they should [personal interview].

Allen's experiment paid off in that both the film and Keaton, with her physical transformation, succeed in conveying the darker side of creative genius. *Interiors* teaches, in Allen's words, that "art doesn't save you," that art without humanity is an empty pursuit (qtd. in Bjorkman 103).

Manhattan

Allen continued his thematic exploration of art and the artist with *Manhattan*, which some critics consider his masterpiece. He both directs and stars this time, serving up his message that art can't set you free, with a serious but lighter touch than in *Interiors*. In *Manhattan*, Allen plays Isaac Davis, a writer who feels like he has compromised his art by writing comedy bits for a television show he detests. He is a decent guy adrift in a sea of amorality trying to answer the universal question: Why is life worth living? He really wants to write a book about New York as a metaphor for the "decay of contemporary culture." His deep veneration for the past sets him in direct conflict with the escalating crime, drug use, loud music, and corruption of the human condition he sees around him in the present. In spite of it all, Isaac still views New York as a "town that existed in black-and-white and pulsated to the great tunes of George Gershwin." He believes that people should mate for life, "talent is luck," and courage is the most important thing in life.

The only calm center in his life is his seventeen-year-old girlfriend, Tracy (Mariel Hemingway) whose humanity and compassion make Isaac a better person. She

gives him a harmonica to bring out "that side" of him, shares his passion for old movies, and gets him to take buggy rides in Central Park. Isaac broadens Tracy's worldview as well, introducing her to a new world of literature and art. In one scene, they share a tender moment in bed together looking at photos. When Tracy comments on someone's old face, Isaac gently tells her that "old faces are nice," something Allen learned himself from Keaton. Tracy supports his decision to quit his job and write his novel, but Isaac throws Tracy over for the elusive Mary Wilke (Keaton). By the time he realizes his mistake and finds the courage to tell Tracy that it's her face that makes life worth living, it's too late. She's on her way to the London Academy of Music and Performing Arts to study acting.

Most of Isaac's friends are artists, too, and, in some way, they all sell out their ideals and dreams for immediate gratification. Yale (Michael Murphy), for example, wants to write the definitive biography of Eugene O'Neill and start up a magazine. But he buys a fancy sports car and has an extramarital affair instead. Yale's great passion is Mary, a waffling, insecure journalist from Philadelphia whose intellectual posturing initially makes Isaac want to throttle her. She trivializes everything that Isaac loves, including Ingmar Bergman. She is both "attracted and repelled by the male organ"; her self-esteem is a "notch below Kafka's," as Isaac tells her; she's seeing an analyst named Donny who calls *her* for advice; and she can't plan four weeks in advance. When Yale temporarily returns to his wife, Emily (Anne Byrne), Isaac starts up a romance with Mary. He thinks he can "fix" her. But Mary warns Isaac: "I've got too many problems. I'm not the person to get involved with. I'm trouble." And she is. Yale and Isaac soon learn that Mary is as temperamental and high maintenance as Yale's new Porche. The same justification Yale makes about purchasing the car might apply to Mary as well: "It's a meaningless extravagance, but I had to have it."

If the role of Renata came easily to her, Keaton found the brilliant but bitchy Mary Wilke near impossible to capture. Reflecting on the casting, Keaton thought that Allen was really looking for someone "more intelligent."

> You know, he was looking for somebody whose verbal skills were more—probably he was looking for Judy Davis, but she wasn't available. He got stuck with me, and I got the part. He just kept shooting scenes with me until finally I got it right. It wasn't easy for me to play that, I guess, kind of troubled, neurotic, brilliant person [personal interview].

The comment suggests that though these characteristics have become part of Keaton's on-screen persona, she doesn't necessarily see herself that way. Enacting a character like Mary Wilke, however, has greatly contributed to the public's perception of Keaton as a complex, intelligent, paradoxical star image.

Once again, Keaton is playing the modern American woman trying to find an outlet for creative expression while looking for love in all the wrong places. Unfortunately, Mary has no true sense of self-worth and so must constantly tell everyone how beautiful and talented she is, just to believe it herself. For example, when we first meet her, she and Yale are snatching a few stolen moments at a photography exhibit when they run into Isaac and Tracy. Mary's first impulse is to impress Yale's friends with her knowledge of art but ends up sounding like a badly written review: "I really feel like [the exhibit] was very derivative. It looked like it was straight out of Diane Arbus, but it had none of the wit." On the other hand, Mary likes the steel cube: "That was brilliant to me. Absolutely brilliant. To me it was textual, you know what I mean? Perfectly integrated and had a marvelous ca-

pability." She doesn't let up as the four of them continue their discussion of art while walking along the street. Isaac thinks Bergman is a genius; Mary tells him to "outgrow" it:

> You're so the opposite. You write that absolutely fabulous television show. It's brilliantly funny. His view is so Scandinavian. I mean, it's bleak. My God, all that Kierkegaard. You know, real adolescent. Fashionable pessimism. I mean, the silence, God's silence. Okay, okay, okay. I mean, I loved it when I was at Radcliffe, but, I mean, all right. You outgrow it.... Don't you see? Don't you guys see that it is the dignifying of one's own psychological and sexual hangups by attaching them to these grandiose philosophical issues?

In response to Isaac's angry reaction to her diatribe on Bergman, Mary falls back on her all-occasion, stock comment: "I'm just from Philadelphia. I believe in God." According to Julian Fox in *Woody: Movies from Manhattan*, the character of Mary was loosely based on Allen and Marshall Brickman's long-time friend, Susan Braudy:

> She had, in fact the same shaggy hair style and speech patterns as Diane, while Mary's Braudy-ish line, "No, I'm from Philadelphia. We never talk about things like that in public," comes to the screen all but verbatim [112].

As Mary, Keaton *looks* the part of the New York intellectual in her tight jeans, tailored blouse buttoned to the starched collar, and dark blazer. Her frizzed, *au naturel* hair is shoulder-length and loosely pulled up at the sides with a thick fringe of bangs. But there is really nothing very natural about Mary. She is all affect. She is an optical illusion, like the shot of her and Isaac sitting in silhouette on a bench next to the Queensborough Bridge in the early hours of the morning. One moment they appear to be looking out toward the East River; the next moment they appear

Manhattan (MGM/UA, 1979). Many of the characters Woody Allen plays find themselves at odds with contemporary culture as they strive to separate the real from the artificial on their quest for truth and meaning. Their running commentaries and observations about life and art often puncture pretentious pseudo-intellectual babble. In *Manhattan*, his Isaac Davis bumps up against the icon of pretension and artificiality in Mary Wilke, played by Keaton. She tells him: "I'm not the person to get involved with. I'm trouble." She's right, but Isaac learns this too late and loses the one "real" person in his life, his younger girlfriend Tracy.

to be looking toward the camera. Allen frequently shoots Mary in shadow or high-contrast lighting with shafts of darkness across her face. Sometimes we hear only her voice as she talks to Isaac from another room, suggesting a dislocation in their relationship. Neither Isaac nor the audience can anticipate her next move.

Appearance and reality are polarized in Mary. In essence, she is an unpredictable phony, and her bravado is a sleight of hand trick—which is possibly the real key to why Keaton had such a difficult time with the characterization. Meryl Streep who also stars in *Manhattan* as Isaac's ex-wife, Jill, and who stars opposite Keaton again in *Marvin's Room*

(1996), explains that Keaton "displays 'incredible honesty' in both acting and in her personal life." *Marvin's Room* director Jerry Zaks agrees, pointing out that "it's difficult for her to lie" (qtd. in Karen Thomas D1). Mary, then, seems far removed from Keaton's own personality as she lies to herself and everyone around her.

In one scene, Mary postures pseudo-eloquently in her dark sunglasses, one hand on her hip and the other gesturing in the air, saying "I say what's on my mind. If you don't like it, fuck off." In the next, she admits, "I never thought I was very pretty." Her insecurity manifests itself in her comments about her intelligence and physical appearance. On the one hand, she boasts about them; on the other, she seeks constant reinforcement. Caught in a rainstorm, Isaac and Mary seek refuge in the Hayden Planetarium. Drenched, she asks: "What do you think? You think I look terrible?" Walking amidst the stars and planets, we see only their silhouettes, as she asks: "You probably think I'm too cerebral. You think I have no feelings, right?" After an argument with Yale, Mary says: "I'm beautiful, and I'm bright, and I deserve better. I'm from Philadelphia. My family's never had affairs. My parents have been married 43 years. Nobody cheats at all."

But Mary does cheat. She succumbs to Yale's charms and goes to a motel with him one afternoon, calling herself a "pushover." Later, at a little sidewalk café, Yale breaks off their relationship and all of Mary's guilt, doubts, and insecurities surface at once as she tells him:

> Of course I'm going to be all right. What do you think I'm going to do, hang myself? I'm a beautiful woman. I'm young. I'm highly intelligent. I've got everything going for me. The point is—I don't know— I'm all fucked up. The point is, what the hell am I doing in this relationship anyway. My phone never stops ringing. I could go to bed with the entire faculty of MIT if I wanted to.

In this single moment, Keaton captures the essence of a woman pinned between colliding forces of traditional values and modern choices. Her traditional Philadelphia upbringing has taught her that dating a married man is wrong. In the competitive, cosmopolitan big city, however, she finds that people often compromise their principles for instant pleasures. Though she wants to do the right thing, Mary can't make a personal sacrifice for anyone else's happiness—and her choices have left her damaged and broken. In an over-the-shoulder medium close-up, we see her shoulders hunched forward as her eyes dart from left to right and then

downward as she shakes her head. Collecting herself, she meets Yale's gaze, but it is the demeanor of an unhappy, troubled woman which registers in Keaton's every tone and gesture. The scene is a direct contrast to the one in which Isaac breaks up with Tracy. Self-assured and confident though hurt, Tracy looks directly at Isaac saying, "I can't believe that you met somebody that you like better than me."

Yale and Mary's breakup is short-lived, however. Both of them lie to and betray a trusting Isaac. Mary finally finds the courage to tell Isaac that Yale has called her several times and that she's still in love with him. A stunned Isaac leaves her sitting on her coffee table, holding a drink, and staring guiltily after him. Yale tells Isaac not to turn this into one of his "big moral issues" when Isaac confronts him about the situation. "You're too easy on yourself," Isaac tells him, and Yale lamely responds, "We're just people." Neither Yale nor Mary has the personal integrity that is so important to Isaac, but we get the sense that Mary, at least, feels genuinely bad that she has hurt Isaac. Keaton reveals Mary's fleeting vestiges of decency in a compassionate parting look.

If Allen, the "perfectionist" as Keaton calls him, was frustrated with her performance, it wasn't apparent on the set. *Manhattan* was Keaton's twelfth film in eight years. She was moving from project to project with little time off in between. In the "Faces of Diane Keaton," Natalie Gittelson quotes a member of Allen's production company who commented on their relationship at the time: "Woody's very paternal toward Diane these days.... He's always putting his arm around her, asking if she's tired. Beatty notwithstanding, they're very loving together. I think Woody's still crazy about her" (26). But *Manhattan* would be the last time that Keaton and Allen teamed in leading roles until *Manhattan Murder Mystery* in 1993. (Keaton appeared in his 1987 *Radio Days* only in a cameo role.) Her next director would not be so solicitous.

Reds

By the time *Manhattan* was released in 1979, Keaton was totally involved with Warren Beatty's ten-year obsession, *Reds*, the story of American journalist and communist sympathizer John Reed who wrote *Ten Days That Shook the World* and helped found the Communist party in the United States. She was also totally involved with Beatty romantically. Beatty had seen Keaton's performance in *Looking for Mr. Goodbar* and told director Richard Brooks that he was "overwhelmed" by her talent and wanted to meet her (Kroll, "Best of the Worst" 58).

Thanks to a string of hits, including *Bonnie and Clyde* (1967), *Shampoo* (1975), and *Heaven Can Wait* (1978), Beatty, like Keaton, was on a professional high. Not only did studio executives consider him a first-rate actor, but a shrewd businessman and talented director as well. Beatty also had a reputation as a ladies' man with a penchant for wooing the industry's top female stars: Natalie Wood, Julie Christie, Leslie Caron, and Joan Collins. By the summer of 1978, he had added Diane Keaton to the list. The rumors flew about their new attachment. Accounts of their affair in the press were rife with speculation as to whether Beatty would break her heart or settle down.

Beatty's pattern of behavior with women was so well established in Hollywood that Woody Allen once quipped that he would like to be reincarnated as Warren Beatty's fingertips (Munshower, *Warren Beatty* 5). Prompted by Beatty's friend, producer Charlie Feldman, Allen wrote a screenplay titled after Beatty's now-famous greeting to women: "What's new, pussycat?" (Lax, *Biography* 206). Nevertheless, most of Beatty's former lovers speak fondly of him, describing him as intellec-

tual, sensual, and dynamic. Leslie Caron once said: "Once he was interested in a woman, he would never let go. He enveloped her with his every thought; he wanted total control of her, her clothes, her make-up, her work; he took notice of everything" (qtd. in Parker 1).

John Parker's biography, *Warren Beatty: The Last Great Lover of Hollywood*, traces Beatty's long string of romances which eclipses in number his relatively shorter list of film credits. Each liaison follows a pattern which may or may not be intentional on Beatty's part, Parker suggests. In most cases, Beatty chose a project and then set about to court the leading lady *before* filming began. Parker postulates: "Was romance a preamble to everything, to ensure some electricity and fire between them as the cameras were running?" (239). The question implies a "complicated foreplay" hard to dismiss in light of the frequency of the pattern. As Parker argues:

> Although the plots of his movies have been cast in wide and various settings, entailing all measure of sex, violence and social upheaval, they basically boil down to relationships between the two leading characters.... Looking back over his collection of work, it is possible to see the pattern emerging almost from the beginning, when Elia Kazan threw Natalie Wood into his arms and admitted, "I knew they had become lovers—and I didn't worry because it helped their love scenes" [239].

Was Diane Keaton just part of the pattern? Perhaps the answer is not so simple. Beatty had always been attracted to intelligent, complicated, talented, successful, independent women—reflections of his own personality.

Keaton was America's current sweetheart. The public saw her as shy and vulnerable, and they loved her for it. Those who covered the Hollywood beat doubted that she could withstand the advances of Beatty's charm and voiced those doubts in the trade papers and gossip columns. But Keaton was 32 years old, and, like Beatty, had no history of a long-term relationship. The idea of marriage appealed to her; it didn't consume her. Later, she would say that she never bought "the fantasy of Prince Charming and all that garbage" (qtd. in Collins 98). In a few short years, the naiveté and insecurity that surfaced in early interviews was gone. Though well-intentioned, the protective instincts of Keaton's friends and fans toward her emotional welfare were unnecessary. Keaton appeared capable of taking care of herself, even with the formidable Warren Beatty.

Keaton and Beatty were actually similar in many ways. Writing about their house hunting expeditions in New York, Marilyn Beck said in the *Star-Ledger* that the "couple has two major things in common: frugality and perfectionism" ("Diane, Warren" 44). Beyond that, both were intelligent, passionate, charming people, who closely guarded their private lives. Beatty once told Louella Parsons: "I never thought it was fair to talk about people I have a personal relationship with" (qtd. in Munshower, *Warren Beatty* 27). Keaton expressed the same sentiment well before her involvement with Beatty. Neither Keaton nor Beatty felt comfortable with fame or with talking to the press. Like Keaton, Beatty said:

> I was not prepared for [fame].... I was not ready for the agony, the coarseness, the vulgarity, having to do things here, being pressured there until finally they rub out your talents. I was insecure.... I felt like I was being sold like a can of tomatoes [qtd. in Parker 90].

Critics suggested that Beatty and Keaton were in the wrong profession if they resented questions about their personal lives. In response, they persistently kept the focus of interviews on their work, refusing to compromise their beliefs or cash in on their relationships. They chose projects based on quality and personal interest rather than their potential for commercial success. Beatty has turned down far more projects than he has accepted, *The Godfather* and *Butch Cassidy and the Sundance Kid* among them. In many ways, Keaton and Beatty seemed well-suited for each other, even down to their strong belief in analysis. The familiarity of all this suggests that Keaton had hooked up with another Woody Allen, albeit the beautiful lothario version that so many of Allen's characters fantasized themselves as on the screen.

The talk about Beatty in the press, however, and his intentions towards his new love interest finally prompted him to speak out about his relationship with Keaton:

> I think I've finally reached a point in life when I'm learning to control my own restlessness ... both in my work and with women. Maybe with Diane, more than with any other woman I've been involved with, I've learned that it's not necessary to keep running after something else [qtd. in Gittelson 255].

But he did, and, for all of its promise, their love affair ended. Beatty's obsessive behavior while making *Reds* and his inability to remain faithful to one woman for long are largely thought to have destroyed their relationship. But they have remained friends over the years. Looking back on their time together, Beatty said: "I loved Diane Keaton ... she made me laugh and made me cry.... If she had not made *Reds*, I do not know what I would have done" (qtd. in Parker 312).

Set between the years 1915 and 1920, *Reds* covers the events leading up to, including, and following the 1917 Russian Revolution. The real focus of the film, however, is Reed's rocky romance with writer and women's liberationist Louise Bryant. As David Thompson writes in *Warren Beatty and Desert Eyes: A Life and a Story*, "No other Beatty film contains so large or troubling a portrait of a woman, or is so concerned with sexual politics" (342). Keaton, who plays Bryant, was Beatty's only choice for this portrait, and she was with him early in 1979 as he traveled throughout Russia, Spain, England and other countries scouting locations for the film that he would control as producer, director, and star. Keaton says of Beatty at the time, "He was possessed by this movie. He was consumed by this movie. He wanted to make a great movie, and he spent a year shooting [it]" (personal interview).

Beatty's interest in Jack Reed had begun in the early sixties when he first traveled to Russia with his Russian-born love interest at the time, Natalie Wood. Christian Williams reports in the *Washington Post* that Beatty wrote a first draft of *Reds* ten years after a trip to Russia in the late '60s (B:1). Though British playwright Trevor Griffiths wrote the initial screenplay, Beatty, with the help of former cowriters Elaine May (*Heaven Can Wait*) and Robert Towne (*Shampoo*), revised the script from the moment shooting began on August 6, 1979. Like Woody Allen, Beatty liked to keep his plans close to the vest, so only he and Keaton and Jack Nicholson (who plays Eugene O'Neill) had scripts. The other actors had to rely on Beatty to constantly fill them in on what they were supposed to be doing. When Edward Herrmann, who played leftist radical Max Eastman, complained to Keaton, she allegedly told him, "It doesn't matter. It's all in Warren's head anyway. He keeps changing it all the time" (qtd. in Munshower, *Warren Beatty: His Life, His Loves, His Work* 124–25). When the Russians demanded to see the script before granting Beatty permission to film, Beatty refused and shot the revolution scenes in Helsinki instead of St. Petersburg (D. Thompson, *Warren Beatty and Desert Eyes* 342).

According to Suzanne Munshower in *Warren Beatty: His Life, His Loves, His Work*, Beatty made several trips to Russia, studying the language as well as the man, Jack Reed. He also began interviewing contemporaries of Reed, including writers Henry Miller and Will Durant; statesman Hamilton Fish; Roger Baldwin of the ACLU (neighbor); Dora Russell, widow of philosopher Bertrand Russell; Rebecca West; and George Jessel (Munshower 114–15). Thirty-two of these "witnesses" appear in *Reds*, their commentaries and recollections of Reed and Bryant serving as historical background and transitions from one scene to another in Beatty's sprawling 3-hour-and-19-minute epic.

The story begins in Portland, Oregon, Reed's birthplace, at the end of 1915. Jack Reed is already one of the most famous journalists in America, having covered everything from labor disputes in the United States to Pancho Villa's uprising in Mexico. He returns home for a visit where he meets Louise Bryant, a modern-minded woman married to a traditional dentist, who chastises his wife for showing nude photographs of herself in a gallery exhibit. Her husband is shocked not only by the photographs, but by the thought of "an emancipated woman in Portland." When one man asks Louise why the photographs are out of focus, she quickly responds, prophetically as it turns out, "The dream dominates the dreamer." Like Mary Wilke, Louise is all flash and pose. Prickly and pretentious, she has trouble living up to her own dreams and aspirations of being an artist, feminist, and journalist. Her badge of freedom is a small *pied-a-terre* in town where she can have some privacy and practice her art.

Louise meets Jack at The Liberal Club and promptly invites him back to her studio to interview him. They talk about politics until dawn. When she asks him if he is married, Reed replies: "I don't believe in marriage." She responds: "How can anyone believe in marriage." But when they encounter each other again at a small dinner party, Reed is amused to discover that Louise is married. When he challenges her about her idea of freedom, Louise promptly says: "I'd like to see you with your pants off, Mr. Reed," and they consummate their beginning relationship in a church courtyard.

Keaton's trademark combination of toughness and vulnerability work well in her portrayal of the conflicted Louise Bryant, whose act of bravado in seducing Reed was to save face as much as it was to fulfill any sexual attraction she had towards him. For example, the next morning Reed is in the bathroom shaving, humming "Onward Christian Soldiers" while Louise is nervously gathering up her things to make an appointment. Suddenly she's skittish and shy. The *mise-en-scène* illustrates the duality of Louise's personality. As she is walking down the stairway, Reed is looking over the balcony railing at her. She has backed herself into a corner, literally and figuratively. The high-angle shot suggests her vulnerability, but when Reed asks her to come to New York with him, she flashes, "What as? Your girlfriend? Your concubine?" She's like a cornered animal, almost hissing the words. The self-assured Reed makes a joke of it: "Well, it's almost Thanksgiving. Why don't you come as a turkey?" The scene sets the tone for their life together: she, tormented and troubled, he, confident and charming. Louise does leave her husband to live with Reed in Greenwich Village, but she is in way over her head with Reed and his brilliant circle of friends who include Eastman, O'Neill, and the radical feminist and political activist Emma Goldman (Maureen Stapleton).

Keaton played Louise as she saw her, not necessarily as history has depicted her, as is evident in Keaton's following analysis of her character.

> My feeling about Louise Bryant is contrary to all the stuff that was written about how she fell in love with [Reed] and blah, blah, blah. See, I didn't believe that. I felt that she was a very competitive woman, that she was not a great artist, yet she wanted to be a great artist. It was kind of like that *Amadeus* theme. She was around this guy who was a great artist. It just broke her spirit, and she couldn't stand it. She wanted so much to be him, or to be like him, or to be as talented as him. So it was torture for her. It was torture. She constantly compared herself with him, and she was constantly belittled by that, and she got back with anger. In the movie, they let love conquer all— and maybe it did. I don't know. But that was her struggle. Her struggle was to find herself as a person, and when she found herself as a person, as an artist and writer, and to respect what she was doing, then she could love him—and I think that was really interesting. I really think that's an interesting problem. It makes her a not very likable, but very real, woman in my opinion [personal interview].

One scene in particular illustrates Keaton's assessment of Louise Bryant. The build up to it is a montage showing Bryant and Reed dancing at a round of parties. With Jack, she is laughing and gay; however, she contributes nothing in conversations with his friends because they intimidate her. If they ask what she does, she replies, "I write." They quickly lose interest and turn away. Beatty often shoots her to either side of the frame, on the periphery, suggesting her place in the group. If she does fill the center of the frame, her back is to the camera or shadows fall across her face. She lives in his world, in his shadow. Beatty usually shoots his character from low angles, giving him the dominant position in the relationship. Louise soon grows dependent on and jealous of Jack, his successful career and his easy, charming way with people. When he tries to help her, she resents his interference, resisting and refusing his constructive criticism of her work.

The illustrative scene takes place when Jack returns a few days late from a trip and finds Louise at the breaking point. The setting sun filters through the bedroom window throwing dancing pools of light on the walls and shadows across

Louise's face as she sits waiting on their bed for him to
return. Poised for a fight,
perhaps a subconscious
effort to get his attention,
she pounces immediately
upon seeing him standing
in the bedroom doorway
with a handful of white lilies,
her favorite flower. They
argue about where he's been
until, desperate, Louise sinks
on the edge of the bed with
her back to him and the
camera. The form is closed;
the framing is tight. With
the dresser, window, and
lamp in front of her and the
bars of the footboard to her
left, Louise has nowhere to
go. She hangs her head and
cries: "Look at me. Oh,
God. I'm like a wife. I'm
like a boring, clinging, miserable little wife. Who'd
want to come home to me?"

Jack's assurances are
to no avail, and Louise tells
him: "I'm just living in your
margins. I don't know what
I'm doing here. I don't know
what my purpose is." When
he asks her what she wants,
she turns to face him: "I
want to stop needing you,"
she says. "I can't work
around you…. I'm not taken
seriously when you're
around." But Jack refuses
to take the blame for her
own lack of initiative and
begins to push back, yelling:

Reds (Paramount, 1981). Keaton spent a year of her life shooting *Reds* with Warren Beatty, who had long been fascinated by
the life of journalist and communist sympathizer Jack Reed and
his wife, Louise Bryant. Keaton says that she played Bryant as
she saw her—a tortured, competitive woman, desperate to escape the shadow of her talented, famous husband. The shoot
was grueling, with Beatty often doing 30 takes at a time. "It
was tough. It was a tough, emotional movie," Keaton remembers, but the performance won her an Academy Award
nomination for Best Actress.

Maybe if you took yourself a little more
seriously other people would too…. Why
do you even expect to be taken seriously
if you're not writing about serious
things?… I'm not even sure I know what
things you're serious about. One day

you're writing about the railroads, and
you don't even finish the piece. The next
day you're doing a piece on an art exhi-
bition that happened three years ago.
Look, why do you give me anything to
read anyway? If I criticize it at all, you
tell me you like it the way it is. And if
we're out with other people, if somebody

doesn't ask you a direct question, you tell me you feel ignored. But with everything that's happening in the world today, you decide to sit down and write a piece on the influence of the goddamned armory show of 1913. Are people supposed to take that seriously?

As Jack speaks, Louise keeps edging away from him toward the window, her head down in profile. She knows he's right, but she won't admit it. Instead she provokes him further with threats of finding her own apartment or taking an assignment in France. Finally, the argument explodes into shouting and door slamming with them standing on either side of the bedroom door in silence. When Louise opens the door, Jack softly says: "Honey, can we just get out of New York? Let's go somewhere and write what we want to write." In a tight close-up, we see Louise's face smiling up at him. She has won this round.

In this scene, Keaton captures all of Louise's fragility and strength. One moment she pushes and challenges; the next she looks beguilingly vulnerable and helpless, her eyes filled with tears. Her upswept hair—pieces falling loose in tendrils around her face—is backlit, softening her hard edges. As Keaton plays her, it is easy to see why both Reed and Eugene O'Neill were attracted to Louise Bryant. She spews feminist ideology but is not above using a few tears to get her way.

During the summer of 1916, while Reed was off on one of his trips, Bryant had an affair with O'Neill (Nicholson) at the Provincetown cottage she shared with Jack. As in their Greenwich Village flat, Louise and Jack were constantly surrounded with the brilliant and famous at their beach cottage. They discussed politics, sang, swam in the surf, and wrote plays in which they all performed. In one scene, Louise sings "I Don't Want to Play in Your Yard"; in another she acts out a part from one of the plays O'Neill is directing. He tells her: "You're supposed to

be looking for your soul, not an ashtray." She doesn't resist or challenge O'Neill's criticisms as she does Jack's, and they begin a brief but intense love affair. We see a series of shots showing Louise and Gene walking along the beach, making love on the sand dunes—doing all of the things that she did with Jack. For Louise, Gene substitutes for the man she really wants. Their affair promptly ends when Reed returns, and Louise runs to greet him. Realizing he's lost her, the hurt and drunken Gene finally staggers out of the house leaving Louise and Jack together.

Jack Nicholson as a wounded lover is an unusual sight, but he turns in an exceptional performance as the lovesick playwright. He follows Louise to Croton-on-Hudson, New York, where she and Jack are living. Not realizing that they have secretly married, he hands Louise a poem that he has written for her and professes his love: "I'd like to kill you, but I can't. I won't be possessive, and I won't be jealous. You can do anything you want to—except not see me."

Keaton's scenes with Nicholson are some of the film's best since both actors are noted for their ability to convey a feeling with a single glance. In this particular scene, all the nerve endings are exposed. Louise timidly tells him that she's married Jack. She's on her knees, unpacking boxes, trying to find Gene a glass for his scotch. She can barely meet his gaze. Pathetically, she hands him a cup and asks if it will do. Gene, like a cat playing with a mouse under his paw, says "no." She finds a glass and, with shaking hands, pours the scotch all over him. He calls her a "heartbreaker" and an "Irish whore from Portland" who used him to get Jack to marry her.

Keaton has said of Nicholson: "Jack is someone who's there for you. He has a lot of energy and hangs in and stays with the scene and, when it's somebody's turn for a close-up, he's there and he gives you as much as he can" (qtd. in Kroll, "Thoroughly Modern Diane" 58). According to Jack Kroll's *Newsweek* profile on Keaton, Nicholson wrote poems to Keaton as O'Neill did to Bryant but asked her not to show them to anyone. He has said of Keaton: "She has intense vulnerability and at the same time a very strong spine inside. That juxtaposition of fragility and strength is very attractive in a woman. She's very easy to fall in love with" (qtd. in Kroll, "Thoroughly Modern Diane" 58).

Reed and Bryant married in November of 1916, but spent more time apart than together. In *Queen of Bohemia: The Life of Louise Bryant*, Mary Dearborn says that one of the couple's problems was that while Bryant saw nothing wrong with her affair with O'Neill, she couldn't deal with Reed's indiscretions. It took the Russian Revolution to reunite them. *Reds* suggests that the year they spent in Russia covering the revolution of 1917 was the happiest of their relationship, which Beatty illustrates in another montage of Louise and Jack attending rallies, covering events, writing, playing, and making love. They have a common cause. Louise, more self-assured, finally accepts Jack's critiques of her work. At the end of Part I, their silhouettes merge in a kiss and fill the screen. We cannot tell where one person begins and the other ends. Their happiness, however, is fleeting. The lovers are swept up by a tide of events neither can control. Beatty visualizes this throughout the film by showing Jack and Louise constantly surrounded by a sea of people who bump into them and keep them apart. Often, we see them pushing through a crowd trying to reach each other, as in the final scene at the train station just before Reed dies of typhus with Bryant at his side.

Neither Reed's nor Bryant's life ended happily. Reed was not quite 33 years old when he died in 1920. He was buried in Red Square, a hero of the Russian Revolution. Lenin called *Ten Days That Shook the World* "a truthful and most vivid exposition" (qtd. in C. Williams, "*Reds*" B1). Bryant's account, *Six Months in Russia*, has been overshadowed by her husband's book. According to her biographers, Bryant became a foreign correspondent after Reed's death and was one of the first journalists to interview Mussolini after his successful coup. She married millionaire William C. Bullitt, Jr., of Philadelphia who eventually left her, taking their daughter with him. Bryant succumbed to drugs and alcohol and died destitute in Paris in 1936. She was 50.

Keaton credits Beatty for helping her portrayal of Louise Bryant, but she says that making *Reds* was "a raw experience" (personal interview). She explains:

> [Warren] helped my performance because he wouldn't stop doing takes. He just kept pushing and pushing and pushing and pushing and trying all different things. You know, he was never satisfied. We would average, you know, on a set up, we would average like 25 takes. People only usually do five at the most. Sometimes you'll do nine. So to do almost 30 every single time out on just a set up is just unheard of.... You never knew for sure what was wrong. What was wrong? Why wasn't I doing it good? It was tough. It was a tough, emotional movie.... I didn't feel that way about *Marvin's Room*. I felt that I was the author of my own work on that one. But on *Reds*, I felt that Warren was the author of my work. He did a good job [personal interview].

George Plimpton, who plays editor Horace Whigham, at the time observed: "Diane almost got broken. I thought he [Beatty] was trying to break her into what Louise Bryant had been like with Reed" (qtd. in Munshower, *Warren Beatty* 123–24).

Reds won three Academy Awards: Best Director (Beatty), Best Supporting Actress (Stapleton), and Best Cinematography (Vittorio Storaro). The Oscar for Best Film went to Hugh Hudson's *Chariots of Fire*. Though Keaton won a Best Actress nomination for her portrayal of

Bryant, she lost out to Katharine Hepburn for *On Golden Pond*. She also received British Academy Award and Golden Globe Award nominations for Best Actress.

While Beatty may not have been as solicitous toward Keaton as Woody Allen, he paid her the highest tribute after accepting his Oscar for Best Director:

> Miss Keaton, I know that public expressions like this can be embarrassing and that my chances of speaking with you in private are at the moment excellent, but I do want to tell you that you make every director you work with look good ... and I think what they're trying to tell me here tonight is that I'm no exception [qtd. in Janos 233].

Though Keaton and Beatty went their separate ways romantically, their paths have crossed over the years. Twenty years after making *Reds*, they re-teamed as a married couple in Peter Chelsom's romantic comedy, *Town and Country*—about a philandering husband and his socialite wife.

It was in this phase of Keaton's career that the public's perception of her as Annie Hall started to change. Audiences who had not seen her performances in *Goodbar* or *Interiors* but had caught her portrait of Louise Bryant saw an actress as adept at drama as she was comedy. If they read her press, they also would have noticed the confident, self-assured tone. The hesitant stammer, the naive comments, the unfinished thoughts that marked her early interviews were gone. Keaton was building a reputation as a serious, honest, no-nonsense actress determined to tackle tough, challenging roles and hard-hitting material. Throughout the eighties, she would play a string of complex, troubled, not necessarily likable, but real, women—just like Louise Bryant. Together they had enough "strange tics" to interest even Keaton.

CHAPTER 5

1982–1986

The Evolving Star Image

She's an original. Diane is not a version of anyone.
—Michael Lindsay-Hogg, director
(*Los Angeles Times*, Oct. 4, 1992)

Film critic Molly Haskell once said that the women Diane Keaton plays "are likely to have been divorced, widowed, analyzed, uprooted, and otherwise tampered with before the opening credits" ("Venus Substitutes" 38). The observation aptly describes Keaton's next four film roles. In *Shoot the Moon* (1982), *Little Drummer Girl* (1984), *Mrs. Soffel* (1984), and *Crimes of the Heart* (1986), she enacts a grab bag of bruised and damaged women whose happiness hangs by a slim thread. In each case, these characters are struggling to pick themselves up after some chain of events has left them wary—and weary—of life.

None of the films are blockbusters. For the most part, they are small, intimate character studies and family dramas that speak to the human condition—and none of them end happily ever after. *Shoot the Moon* is a portrait of a marriage coming apart at the seams. *Little Drummer Girl* is about an actress caught up in the escalating Israeli-Palestinian conflict. *Mrs. Soffel* and *Crimes of the Heart* both address the restrictions placed on women in patriarchal societies. Like most serious actors, Keaton prefers roles that give her a chance to flex her acting muscles instead of Hollywood formula films which often require a very limited acting range. The characters in these four films, all modern American women with a number of strange tics, provided Keaton a chance to explore the boundaries of her acting talent. She received high critical praise for her performances in *Shoot the Moon*, *Mrs. Soffel*, and *Crimes of the Heart*. *Little Drummer Girl* proved too much of a stretch. The failure of the film had as much to do with the convoluted script as Keaton's inability to enact a believable spy. Unfortunately, however good her reviews, the films didn't do well at the box office.

The 1980s represented a new era in Hollywood, one heavily influenced by a new political administration. Ronald Reagan's right-wing, Republican ideology inspired a wave of military films and white, action-adventure, tough-guy heroes like

Sylvester Stallone and Arnold Schwarzenegger. Female stars were often masculinized, like Sigourney Weaver in *Aliens*. Even Goldie Hawn went to war in *Private Benjamin* (a comedy about a wealthy, pampered Jewish princess whose stint in the Army gives new meaning to her life). Female audiences, given little to go to the theater for, turned to television and the VCR. The film industry had become a microcosm of big business dealings in America where the bottom line was all consuming, often at the expense of quality. Like many United States corporations, Hollywood studios went global, realizing huge profits in the foreign market, especially with action-adventure films which seemed to play well in any language.

A great divide developed in the way films were financed and marketed. With escalating movie budgets, studios and investors were less likely to take chances on films unlikely to garner enormous profits—like the small, thoughtful, intimate, socially conscious films that Keaton was drawn to. Instead, the studios poured money into the production and marketing of movies that would return their investment many times over, and, for the moment, those commercially successful films were military blockbusters like *Top Gun* and *Rambo*. These films by men and about men didn't require a whole lot of thought, but they embodied the values and agenda of the top man in the country.

In *Hard Bodies: Hollywood Masculinity in the Reagan Era*, Susan Jeffords argues that the images of the Reagan administration influenced the images coming out of Hollywood. Photographs or news footage of Reagan himself riding tall in the saddle or chopping wood or striding across the White House lawn signified what Jeffords calls the "hard body," which stood for "strength, labor, determination, loyalty, and courage" (Jeffords 24). Jeffords contends that these images of Reagan came to symbolize not just the American hero but also the tough, aggressive national character he was shaping. And this national character was diametrically opposed to that of the softer, "feminine" Carter administration "in which the United States government was brought to a standstill by a Third World nation" (Jeffords 25). Reagan's idea of a strong nation "capable of confronting enemies rather than submitting to them, of battling 'evil empires' rather than allowing them to flourish, of using its hardened body—its renewed techno-military network—to impose its will on others rather than allow itself to be dictated to" became the stuff of Hollywood (Jeffords 25).

The political climate of the Reagan years wasn't favorable for the "softer" female stars like Diane Keaton. As she pointed out, she wasn't right for the popular action-adventure genre of the time. It is virtually impossible to imagine Keaton as the gun-toting, butt-kicking Ellen Ripley of *Aliens* or the equally buff Sarah Conner (Linda Hamilton) of *The Terminator*. With their gritty, provocative style and muscle shirts revealing bodies as hard as any male action hero, they are the antithesis of Keaton in her soft layers of clothing, her trademark starched shirts buttoned to the neck revealing nary an inch of flesh, hard or otherwise. Her various turns of vulnerability and almost hysterical toughness would be no match for a relentless demon from outer space or a mechanical warrior from the future.

The image of Keaton as action hero just didn't compute with her previous on-screen images, which is probably why critics found her military scenes in *Little Drummer Girl* unbelievable. Peter Travers wrote: "Her scenes in training at a PLO camp should send shivers down the spine; instead they come off like outtakes from *Private Benjamin*" (Rev. *Little Drummer Girl* 10). As Natalie Gittelson wrote in "The Faces of Diane Keaton," she is "a throwback to a softer, gentler female of yesterday and a foretoken of tomorrow" (28). For the present, however, Keaton stayed with dramatic roles that, with few exceptions, at least earned her critical praise.

Work was steady but not as frenzied as in the seventies. Instead of making at least one film per year, Keaton often went two years between films. Financially secure, she had the time to pursue other interests, one of which was volunteering her Tuesday and Thursday nights at The Jewish Home and Hospital for the Aged on 106th Street in New York. Keaton's friend Kathryn Grody said: "I went and found it tremendously depressing, but Diane finds it inspiring. She is extraordinary with them and they love her" (qtd. in Jerome, "Diane Keaton" F4). But it is in an interview with Leo Janos that Keaton permits us a rare glimpse of the woman behind the on-screen persona and her personal concern for the country's elderly:

> I think it's hideous how we treat old people. They are left alone, completely isolated. So I decided to do this small thing as a kind of memorial to my grandmother. I like it. I just sit there and talk. I go to a dance on Thursday nights. The down side is, I'll ask for a particular person, and the room is cleaned out, and it's as if he or she never existed. They've disappeared in the night. Literally [qtd in Janos 232].

Keaton also used her time between films to build up work outside of acting, cultivating her life-long interest in photography and her dawning interest in directing. Considered an art photographer rather than a commercial photographer, she visualized that same sense of isolation and loneliness she found at the Jewish Home and Hospital in her first collection of photographs, *Reservations*, published by Knopf in March 1980. As her subject matter, Keaton chose forgotten, run-down American hotel lobbies from Atlantic City to Pasadena and points in between. Reviewing the book for *Newsweek*, Douglas Davis writes that "everywhere is a sense of loneliness—empty sofas, TV sets

turned off, a bank of telephones, unused and unanswered" (96). Keaton says: "I really was seeking these rooms out ... places that are sort of borderline, once were high-style, you know" (qtd. in Davis 96). Hotel managers often threw her out, even when they recognized her.

The idea for *Reservations*, Keaton explains, grew out of a photo essay she did for *Rolling Stone* on Atlantic City. Afterwards,

> I showed Bob Gottlieb and Knopf about ten photos of just interiors of hotels because it was just this idea I had, and he said to go ahead and do the rest. He said he would do a book.... It was about just exploring the city and how amazing Atlantic City was at that point. It was before gambling set in, and they had all these extraordinary hotels that were still there. It was sort of a graveyard place and nobody went there anymore, but these relics were still standing that were these extraordinary structures.... It grew out of being inside those hotels [personal interview].

The prestigious Castelli Graphics Gallery in New York exhibited 19 of the book's 44 photos.

Poetic and haunting, Keaton's images capture the frayed remnants of a society obsessed with newness, a society known the world over for tossing out things that are the least bit worn or used. More importantly, perhaps, the photographs in *Reservations* reflect Keaton's compassion for the neglected or unwanted. Like the character Uncle Arthur (Maury Chaykin) in her feature-length directorial debut, *Unstrung Heroes* (1995), Keaton is a collector of castoffs. Whether people or clown paintings or plastic bananas, she has an eye for the oddball and the abandoned. In a sense, her photographs are a way of collecting images, of documenting people and places so that they won't be forgotten.

All of her edited collections of photography reflect this sensibility. Her latest book, *Local News: Tabloid Pictures from the Los Angeles* Herald Express *1936–1961* (1999), offers a stunning array of "forgotten faces" and headlines from one of William Randolph Hearst's famous newspapers. Many of these pictures provoke an overwhelming sense of sadness, like the one of a slain woman's dirty shoes and beaded necklace—the only clues to her identity. In her introduction, Keaton writes that this book "honors the pretty, the hopeful, the ordinary, the murdered, the ugly, the tortured, the smug, the guilty, the lost and found.... Each human face is a compelling mystery that looks back at us like a mirror reflecting the absolute fact that we live, we die, and we are forgotten.... This book is for those who slip away unnoticed."

Keaton did a number of photography and art exhibitions during the eighties, including a series of portraits of her friend, Carol Kane, and a collection of religious paintings that Keaton thought up and artist R. D. Huggins executed. Their work was displayed at New York's Daniel Wolf Gallery. The show was a prelude to Keaton's 1987 documentary, *Heaven*, a collage of images and interviews with various people on the concept of heaven. The same poetic sense of isolation and clean, spare, slightly off-center composition style we see in her *Reservations* photographs can be found in *Heaven* and especially in her later work behind the camera.

Two other projects occupied Keaton's off-screen time during this period; one was a collection of photographs called *Still Life* (Calloway 1983) that she coedited with art dealer Marvin Heiferman and the other a 20-minute movie she directed called *What Does Dorrie Want?* about her sister Dorrie. It was shown at the Filmex Festival in Los Angeles in 1982 and was the first of many small projects Keaton undertook in the coming decade to steadily build her skills as a director, which included two music videos for Belinda Carlisle: *Heaven Is a Place on Earth* and *I Get Weak*.

For the moment, her love of the camera manifested itself in choosing the images for *Still Life*, a collection of photos that captures what her creative partner Heiferman calls "a portrait of middle-class American life after the war as drawn by the movies" (qtd. in "The Way We Were" 23). Keaton and Heiferman went through hundreds of studio files and private collections and thousands of photos to select the 64 color prints that appear in *Still Life*. All of them reveal the vacuous glamour that Hollywood was selling to the American public post World War II.

In a publicity shot from *The Thrill of It All* (1963), for example, Doris Day stands smiling, holding a box with the word "Happy" printed across it, next to a bright, shiny-new washing machine. With her beige hair, beige dress and pearls, Day was photographed against a bright-yellow wall filled with white daisies. For Keaton, images like this one were death-like, "just representations of the idea of the scene" (qtd. in Pacheco 106). In her 1993 collection, *Mr. Salesman*, it is the Willy Lomans of the world who similarly stare back at us "from under the atrophy of living within the boundaries of The American Dream," as Keaton writes. In her selection of photographs, Keaton reveals an uncanny ability to capture and expose the emptiness of our materialistic pursuits. The Whitney Museum exhibited 44 of the photographs from *Still Life* in November and December of 1983.

Keaton's off-beat vision was at cross purposes with the current direction of the country. Unfazed, she made choices that were interesting to her at the time, choices that would allow her to grow and evolve, regardless of whether they reflected popular tastes. While her next four films didn't score big profits at the box office, Keaton herself was doing consistently good work, the key to a long career in the movie business.

Shoot the Moon

Alan Parker (*Fame*, *Midnight Express*) wasn't shooting for a feel-good movie with *Shoot the Moon*, which was scripted by Bo Goldman (*One Flew Over the Cuckoo's Nest*). Set in scenic Marin County, California, near San Francisco, the film unsentimentally exposes all the raw nerve endings of a disintegrating upscale marriage. All that seems to connect Faith (Keaton) and George Dunlap (Albert Finney) after 15 years together are four young daughters and a restored Victorian farmhouse. Parker allows his film to unravel as slowly as the Dunlap's marriage, and the result is so realistic that it caused Pauline Kael to write:

> There isn't a scene in his new picture ... that I think rings false.... The characters ... aren't taken from the movies, or from books, either. They're torn—bleeding—from inside Bo Goldman and Alan Parker and the two stars, Diane Keaton and Albert Finney, and others in the cast [*For Keeps* 924].

In fact, Parker confessed that the film mirrored his own life more closely than any film he had ever made: "It's the only film I ever did where every single day I knew every line everybody should be saying because I'd probably already said that line the day before" (qtd. in Hall C1). Keaton, too, found herself caught up in the story, writing pages of notes to screenwriter Bo Goldman which he later described as "good as any I've ever seen. Simple thoughts, always presented in the most matter-of-fact, practical way" (qtd. in Kroll, "Thoroughly Modern Diane" 114). She told Joey Berlin of *The New York Post*, "I want to have a participation in the story, not just my part. I rattle on and write these notes to everybody. I have a lot of opinions" (qtd. in "Another Mother" 41). When it comes time to shoot, however, she puts herself in the hands of the director: "I usually have a say in the story, but when you act, you're the actor. The director's the director, and that's that," she declared (qtd. in L'Ecuyer, "Diane Keaton" 38). This was Parker's film, though in all probability Keaton drew upon her own recent breakup with Warren Beatty to help create the character of Faith Dunlap.

The opening images of *Shoot the Moon* set the tone. An extreme long shot reveals the house at the end of a long and winding driveway. It stands alone amid the misty rolling hills, bathed in twilight. The camera slowly zooms in on several ducks swimming silently in a pond; a solitary car parked in the drive; an overturned bicycle with its wheels spinning slowly; an empty porch swing still moving as if someone had just gotten out of it; and a teddy bear tossed aside and forgotten. The images of loneliness, the thickening fog, and the plaintive theme song, "Don't Blame Me," picked out with one finger on a piano, all create a feeling of uneasiness that never goes away, not even after the film has ended. We have an immediate sense of unseen forces working on the inhabitants of this world, and it makes us nervous, uncomfortable.

George Dunlap is a temperamental, successful writer who has taken a mistress named Sandy (Karen Allen) as well as an award for his latest novel, ironically titled "The Court Game." The experiences of writing and keeping his other life a secret have left him exhausted. Parker often frames him tightly through doorways or in small spaces; he is a cornered, conflicted man. He "worships" his wife but can't say why he's leaving her, except that she always remembers "the wrong things." George is the kind of father who steps in for the fun part of child-rearing. He tells Faith one night: "You had four children, four children, and you raised them with the back of your hand—and you made it look so goddamned easy.... I was never there. I was a bystander, an outsider in all this." Like Renata in *Interiors*, George's art needs isolation, and, indeed, though he is often surrounded by people, he is as isolated as the exquisitely renovated farmhouse he treasures.

Faith Dunlap is a used-up housewife who has been cast aside for a younger woman. She has invested in George, not herself, spending years taking care of their house and four children so that he could make something of himself. The experience has left her exhausted. In truth, she reigns tenuously over a rowdy bunch. Her husband's temperamental outbursts and her precocious, boisterous brood of daughters would be enough to exhaust anyone. Throughout the film, we see Faith picking up after her children, vacuuming, and doing dishes in baggy, paint-splattered jeans, an old shirt (buttoned to the collar), and a worn, brown cardigan—a classic case of a wife and mother who spends little time on herself. She tries to pick up the pieces of her own life only after she thinks there is no longer hope for a future with George. Reluctantly, she moves on with a younger man, Frank Henderson, whom she has hired to build a tennis court that she has always wanted. The song "Play with Fire" by the Rolling Stones provides the background music for their awkward seduction scene and presages the outcome of their affair.

When we first meet George and Faith Dunlap, they are preparing for an award dinner. Faith's four daughters are gathered around her dressing table, "helping" her get ready. Arms, lipstick tubes, and powder brushes fly around her. Their constant chattering, overlapping dialogue is as natural as Keaton's own way with children. Though she was not a mother at this point in her life, she did come from a household with four children, and her interaction with young people in all of her films seems unforced and real. As she looks in the mirror, she declares: "I hate the way I look," and we wonder, given the way Faith is dressed, how much of the costume decisions were Keaton's own.

Faith wears an ensemble that could have been pulled out of Keaton's closet: a blue and red stripe, fitted, two-piece suit cinched at the waist with a Davy Crocket belt and accented with red gloves. Her shoulder-length, bobbed hair is fringed with thick bangs. She has the look of a woman who could be pretty, but her eyes and mouth are pulled down at the corners as if by the sheer weight of discovering her husband's infidelity.

The only thing forced is Faith's smile as she trots along after George at the awards banquet trying to obey his instructions, "Smile, goddamnit," and George's acceptance speech upon winning the book award. From the podium, he thanks his wife "so aptly named" and blows her a kiss for the cameras. Their uneasy silence is broken—along with the china—the next morning as Faith confronts him about his "lady friend." Fearful that his response will generate an outcome she is not prepared for, Faith catches herself, refusing to meet his gaze or to discuss it further. Instead, she turns her back to the camera and George, plunging her hands into a sink full of dishes.

George wants a showdown and provokes her into facing the situation by smashing dishes until the floor is strewn with glass and shards of porcelain. Faith turns her back once again and, holding onto the countertop, doubles over in her old brown cardigan and weeps. Parker cuts back and forth between Faith sobbing in the kitchen as she tries to clean up the mess and George hesitating at the front door. He cannot leave, yet cannot stay, because so many things still connect him to this woman: the kids, the house, the in-laws, their travels, and the thousand day-to-day decisions—like where to move a sofa—that they've shared over the years. It's a classic case of not being able to live with or without each other. George is paralyzed with indecision until, finally, he walks out.

Eldest daughter Sherry takes the

Shoot the Moon (MGM/UA, 1982). George and Faith Dunlap can't seem to make a clean break of their marriage. Four rambunctious daughters, a restored Victorian farmhouse, and 15 years of memories and habits keep pulling them back together. The composition of this shot shows the couple in the foreground, in sharp focus compared to the dining patrons around them. George (Albert Finney) and Faith (Keaton) are in profile, locked on each other, oblivious to how loud and obnoxious they are getting. Struggling to sort out what went wrong, they fling accusations as easily as they share their cuisine. Each occupies half of the frame, suggesting that there are two sides to this story. But when an attack comes from one of the offended diners, the Dunlaps defend each other with all the fury and passion of a loving couple.

breakup the hardest. When she asks Faith why George left them, we see Keaton embody the disillusionment of a woman whose life didn't work out the way she thought it would and the tenderness and compassion of a mother who wants to lift the blame from the shoulders of her children:

> FAITH: He left me, not you. When two people love each other, it's like going through doors. And, first, you go through doors together. Then one person gets ahead.
> SHERRY: But if they love each other, why don't they wait for each other?
> FAITH: I don't know.
> SHERRY: Do you wish for you and Daddy?
> FAITH: No.

> SHERRY: Frank?
> FAITH: No.
> SHERRY: Did you stop wishing?
> FAITH: No. I hope I never stop wishing. It's just that when you get older, you learn to take things as they come. George always said that wishes are sometimes all that we have.

As Sherry tries to work through her anger and frustration over her parents' split, she resists all of her father's attempts to reconcile with her until he breaks into the house one night and beats her into submission.

Faith and George reconcile once, briefly after the death of Faith's father. Bound by ties to family and habits that are hard to break, George attends the funeral and ends up sharing a dinner table as well as the food on his plate with his soon-to-be ex-wife. We see the flip side of Faith's character here in what has become Keaton's trademark feisty scene. No matter how wounded or vulnerable or depressed, her characters muster up the strength at some point in a film to verbally dress down an opponent. With an 80-year-old piano-playing chanteuse warbling "Don't Blame Me" in the background, George and Faith reminisce, laugh, blame each other, shout accusations, and totally ignore the other patrons' requests to pipe down. They end up in a brawl with another couple, fiercely defending each other against outside attack. At one point, Faith yells: "Fuck you, woman. Fuck you," as she gives her the finger. Somehow the experience unites George and Faith. They declare themselves the winners, sit down, order lobster and wine, hold hands, giggle, and walk through the door of her hotel room together for one last night of lovemaking.

Keaton describes the movie as "the war of a man and a woman who are breaking up and how the woman is crushed by this man going off and having an affair with someone else." She sees it as a realistic depiction of "a marriage when a marriage starts to fall apart and the pain is involved and all of that—how it affects the kids" (personal interview). And while George and Faith go on to other partners, it is the children who suffer in this film. Emotionally tied to their mother, they desperately try to please their father and appease his rages, even as George lies bleeding on Faith's newly built tennis court. In a fit of jealousy over Faith's relationship with Frank, George destroys the tennis court with his car until Frank beats him. The final scene does suggest a battleground. George lies amidst the wreckage he's created, including his children, calling Faith's name as the fog surrounds them.

After seeing *Shoot the Moon*, Pauline Kael wrote: "Diane Keaton may be a star without vanity; she's so completely challenged by the role of Faith that all she cares about is getting the character right" (*For Keeps* 927). Several of Keaton's key scenes in the film substantiate Kael's assessment of her growth as an actress:

> Very few young American movie actresses have the strength and the instinct for the toughest dramatic roles—intelligent, sophisticated heroines. Jane Fonda did, around the time that she appeared in *Klute* and *They Shoot Horses, Don't They?*, but that was more than ten years ago. There hasn't been anybody else until now. Diane Keaton acts on a different plane from that of her previous film roles; she brings the character a full measure of dread and awareness, and does it in a special, intuitive way that's right for screen acting. Nothing looks rehearsed, yet it's all fully created [*For Keeps* 927].

Almost without exception, reviewers singled out the bathtub scene as an example of Keaton at her finest. George has returned to pick up his books and a few other belongings. Faith helps him pack. One of the books triggers memories of a vacation they spent together in Provence, France. Tentatively, they begin to sing the Beatles' song, "If I Fell," in French. Later, after he has left and taken the girls for a visit, Faith lies in her claw-footed tub smoking a joint and singing the song first in French, then in English. Slowly, as her face registers a dawning awareness of how much the words echo her own relationship with George, her voice catches and she begins to weep.

Michael Sragow wrote in *Rolling Stone*: "This is screen acting at its peak" (27). Gary Arnold for *The Washington Post* said: "Keaton plays her greatest single scene—it's bound to become a classic.... Faith begins crooning the lyrics of a Beatles song—'If I Fell'—to herself, and each word seems to evoke a fresh, spontaneous note of regret and sorrow" ("Love's Bitter Season" D1). Carla Hall called it "an exquisite moment" ("Director Parker" C1). In a 1997 interview with Keaton, Robert Denerstein of *The Rocky Mountain News* told her: "That image stayed with me like a great painting, a lingering portrait of the American woman in the '80s" ("At 51" D6).

Neither Keaton's performance nor the film garnered Academy Award nominations. Meryl Streep won that year for *Sophie's Choice* out of an actress pool that included Julie Andrews (*Victor/Victoria*), Jessica Lange (*Francis*), Sissy Spacek (*Missing*), and Debra Winger (*An Officer and a Gentleman*). Jessica Lange and Sissy Spacek would costar with Keaton in *Crimes of the Heart*. *Gandhi* took home the Oscar for Best Picture, beating out *E.T.*, *Missing*, *Tootsie*, and *The Verdict*.

Little Drummer Girl

Reviews for Keaton's performance as Charlie in *Little Drummer Girl*, directed by George Roy Hill (*Butch Cassidy and the Sundance Kid*), were polarized. Critics either loved or hated her interpretation of John Le Carré's British repertory actress and pro–Palestinian sympathizer who becomes a spy for Israeli intelligence. On the one hand, Jack Kroll of *Newsweek* called Keaton's performance "vivid and powerful" and "Oscar caliber" ("In the Theater of the Real" 118). On the other hand, in his review of the film for *People*, Peter Travers wrote: "Forget that the movie doesn't live up to the book (few movies do), but how can we forgive Keaton for a comically intense performance that distorts what may be Le Carré's most complex work?" (10).

In truth, Loring Mandel's screen adaptation of Le Carré's novel is as incomprehensible as Paul Attanasio's comment: "Diane Keaton gives the performance of her career" ("Daring *Drummer*" B1). Le Carré's complex, 500-page detailed thriller

about the Israeli/Palestinian conflict would be better served up as a mini-series marathon instead of a 2-hour and 10-minute movie. The characters here have more names than those in a Russian novel, and huge chunks of the book have been condensed to a whirlwind tour of location sites. The film opens in Bad Godesberg, West Germany; quickly moves to Dorset, England; cuts to Munich; and before we can say Apollo wine, Charlie is in Mykonos, Greece, making a wine commercial. After a brief stop at the Parthenon in Athens, she's back in London briefly before a stint at a PLO camp in Beruit where she teaches Palestinian soldiers to sing Petula Clark's "Downtown," then on to Jerusalem for the climax, and finally home for the denouement. The material is so hacked up that it takes at least a couple of viewings to determine who's on first.

The script leaves little time for an actress with a predilection for small, psychological dramas to get inside her character's head. Given the rich possibilities of a novel that seriously examines the long-standing, volatile middle-east political dilemma, the results are disappointing. Keaton is out of her element. For one thing, the original Charlie is British, and, because Keaton has no facility with dialects, Charlie becomes an American actress doing British repertory theater in London for the film version. This is all very odd since she still strives for a British accent in the scenes showing her acting on stage. The juxtaposition of her scenes with those of her fellow actors and friends only serves to point up how unfortunate her attempts are.

Keaton's look here also defies explanation. With one dangling earring and one stud; tight, black stove-pipe pants; spike heels; jackets with huge shoulder pads; and a permed, cut-over-the-ear coif, she comes off as a cross between a punk rocker and a Philadelphia quarterback. Her PLO fatigues, belted tightly and fashionably at the waist, simply look absurd.

Little Drummer Girl (Warner Bros., 1984). Hill's film version of John Le Carré's novel doesn't work—neither does Keaton's interpretation of Charlie, an actress and Palestinian sympathizer who becomes a spy for Israeli intelligence. Keaton's physicality, especially, doesn't fit the action genre, which is one of the reasons some critics and audiences didn't buy her scenes in the PLO camp where she trains the troops in guerrilla warfare. Looking back on the characters, she admits: "I just didn't pull that one off."

The name Charlie itself conjures up images of military CB radio code that could stand for anything, like Charlie the actress. She's a Palestinian sympathizer until she meets Joseph/Gat Becker (Yorgo Voyagis) with whom she immediately and inexplicably falls in love. The range of his expressions sweeps the spectrum from glum to morose. At first Charlie thinks Joseph is the Palestinian, Michele, who lectures in a black ski mask. Then she discovers that he is really a member of an Israeli spy ring led by a man called Marty (Klaus Kinski). Joseph kidnaps Charlie, and, en route to their secret hideout, she cries: "Stop this car. I'm getting carsick, and I'm out of my depth"—a fitting epitaph for the movie.

After a long night of grilling, Charlie agrees to accept the part of a lifetime: act as bait for the Israelis who are trying to track down the Palestinian terrorist, Khalil (Sami Frey), who has been blowing up Israeli statesmen. It turns out that Khalil is the brother of Michele, who the Israelis capture and finally kill. Also, surprise, we discover that Charlie isn't who she says she is. Instead of the well-bred young woman who attended a private school in Virginia and whose life was rocked by scandal when her father went to prison, we learn in this scene that she went to public school in Ames, Iowa, where she was suspended for being "too available to local boys." In a 1987 interview for *Film Comment*, Keaton described Charlie as "'pathetic, all ambition and no gifts. No brains. No nothing'" (qtd. in Glicksman 36). Keaton added that of all the characters she had played in this phase of her career, she found Charlie "interesting" but the least likable "because she was somebody who was so lost" (qtd. in Glicksman 37).

Little Drummer Girl gives Keaton, as the brassy Charlie, a chance to swear and scream and fly into hysterics for at least half of the movie, but it all seems forced and unbelievable. However, there are several scenes in which she captures the sheer terror of a confused and naive woman whose lofty talk and ideals come crashing down around her in the harsh reality of international politics where nobody wins. One side can be just as right or wrong as the other. Charlie finally realizes that she is little more than a pawn, a means to an end, for both sides. She assumes the role of the dead Michele's girlfriend so that the Israelis can capture a terrorist, but, once she crosses the line, the Palestinians test her loyalty and use her to carry out their acts of terrorism.

Charlie is forced to watch acts of violence in both camps. She must watch the Israelis inhumanely strip the captive Michele and clinically point out all of his scars and body markings, in case Khalil tests her about her relationship with his brother. In Keaton's face, we see every person's reaction to such insensitivity as she looks on only as long as she has to before running to the bathroom where she gets physically sick. At the PLO training camp, she cannot run from the horror. To make her loyalty to the cause believable, Charlie must stand by and watch as the Palestinian soldiers shoot a captured Israeli spy. Keaton's depiction of controlled revulsion is another example of her ability to register conflicting emotions simultaneously. Charlie stands in profile watching the scene through a window of a hut with the Palestinian captain next to her watching her every move. The shot fires, and, for a split second, she looks down, begins to shake, gains control of herself, and feigns indifference. It is a marvelous

bit of acting topped only by her performance in the climactic scene.

After Charlie connects with Khalil, masquerading as Yano, they briefly reminisce about Michele and then fall into each other's arms. After a night of lovemaking, Khalil hears a noise, grabs his gun, and realizes that something is terribly wrong. Lying in bed, Charlie tries to calm him, but she says all the wrong things. Her radio/recorder that he's taken the batteries out of now works. Dawning suspicion compels Khalil to ask: "Who do you work for, Charlie?" Keaton's portrait of a woman trapped, her fear so palpable that she almost cannot speak, does send shivers down the spine.

Shaking, Charlie confesses that she never even knew Khalil's brother. Khalil responds, "You believe in nothing." In that moment, just as Charlie's face registers a full understanding of her life of lies and deceit, Joseph breaks in and shoots Khalil, whose blood symbolically washes over the screaming Charlie, spurting in her eyes and mouth. She has blindly become the instrument of his death, and the impact of her actions manifests itself in Charlie's ultimate inability to return to acting. She can no longer give voice to her characters on-stage again. Keaton's performance achieves terrifying realism here, but, overall, she never quite manages to sustain a believable characterization throughout the film. In 1987, she told *Rolling Stone*: "I just didn't pull that one off. I tried very hard, but when I look back on that one, it was just effort" (qtd. in Edelstein 24).

Mrs. Soffel

Mrs. Soffel was an entirely different experience for Keaton. *Little Drummer Girl's* location shoots had kept her out of the country for months since filming began in the summer of 1983. Like her friend Woody Allen, Keaton doesn't like to be away from home for long periods, and that combined with the tension of trying to create a character she never did get a handle on made for a frustrating experience. The excitement of working with Australian director Gillian Armstrong, whom Keaton calls "the single best female director," revived her spirits (personal interview). Armstrong's first feature-length film, *My Brilliant Career*, starring Judy Davis, launched her own career and won the British Critics' Award for best first feature film as well as seven American Film Institute awards, which included best director and best film.

Keaton says that Armstrong is so "imaginative and so brilliant visually, and her point of view is so female. Her stories are so strongly rooted in female problems, difficulties, sexuality, romantic fantasies. I just think she's really amazing" (personal interview). Almost as soon as filming began in February of 1984, Keaton said she paid close attention to Armstrong's directing style, often following Armstrong around and making notes on her shots for her own future reference.

Keaton was proud of her work in *Mrs. Soffel*, a dark period piece and psychological drama inspired by real life events that took place in Pittsburgh, Pennsylvania, at the turn of the century. Keaton was the first choice of screenwriter Ron Nyswaner and producer Edgar Scherick to play Kate Soffel, a mother of four who escapes her cloistered, stifling life as the wife of Allegheny County Prison Warden Peter Soffel (Edward Herrmann) by running off with convicted murderers Ed (Mel Gibson) and Jack (Matthew Modine) Biddle.

As the story goes, the Biddle brothers were robbers, not murderers. They gained a following, especially of young women, who felt that they were innocent of shooting a local grocer in the head. Armstrong visualizes the Biddle fervor with signs in front of the prison reading: "Biddles must not hang." Families pray

for the innocent boys inside. Women swarm a guard asking to see Ed and Jack, while handing him care packages to deliver to the brothers. The Soffel cook thinks Ed Biddle is handsome, and, in one scene, Kate finds her daughter, Margaret, under her bed compiling a scrapbook of "all the injustices against the Biddles." Supposedly, Kate Soffel also succumbed to their charms, especially those of the charismatic Ed Biddle who aroused sexual passions that her cold and rigid husband could never inspire. She ended up sacrificing her children and her reputation for a grand passion.

If critics faulted Keaton's performance, it was for being too modern in her actions and demeanor for a period piece. Writing for *Maclean's*, Lawrence O'Toole said, "When she speaks, her grand illusion of being the stifled Victorian woman falls apart. Keaton sounds too modern, and her physical mannerisms and carriage betray her as well" ("Passionate Partners" 51). Pauline Kael also wrote at the time: "Diane Keaton has trouble with the period role: her fast, distraught manner of speaking, the words she emphasizes, the ones she throws away—it's all very specifically modern" (*For Keeps* 1035).

Kael also suggests that Keaton has "freakishly inspired" moments on screen that more than compensate for any modern sensibilities. In one scene, for example, Kate has brought Ed a file hidden in her laced boots. She stands close to the prison bars reading a Bible passage while Ed crouches down and seductively removes the file. Kael writes:

> Ed has been holding her against the bars and she has been speaking like a moral exemplar when suddenly, in mid-sentence, she lets out a dirty little giggle. We know then that Kate is living in a fever dream and doesn't want to wake up. And the post-hippie diction and the other surface flaws in Keaton's performance fade into relative insignificance, because the things that come from inside are so startlingly right [*For Keeps* 1035].

Keaton loved the idea of playing a woman who gives way to her deepest desires. She says: "I've never done anything like that. I was just so glad to get that thing off and thrilled and excited about it. It was really wonderful" (personal interview). The film was a critical success, but Keaton claims it didn't do well at the box office.

> That was another movie that made not a nickel, by the way. It was a bomb. Nobody went to see that movie. Nobody. Nobody. And it's so interesting because, what, about five years later, Mel Gibson became a huge giant. Nobody wanted to see it. I don't know why.... It's disappointing when people don't seem to like it. I think what happened is that they screened it, and people didn't take to it. It was too dark. I don't know. I thought it was beautiful [personal interview].

From the film's opening credits, the images are beautiful—and unrelentingly dark. A low rumbling of drums heralds a virtual slide show of a factory town at dawn: a burst of light from a blast furnace, a tower topped with a cross, a loaded train slowly moving past a horse and buggy. Blue filters on the camera lens cast a cold shadow over the action. As Kate will later tell Ed during their escape to Canada: "It's like the snow's inside my skin." Movies this dark are probably an acquired taste.

The world inside the prison is darker still. Armstrong uses mostly natural light sources, like windows and oil lamps, so that the images are at times barely perceptible, creating a sense of claustrophobia and entrapment. As wife of the prison warden, Kate lives in prison quarters with her family. When we meet her at the beginning of the film, she has been in bed for three months suffering from neurasthenia. We get an extreme close-up on her eyes opening before we hear her scream. She's had a dream, a prophetic one at that. She tells her husband, who is spooning laudanum down her throat: "I was lost in a snow storm. I couldn't breathe. Some-

body pulled me out to a clear spot. I know what God's telling me. God was telling me he's not going to let me die."

Kate is like the walking dead. By day, she moves through the prison corridors like a specter, dressed from head to toe in black, delivering Bibles to inmates she knows by name. Only her shadow precedes her along the cold, stone slab walls. By night, she moves like a ghost through the family quarters checking on the children, tucking them into bed, praying with them. Again, Keaton's natural way with children infuses these scenes with tenderness as she gently counsels them and teaches them to pray. But Kate's prayers are just empty words; she cannot quite convince herself or the literal Ed Biddle that misery on earth leads to heavenly rewards. We get the sense that all the passion has been squeezed out of this woman's life, leaving just a shell, until she meets Ed. Their kiss through prison bars almost literally restores her to life, filling her with renewed energy and purpose as she fights for a re-evaluation of his case.

At first Ed's honeyed words are as empty of meaning as Kate's own, but they are all he has to win her support. She's his ticket to freedom. She's also older than Ed, and even the soft, amber filters cannot hide the lines around her eyes and mouth which he sees through the bars of his cell. But they fill a need in each other, connecting both on an emotional and sexual level so that when Ed and Jack do escape, he takes her with him to Canada. The extreme long shots and long shots of their sleigh, usually driven by Jack, moving north through miles of white snow and open space are in direct contrast to the tightly framed prison images.

Armstrong often shoots the lovers huddled in the back of the sleigh. The light splashing only across their faces, with all else in darkness, suggests that Kate and Ed are in a world of their own. They can no longer exist without each other. Pauline Kael accurately sums up

Mrs. Soffel (MGM/UA, 1984). In one of Keaton's few period pieces, she plays the tragic Kate Soffel, wife of a Pittsburgh prison warden and mother of four who falls in love with the condemned Ed Biddle. But Armstrong does not sentimentalize their doomed romance. Instead, she has the characters play their most romantic scenes while on opposite sides of Ed's prison cell with the hard, steel bars between them or in the spacious but snow-covered, freezing countryside. Here, Kate (Keaton) shoots a gun to clear off the townspeople as she flees with Ed (Mel Gibson, center) and his brother Jack (Matthew Modine).

their actions: "They're killing each other by staying together, yet you can see that staying together is all that matters to them" (*For Keeps* 1036). Stopping to rest at a farmhouse, Kate, wearing a white dress, undoes her tightly upswept hair which falls softly to her waist and makes passionate love to Ed. Their words are finally fraught with meaning. Ed professes his love and asks for her forgiveness, and Kate, knowing what fate awaits them, says: "Don't you let them take me alive, Ed." Though her psychological journey with Ed liberates Kate emotionally, their physical journey together can only end in disaster.

Armstrong brings the film full circle when Kate ends up where Ed Biddle began, in a prison cell. As her dream foretold,

God does not let her die, although Ed keeps his promise and shoots her before he and Jack are hunted down and slaughtered like animals. Framed between the bars of her cell, dressed in black once more, Kate tells the guard. "I don't want to see that preacher. I don't need his prayers." Kate has replaced her prayer book with a poem that Ed has written to her about "true hearts" beating beyond the grave.

The on-screen chemistry of the two stars makes the attraction between Kate and Ed believable despite their age difference and disparate backgrounds. Keaton says of her co-star: "Mel Gibson was so great. I loved him in that movie. He was just so beautiful and fresh. God, any woman would fall in love with him" (personal interview). She never got close to Gibson while filming *Mrs. Soffel*, however. She told Dominick Dunne at the time that not knowing her co-star well off-screen actually helped their performances: "I wanted to keep a distance from being friendly with him. If you start hanging out together you lose the kind of tension it takes to play a part like that" (qtd. in "Hide and Seek" 38).

Crimes of the Heart

Mrs. Soffel was released on December 26, 1984, only two months after *Little Drummer Girl* opened. It was the seventh in a string of intensely dramatic roles for Keaton. This particular body of work shadowed Keaton's early comedies and inspired Sally Hibben of *Film Dope* to write in 1984 that it was "misleading" to call Diane Keaton a comedienne. Hibben compared her to Sandy Dennis, ten years Keaton's senior, who played a bevy of "willowy depressives" both on stage and on screen (39). Dennis, who won a Best Supporting Actress Oscar for *Who's Afraid of Virginia Woolf?* (1966), also starred in *Up the Down Staircase* (1967), *Sweet November* (1968), and *The Out-of-Towners* (1970). She won two Tony Awards for *A Thousand Clowns* and *Any Wednesday*, but the neurotic women Dennis plays differ from Keaton's in that Dennis's neuroses are unrelieved. Her characters never give us even a glimpse of the warmth or vulnerability that underlies so many of Keaton's dramatic characters, and Dennis's halting, stuttering style of speaking seems to stem more from a fuzziness of thinking rather than any shyness or awkwardness.

Keaton's next project broke her dramatic streak and marked the return of the comedienne. *Crimes of the Heart* was directed by Australian Bruce Beresford, best known for *The Getting of Wisdom* (1977), *Breaker Morant* (1980), *Tender Mercies*

(1983), and *Driving Miss Daisy* (1989). Beresford and Gillian Armstrong were part of the New Wave of Australian filmmakers whose talent revived an all but derailed national film industry in the mid-seventies. Beresford, especially, is known as an actor's director who prepares well and elicits Oscar-winning performances from his stars with his patient, affable style. His willingness to listen to his actors and give them room to experiment paid off in *Crimes*. Keaton, along with her costars, Sissy Spacek and Jessica Lange, play the Mississippi MaGrath sisters of Beth Henley's Pulitzer Prize–winning play of the same name and do some of their best ensemble work under Beresford's direction.

To capture all of the nuances and complexities of sisterhood, Southern-style, for example, Beresford kept the set relaxed and loose. Sissy Spacek said, "I never felt a panic for time, pressure. And he had a really good relationship with all of us. Separately and together" (qtd. in Rochlin 38). Beresford had the actresses submit suggestions for their characters and gave them some freedom with the dialogue. Keaton said, "He let us overlap so much, and I thought it was really freeing.... That happened a lot with the movies I did with Woody Allen" (qtd. in Rochlin 53).

Beresford also brought the actresses together as a family off-screen. Instead of giving them each separate trailers, which tends to isolate actors, Beresford rented a house for them while on location in Southport, North Carolina. They had their own dressings rooms but shared the rest of their living quarters, which worked out well by all accounts. Tess Harper, who plays cousin Chick, told David Sterritt of *The Christian Science Monitor*: "If the people who see this film enjoy it anywhere near the way we enjoyed making it ... it will be a tremendous success. I've never been on a set full of such camaraderie, enjoyment of each other" (qtd. in "Actress Tess Harper" 22). As a result of

Beresford's efforts, the actresses come off looking comfortable and natural with each other, giving an authenticity to their scenes as loving, chattering, bickering on-screen sisters. Nothing about this film looks artificial or posed.

For Keaton, *Crimes of the Heart* had several things going for it aside from its director and her costars, all of whom she admired. The ensemble piece about the dynamics among three sisters interested her from the beginning. She said, "I have two sisters, and that kind of psychological make-up—the kind of rivalries and love and envy, in particular Lenny's envy of Meg—is fascinating to me" (qtd. in Golightly 35). According to Margy Rochlin's article "Tender Crimes" for *American Film*, Keaton was involved with the film project ever since the play's off–Broadway production in 1980. Her manager at the time optioned it for her, but nothing came together until producer Freddie Fields got involved in 1983. Beresford then signed, and he and Beth Henley shaped the script (38).

In addition to the relaxed atmosphere of the set, the material itself gave Keaton the opportunity to lighten up and let go a little. For the first time in years, she returned to comedy, albeit a tragic-comedy in the Southern grotesque style of Flannery O'Connor and Eudora Welty. Life in Henley's Hazelhurst, Mississippi, doesn't always inspire faith in any rational, moral code of the universe for the MaGrath sisters—or in their fellow men—and they're prone to having "real bad days." Their abusive father left them, and their mother hanged herself (along with her yellow cat) when they were children. The event made the national news and the front page of the *Enquirer*. Granddaddy (Hurd Hatfield) raised them with an iron fist in a big old Victorian house, and now he's lying near death in a hospital bed.

The MaGrath girls have grown up with eccentricity bred in the bone and madness in the genes. Youngest sister Becky "Babe" Botrelle (Spacek) documents all of the unhappy events in her life in a giant photo album adorned with a big red heart on the cover. "I just like to keep an accurate record," she tells her sisters. Babe also wears party hats while playing the saxophone—badly. She has a passion for lemonade with lots of sugar and a fifteen-year-old black boy named Willie Jay. Her abusive husband, Senator Zachary Botrelle, she says: "Just started hatin' me cause I couldn't laugh at his jokes." He has a long history of beating Babe around, but when he kicks around Willie Jay, Babe shoots him in the liver. She was aiming for his heart, but missed. Calmly, as he's writhing on the dining room floor, Babe makes up a big pitcher of lemonade to quench her "powerful thirst." Always a lady, she offers Zachary some: "I made up some lemonade. Would you like some? No? Would you like a coke instead?" In jail, awaiting bail and big sister Lenny (Keaton), Babe is the picture of a Southern belle in her white dress, white gloves, and pearls.

The incident brings middle sister, Meg (Lange) home from Hollywood where she has been trying to make it as a singer and actress. According to eldest sister Lenny, Meg is the one who always got what she wanted: singing lessons, dancing lessons, men (especially Doc Porter played by Sam Shepard), and twelve golden jingle bells sewed onto her petticoats while she and Babe only got three. But talent in Hazelhurst and Hollywood doesn't necessarily mean the same thing. Meg ends up working in a dog food factory and spending time in the L.A. County Hospital psychiatric ward after she has a little breakdown. With her shagged, over-bleached blond hair, short skirts, jean jacket, and dark shades, Meg gets off the bus looking like she's "been around the block" a few times, a latter-day Blanche DuBois (a role that Lange played in her 1992 Broadway debut in *Streetcar Named Desire*). Meg may look vastly different

Crimes of the Heart (DeLaurentiis Entertainment Group, 1986). Diane Keaton is beloved by men *and* women. Those who have worked with her comment on her professionalism as well as her fun-loving spirit. But some of Keaton's most natural on-screen moments appear in female ensemble films like *Crimes of the Heart*, based on Beth Henley's Pulitzer Prize–winning play about three Mississippi sisters. The conversation and laughter around the MaGrath kitchen table in this scene seem so spontaneous that Keaton (Lenny), Spacek (Babe), and Lange (Meg) hardly appear to be acting. Drawing on her own experiences growing up with two sisters, Keaton beautifully projects on film the often enigmatic bonds and rivalries of sisterhood. Keaton's other "sister" films include *Interiors, The Lemon Sisters, The First Wives Club, Marvin's Room*, and *Hanging Up*.

from her two sisters, but, like them, she has deep scars.

Lenny MaGrath is the sister who stayed home to care for the tyrant Granddaddy, who has convinced her that no man will ever want her because of her shriveled up ovary. The wonderful thing about the screenplay is that nothing is overtly stated. The audience must make inferences about character and relationships based on perhaps one line or a look from an actor. Meg's line about her "bastard" daddy's smile and big white teeth, for example, and the subtle turn of her head, clenched jaw, and almost imperceptible shudder suggest a woman who might have been sexually abused as a child. In

Lenny's case, we get the distinct impression that Granddaddy knew exactly what buttons to push to keep Lenny at home and tending to his needs. On top of a shriveled ovary, her hair is falling out, too. It doesn't take much to convince her that no man will ever look at her.

Unlike Charlie in *Little Drummer Girl*, this *is* a part Keaton was born to play. As Rita Kempley wrote in her review of the film, "As the frumpy Lenny, Keaton eases smoothly from New York neurotic to southern eccentric" ("Twisted Sisters" N39). She wears layers and layers of loose clothing: long skirts with ankle socks and penny loafers; blouses always buttoned to the top, often with a cameo or brooch at the collar; big, baggy sweaters; floppy garden hats; and green garden gloves. She frequently touches her abdomen as if to protect her one good ovary. In one scene, Babe and Meg watch Lenny working in the garden. Babe might be slightly insane, but, intelligent and insightful, she can size up the truth of the situation. Lenny is becoming her grandmother. She tells Meg, "Lenny works out in the garden wearing the lime green gloves of a dead woman."

The high strung Lenny, as Keaton plays her, can also go from sweet to hysterical in a heartbeat. When Doc Porter brings her a bag of pecans, she coos and flirts, looking down shyly and looking up through her lashes, until he mentions Meg's name. His interest in his former love irritates Lenny. After all, he's married now with two children. The real reason for her irritation, though she won't admit it, stems from her long-standing crush on Doc. She also resents the fact that Meg left him for the lights of Hollywood, especially after Meg was partially to blame for Doc's bad leg. It seems Meg wouldn't leave a building during Hurricane Camille, and Doc wouldn't leave her. When the roof collapsed, his leg was crushed. Lenny tells Babe: "He loved her. And then she left him to go to California. That's what she did."

When Doc mentions that he'd like to call on Meg when she comes home, Lenny's mood instantly shifts from demure to distressed; she lashes out at him and falls onto the lawn swing in a heap of tears. Lenny's been having a bad day. Granddaddy's dying, Babe shot her husband, Doc's still interested in Meg, and Lenny's old horse has been struck by lightening. To top it off, it's her birthday, and she must celebrate alone. In one poignant scene, Beresford shoots Keaton in medium close-up at the kitchen table as Lenny carefully tries to put birthday candles on three very hard chocolate chip cookies. When they crumble, she doesn't give up.

Instead, she strikes a match and melts the wax on the bottom of the candles, gently sticking them on three new cookies. She begins to sing "Happy Birthday" softly to herself as the camera slowly pulls back, framing Lenny alone through the kitchen doorway. Aside from an uneven Southern accent, Keaton beautifully captures the portrait of a spirited woman twisted into spinsterhood by forces beyond her control.

After interviewing Keaton for *Lear's* in 1993, Marcelle Clements wrote:

> When Keaton talks, it's a multimedia performance. Her body and her facial expressions remain in constant and playful counterpoint to the content of her monologues. She gestures, she purses her lips, she jiggles her leg, her fingers flutter toward her throat, she brandishes her spoon. For real emphasis, she occasionally crosses her eyes [84].

Keaton brings these same twitches and mannerisms to her characterization of Lenny. In one scene, she gleefully hops back and forth from one foot to the other, simultaneously screaming and laughing, while she and Babe look at grotesque pictures from Granddaddy's book on skin diseases. In another scene, exhausted and "depressed," she and Babe break down in nervous laughter when they tell Meg that Old Granddaddy fell into a coma. Lenny laughs so hard she snorts, almost falling backwards off her chair.

Later, when she finds out that Babe has told Meg about her one true love, she stomps her foot and slams her hand down on the table, shouting, "I'll never be happy!" It seems Lenny did find a man when she joined the Lonely Hearts Club of the South, and she and Charlie, who works in a boot factory, actually "did it" one weekend. But Lenny, fearing that she can never have children, breaks off their relationship. She's furious with Babe for betraying her trust, and, when Meg tries to console her, Lenny screams, "I just didn't want him not to want me. Don't talk to me anymore because I'm going to vomit. I just hope this doesn't cause me to vomit," as she runs into the bathroom.

The MaGrath sisters may have their petty jealousies, but it is the bond of sisterhood that ultimately sees them through the bad days. Together they make discoveries and work through their problems. After an amazing sequence of thwarted attempts by Babe to kill herself, for example, she finally realizes why Momma MaGrath hanged the family cat: she didn't want to die alone. Meg and Lenny rally around Babe, hiring the young, sharp lawyer, Barnett Lloyd (David Carpenter) to defend her. Meg makes peace with herself and Doc. And, surrounded by her sisters, Lenny finds the courage to finally stand up to bitchy Cousin Chick (chasing her up a tree with a broom) and call Charlie who confesses that he never liked children in the first place.

Their happy time together is fleeting, and they know it as they gather around the kitchen table to celebrate Lenny's birthday with a real cake that Meg has bought. Lenny's wish as she blows out her candles captures all the fragility of their future:

> I guess it wasn't exactly like a specific wish. It's just this vision just came over me. I don't know exactly. Something about the three of us, and, oh, we were all just smilin' and laughin' together. You know somethin'? It wasn't for every minute; it was just for this one moment. And we were all laughin'.

Beresford's freeze frame of the final tableau of the sisters laughing and eating cake becomes a snapshot in Babe's album, documenting their moment of unity, their future uncertain.

In an interview, Keaton once con-fessed that although she has an ego, she's not sure it applies to her work. She never worries, for example, whether she has a good side for the camera. "If you worry about [that], you're involved in a kind of acting I'm not interested in," she said (qtd. in Cohn, "All Business Actress" 9). Neither Sissy Spacek nor Jessica Lange seemed to be interested in this kind of acting either, which is probably another reason why the three got along so well. They stayed focused on finding the truth of their characters, and Beresford gave them the freedom to do so.

Keaton has said that the best kind of acting comes from this kind of experience:

> I think when you're out there you don't want to be censoring yourself while you're doing it. You just want to fly with the material; you just want to keep yourself open and don't get in your way. In other words, don't start thinking is this good enough or should I not go that far, or is this the wrong thing to do right now [personal interview].

Her approach worked in her portrayal of Lenny, a character who never censors herself. Lenny always operates on full throttle, flinging herself in the moment, saying whatever is on her mind, taking her sisters on the emotional roller-coaster ride with her.

The role for Keaton marked a turn—if not a full turn, then at least a half turn—toward comedy again and provided a nice transition into the mix of comedic and dramatic parts she would play in the late eighties. For now, however, Keaton was gearing up for a project that had obsessed her since the idea was conceived in 1982. *Heaven*, her documentary about the hereafter, would pave the way to the director's chair but not without great personal anguish and disappointment.

CHAPTER 6

1987–1989

The Importance of Being Honest

One thing remains certain in the movies, and that is that it's very important to be a huge star in order to get anything done at all. It's unbelievable how the value of a name is everything. That was the law of the land in the beginning, and that is the law of the land now.
—Diane Keaton (Personal Interview, 1998)

London's newspaper *The Guardian* once saluted Diane Keaton's work, remarking: "We loved her Louise Bryant in Warren Beatty's *Reds*, a performance so real in its complexity it's a wonder Keaton was ever cast by Hollywood again" ("Weekend" 17). Though it was meant as a supreme compliment, the comment characterizes Keaton's leading lady status in Hollywood by the end of the 1980s. She was considered one of the best actresses around, but fewer and fewer good screen roles came her way. She accepted a cameo role as a nightclub singer in Woody Allen's new movie, *Radio Days* (1987). She starred as an aggressive New York businesswoman who gets it all in the 1987 comedy *Baby Boom*. And she played a mother who loses it all in the 1988 drama *The Good Mother*. Centered by her family, her work ethic, and her years of act-

ing experiences, Keaton refused to give up. She continued to move forward, taking on diverse projects that reflected her interests, and kept herself busy.

At the time *Crimes of the Heart* was released in 1986, Diane Keaton was forty, and Hollywood has never been a 40-friendly place for leading women on screen. Jessica Lange bemoaned the lack of opportunities for women in a male-dominated and youth-obsessed industry and culture, saying: "Actresses have to assume that once they're past a certain age, they'll just do character roles. I mean, they certainly won't be doing romantic leading roles like men in their 40s, 50s, and 60s are still doing" (qtd. in "Power Dessert" 60). Lange was referring to actors like Sean Connery who, at sixty-something, is still considered a sexy leading man. The older he gets, the younger his leading lady. In 1999, he starred in *Entrapment* with Catherine Zeta-Jones, thirty years his junior. Seldom in American cinema do we see an older actress with a younger leading man, a scenario that challenges the laws of the patriarchy. And when we do, critics tend to focus on the age disparity. For example, Leonard Maltin calls *White Palace's* ending "improbable" when love wins out between a sexy, 43-year-old waitress (Susan Sarandon) and a rich, 27-year-old yuppie (James Spader) (*Movie and Video Guide* 1482).

Many of Keaton's contemporaries opted for plastic surgery to maintain their looks as well as their leading lady status. To date, Keaton has resisted temptation:

> I think aging in particular is a tricky area. There's a huge denial and an instant craving to get away from aging of any sort because basically it's a young person's medium in terms of the acting.... A lot of people have taken that route of trying to stay young by having face lifts, which, of course, to me just doesn't work.... You have to represent some sort of authentic life. I think it's really important that there are a few out there who choose not to become part of that plastic surgery kind of solution [personal interview].

Keaton's views on the subject compelled her to write an article in 1993 entitled "The Mask" for *Mirabella* magazine in which she likens getting a face lift to wearing a mask—forever. She calls the plastic surgeon "the country's resident esthetic dispenser" and explains, "His work is sought out by the monied and not-so-monied. After he has chipped away at another anxiously hopeful face, that face is suddenly and irretrievably introduced into the world of immobility" (55).

One of the key elements of Keaton's personality lies in her desire "to represent some sort of authentic life." In interview after interview, her family, friends, lovers, former lovers, costars, directors, and interviewers themselves—basically everyone who comes into contact with her—comment on Keaton's absolute honesty in both her professional and personal life. The following excerpt from her article reveals a woman who has given considerable thought to the real price of plastic surgery: the loss of authenticity.

> Some people prefer to look as if they haven't experienced life. It's the more accepted way to go now. But my question is, why? What's so great about wiping the marks of experience off your face? Why do we want the same things we wanted when we were adolescent? Isn't it awful to be caught repeating the tired complaint, "Men age better," at miserable, self-involved dinners endured with other frightened, middle-aged women? There must be something more emotionally relevant, and challenging, than pursuing men. Why do we want to airbrush, erase, scrape, sandblast and basically eliminate our faces to put on a mask of dubious authorship? What's so great about staring in the mirror at a freshly cut generic face that can barely adjust to the joy, despair, shame or pride you feel but can't see? ["The Mask" 54].

American women are conditioned to want the beautiful, sexy images immortalized in films and photographs, which, for Keaton, impede individuality and thought. No matter how right Keaton may be, the ultimate truth is that in an industry built on glamour with a little talent on the side, good leading parts for middle-aged actresses are as hard to find today as they were in the late 1980s.

As the country eased out of an era dominated by Ronald Reagan's macho ideology, however, a change was taking place in Hollywood indicated by a noticeable upturn in the female presence—especially *behind* the camera. Dawn Steel became president of Columbia Pictures. Penny Marshall made her directing debut with *Jumpin' Jack Flash*, starring Whoopi Goldberg, and followed it up with the blockbuster *Big*, starring Tom Hanks. Ruth Prawer Jhabvala won her first Best Screenplay Oscar for *A Room with a View*.

Lizzie Borden coproduced and directed *Working Girls*. Lillian Gish, at 91, starred in *The Whales of August*. Jessica Tandy, in her 80s, won a Best Actress Oscar for *Driving Miss Daisy*, produced by Lili Zanuck. And Euzhan Palcy, a black woman, directed studio feature *A Dry White Season* ("Women in Hollywood: A Timeline" 56–57). Linda Seger summed up the prevailing attitude of industry women in *When Women Call the Shots: The Developing Power and Influence of Women in Television and Film* when she wrote: "Women want more diversity in films. We don't want to remove the male action film, but we ask for the opportunity to create different kinds of films *in addition to* the usual" (141–42).

Most of these women didn't ask for opportunities. They seized them. When actresses, especially those closing in on 40, couldn't find good roles, they created their own production companies and optioned material that reflected their interests and concerns. Meg Ryan, who founded Fandango Films, says that most of the scripts Fandango produces address

> contemporary questions that women of our age are dealing with, whether it's how we live our lives, how our spirituality is manifested, how we have our families, how we are with our friends, our connection to nature, our social orientation and morality, or how our professional identities are formed or impressed upon by the world around us [qtd. in Seger 116–17].

Filmmaker Oliver Stone applauded films with a strong female voice: "If it were all men, perspectives would be skewed. It's a need for balance, in order to be truthful to the world" (qtd. in Seger 85).

Barbra Streisand, Jessica Lange, Bette Midler, Glenn Close, Sigourney Weaver, Goldie Hawn, Susan Sarandon, Meg Ryan, and Michelle Pfeiffer were only a few of the actresses advocating change for women in the industry, championing the "need for balance," generating their own pro-

jects, and insisting on being judged for their work and not their physical appearance alone. In her 1992 address for Women in Film's Crystal Awards Lunch, Streisand took a hard look at the status of women in Hollywood as well as American culture. Angry about the inequities but optimistic about the future, she said:

> I look forward to a society that is color- and gender-blind, that judges us by the value of our work, not the length of our legs. That accepts the fact that a woman can be many, many things: strong and vulnerable, intelligent and sexy, opinionated and flexible, angry and forgiving. Deep thinking as well as deep feeling ["We Are the Girlz in the 'Hood" 27].

Streisand's comments crystallize Keaton's own complex, paradoxical star image that evolved through her on-screen characters, critical reviews of her films and acting, as well as interviews with the star herself. The public already accepted the fact that she was a woman of many, often conflicting, parts. Like Bette Davis before her, she became an icon precisely because of those opposing traits: strength and fragility. Neither Keaton nor her predecessor are considered great beauties, but they are valued for their candor, talent and dedication to their craft. In fact, both stars are known for their no-nonsense approach to work as well as their uncanny ability to tap into the collective consciousness of female audiences at any point in time, enacting on-screen their problems, fears, and anxieties. As Bill Hagen wrote of Keaton: "She usually plays the prototype of whatever decade she happens to be working in" ("Keaton Explodes" D8). The movies Keaton had been making were those "different" kind of movies that Linda Seger envisioned for women and that Fandango Films now looks to produce. Her movies addressed contemporary questions about contemporary women. In short, she has been swimming against mainstream for years; the rest of the pack just caught up.

Woody Allen says of her: "She has a phenomenal gift—just a very big talent—more than most of her contemporaries. Plus, she's smart and dedicated" (personal interview). Quietly, through hard work, self-education, and persistence, the Keaton star image took on a new depth. Keaton's last few films, while not exactly box office hits, did enable her to transgress her previous on-screen persona as Woody Allen's comic foil. Critics no longer talked about her in terms of *Annie Hall*. Of course, there remained certain redundancies from one performance to the next: the layers of clothing; the wide, shy smile; the flirtatious delivery of a line; the coy, sideways glance; the hand gestures that punctuate a monologue; the note of hysterical anger that suddenly erupts with moral outrage. These traits are part of the Keaton core and surface at times in all her characters. On the whole, however, as Laura Morice noted in one interview with Keaton:

> The fumbling, scatterbrained persona she turned into high performance art early in her career has given way to a woman who seems more comfortable with herself, a woman who has strong ideas and is perfectly able to express them in complete declarative sentences [78].

When Keaton found the times changing, she changed with them. Never one to waste much time complaining, she remarked philosophically: "The interesting thing to do, like some movie stars have done, is generate your own things or make your own projects" (qtd. in Jerome, "Diane Keaton Booms Back into Comedy" F4). The negative publicity she received for her own first major project behind the camera, *Heaven*, however, might have sent any of the powerful and mighty in Hollywood reeling. But realism and optimism seem to reside simultaneously in Keaton. They must have seen her through the barrage of criticism she endured for *Heaven*, which David Ansen

described as "part freak show, part collage ... less a traditional documentary than a Keaton-designed objet d'art" ("Are There Diets in Heaven?" 79). Devastated but determined to do better next time, Keaton barely broke stride. She took her lumps—and moved on.

Radio Days

After *Crimes of the Heart*, Keaton made a brief cameo appearance in Woody Allen's nostalgic *Radio Days*, starring Mia Farrow, Danny Aiello, Dianne Wiest, and old friend Tony Roberts (*Play It Again, Sam* and *Annie Hall*). It took all of one-half day to film her scene in a 1940s ballroom. Carlo Di Palma's camera, which has been panning the crowded room, finally locks onto a solitary figure standing before a mike in front of a full orchestra singing Cole Porter's "You'd Be So Nice to Come Home To." Dressed in a high-neck, long-sleeve, forties-style white gown fitted at the waist, Keaton is big-band singer Monica Charles. After her song, she smiles shyly at an appreciative audience, whispering "thank you, thank you" over the applause.

It's a sweet performance, if not a long one. Keaton says, "'I came in and sang it three times, and I was out'" (qtd. in Edelstein 64). She is on screen for approximately two minutes, but critics were impressed. David Sterritt's review of the film mentions that Keaton "shows up just long enough to stop the show with a song" ("Woody Allen's Evocative *Radio Days*" 23). Keaton admits that she enjoyed the experience because it reminded her of her dream of being a singer. She enjoyed the experience of making *Heaven*, too, but the reviews were not as kind.

Heaven

Bruce Williamson of *Playboy* called *Heaven* a "provocative and diverting documentary" (Rev. of *Heaven* 17), but most critics were scathing in their comments. *People* magazine said that Keaton's film was "pure prattle, alternately exploitative or patronizing," ending with this comment: "A recent poll by *USA Weekend* reported 67 percent of Americans believe in hell. If they sit through this maddening film, the other 33 percent are bound to come around" (*People,* "Heaven" 10). Though she was hurt by the negative reviews, Keaton tried to focus on the positive part of the experience, which for her has always been the process of making a film. She told Jack Mathews of *The Los Angeles Times*: "I really enjoyed doing it ... and you couldn't take that away from me, even if everybody hated it" (qtd. in "Secure" 3).

Heaven actually went over well with European audiences which tend to be more accustomed to artistic fare, but the main problem in the States was that most people didn't know what to make of the film. *Heaven* is a bit hard to explain, even for its director who calls it "a strange little movie" (qtd. in Glicksman 34). It tends to defy category. It lies somewhere between a documentary and an art film, and there is a lot of territory between these two extremes. Keaton layers interviews with assorted friends, family, strangers, and street people; old film clips depicting images of doom and death, salvation and heaven; and a sound track that includes everything from screaming fundamentalist preachers to heavenly harp music. The result, as many critics noted, is reminiscent of Keaton's collages and photography work which reflect her original view of the world.

Actually, Keaton's interviewees look as though they just stepped into a series of life-sized abstract designs. The sets look much like those in Woody Allen's futuristic film *Sleeper*, all white with geometric shapes forming oblique angles that give the frame depth and perspective. Laser beams of various colored lights throw more patterns across her subjects, creating a tissue-paper collage effect. In some instances, Keaton includes a weirdly-shaped video screen in the background showing white, fluffy, rolling clouds or planets and stars moving through space. Her interviewees, positioned to the sides or bottom of the frame, look like they could easily drop out of her off-center compositions—into infinity. The overriding sense is one of imbalance and, given the subject matter, spiritual confusion. The human subjects are pushed to the insignificant margins of the frame, overwhelmed and overpowered by the sheer weight and magnitude of the questions they are trying to answer.

These questions act as title cards, dividing the film into several parts or episodes and acting as transitions from one section to the next. Each section contains a series of interviews intercut with old film footage that corresponds to the question being asked. The questions include: Are you afraid to die? What is heaven? Do you believe in heaven? How does an expert view heaven? Can heaven be on earth? Have you had a vision? What is God like? Is there love in heaven? Is there sex in heaven? What are the rewards of heaven? Can you prove there's a heaven? How do you get to heaven? As Keaton's interviewees wrestle with defining the intangible, the real question behind the film seems to be: Where do we get our ideas about heaven?

Keaton got the idea for her film in 1982 when she and a friend visited the Mormon Temple in Salt Lake City and watched one of their promotional films on heaven. "It was like a surreal dream," she told Marlaine Glicksman. "These people sort of floating in the clouds. It just sort of grew after that, just sort of sparked my imagination" (qtd. in Glicksman 33). Keaton then went "shopping" for more images. Film historian William Everson helped her find films that were in the public domain so that she didn't have to pay the exorbitant fees to obtain the rights to newer material. Some of those old films include David Niven's *Stairway to Heaven*; Vincente Minnelli's African-American musical *Cabin in the Sky*; *The Green Pastures*, with another all-black cast; *A Guy Named Joe* with Spencer Tracy; and Raoul Walsh's *The Horn Blows at Midnight*, starring Jack Benny.

Some of the images from these films include Hollywood's notion of the city of heaven, choirs of angels, as well as a dance number from *Top Hat* with Fred Astaire gliding Ginger Rogers across the floor in her white ostrich-feather dress. Other images are apocalyptic: explosions, tidal waves, buildings crashing, people dying. Still others are taken from religious television programs of the fifties. In one, three elderly, silver-haired men wearing dark suits and glasses discuss the rewards of heaven. Moderator Russell Pollack looks into the camera and says sweetly, "Hello, friends. We would like to talk over with you some of the promises of God." Another clip from this era, for which Keaton took a lot of criticism, depicts a macrocephalic woman named Evelyn who comes forward in her wheelchair and begins to sing: "One of these days, I'm going to walk with my Lord." Some critics found Keaton's choice insensitive.

Paul Barnes and Keaton edited the film, Skip Lievsay worked on sound, and RCA financially backed the project. These are some of the best people in the business, but the film has Keaton's signature all over it. When Stephanie Mansfield of *The Washington Post* asked Keaton if she thought her film would ever have gotten off the ground if her name were still Diane Hall, Keaton responded: "No. No way" (qtd. in "Up from *Heaven*" C1). It was an indirect admission at least that she had capitalized on the law of the land. She was a famous star, and her name could green light a project.

Keaton also went shopping for people to interview. She found them in her own pool of family and friends—as well as on the streets of Hollywood. Many of these people were the lonely, the unwanted, the cast-offs of society, the types no one else but Keaton would bother to recognize, let alone ask for an opinion. The interviews, which she conducted between acting jobs in 1984 and 1985, are as surreal as the film images. None of the interviewees is identified, though at the end of the film, an elderly woman named Grace says good-bye to certain people as they momentarily flash on screen.

Keaton's sister Dorrie, her parents Jack and Dorothy Hall, and her grandmother Mary Hall are recognizable. In one scene, her mother admits that heaven isn't something she thinks about or gives much "credence" to. In another, her father says, "If there is something after death and you've led a good life, I can't conceive we won't be together." But it's Grammy Hall that the camera lingers on. Keaton gets the camera in close and tight on Mary's face as she says, "Heaven is just open space.... Nobody ever came back and said, 'Well here I am, and I'm so glad to see you.'" When asked about hell, Mary quickly responds, "Where would I find hell? I found the biggest hell right here on earth." In one of the last scenes in the film, Mary talks fondly about her sister Sadie: "When I lost her, I thought I lost everything, which I did. But I had to go on." Mary Hall died shortly after this interview.

In most of the interviews, Keaton alternates between extreme close-ups that fragment a subject's facial features and medium to full shots that isolate individuals within the abstract patterns and shapes. It is another way of layering, of creating a collage-like effect within the interviews themselves. Some of the more memorable people include a hippie who argues that "things are lining up right now to bring about heaven manifested on earth." He chides the disbelieving young man next to him for upsetting the balance of things. "Cows are lawnmowers ... created to eat grass.... You're killing them and making leather jackets." A Salvation Army couple describe death as being "promoted to glory."

An elderly man claims that his spirit left his body during a near-death experience. "I saw the geographical location of heaven," he says. "It wasn't crowded. There's plenty of room." One young woman reveals that Christ is on the planet "living in a Pakistani community at this time in London awaiting, specifically, for the media as representing humanity to seek him out and have a press conference with the entire world." Still another woman with long brown hair and white eye shadow likens God to Groucho Marx, "always playing tricks on us. When we think we've got it," she argues, "we're sitting in a pile of cow manure. He really is a practical joker.... Until you can love a gnat as much as you love yourself, you will not know God." This is the same woman who later, when asked if there is sex in heaven, responds: "We're going to have an orgasm that you can't even comprehend."

Though Keaton is off-camera asking the questions, some of the interviewees address her by name or implication. For example, one man with noticeable gold fillings, says to her: "If you want me and I want you, it's up to us.... They think you're married to Mel Gibson ... but he loves Sissy Spacek. He does." When asked if there is sex in heaven, a bearded preacher tells her: "You ask this question because you're ignorant." In one scene, she has a screenwriter and a fundamentalist (Reverend Hands) debating the existence of heaven. The fundamentalist, directing his comments to the screenwriter and Keaton, says: "When you people start talking about heaven, you people botch it up.... You put your feelers out and get a whole lot of nothin'." Keaton told Glicksman that Rev. Hands was "a little annoyed" over the interview: "I asked

him questions that put him on the spot. I asked him about homosexuality. Because he knows that they're the kind of questions that get people upset. And get him in trouble" (qtd. in Glicksman 36).

Heaven ultimately reflects Keaton's artistic visual style, her interest in the unusual and unwanted, her sense of humor, and her personal thoughts on heaven and hell. She admits to being an agnostic, though she says she understands "the longing and the need for more, for something better" (qtd. in Buck 107). She does not condemn others for their beliefs and doesn't shy away from expressing her own. In one interview, Keaton revealed: "Heaven was created because everybody is afraid to die. Otherwise, no one would think of heaven" (qtd. in Demaris 5). With her usual candor, she calls the whole idea of eternity, life without conflict, "bone chilling" (qtd. in Edelstein 24).

Baby Boom

The 1987 *Baby Boom* was written by Nancy Meyers and Charles Shyer. A team both professionally and personally, Meyers and Shyer wrote the screenplay on speculation and sold it almost immediately to United Artists. Produced by Meyers and directed by Shyer, the film reflects their own experiences of trying to juggle a career and a family (Janusonis L12). The duo never anticipated *Baby Boom's* far-reaching effects. The film ushered in debates about the place of women and motherhood in the corporate structure. It inspired a television sitcom of the same title starring Kate Jackson, and it impelled Minneapolis marketing executive Julia Knight to found Growing Healthy, a baby foods company. She claims: "I really did get the inspiration for founding my company while I was watching the movie *Baby Boom*.... I'm watching and I'm thinking, Hey, why hasn't anybody really done this?" (qtd. in "Julia Knight"

73). Six years later, according to an article in *Working Woman*, Knight's company sold more than a million dollars worth of "fresh-frozen, additive-free, microwaveable baby food" (Stesin 60).

The well-written screenplay also inspired Diane Keaton's light-handed, perfectly-timed comedic performance. J. C. Wiatt is one of her signature roles, showcasing her paradoxical persona. Meyers and Shyer noted that Keaton worked best with little rehearsal: "She's more spontaneous and totally cooperative…. The great thing about Diane is the degree of amazing choices she gives." Shyer also called Keaton very "un-actressy." He said: "She'd go in line at lunch, didn't cut, knew all the crew's names" (qtd. in Jerome, "Diane Keaton Booms Back" F4).

With *Baby Boom*, Keaton made a 180-degree turn from the frumpy Lenny MaGrath in *Crimes of the Heart* to the sleek, super-charged Madison Avenue ad exec with a corner office at Sloane, Curtis & Co. and a six-figure salary. Sporting designer suits by everybody from Armani to Matsuda, the fast-talking, fast-walking J. C. Wiatt reminds us of Rosalind Russell's Hildy Johnson in *His Girl Friday*. Perhaps it's the costumes or the soft bobbed cut with wispy bangs or the soft-focus lens, but Keaton *looks* a good ten years younger than the spinsterish Lenny. All energy and bravado, her J. C. Wiatt

Baby Boom (MGM/UA, 1987). Keaton as the lean and hungry Tiger Lady J. C. Wiatt tosses out marketing statistics for The Food Chain account with the speed of a rapid-fire weapon and a look that would stop a question in its tracks. Here in her element, the corporate boardroom, she's as sleek as a cat about to spring. J. C.'s predatory instincts change, as do her costumes, once she adopts baby Elizabeth and moves to the country. Costume designer Susan Becker softens her look with long dresses and tweeds to illustrate the character's evolution from a hard-edged advertising exec to a mother *and* businesswoman.

is the antithesis of the whining, paranoid MaGrath sister. Whirling through the halls in a flurry of files and phone calls, she leaves weary and wonderstruck underlings in her wake as she commands, "Get me the CEO of IBC—ASAP!"

She's known in the advertising business as "Tiger Lady." Married to her job, she works 5 AM to 9 PM. Her boss, Fritz (Sam Wanamaker), wants to make her a partner, which means even longer hours. No problem. But Fritz hears J. C.'s biological clock ticking and warns her that while he can have it all because he's a man, she can't. There's no room for motherhood in the corporate structure. He tells her:

> A man can be a success and still have a personal life, a full personal life. My wife is there for me whenever I need her. I mean, she raises the kids, she decorates ... I don't know what the hell she does, but she takes care of things.... I'm lucky. I can have it all.

No problem. J. C. lives with an investment banker married to his job. "We eat, sleep and dream our work. That's why we're together.... I don't want it all. I don't," she reassures a doubtful Fritz. Certainly, lovemaking doesn't take up much of her time. She and significant other Steven (Harold Ramis) have streamlined their sex life to a four-minute marathon. Start: 11:46. Stop: 11:50. When J. C. suddenly inherits a baby from a distant relative, she says: "I can't have a baby because I have a 12:30 lunch meeting."

Costume designer Susan Becker wanted J. C.'s suits to imitate the New York skyline with their "straight lines, authoritative shoulders and lean-and-hungry shapes" (Barnett 9). When she belted the suit jackets to show off Keaton's small waist, the trend caught on. Keaton was once again the topic of the fashion world. Critics commented on her great set of legs, which they so seldom glimpsed. One critic gushed: "Does anyone look better in clothes than Keaton? She could well start another fashion trend, as she did with *Annie Hall*" (Hagen, "Keaton Explodes" D8). When J. C. leaves the city for a life in rural Vermont, Becker softened the look with long skirts and blouses.

In addition to her look in *Baby Boom*, critics also raved about Keaton's performance. Molly Haskell said: "Keaton has aged with a bold, decisive grace from the

flapdoodle sweetheart in *Annie Hall* to a workaholic executive in *Baby Boom*, a role as tailor-made for her as any studio vehicle" ("Venus Substitutes" 38). Jim Emerson of *The Orange County Register* called her "magnificent," adding:

> This is Keaton's most accomplished screen work, a virtuoso performance in which she masterfully orchestrates every behavioral detail—posture, facial expressions, vocal inflections—without coming across as fussy or mannered ["Diane Keaton Babies Her Expanding Career" L1].

David Ansen wrote, "From first to last, it's Keaton's movie, and she makes a delightful return to comic form" ("Man, Money and Motherhood" 84).

In the late eighties, several romantic comedies, including *Baby Boom*, dealt with what was happening to women in corporate America. After almost three decades of lying dormant, the sassy, smart, lovable, slightly neurotic romantic comedy heroine returned in the form of Jane Craig (Holly Hunter) in *Broadcast News*; Tess McGill (Melanie Griffith) in *Working Girl*; and J. C. Wiatt in *Baby Boom*. Jane Craig shows us what happens when a highly principled, successful television news producer tries to juggle her career and love. Tess McGill teaches us that a woman doesn't have to be cutthroat in order to climb the corporate ladder or be a good boss. And J. C. gives women sitting in the audience options. She uses her intelligence, her education, and her experiences to start her own successful business and ends up with it all: a farm in Vermont, a baby she adores, a baby food empire, and the local vet (Sam Shepard), who likes her "bull terrier" approach to life.

As writer/director Nora Ephron contends, these are strong female characters. She explains that the romantic comedy genre has always provided strong images of women because the films are based on conflict, and conflict needs two equally-matched characters. Women have to be as smart and clever as the men to make the story work (Seger, *When Women Call the Shots* 216). Writer Treva Silverman adds that much of the conflict in romantic comedies takes the form of verbal sparring and antagonism: "It's a kind of foreplay, a kind of dance" she says. Sparks might fly over "class, values, different backgrounds, a misunderstanding or misinterpretation, or just bad timing" (qtd. in Seger, *When Women Call the Shots* 217). The audience knows immediately that these two people belong together and will usually find a way to work through their conflict and create a lot of entertaining sexual tension along the way.

Baby Boom's snappy banter and feisty heroine are reminiscent of early romantic comedies, like Ernst Lubitsch's *Trouble in Paradise* and Frank Capra's *It Happened One Night*. Yet *Baby Boom* is a romantic comedy for the eighties with Keaton's dual persona perfectly in sync with the film's contemporary question: Can women have it all? As the film opens, J. C. strides confidently down Madison Avenue reading the morning news as a female narrator lays out this issue:

> Fifty-three percent of the American workforce is female. Three generations of women have turned a thousand years of tradition on its ear. As little girls, they were told to grow up and marry doctors and lawyers. Instead, they grew up and became doctors and lawyers. They moved out of the pink ghetto and into the executive suite. Sociologists say the new working woman is a phenomenon of our time.

After introducing J. C. Wiatt as an example of this phenomenon, the narrator adds: "One would take it for granted that a woman like this has it all. One must never take anything for granted."

The issue of how women balance their personal and professional lives is central to Meyers' and Shyer's intelligent, witty, and timely script, and Keaton manages to visualize the dilemma with comedy and

compassion. Keaton's scenes with the baby Elizabeth (played in turns by Michelle and Kristina Kennedy) in particular are some of the film's most hilarious and tender—illustrating the demands of work and motherhood as well as Keaton's wonderful facility with broad, slapstick humor.

In one scene, J. C. hands Elizabeth over the coat-check counter, bribing the attendee with her Visa card if she'll watch her while she has lunch with the CEO of The Food Chain, a potential client. In another scene, J. C. weighs the baby on the grocery store vegetable scale. After a full day at Sloane & Curtis, J. C. makes Elizabeth a fine dinner of linguini with clam sauce which the baby systematically makes a mess of. No problem. J. C. simply sprays her little hands with Fantastik. When she can't get Elizabeth's diaper to stay on, she uses duct tape. And when Elizabeth gets a cold, it's J. C. who sits up with her. With the naked child over her lap, J. C. downs a Valium with baby juice from Elizabeth's bottle, closes her eyes, and squeamishly sticks a thermometer in the baby's bottom.

The tough Tiger Lady grows a heart when she meets Baby Elizabeth, but she has every intention of putting her up for adoption. Sitting in the adoption agency with Elizabeth on her lap, J. C. tries to explain that she works 12 to 14 hours a day and she's "not natural" with children. She's comfortable with her decision. "Guilt's not a part of it. Guilt's not a word in my vocabulary," she says. "I mean, please, guilt?" Famous for her ability to say one thing and express another in a single gesture, Keaton dons her dark sunglasses, puncturing J. C.'s pretensions and hiding her guilt.

It's when she meets the adoptive parents (who look like they could have posed for *American Gothic*), that J. C. decides to keep Baby Elizabeth. Leaving the adoption center with Elizabeth precariously tucked under her arm, J. C, who claims she is "not really great with living things," warns her new child: "Just don't expect too much." She tells Steven: "Suddenly I saw her in frosted lipstick wearing a Dairy Queen uniform.... I just couldn't give her to a woman who called her husband 'sir.' It gave me the creeps." She knows that with them, Elizabeth will never have a chance to move out of the pink ghetto. J. C.'s choice, however, comes with consequences. Steven moves out, and J. C. gets squeezed out of the executive suite by the sharks who think she's lost her edge and gone soft.

The resilient J. C. moves baby and belongings to Hadleyville, Vermont, population 319, but nothing works out quite the way she envisioned it. Her dream farmhouse is falling apart, and the repairs are draining her bank account. She finally snaps when Mr. Boone, the local handyman, tells her that her well has dried up. Keaton is at her best in this scene, delivering her lines with both a deadpan seriousness and all the nuttiness of a modern-day Carole Lombard. Dressed in an oversized coat and boots, she marches through the snow drifts around her well, waving her arms in the frigid air as she responds: "Oh, good. I thought it was something serious. You can just fill it up. There's a hose right around the back. You know what I mean?" Mr. Boone laughs, "Lady, you're out of water. You're going to have to tap into the county line, and that's three miles down the road." In other words, it's going to be expensive. J. C. loses it. "I've had it," she screams.

> I can't make it here. I'm not Paul Bunyan. I need to work. I need people. I need a social life. I need sex.... I used to be cute. I'm not prepared for wells to run dry. I just want to turn on the faucet and have water. And I don't want to know where it's coming from.

When she finishes this hysterical tirade, she faints, falling backward into a snow-drift.

The incident brings her together with Dr. Jeff Cooper (Sam Shepard), the town veterinarian, and their inevitable romance gets off to a rocky start when J. C. mistakes him for a "real" doctor and spills her guts to him about her problems. Their smart, clever banter illustrates some of Meyers' and Shyer's best writing, like the scene in which J. C. rebuffs all Dr. Cooper's attempts to help her change a flat tire.

> JEFF: You kind of remind me of a bull terrier sometimes. You're feisty, and hard to get along with...
> J. C.: Yeah, I bet you say that to all the girls.
> JEFF: Even a bull terrier, once they warm up to you...
> J. C.: What? They bring you your slippers?
> JEFF: Look, is there something I've done to you that I don't know about?
> J. C.: Right. You don't know that I've been completely humiliated?
> JEFF: Why, because you told me you haven't had sex for over a year?
> J. C.: It hasn't been over a year. Where did you hear it was over a year? At the town meeting?

When Dr. Cooper persists, J. C. stops pumping the jack handle, looks him in the eye and says:

> I am a tough, cold, career woman. I have only one thing on my mind at this point in my life, and that is to get out of this moth-eaten town. And nothing here—including you, Dr. Charm—holds any interest for me whatsoever. So what do you think about that?

He grabs her, kisses her, and says, "See you around." Of course, she begins to see his charm, and they realize that they are made for each other. When some critics saw the film as an anti-feminist statement, Meyers and Shyer quickly responded in a letter to the editor in the *New York Times*:

> In *Baby Boom*, the Keaton character was forced to leave her executive position in New York because the company for which she worked was rigid and unyielding with

regard to working mothers.... However, she doesn't give up or give in. She starts her own business and eventually succeeds as an entrepreneur, finding a way to have the two things she wants most—her career and motherhood. The Shepard character provided romance in her life. He didn't compensate for or take the place of her career. At the end of the film, Keaton's character is completely self-reliant. In *Baby Boom*, we endeavored to move the audience to think and recognize the increasing prejudice women face today ["Feminist Heroines" 2:3].

Keaton agrees with Meyers and Shyer, but sees the film more in terms of what it says about human values and a person's ability to give love unselfishly.

Keaton has also been surprised at the film's endurance over the years. She claims that while it was not a huge hit when it first came out, it has had another life in video:

> *Baby Boom* was not a hit. *Baby Boom* came out the year *Three Men and a Baby* came out. *Baby Boom* came out before *Three Men and a Baby*, but the hit was *Three Men and a Baby*.... It sort of made a little bit of money, but then what happened was in video, when it came out in video, and over the years people like it. But for some reason, people didn't go to see that darned thing. And we were all very disappointed about that because that was made to be commercial and likable and funny, and I thought it was funny. That movie more than any movie I've ever been in, I keep hearing about it later.... That damn movie, it continues to live on, and when it came out it was a big disappointment. I'm telling you they wrote that well. That was a good part. That was a good screenplay. I had fun on that [personal interview].

The National Association of Theater Owners named Keaton Female Star of the Year in 1988 for *Baby Boom*.

The Good Mother

The Good Mother, based on Susan Miller's 1986 bestseller and adapted for film by Michael Bortman, is another of Keaton's family dramas. Directed by Leonard Nimoy (*Three Men and a Baby*), it is about Anna Dunlap, a middle-aged divorcée, whose primary goal in life is to be a good mother to her six-year-old daughter, Molly (Asia Vieira). Her second goal in life is to be a passionate person. The conflict of these two goals sets up the conflict of the film. Anna, it seems, can't have both. Raised in a strict, New England, WASP family headed by her stern and domineering grandfather (played by Ralph Bellamy), Anna has spent years repressing her sexuality. She's had "nothing sex" with Brian (James Naughton), who left her for another woman. "I never felt very erotic around him," Anna admits to a friend. Things change when she meets sexy, seductive Irish artist Leo Cutter (Liam Neeson), and he strips away years of Anna's inhibitions.

Anna and Leo enjoy a grand passion until two seemingly innocent incidents destroy her world. She is determined to raise Molly differently than she had been raised. "I tried to raise Molly freely. I didn't want her to be afraid of her body," Anna tells her attorney (Jason Robards). So she reads her books about the human body, which, naturally makes the precocious Molly curious about certain body parts. When she sees Leo naked in the shower, she asks him if she can touch his penis, and, Leo, uncomfortable but aware of Anna's feelings on the subject, allows it. In another scene, Molly crawls into bed with Leo and Anna who continue to make love after Molly has fallen asleep.

Molly tells her father about her adventures. He sues for custody. And though Leo tells his side of the story honestly, Anna's attorneys brand him nothing short of a child molester. Terrified of losing Molly, Anna plays along, but this is all to no avail since Anna loses custody of Molly anyway and must agree to rigid visitation rights. Though Leo tries to reach out to Anna, she is inconsolable. Their

The Good Mother (Touchstone, 1988). Keaton's romantic heroines are generally shy, if not a bit neurotic, in the love department. But they will conquer their fears and self-doubts for the love of a good man. In the scene above, the sensuous, soulful Irish artist, Leo Cutter (Liam Neeson), awakens Anna's long-repressed sexual passions. As she gives way to Leo's seductive charms, however, his sculptures loom almost menacingly to either side of the couple—a foreshadowing, perhaps, of the fate that awaits them.

relationship is reduced to a phone call "every now and then late at night," but, as Anna states at the end of the film in a voiceover narration, "His voice always lifts my heart, but somehow we bump up against the impossibility."

Many critics didn't buy the storyline of *The Good Mother*. They found a contradiction between the morally conservative eighties and the ever-increasing divorce rate and number of single-parent households. They asked: Would an otherwise good mother be so severely punished for one mistake in judgment? The answer seemed to be a resounding "No." Critics found the plot implausible for the times. They praised Keaton's performance but wrote the film off as tedious and unconvincing. David Denby argued: "What comes through the miasma of frustration is a generalized sense of female victimiza-

tion and an almost masochistic acceptance of the most severe punishment—losing a child—for sexual pleasure" ("Paying the Price for Pleasure" 30). Pauline Kael called the ending a "victimization fantasy" ("Trials" 107). Even Keaton exclaimed: "Honestly, in the movie, I can't imagine that somebody wouldn't give her her kid back.... I mean, what was it? It was hardly anything that she did" (personal interview). The consensus was that the punishment didn't fit the crime.

Anna gives up both her child and her lover too easily in the film, and that was difficult to accept for critics or audiences. In some respects, Anna's total resignation to her fate by the end contradicts her strong-willed, determined nature throughout most of the film. In scene after scene, we witness Anna's efforts to make it on her own, to support herself and her daughter

The Good Mother suggests that Anna abandons good judgment for a grand passion. She smiles dreamily with eyes closed while Leo reads to the curious, precocious Molly (Asia Vieira). This intimate snapshot, a family bonding experience, turns into a nightmare when Leo is falsely accused of child molesting, and Anna pays a terrible, albeit unrealistic, price for her passion.

with little help from her well-to-do family from Cambridge. In one scene, she is visiting her grandparents when her grandfather calls her into his study. He wants to give her some money to help out with child care expenses. She refuses his offer. Surprised and angry, he chastises Anna for her "bohemian pretense. It's tiresome in someone your age.... You suffer from some romantic ideas about poverty." Ralph Bellamy, the actor who played all those sappy third-wheels in movies like *His Girl Friday* (1940), is anything but sappy here. He is cold, stern, dogmatic. He gives Anna a look that would freeze anybody's blood, but she finds the courage to stand up to him. "It's not poverty. It's independence. It's being my own person," Anna tells him.

In another scene, Leo criticizes Anna's lack of commitment to any kind of "mean-ingful" work. Indignant, Anna lashes back passionately:

> You just listen to me for one minute, Leo. I remember it used to be that men would say I want a woman who ... and the list would be slightly different. I want a woman who can cook and who can sew or entertain my friends. But it's still the same thing. It's still the same thing. It's still your list. It's still your rules. It's still your game. It's still a man's list, even though the list has changed.... I wasn't good enough in music. I made a different kind of commitment with Molly. She is my commitment. I really hate to be told that there's no honor in it.

Keaton has had a lot of practice with scenes like this one in which her character erupts into an angry tirade. Words tumble out quickly and sharply, hitting her usually stunned target from all directions as she punctuates a word with a wave of her hand. She can give a person whiplash. Dressed in a black shirt, a short, tight skirt, and a blue cardigan cinched at the waist with a wide, black belt, Anna looks and sounds like a woman of substance, a woman ready to defend the choices she has made in life—all the more reason we are disappointed by her utter cave in at the end.

Anna, like most of Keaton's characters, is a complicated woman. She is strong and independent, but she virtually disappears into those she loves. And, when she does, she tends to lose herself. She swings too far in either direction and can no longer center herself. With Leo, she abandons all good sense for passion, much like Kate Soffel. She tells her counselor that Leo changed her life. She wasn't frigid anymore. "I was beautiful. Our sex was beautiful," she confesses. "I didn't feel with Leo there was a need for all the rules." As Keaton once remarked, "It's an intoxicating thing that drives people to passion. Your life is richer for it.... But you often pay a price" (qtd. in Garis, sec: Features). Anna pays an unbelievable price: her daughter.

Anna sacrifices herself and Leo for what she feels is her one worthy creation: Molly. Having invested all of her own hopes and dreams in her daughter, she has little left when that is taken from her. Standing on the Maine coastline at the family's summer home, she is a shell of a woman, living only for her visits with Molly. She says she "can't make use of Molly's misery to get her back," and Leo's presence is too painful a reminder of what she lost. All she has are her grandmother's comforting words: "Everybody knows you're a good mother, Anna." In a revealing comment to movie critic Jay Carr, Keaton, separating herself from her on-screen character, admitted: "Now me, Diane, if I had that situation, I'd have fought it" (qtd. in Carr, "Diane Keaton Puts Her Fears Aside" CN:L).

Several reviewers felt that both Keaton and Liam Neeson "outclassed" the material, though Keaton was initially worried about whether audiences would accept her as a romantic leading lady at her age: "I had an enormous hesitancy at this point in my life if I could play those scenes with a guy, if anyone would buy that" (qtd. in Carr, "Diane Keaton Put Her Fears Aside" CN:L). She and Neeson have several steamy scenes together. One, in particular, might arguably be one of the most erotic seduction scenes on film. Leo has just shown Anna his side of town, a world filled with artists and free spirits like himself. He brings her back to his apartment, puts on some music, dims the lights, and begins to help Anna unwind and relax. As he stands behind her, Leo slowly moves back and forth, whispering in her ear as they make shadow sculptures on the wall. Pauline Kael observed that Neeson has "a graceful male-animal presence—silent, erotic" ("Trials" 108). Neither critics nor audiences had any trouble understanding why Anna would fall for this man.

Keaton admits that, overall, her Anna Dunlap is more likable and sympathetic than the character author Susan Miller created, just as her Theresa Dunn was more sympathetic than Judith Rossner's in *Looking for Mr. Goodbar*. "In the movies, they have to try to make you more likable," she states (personal interview). Always excellent when working with children, Keaton's scenes with Asia Vieira (Molly) look completely natural, depicting Anna as a warm and tender mother. Hal Hinson of the *Washington Post*, discussing Keaton's work in *The Good Mother* and *Baby Boom*, wrote:

> All the signature Keaton mannerisms— the hesitations and stammers and idiosyncratic, amusical phrasings, the hair business, the seductive coyness—are there in both performances, as they were whenever Bogart was on screen, or Davis or Hepburn. But added to them is a very

modern sense of authenticity ["'The Good Mother' and the Far Better Keaton" B1].

Hinson comes as close as anyone to summing up Keaton's star image at this point in her career. Once typecast as the flaky but lovable ditz of Woody Allen's films, Keaton veered off into a rich variety of character roles that, in some cases, were anything but lovable. For over a decade, she had chosen parts in films that were less than Hollywood blockbusters, and these parts provided her with opportunities to expand her range and hone her technical skills. While Keaton brought certain core characteristics with her from film to film, and while she continued to play modern women with contemporary problems, she played characters as different as J. C. Wiatt and Anna Dunlap. At the same time, she had what Louis Giannetti calls star appeal: "enormous personal magnetism, a riveting quality that commands our attention" (265). Roseanne Barr's comment to Keaton when the actress appeared on her talk show illustrates Giannetti's point. "My God, how we love to watch you," Barr gushed.

In 1988, after years of contemplating a permanent return to her home state of California, Keaton moved out of the San Remo in Manhattan and into a home in the Hollywood Hills designed by Lloyd Wright (son of Frank Lloyd Wright) in 1926 and once owned by silent film star Ramón Navarro. Whether she would admit it or not, she was by now a huge star. As an icon of popular culture, she stood for the "authentic life," both on-screen and off. Her face, untouched by the plastic surgeon's scalpel, was maturing but still beautiful, expressive, and photogenic. And her work still elicited rave reviews. Her name held value and power, and though her reputation and status did not necessarily buy her great leading roles, especially in the first half of the nineties, they would enable her to chart new territory in television and continue to work steadily on her directing skills.

CHAPTER 7

1990–1995

The Director

I'd like to direct more. It's frightening, But the fact that it's frightening is a very compelling thing for me. I've always liked doing something I'm afraid to do.
—Diane Keaton (*Boston Globe*, Sept. 15, 1996)

Keaton kept a frenetic pace in the early nineties, diligently pursuing directing projects while maintaining her acting career. She edited another photography collection called *Mr. Salesman*, curated art shows, as well as created and produced a feature film, *The Lemon Sisters*. In addition to signing on for *The Godfather: Part III*, she starred with her friend Steve Martin in *Father of the Bride*, parts one and two, and reteamed with Woody Allen in *Manhattan Murder Mystery*. She took on the voice of Daphne the dog in *Look Who's Talking Now* and branched out into a new medium, television, with starring roles in HBO's *Running Mates* and TNT's *Amelia Earhart: The Final Flight*. More important, perhaps, Keaton built an impressive resume of television directing projects, including Lifetime's *Wildflower*. She won an Emmy nomination for directing the CBS Schoolbreak Special, *The Girl with the Crazy Brother*, which debuted on January 30, 1990. It concerned a young girl trying to cope with life and a schizo-

phrenic brother. The positive critical notices she received for directing these two television movies, as well as her episodes of *China Beach* and *Twin Peaks*, led to her first feature-length film, *Unstrung Heroes*, in 1995.

If she found challenging leading roles harder to come by than in the past, she shrugged it off, saying that good roles come and go. She was resigned to having to work harder and search for jobs with a wider compass. Her dilemma was twofold. First, though romantic comedies were making a comeback in the nineties, Meg Ryan and Julia Roberts had replaced Keaton as heroines of the genre. Beautiful and plucky, Ryan and Roberts appealed to a post-feminist generation of independent, savvy working women who found themselves a bit bewildered by the challenges of juggling a career and a relationship and who were willing to suspend their disbelief long enough to watch their romantic fantasies played out on-screen. Roberts's *Pretty Woman* (1990) and Ryan's

Sleepless in Seattle (1993) were two of the highest grossing romantic comedies of all time. Second, Hollywood was increasingly reluctant to invest in the small, intimate dramas that marked Keaton's career in the eighties because the returns were minimal. The huge film budgets of the 1980s skyrocketed into the nineties, driven by soaring star salaries and the insane belief that if a movie didn't gross at least $100 million it was a disappointment. Keaton's response to her predicament was "Yeah, it's hard to find good roles, so what's next?" (qtd. in Willens 4).

One of the striking aspects of Keaton's persona is her refusal to quit or get lost in the new wave of talent and onslaught of changes taking place in Hollywood. Keaton's long-time friend, Carol Kane, once said of her: "She never wastes a day. The sun comes up and she feels she ought to be up with it" (qtd. in Collins 98). Between jobs, Keaton worked on her library of photography books, frequented bookstores and swapmeets, relaxed on the beach, visited her home in Arizona, and often went to movies alone. Her family ties were stronger than ever. After her father, Jack Hall, died in September of 1990, Keaton spent more and more time with her mother who also had a small home near Keaton's in Arizona. More of her work time was spent on projects behind the camera.

After the critical failure of *Heaven*, Keaton did not give up on directing. If anything, the negative reviews made her more determined than ever to keep working at it. Keaton explained that photography sparked her interest—that and watching Gillian Armstrong at the helm of *Mrs. Soffel*. After that, Keaton begged her agent to find her work, anything to get "in." "It was very slow," she said. "I started doing MTV videos. I did episodic TV, and then I directed a TV movie. It was just a slow process of wanting to try it—the way I think most people would do it—slow and steady" (personal interview). Keaton

claims she had to prove herself in television before working in feature films.

The rewards of directing far outweigh its demands or her fear of it, according to Keaton. She has discovered that it gives her a chance to get involved with something other than herself, to see out rather than in. In one revealing quote, Keaton confesses that she enjoys directing because, as she puts it, "I like using my mind more than my feelings, which dominate my acting" (qtd. in L'Ecuyer, "Her Film *Heaven*" J1).

On the set, she keeps things "loose and sloppy" though her actors—including Michael Richards, John Turturro, Maury Chaykin, and Andie MacDowell who star in *Unstrung Heroes*—will say that she knows exactly what she wants and has mapped out her shots well beforehand in huge notebooks, much like Alfred Hitchcock's exacting storyboards of his films. Images must be put together to make the piece work, she claims, in a way that won't bore the audience (Buck 107). But she makes sure that the actors have room to experiment.

Keaton has often argued that directors who give too much direction can inhibit a performance, so, like Woody Allen, she keeps her comments to a minimum and doesn't rehearse her actors. She explains:

> The one thing that I don't like is when a director talks too much to me. It stifles whatever spontaneity I have going.... I like the actors to do a lot of different things with a take—because you don't know what you're gonna get, and that's the fun thing about it [qtd. in Ebert, "'Unstrung'" NC5].

Allen once said that he doesn't rehearse at all on his sets. "I always encourage the actor to use the script only for the sense of information I have to get across. 'Just don't stray from the character,' I say, but talk in your own words. Yell over people" (qtd. in Insdorf, "Play It Again, Woody" NC1).

Keaton in the Editing Suite. Possibly Keaton's favorite part of directing is the editing process, arranging the fragments of film into an artistic, coherent whole. And she brings all of her talents—her work ethic, discipline, poetic vision, sensitivity to actors and their craft, and years of acting experience—to the task. Today she is among the few who have carved out a double track in Hollywood, as actor and director.

There are several striking similarities between Keaton's directing style and Allen's, aside from their approach to directing actors. Extremely budget-conscious, neither wastes a lot of money on slick opening credits, preferring simple black title cards with white lettering instead. Both are organized and detail-oriented. Allen, famous for being fast and focused, works with relatively small budgets by Hollywood standards and brings his movies in on time. According to Michael Richards who starred in *Unstrung Heroes*, Keaton was "very organized, which made the picture-making process very easy for us. She brought the picture in early" (qtd. in Parks, "*Unstrung* Director" Zest 12).

Both Keaton and Allen give their total attention to the directing process, seldom, if ever, socializing with the cast or crew.

Those who have worked with Allen say he comes onto the set or into the editing suite focused immediately on the task at hand, barely pausing to nod. Hugh Grant, who costars in Allen's *Small Time Crooks* (2000), says that Allen is virtually silent on the set. "I'm used to directors who come up to me after every take and tell me how marvelous it was," Grant joked on the *Today Show*. "Woody doesn't do that." Keaton explains that directors must focus on a million different details. "There's only so much time you have in a day," she argues. "You can't relax on the job—not that job" (qtd. in "Greek Goddess" G1).

Keaton claims that while she has none of Allen's talent or imagination, he did teach her several valuable things about directing, such as discipline and decisiveness. "He is the most disciplined person

I have ever come across," she says. "Every day is a work day for Woody, and he taught me how to work in the sense that it is a consistent regular thing" (qtd. in R. Stein E1). Allen also taught her how to trust her instincts. "He is a very decisive person. He knows what he likes immediately," Keaton says (qtd. in R. Stein E1). In several interviews throughout the years Keaton has described herself in the same terms: a decisive person who knows what she likes immediately. Both also profess to enjoy the editing process.

One difference, however, between Allen and Keaton is that Allen has directed himself in many of his films, and Keaton has persistently said—until recently—that she has no desire to direct *and* star in a movie because it's too difficult for her to switch roles. However, in 1999, she finally decided to wear both hats, directing herself, Meg Ryan, Lisa Kudrow, and Walter Matthau in Nora and Delia Ephron's *Hanging Up*, released in 2000. The film is about three sisters in a dysfunctional family trying to cope with each other and their dying father.

Keaton's other directorial influences have tended to be more American than Allen's, which are essentially European. Here, she talks about some of the films and directors who have influenced her and why she considers herself an American director.

To Kill a Mockingbird [dir. Robert Milligan] is the outstanding influence for me of all movies. I think it is beautiful to look at. What it is about is amazing. The music is incredible. The visuals are great, and yet it is all about this family in this small town—and yet big scenes, huge scenes. I guess I'd have to say that's the most influential movie to me. And *A Place in the Sun* [dir. George Stevens]. And yet *A Place in the Sun* has nothing to do with anything I've ever done. It's much bigger, and I like what *A Place in the Sun* is about and how beautifully directed it is and how really amazing it is to me and the mood of the piece and the way he shot it. I think George Stevens was a great direc-

tor—a great American director. I've seen a lot of great European films but I'm more drawn to American films and American directors just because what they're about interests me more because it's more identifiable to me. For me as a director, I think I'd have to start smaller, and smaller is what I know more [personal interview].

As in the case of her acting, Keaton's modesty toward her own work as a director seems to inspire loyalty and ignite the protective instincts of her fans, friends, and family. One smitten reporter, miffed at the frequent comparisons to Woody Allen and/or Warren Beatty and the more frequent questions about what she learned from them, wrote:

It doesn't seem to have occurred to these people that Allen and Beatty may have learned more from her than she ever learned from them. Nor has it occurred to them that Keaton is a wild and rare and precious original in American movies and that her well-developed aesthetic sense may well have exceeded, in some ways, those of her old boyfriends [Jeff Simon, "A Sampling" D1].

Even Maury Chaykin, who starred in *Unstrung Heroes* (Uncle Arthur) and worked with Keaton on *Northern Lights* (1997), commented: "I've worked with Woody Allen ... and I've worked with Diane Keaton—and Woody Allen is no Diane Keaton" (qtd. in Kirkland, "Heroes' Welcome" 46).

Ultimately, the first half of the nineties was a time of both reflection and activity for the star. She likened the period to a learning experience: "I feel like I've been going to school for a while, and I sort of feel that way about my personal life too. And I'm trying to learn some new ways of approaching how I live the remainder of my life" (qtd. in Clements 104). The decisions she was making at this transitional point in her career would open up new opportunities and eventually lead to the success Keaton experienced toward the end of the nineties, as an actress and as a director.

The Lemon Sisters

Keaton took another critical hit in September, 1990, with the release of *The Lemon Sisters* which she produced as well as starred in with long-time friends Carol Kane and Kathryn Grody. The story evolved from their friendship and their love for Atlantic City. Carol Kane explained that the three of them went to Atlantic City with scriptwriter Jeremy Pikser, who had worked on Warren Beatty's *Reds*, to discuss story ideas. The result was a screenplay about three friends who grow up in the carnival atmosphere of Atlantic City's heyday and agree to meet every Monday for the next million years. It shifts back and forth between 1959 and 1982, when we see the three still together and performing as the singing Lemon Sisters each Monday night at Tony's Paradise. They eventually have a falling out and realize that, as Nora's mother pointed out when they were children, "One alone is just a lemon, but three is a jackpot."

Kane attributed the realization of the project to Keaton: "Diane did it. She made it real" (qtd. in Kasindorf Part II 15). Although Keaton didn't consider the job of producer her "bag," she did admit that it offered her "a chance to do more films and stay busy instead of sitting around and waiting for the phone to ring" (qtd. in Janos 232–33). It also gave her another chance to sing several numbers on-screen, including a syrupy rendition of "You've Got to Have Friends" with her pals.

The Lemon Sisters was not a hit. Beset by financial problems and script changes, the film was originally scheduled for distribution in the summer of 1989 but was postponed while director Joyce Chopra (*Smooth Talk*) added the film's black and white flashbacks of the three characters as young girls. The flashbacks keep interrupting the main story line, never giving it a chance to develop fully. And their sheer number in addition to their slim connection to what is happening in the present give the impression that we are watching two separate films.

The reviews were brutal, often playing on the film's unfortunate title. Keaton admitted that *The Lemon Sisters* is "not a high-concept film.... It's about friends and dreams, and how friendship pulls you through life's tough moments" (qtd. in Janos 232–33). In truth, the film seems little more than an excuse for three friends, who met while making *Harry and Walter Go to New York* (1976), to work together again. And while their friendship, the focus of the piece, might be of paramount importance in their lives, the banal theme about the whole being more than the sum of its parts did not interest either critics or audiences.

The film opens in 1959 under the boardwalk as three young girls—Eloise Hamer (Keaton), Nola Frank (Grody), and Franki D'Angelo (Kane)—swear on three lemons to be friends forever. Nola, whose parents own a salt-water taffy shop, narrates the story. She introduces each of the characters, often commenting on their past and present exploits with the tone of a tolerantly amused mother. The sensible one of the group, Nola has grown up and settled down with husband Fred Frank (Elliot Gould) and kids. But the taffy business isn't what it used to be, and the shop is on the brink of financial ruin.

Eloise's mother died when she was two, which, according to Nola, explains why she "went her own way even as a kid." She is raised by her father, Wild Bill Hamer, a host of children's talent shows and an eccentric collector of television memorabilia which includes Mr. Ed's feed-bag, Ralph Cramden's bus driver's uniform, Jack Benny's violin, and Captain Kirk's chair. Eloise grows up to be, yes, an eccentric collector who zealously guards (and talks to) her now deceased father's prized possessions because they're all she has left of him, save for a few old home movies. Still living in her huge family home, full of cats that she's allergic to, Eloise can't quite seem to communicate or get together with C. W. (Rubin Blades), the taxi driver who loves her. All of their conversations go something like this, regardless of who initiates them:

> C. W. OR ELOISE: Call me if you make up
> your mind.
> C. W. OR ELOISE: Do you want me to call
> you?
> C. W. OR ELOISE: Only if you want to call
> me.
> C. W. OR ELOISE: Do you want me to
> want to call you?

They sound like an old 78 stuck in the same groove. Neither wants the other to know how much he/she cares.

Franki, the third member of the trio, is like a water sprite who belongs to no one but the elements. Her background is uncertain since Nola never gives us any details, nor is Franki ever shown with family or other friends. All we know is that she was named after Frank Sinatra and has been on her own for a long time, eking out a living by snapping photographs of clientele in some of the local casinos. A tiny, wide-eyed waif with long, blond, wavy hair, Franki is totally ungrounded in reality. She is determined to be a star (though she has so little talent) and drag her two friends with her. Franki's dream is for the three of them to open their own nightclub in which they will perform. Enter Frankie McGuiness (Aidan Quinn), the handsome huckster who decides to manage her career in exchange for a new suit and a little lovin' on the side. His advice? "Sell the sex." In no time, he has Franki undulating on stage to the tune of "Wild Thing" and making the rounds of auditions.

But Frankie McGuiness is not the bad guy in *The Lemon Sisters*. If there is an antagonist in the film, it is change itself,

a theme that Chopra bludgeons us with. The black-and-white, fun-filled shots of happy 1950s Atlantic City tourists engaged in riding rollercoasters and watching parades down the boardwalk are frequently juxtaposed with a colorful but ominous collage of skyscrapers and casinos that tower menacingly over the little mom and pop shops that they've put out of business.

Property along the boardwalk is at a premium, and when Eloise and Nora accept offers to buy their store-front real estate for $100,000 each, the trouble begins. Franki wants them to sink their newfound cash into her dream, The Lemon Club. Nora's husband has other ideas that include opening another shop in a new location and selling "taffits," taffy rabbits. He and Nora lose everything, including their home, when the casino a few doors down begins giving away taffy. Eloise can't save them because she's spent most of her money on "Greco-Roman trash," as Nora calls it. Taking her own collecting seriously, the "unpredictable" Eloise has redecorated her home with huge plaster statues or parts of statues, like the large white hand that extends from her glass coffee table. It looks like a permanent split for the three friends.

What makes *The Lemon Sisters* somewhat palatable, however, are several slapstick scenes featuring Keaton, and Kane's performance of "Rawhide," which are wonderfully funny. Keaton has said: "I'd personally be happy to do a couple of parts where I fall down a lot. In the early Woody Allen movies I was just an idiot, and I enjoyed that very much" (qtd. in Hirschberg 42). Allen himself has said of Keaton: "She's just a major, major comedienne in every way. She moves funny, she ad-libs funny, she sings, she dances, she's hilarious" (qtd. in Decurtis 46). More recent films like *The First Wives Club*, *Northern Lights*, and *The Other Sister*, have given her the opportunity to do what she calls "really wildly physical comedy" (personal interview). With *The Lemon Sisters*, Keaton began moving again in that direction.

In one scene, Eloise, an encyclopedia of television trivia, gets talked into becoming a contestant on a game show. She stands nervously next to Host Bob in her red suit with the proverbial wide shoulders, tapered waist with peplum and straight skirt—a stark contrast to her cool opponent, a cocky 12-year-old boy named Scotty, as slick as his greased hair. Sitting awkwardly in two gigantic arm chairs, they have to run up to a buzzer a few feet in front of them and then answer the question. Keaton's comic timing is impeccable here as an excited Eloise answers the questions before hitting the buzzer, thus giving her opponent the points. At one point she jumps up and runs for the buzzer but trips and falls on the way. She picks herself up and in between embarrassed giggles, she apologizes sweetly: "I'm sorry, Bob. I'm sorry." When she sits down again, she falls backwards in her huge chair, her legs and arms flailing in the air.

Keaton also has the ability to save a scene from cheap sentimentality by using a bit of physical humor or irony. For example, Eloise eventually ends up in the hospital with asthma because of her cats. Sitting up in her bed, underneath the oxygen tent, she looks lost and vulnerable. When Nola and Franki come to visit, she does a funny little mime routine against the plastic tent. And when a misunderstanding separates the three friends, Eloise lurks in the shadows or slinks around in the margins watching her friends from afar. As Allen says, Keaton moves funny, a trait she takes advantage of when Eloise launches her health kick with speed walking. Her funny, awkward gait is matched only by her attempts to make a wheatgerm milkshake, which explodes in her face when she forgets to put the lid on the blender.

She is truly alone now, but the *mise-en-scène* in one scene parodies her solitude. Curled up in a big yellow chair, Eloise sits to the far right of the frame. The dominant image instead is a giant cardboard cutout of The Lone Ranger on his horse Silver. On-screen moments like these make it tempting to speculate on what might have been if Keaton had stayed focused on comedies after her early films with Woody Allen.

Carol Kane's rendition of "Rawhide," with her twirling microphone wreaking havoc in Caesar's Palace, actually steals the film, but neither Kane's facility with slapstick nor Keaton's can save *The Lemon Sisters* from its predictable end. Eloise, of course, sells off most of her father's collection of memorabilia to save Nola's house and their friendship. "It's just stuff," she learns as she hands her friend a paper bag full of money. Though not quite as unwatchable as most of the review headlines suggest, *The Lemon Sisters* is one of the more mediocre movies in Keaton's oeuvre.

The Godfather: Part III

Not long after the spectacular success of *The Godfather: Part II* which premiered in 1974, Charles Bludhorn, Chairman of Gulf & Western Industries, Paramount's parent company, began thinking about a *Part III*. Almost 17 years and about as many script incarnations later, it finally happened. Frances Ford Coppola and Mario Puzo, who initially had no interest in doing a *Part III*, teamed up once more and went to work hammering out the continuing saga of the Corleones. This time Michael wants to go legitimate but finds himself surrounded by crime, even in Vatican City.

Coppola began filming *The Godfather: Part III* in Rome in late November, 1989, with most of the original cast and crew members. Robert Duvall (Tom Hagen) wanted too much money, so his character was replaced by another: financial advisor B. J. Harrison, played by George Hamilton. Coppola's daughter, Sofia, got the role of Mary, Michael and Kay's daughter, when Winona Ryder fell ill.

Keaton was reluctant to play Kay Corleone again, not because her character would now be about 60 years old but because she "always found her to be such a sad character." Ultimately, she said that she was glad she did it.

> The part was about a shared past that didn't work, and I liked that. Michael and Kay meet again after many, many years. You know how that is.... When you've been very close to somebody? I don't think she ever got over him.... Making that movie was so bittersweet. It's sort of the end of the trail for us [qtd. in Garis, "Keaton's Single Spirit" sec: Features].

Keaton might easily have been commenting on her own relationship with costar Al Pacino. They had dated for a while in the seventies, but eventually went their separate ways.

Sometime during the late eighties, Diane Keaton began seeing Pacino again romantically. They broke up again on the set of The Godfather: Part III. According to Harlan Lebo's The Godfather Legacy, the situation reached a crisis point in Italy.

> For several years, Diane Keaton and Al Pacino had struggled through an on-again off-again relationship. The main conflict seemed to be a long-term commitment; Keaton wanted one and Pacino didn't. The result was a strained relationship between the two that was soothed in part by misfortune: Pacino's beloved grandmother died during production, and Keaton accompanied him to New York for the funeral. While they were gone, they settled their differences and forged an uneasy personal truce that would last for the duration of the film [251].

Perhaps Keaton and Pacino brought much of their own angst to Kay and Michael's love-hate relationship, but there are no substantiating details. Both stars are very private people who would find that kind of speculation an intrusion.

Most, if not all, of Keaton's scenes in The Godfather: Part III are with Pacino. Kay and Michael are reunited after eight years when Michael invites her and their grown children, Tony and Mary, to attend yet another Corleone ceremony. This time it is his own as he receives the Order of St. Sebastian Medal from the Catholic Church after donating $100 million for the poor of Sicily. Michael is trying to buy his redemption. Having ordered the death of his brother Fredo, Michael's life has become a Greek tragedy, and he is haunted by his sins. As Coppola explained, it is a different Michael we see in Part III. Now in his sixties, he hasn't made things right, and he needs to put his house in order before he dies (A Look Back). But no amount of money can buy back his innocence as Kay, ever his conscience, tells him when she finally gets him alone in his study: "I didn't come here to see you disguised by your church. I think that was a shameful ceremony."

Kay has come to plead her son's case. Tony doesn't want to be a lawyer. He has a voice for opera. Michael must let him go. As she begins to talk, Kay is leaning against the door to the far right of the frame. She has always been framed in the background or in the margins, suggesting her position in the family. She has never belonged, yet she is the mother of his children. And once a Corleone, no one ever really leaves. If Michael keeps getting pulled back into the life of crime, Kay keeps getting pulled back into the family.

We first see her in this scene, for example, as a reflection in the glass of a family photograph which shows her posed awkwardly to one side of her husband, looking out of the frame, deep in thought. It is only in her most intimate conversations with Michael that Kay takes up the center of the frame, as she does in the heat

The Godfather: Part III (Paramount, 1990). Coppola had his problems with the third install-ment of *The Godfather*, a film he never wanted to make in the first place. Sixteen years after the release of *The Godfather: Part II*, Coppola and Mario Puzo agreed to write the screenplay, which they kept revising during filming. The budget escalated. Winona Ryder got sick and bowed out, so he cast his inexperienced daughter, Sofia, to play Mary Corleone. The critics weren't kind. Robert Duvall passed on playing Tom Hagen again because he wasn't offered enough money, so Coppola brought in George Hamilton to play Michael's lawyer. Audiences were disappointed. And Diane Keaton and Al Pacino were ending a real-life, long-term relation-ship on the set. The bright spot seemed to be newcomer Andy Garcia, who plays Michael's nephew, Vincent Mancini. Here, bathed in light from a doorway, he watches over his family, who appear to be lost in their own thoughts.

of the argument over Tony's future. Kay has returned stronger, more self-assured than in the old days. The tailored suits—with the wide shoulders and narrow waists—in varying shades of brown and cinnamon that Kay wears throughout the film suggest a sense of power and directly contrast the girlish, bright-colored dresses she used to wear as Michael's wife.

Yet, there is something still vulnera-ble about Kay. She looks younger than her years, with her upswept hair softly curled around her face. But it's the con-cern on her face and the tender emotions that well up after years of being suppressed that gives away her vulnerability as she stands in the hospital room watching a stricken Michael lying in bed after his heart attack. She still loves this man. He says, "I never expected you," to which Kay replies: "No. I know. But I'm here." It's a line she will repeat later in Sicily where their son Tony is debuting in *Cav-alleria Rusticana* at the Palermo Opera House.

Like Keaton and Pacino themselves, Kay and Michael call a truce in Sicily. Cautious at first, unsure of herself or his motives, Kay spends a day touring the cobbled streets of the city where Michael's father was born. He wants to show her the "real Sicily" so that she can better "understand the family history." Kay quickly responds: "Oh, I think I understand it well enough." Cautions fade and tensions ease, however, as they stroll along talking of their past and their children and even stopping to dance in the plaza. But signs of danger and doom surround them. An innocent puppet show turns into a violent story about vendetta, and Michael's friend, Don Tomasino, is murdered on his way to his villa to meet Michael and Kay who wait for him there.

It is at the villa that Kay and Michael declare their love for each other after years of separation. Michael finally asks for her forgiveness, what he has been looking for all along: "I love you, Kay. Don't dread me anymore. You know, every night here in Sicily I dream about my wife and my children and how I lost them." And Kay, her defenses down, declares through tears: "I guess if it's any consolation, I want you to know that I always loved you, Michael—and, you know, I always, always will." He grabs her hand, but they are interrupted when friends come to request revenge for the murder of Don Tomasino.

Kay stands watching the request, as she has in the past, through the doorway of a nearby room. This time, however, when she realizes the meaning of what Michael is about to undertake, she utters, "It never ends," and walks out of the frame before a door can close on her. An assassin's bullet underscores Kay's prophetic words when, after their son's triumphant performance, Mary is shot on the steps of the opera house. The image of Keaton's and Pacino's intensely realistic performances as Kay and Michael, who lie screaming on the blood-stained steps over their loss, lingers long after the closing credits. Any hope of their reconciliation ends with the violence and horror of Mary's death.

Although Kay has been called the moral compass in The Godfather films, Keaton sees her as a "peripheral" character who pays a terrible price for her association with Michael Corleone. "They lose a daughter," she explains. "So in a

certain sense it's a very tragic tale in that you should just stay away from the Mafia. It's horrible. He's a murderer and a killer. He's the worst of the worst" (personal interview). For Keaton, who has definite opinions about the Mafia, The Godfather films are brilliant, but they have a tendency to romanticize this world of crime:

> The best one about the Mafia is Good-Fellas because it really shows you how disgusting it is. I mean, I sat there watching it and said "I hate them because they're the worst kind of lowest humanity," and he [Martin Scorsese] really brought that to life better than anyone. I mean, to me, that's how you should view the Mafia, and that's the way they should be seen. It didn't romanticize them for a second [personal interview].

Unlike the first two films in the trilogy, which received high critical praise, The Godfather: Part III met with a lukewarm reaction, largely due to its convoluted plot.

Directing for Television

Diane Keaton is not a snob about working in television as some film stars are. In fact, she argues that television has been good to her, providing opportunities to act and direct and to work with material that no one in the film industry would touch because they think it wouldn't make any money. "If there's material you totally love, and if no one else will do it, and if they want you enough, then maybe they'll let you do it. And that's what you can have with television," she claims (personal interview).

Keaton has starred in three made for television movies: Running Mates (1992), Amelia Earhart: The Final Flight (1994), and Northern Lights (1997). She also credits television for her start in directing. Her MTV videos for Belinda Carlisle, her Schoolbreak Special, her episode #23 of Twin Peaks (aired February 9, 1990), and her "Fever" episode of China Beach (aired

November 3, 1990), all led to her job directing *Wildflower* which premiered on December 3, 1991, on the Lifetime channel.

Adapted from Sara Flanigan's novel, *Alice*, set in rural Georgia in 1938, *Wildflower* stars Patricia Arquette (Alice Guthrie) as a seventeen-year-old epileptic whose seizures prompt her abusive stepfather (Norman Maxwell) to keep her locked in a shed. Her mother, Ada Guthrie (Susan Blakely), is too afraid of her husband to help her daughter. Two neighboring teens, a brother and sister played by William McNamara (Sammy Perkins) and Reese Witherspoon (Ellie Perkins), have their own troubles. Their father, played by Beau Bridges, has taken to the bottle after his wife dies and is too distracted by his grief to pay attention to what his children are doing. Sammy and Ellie find Alice and gradually bring her back into the world.

Most of the reviews had high praise for Keaton's sure-handed directing style, and Joe Stein called *Wildflower* "top-rate, certainly a cut above the usual TV-movie" (D6). Most important, Keaton's job on this television movie caught the attention of Susan Arnold and Donna Roth, two of the producers of the soon-to-be developed *Unstrung Heroes*, another complex family drama. Based on what they saw here, Arnold and Roth would insist on Keaton to direct their feature film.

Father of the Bride and Father of the Bride: Part II

In *Father of the Bride* (1991) and *Father of the Bride: Part II* (1995), Keaton was reunited with producer Nancy Meyers and director Charles Shyer with whom she had worked on *Baby Boom*. It was a charmed union. Keaton's comic timing and facility with fast, sharp, witty dialogue was in perfect sync with Meyers and Shyer's contemporary, sophisticated screwball comedies, throwbacks to those of predecessors Billy Wilder, Ernst Lubitsch, Howard Hawks, and Preston Sturges. Their wise-cracking, intelligent, slightly daffy heroines—like Barbara Stanwyck in Sturges' *The Lady Eve* or Katharine Hepburn in Hawks' *Bringing Up Baby*—were forerunners of the Keaton persona played out as J. C. Wiatt in *Baby Boom*. The unpredictable antics of these screwball heroines kept the men in their lives in a constant state of wonderment.

Meyers and Shyer reverse the roles in the *Father of the Bride* films. They tone down the eccentric, daffy side of their heroine but retain the intelligence and wit in order to counterbalance their "over-reactor" hero George Banks (Steve Martin) and outrageous wedding consultant Franck Eggelhoffer (Martin Short). *Father of the Bride* and its sequel are definitely Steve Martin vehicles, but to suggest that Keaton is "wasted" or "invisible" in them, as some critics have, is to miss her subtle comic performance and underestimate her character's importance in the films.

Meyers and Shyer wrote the screenplays based on Vincente Minnelli's *Father of the Bride* (1950) and *Father's Little Dividend* (1951), both starring Spencer Tracy, Joan Bennett, and Elizabeth Taylor. The remakes have that 1950s feel about them, but the circumstances are decidedly modern. Keaton plays Nina Banks to Steve Martin's George, sort of an Ozzie and Harriet of the nineties. They have it all: a stable, happy marriage and two beautiful children, Annie (Kimberly Williams) and Matty (Kieran Culkin).

Their home, a Georgian revival at 24 Maple Drive in an upscale neighborhood of San Marino, looks like it might have been the set for the fifties sitcom, *Leave It to Beaver*. In fact, Nina's proverbial pearls and high heels seem like a homage to that ideal American mom, June Cleaver. Like June Cleaver and Harriet Nelson, Nina is the center of this family, calmly maintaining order and stability when

Father of the Bride (Touchstone Pictures, 1991). Woody Allen always claimed that when he acted with Keaton, he became her straight man. But in *Father of the Bride*, Keaton's comedic talents take on more subtlety and restraint to balance the hyperkinetic team of Steve Martin and Martin Short. Nina Banks is the calm center and voice of sanity in husband George's life. She punctures his harebrained ideas and actions with wit and reason. In her soft, pastel suits and dresses, draped with scarves and pearls, Nina is a throwback to those TV moms of yesteryear who maintained the illusion that their screwy husbands were in charge and looked upon their antics with bemused tolerance. Here, Nina sits smilingly with husband George (Steve Martin) and daughter Annie (Kimberly Williams).

things start to go awry. Unlike her fifties counterparts, Nina works outside the home. While George owns a tennis shoe company called Sidekicks, Nina owns her own business.

If George is the over-reactor in the family, Nina is the reactor. They're a perfect match, as George says. Much of the humor comes from Nina's reactions to George's behavior in both films. In *Part I*, daughter Annie returns from studying architecture in Rome and announces her engagement to independent communications consultant Bryan McKenzie (George Newbern) at the dinner table. George, who hates change as much as he loves his daughter, flips out at the prospect of losing Annie, who innocently exclaims: "He's like you dad, except he's brilliant."

But Nina knows her husband all too well. She keeps watching George for signs of erratic behavior while trying to get more information out of Annie about her intended. Sure enough, after his initial, negative reaction, George's imagination goes into overdrive, misinterpreting "independent" for "jobless" and envisioning Bryan as some 45-year-old pervert. When Annie storms out of the dining room, the realistic Nina turns to her husband and gently chides: "George, stop acting like a lunatic father and go out there and talk to her before she runs out that door and marries this kid, and we never see her again." Patiently, she smiles after him, shaking her head tolerantly.

Later, when the new in-laws greet them with, "What a relief. You two look perfectly normal," Nina, in her pink dress and pearls, quickly responds: "I am." Her point is soon made when George, snooping around in the McKenzie study, ends up in the swimming pool with their bank book. Keaton's wide-eyed shock at his predicament outside and her attempts to distract the McKenzie couple from seeing him out the window are as amusing as Martin's own shtick. The two seasoned comedians make quite a good team. Martin and Keaton look like a long-time married couple. Their ease with each other appears natural, comfortable, and unstudied, though this was their first film together. For example, after meeting Bryan, Nina and George climb the stairs to bed, talking and undressing along the way, carrying the conversation into their bedroom, with the rhythm of a couple long used to each other's routines. Nina is elated with the match and tries to convince George that it feels "right." She reminds him of their own courtship and passion and soothes the excitable George, for the moment at least, with a few words and a hug: "I'm happy for Annie. This is a big deal. I think we should at least hug."

Martin and Keaton's on-screen rapport may be attributed in part to their real-life friendship and affection for each other, which also extended to young newcomers Kimberly Williams and George Newbern. Williams, who actually replaced Phoebe Cates when she became pregnant before shooting, told one reporter: "I was scared. I felt very out of my element, and they took care of me" (qtd. in Strickler, "Movie Novice" E2).

The Keaton and Martin partnership is the reverse of Keaton and Allen's. Allen said once, "I always look smaller than normal compared to Keaton. I turn into the straight man" (qtd. in Dowd, "Old Pals Act" 6). With Martin, Keaton plays the straight, centered one, yet her reactions are funny. Allen explains Keaton's on-screen charisma this way:

Her personality is so large, it's hard to see anything else on the screen. It's like you're dancing with Fred Astaire, and you may be a decent dancer yourself, but your eye goes to Astaire. Your eye goes to Keaton. She has such a natural gift, she eclipses everyone [qtd. in Decurtis 48].

We should remember that the comment is coming from Keaton's biggest admirer, but, on second or third viewing, he is right. Even when Keaton is a secondary character as in these *Father of the Bride* films, or even in the *Godfather* films, her performance commands our attention.

When the action cuts away from her, the balance disappears—the softness and warmth and calm that complement Steve Martin's hyper persona. Her voice is lower; the wide smile is more tender. Her whole look is softer, more relaxed. Susan Becker, costume designer for *Baby Boom*, dresses her here in looser-fitting versions of the J. C. Wiatt suit, dresses, blouses and skirts, slacks and sweaters—all in shades of pinks and creams and browns—adorned simply with scarves and pearls. Even Louis B. Mayer, who extolled the virtues of motherhood in his films, would have praised Keaton's transformation into the All-American Mother and object of George's adoration.

While this transformation into the icon of motherhood is so believable and soothing that we begin to think of her in these terms, it does nothing to diminish Keaton's comic performance. In one scene Nina and George are in the kitchen cleaning up after a dinner with Annie and Bryan, when Nina tries to convince him to hire a wedding consultant. Her delivery of a line and physical reactions to his grousing keep the scene light and funny. "I want to call a wedding coordinator to make this thing really, really beautiful, and you want to call Gabe at the Steak Pit," she tells him. But when she cries, "I really can't take this. I'm not used to all this arguing," George relents. As he walks out of the kitchen and up the stairs, still

Father of the Bride: Part II (Touchstone Pictures, 1995). There's a decided symmetry in set and situation in Charles Shyer's update of Vincente Minnelli's 1951 *Father's Little Dividend*. Note the perfect balance of the Banks' living room. One side duplicates, almost exactly, the other as mother (Keaton) and daughter (Kimberly Williams) find themselves pregnant at the same time. Martin Short, center, leads the exercises. Audiences basked in the fifties feel of the two *Father of the Bride* films and their celebration of the idealized American family.

talking, we see Nina wiping down the kitchen counter, nodding. When he finally says, "All right, I'll go," an exasperated Nina collapses in a heap on the counter, bringing a hand up over her buried head to make an okay sign.

Keaton's performance in *Father of the Bride: Part II* is a bit edgier. Nina, now pregnant, must also contend with a husband snapped into mid-life crisis over being a father and a grandfather at the same time. Annie is pregnant, too. When the doctor tells Nina and George they are going to have a baby, George turns to a surprised but elated Nina and says: "And who, may I ask, is the father?" before passing out. He dyes his gray hair brown and sells their home which he later buys back at twice the price.

George's antics and doom-and-gloom scenarios about being an elderly parent, like "Well, we won't have to worry about hearing him come in late," finally get to

Nina. They have been sharing their "good news" with Annie and Bryan when Nina confronts George. The scene illustrates Keaton's ability to pull off neurotic frustration with comic effect. That rising note of hysteria creeps into her voice as she gives George a tongue-lashing without ever losing her warmth.

> NINA: You're so hilarious, George. So sensitive. And I really appreciate your asking how I feel about all this, especially since I'm the one who's going to be having the baby.
> GEORGE: You're right. How do you feel about it?
> NINA: I know how old I am, George. I've already been the mother of the bride. But here I am, at the age I am, and I'm pregnant. And I don't think that qualifies me for the *Guinness Book of Records*, George. So, in answer to your question, I'm very happy. I'm happy. And I'm feeling nervous. And I'm very much alone.

In tears, Nina turns to hug her daughter, "Goodbye, sweetie," and in a sharp tone turns to George, shakes a finger, and says as she is walking out the door: "Do me a favor. Don't follow me, Banks. No!"

Both Martin and Keaton are actors capable of displaying great tenderness which comes across in two scenes in which George tells Nina how much she means to him. Sitting on the floor in her night-shirt—buttoned to the collar—Nina says: "Honey, you've got me worried. I don't know. You dyed your hair. What's next? A 19-year-old girlfriend? Men do those kinds of things. They don't want to grow old with their wives, so they get new wives." George, putting his arm around her, tells Nina in a reassuring tone:

> Nina, I may dye my hair and I may want to move to the beach and I may hate the idea that I'm going to be a grandfather, but never for one millisecond of one day did I ever not want to spend the rest of my life with you. And I'm sorry I've been such a jerk.

And Nina, who never lets George get off the hook easily, sweetly responds: "Oh, that's okay. I'm used to it." Later, when Nina's labor develops complications, a worried George leans over her hospital bed, talking about how he felt on their first date. The camera cuts back and forth from George's face to Nina's as he tries to distract her from her worry over possibly losing the baby. She says, "Thank you, George, for telling me" and he gently tells her: "Thanks for marrying me, Nina."

In the end, *Father of the Bride* and *Father of the Bride: Part II* may not have been the most challenging roles in Keaton's or Martin's career, but they are pleasant, appealing films about family and coming to terms with letting go of your children. Audiences loved them, and said so at that arbiter of popular taste, the box office. For Keaton, the films marked a switch in character type from her usual high-strung neurotic heroines to the more restrained, soothing mother of the bride. Her performances, deceptively low-key, had a great deal to do with the films' success.

Acting for Television: *Running Mates* and *Amelia Earhart: The Final Flight*

In the early nineties, Keaton found two roles that she wanted to play, but no one in Hollywood was interested in making the films. One was Aggie Snow in *Running Mates*, a romantic comedy about an award-winning children's author and illustrator who falls in love with her high-school heartthrob, now a senator running for President of the United States. The other was a character out of American history, Amelia Earhart, with whom Keaton shares some uncanny similarities, not the least of which is her physical appearance. It was television that ultimately gave Keaton the chance to bring these characters to life. *Running Mates*, filmed in June of 1992, debuted Sunday, October 4, on HBO. TNT picked up *Amelia Earhart: The Final Flight*, which premiered Sunday, June 12, 1994. The role of Earhart would win Keaton an Emmy nomination as Lead Actress in a Miniseries or Special in the 47th annual award show held on Sunday, September 10, 1995.

Keaton says that Carol Eastman's "wonderful dialogue" initially attracted her to *Running Mates*:

> She wrote *Five Easy Pieces*. So she's this extraordinary writer. Just this brilliant writer, and this thing had been sitting around. So HBO said we want to do something with you, and I said, "Well, I'd like to do this. I'd like to do *Running Mates*. See if you can get the rights to *Running Mates*." So we negotiated a deal with Paramount, who I think owned it, and they let us have it. It was great to do it because otherwise it wasn't going to get

done. So you can take material that has been sitting around and bring it back [personal interview].

In addition to the well-written script, Keaton fell in love with her character, the artistic and outspoken Aggie Snow. It was fun, according to Keaton, to play a woman who felt it was her right to express herself, no matter how obnoxious she came off to others. Keaton explains:

> What she's about really is someone who's extremely isolated but has very high ideals and moral standards. Like a lot of artists, she's not quite in this world. Then she falls in love with this man who's all about dealing with people and negotiating with the world [qtd. in Willens 4].

Wickedly bright, Aggie is always a step ahead of love interest Hugh Hathaway (Ed Harris), for example. After many years, they encounter each other in a restaurant where Aggie is having breakfast with her off-beat brother, Chapman (Ed Begley), a musician who is having a rough time after his wife leaves him. As Hathaway comes in with his entourage, Aggie hides behind her dark shades and newspaper until her brother makes a scene about finding foreign objects in his omelet and she gets up to reorder for him. Feeling Hathaway staring at her, she knocks over a tray of dishes, and the two meet again—cute.

He's immediately smitten, and she's throwing one-liners to cover her nervousness over his obvious come-on. After all, this is the guy who never knew she existed in high school, the guy whose all-star running back picture in the yearbook carries her lipstick print. When he invites her to Washington "to see government in action," Aggie quickly replies: "I think I just have." When he keeps staring, she tells him, "There's looking, and there's ocular intrusion." And when he asks her I.Q., Aggie whips back: "Yours plus 12."

Keaton said of her character: "This woman never shuts up.... She needs to learn a lesson sometimes" (qtd. in Gardella, "Few Complaints" 44). Several critics likened the romance between Aggie and Hugh to some of Tracy and Hepburn's on-screen relationships, especially in *Woman of the Year* in which the indomitable Tess Harding gets a lesson in humility from Tracy's Sam Craig and learns the meaning of compromise.

It's Hugh at first who needs to learn a lesson, however. When he keeps her waiting, and waiting, in the Senate dining room while he glad-hands with fellow politicians, Aggie hopes to cause a scene that will embarrass him. Standing at the table in the center of the room, she begins: "I want to thank you for the swell time, especially up in the office, Senator." To surprised onlookers, she says, "He just loves it when I strip down to my holster and heels, tie him up to a chair and blow 'I Gotta Be Me' on his bugle.... Be sure to give my number to some of the other boys now, won't you?"

She saunters out, only to be tracked down at home that evening by a contrite and even more smitten Hathaway. "You were sensational," he tells her. "Is it the fact that you have absolutely no respect for me that makes you so damned attractive?" When he proposes that same evening, she snaps: "See a therapist." And he tells his campaign manager: "She's the one. She's smart. She's funny. She's attractive as hell. I'm crazy about her."

Running Mates was a change of pace for Ed Harris who says he usually does parts "filled with angst and pain and violence." His main reason for doing the movie "was the opportunity to work with Diane" (qtd. in Romano, "Ed Harris" B3). Keaton said she also liked the idea of playing someone who is falling in love: "I didn't think I would enjoy it as much as I did, so that was the surprise part for me" (qtd. in Bobbin 5).

But Aggie resists Hathaway's attentions—at first. Like Aggie, Keaton insists she is not a political creature, though, interestingly, Woody Allen describes her as so American that "she would make a good First Lady" (personal interview). When Hugh proposes for a second time, Aggie tells him that she hates politics. She hates parties. She hates social functions in general. She doesn't want to live her life in a "national terrarium." She's afraid of the press. She's afraid of being under a microscope. She never wants to say things she doesn't believe or stand in front of a camera and smile or wear stupid hats. "I want you to be exactly the way you are," he assures her—words that will come back to haunt him.

When Aggie hits the campaign trail with Hugh as his fiancée, the trouble begins. His campaign team wants to muzzle her. "Too feverish," they claim. The outspoken Aggie has become a media darling because of her unpredictable comments, but she has a skeleton in her closet that threatens to destroy his chances of winning the bid for president. It seems that in the sixties Aggie appeared topless in a flag-abusing film by her then-husband. As Aggie tells him, it's her career at stake also. After all, she is a children's author. But Hugh can't think of anything but his own career.

To lie or not to lie becomes the question and another reason Keaton felt so strongly about making *Running Mates*. Should Aggie, a woman almost obsessively honest, lie to save the political career of the man she loves? Keaton, faced with the same situation, says she would lie. "I think sometimes that you have to sacrifice things for somebody you love.... So I believe that it was more important to lie for him" (qtd. in Endrst, "Keaton" C1). As it turns out, Aggie doesn't have to go that far because Hugh steps up, defending her right to free expression and his right to be judged on his own merits and not some art film Aggie made years ago. Harris sympathized with his character's situation, adding that he is more interested in a politician's leadership qualities than his

or her personal life. "I really could give a damn what their past has been like," he claims (qtd. in Froelich, "*Running Mates*" 19).

Running Mates also raises the right-to-privacy issue, the conduct of the press. Captivated by Hathaway's "colorful and controversial" fiancée, they camp out on Aggie's front lawn and snap pictures as she comes out one morning to get her newspaper wearing an old bathrobe and socks. Later, like a swarm of locusts, they chase her into a women's restroom, where she barricades herself from their prying cameras and questions. "How did I sink to these heights?" Aggie cries. But the press turns vicious in the final scene as they crowd in, surrounding the podium where Hugh is standing with Aggie and firing off questions about whether Aggie has the moral fibre to be First Lady. When one particularly obnoxious reporter presses her to respond to rumors that she did, in fact, appear nude in the film, Aggie flashes back: "What part of your humanity did you have to bury in order to ask that question?"

Running Mates may be a light romantic comedy, but this final scene is sheer wish fulfillment for all those who would love to see the press humbled—just once. Standing next to Hugh, the tough Aggie is finally reduced to tears, not from the press but from Hugh's willingness to put himself second to defend her actions. As in most romantic comedies, Hugh finally becomes a man worthy of the heroine as he begins: "I have never met anyone with more integrity than Aggie Snow.... This is the woman I intend to marry." By the time he's finished, it's the reporters who look like they may burst into tears. They burst into applause instead and give ground as Hugh and Aggie walk out of the room together—and presumably into their new home on Pennsylvania Avenue.

A seemingly innocent, rather insignificant little movie in the Keaton canon, *Running Mates* does raise some big issues.

But, more important, it presents a character who appears to be a composite of many of Keaton's former characters. For example, she is playing an artist in *Running Mates*, just as she did in *Annie Hall, Interiors, Manhattan*, and *Reds*. Also, like Kay Corleone or Lissa Chestnut (*Harry and Walter Go to New York*), Aggie is a moral compass for other characters in the film as well as the audience. Independent and honest, Aggie, like Louise Bryant or Anna in *The Good Mother* or even Terry Dunn in *Looking for Mr. Goodbar*, insists on being her own person, not just an extension of someone else.

With her intelligence, wit, and humor, Aggie Snow also could be J. C. Wiatt's Washington, D.C., counterpart. Both are outspoken and quick with a comeback, light-years ahead of their love interests in brain power. In one scene, an angry Aggie refuses to go to a White House reception with Hathaway. "You're supposed to be there with me," he yells. "Tell them I came down with lockjaw," Aggie flashes back. On the other hand, these two characters can be shy and tender. The first kiss in both films is virtually identical: a shy, awkward, hesitant tango of limbs and lips. Only the male partners and the settings change.

Even dialogue uttered in previous films echoes in *Running Mates*. In *The Good Mother*, Anna confesses to Leo her lack of confidence with sex: "I don't think I'm very good at it." Aggie tells Senator Hathaway, "I'm not good in the love department." In *Baby Boom* and *Running Mates*, Keaton's characters say: "I don't dance very well." The repetition of these elements and similarities between characters, whether dramatic or comic, help pinpoint the nuances of Keaton's performances and reinforce her paradoxical on-screen persona of a woman who is simultaneously outspoken and shy, intelligent and flaky, independent and vulnerable, warm and edgy.

Some of the similarities between Kea-

ton's own persona and her next television role, Amelia Earhart, seem almost uncanny. Keaton bears a striking resemblance to America's first aviatrix whose exploits captured the public's attention and fascination. Little, however, is known about Earhart's private life. Lady Lindy, as the world came to call her, set out with her navigator, Fred Noonan (Rutger Hauer), in her Lockheed Electra to circumnavigate the globe by flying along the equator. On July 2, 1937, about 40 days and 22,000 miles into the journey, they left New Guinea for Howland Island in the South Pacific and were never heard from again. She left behind millions of shocked fans and a stunned husband, publisher George Palmer Putnam (Bruce Dern), who was also her manager and press agent.

Amelia Earhart: The Final Flight (1994), directed by Yves Simoneau, focuses on the last two years of Earhart's life. Based on Doris L. Rich's biography, scriptwriter Anna Zandor depicts Earhart as a flawed, complex heroine: temperamental, headstrong, and reckless. When Rich saw Keaton's performance as Earhart, she told the *Washington Post*: "She's just magnificent" (qtd. in Winslow Y7). According to Rich, Earhart lived a frenetic life, moving from one project to the next without a pause. Impatient, she sometimes skipped crucial details, like learning Morse code, for example. As for her disappearance, Rich argues that Earhart just ran out of gas: "She assumed she would be able to home in on Howland Island [by radio signal], but was on the wrong frequency" (qtd. in Winslow Y7).

Earhart was a nervous flier, like the actress who plays her. It is a well-known fact that Earhart was uncomfortable in the cockpit. The movie depicts this in several heated arguments between Earhart and Putnam. In one scene, she turns to him and says: "I'm not this myth that you've created! I'm just a mediocre pilot who you picked out of a crowd nine years ago because I looked like Charles Lindbergh and oh, yes, I could fly just a little bit!" Keaton, known for her forthrightness, plays Earhart with the same sense of honesty and fair play. Tormented because she thinks she's living a lie, she tells her husband:

> I'm not this Amelia Earhart person.... She's just an invention. She's been invented by me, by the press and by all those women out there looking for a heroine. But I'm not, you know. I'm not a heroine. Sometimes I think we're just a business merger.

An even more striking similarity between Keaton and Earhart lies in their sense of style. Costume designer Jill Ohanneson might well have been describing Keaton's own fashion tastes when she says of Earhart, "She wore what she liked, not what convention dictated. She had a real flair for combining things—men's clothes with women's accessories" (qtd. in Patteson E3). And when Keaton says of Earhart, "She had a great personality, those winning American looks," she is unwittingly echoing those who have described her in the same terms (qtd. in Patteson E3).

While the film and Keaton received mixed reviews, the independent, stubborn, conflicted Earhart provided Keaton with what was probably her most challenging role at this stage of her career. It was a role that won her Golden Globe, Emmy, and Screen Actors Guild nominations for Best Actress in a Miniseries or Movie Made for Television in 1995.

Manhattan Murder Mystery

Keaton wasn't scheduled to star in Woody Allen's 24th film about a middle-aged, upper East Side New York couple who get entangled in a murder mystery. Mia Farrow, Allen's long-time romantic partner and costar, was slated to play his on-screen wife, Carol Lipton. Their lives erupted in a public nightmare. The mudslinging and accusations of child abuse began after Farrow discovered Allen was having an affair with her adopted daughter, Soon-Yi Previn, to whom Allen is currently married. Five weeks before filming began in September of 1992, Keaton, who had just wrapped up *Running Mates*, stepped in to help out her old friend. Allen said that working with Keaton again was "great therapy" for him (qtd. in Dowd, "The Return" 2C).

Many friends and co-workers attribute Allen's upbeat mood on the set to Keaton's presence. Anjelica Huston, who plays author Marcia Fox, says the set was a whole lot lighter and more fun on *Manhattan Murder Mystery* than it was on Allen's *Crimes and Misdemeanors*, largely because of Keaton. Huston said, "He showed up in the hair and make-up trailer to tease Diane about her hair and her big photograph books, all diligently marked with yellow Post-it paper.... Around Diane, he was open and accessible" (qtd. in Dowd, "Old Pals" 6).

Their "lucky chemistry," as Allen calls it, was evident on-screen. Critics were delighted with the reunion. Adina Hoffman of *The Jerusalem Post* wrote:

> At least he's cast Diane Keaton. Thank God. Keaton boosts *Manhattan Murder Mystery* up several high-rise floors. Her presence in the film adds some of the wild skittishness that's been missing from Allen's recent movies ["Play It Again" 5].

Craig Macinnis, *Toronto Star*, commented that Keaton "is a comic genius, a ditz-savant who gathers energy to herself and casts it back in erratic waves. Keaton and Allen are, for each other, custom-created foils. Opposites who don't attract so much as collide" (B1). Jay Carr, *The Boston Globe*, noted: "It's as if we're looking in on what life might be like if Alvy Singer had married Annie Hall" ("Allen's Mystery" 41). And Rita Kempley said of Keaton and Allen: They "click like two

Manhattan Murder Mystery (TriStar Pictures, 1993). In one of life's twists of fate, Diane Keaton ended up replacing Mia Farrow in Woody Allen's *Manhattan Murder Mystery*. When Allen and Farrow's personal relationship erupted in a very public way, Allen was left without an actress to play his on-screen wife, Carol Lipton. Keaton, who has remained unwaveringly loyal to her long-time friend and frequent costar of the seventies, stepped into the role at the last moment. Though they hadn't acted together for years, their "lucky chemistry," as Allen calls it, was as evident as ever, much to the delight of critics and fans alike. In this scene, Carol, who suspects Paul House (Jerry Adler) of killing his wife, tries to wheedle some information out of him as Larry nervously looks on.

champagne glasses" ("Allen's Carefree Caper" D6).

Manhattan Murder Mystery also re-teamed Allen with writer Marshall Brickman (*Annie Hall* and *Manhattan*). The two had originally written *Annie Hall* as a murder mystery, but ultimately focused on the romance between Alvy Singer and Annie as a way of tightening the script. Allen, who admits to having "a real junk tooth for murder mysteries," said the idea for the original story never really died and came out of a real-life mystery of sorts:

In the '60s, I was renting a tiny apartment on Park Avenue.... I had two sweet next-door neighbors, an avuncular man and a middle-aged woman. I went to California to play at "the hungry i," and when I came back, he said his wife had fallen out the window. He was in a blue silk smoking jacket, and said, "yes, it was terrible." He seemed so casual. I always thought it was an interesting theme—the impulse to watch him [qtd. in Insdorf, "Play It Again" NC1].

Allen and Brickman use a similar situation in the exposition of their film.

In the beginning of *Manhattan Murder Mystery*, Carol and Larry Lipton return from seeing *Double Indemnity* to find that the sweet, middle-aged neighbor, Lillian House (Lyn Cohen), whom they've only met the night before, has just died of heart failure. Her husband Paul (Jerry

Adler), a stamp collector and owner of a run-down cinema house, seems less than distraught. This sends Carol's imagination into overdrive. "Mr. House seemed a little too perky," she tells Larry (Allen). "This guy should be a wreck. He's too composed for a man whose wife just died." But the only person who will play along with her suspicions is their recently divorced friend and playwright, Ted (Alan Alda), who has had a crush on Carol for years. Together they decide to get to the bottom of what happened to Lillian House.

Larry, a book editor for Harper's, is a little jealous of Carol's relationship with Ted and tells her one night as they're getting ready for bed: "You guys are slipping into a mad obsession." Keaton and Allen's overlapping dialogue, their movement in and out of rooms while in conversation, their spontaneous reactions to each other, seem so natural and comfortable here. It's as if we're watching an old married couple, one of whom wants to put a little spice back into the marriage. The other is quite happy with the status quo, thank you. When Carol turns to Larry at one point saying, "I don't know why you're not more fascinated with this. We could be living next door to a murderer," Larry quickly responds: "New York is a melting pot. I'm used to it."

When Keaton stepped into the role of Carol Lipton, the dynamics of the character changed, according to Allen. Carol was originally the straight, serious character while Larry was the one with the detective instincts. In his biography on Allen, Eric Lax explains that Allen wanted to write the part specifically to fit Diane's persona but couldn't because of the film's tight plot structure. So, instead of changing the script, "they simply swapped roles, with Woody transformed into the straight man, a solemn spoilsport, on the imminent verge of an anxiety attack, and Diane playing the more buoyant, fanatical half of the partnership" (Lax, *Biography* 238).

Though their interaction on-screen appeared perfectly easy and natural, Keaton said she initially had some trouble getting the part down the way Allen wanted it. Keaton immediately went to work with her acting coach, Marilyn Fried, to figure out what she was going to do with the role. She was "completely terrified," she admitted, but Allen, in his "totally honest, totally straight, nonsentimental" way, kept shooting until she got it right (qtd. in Clements 84).

In one scene, for example, Carol and Ted meet at the National Arts Club in New York's Gramercy Park where they discuss the case, as well as his feelings for her, over wine. By this point in the film, they are both convinced that Paul House has done in his wife. Larry has also set up a blind date between Ted and his femme fatale client, Marcia Fox. Carol, who is enjoying her sleuthing escapades with Ted, is trying to hide her pique at her husband's matchmaking, but Ted confesses that Carol, not Marcia, would be his first choice. Keaton must express several emotions at once here. She's flattered, excited, yet a little guilty because she's a married woman. Keaton says she did the scene many times because Allen said it just wasn't good.

Another sensitive area for Keaton seems to be the costumes she wore in the film. For the most part, Carol wears rather sophisticated suits, simple but elegant and appropriate for a woman of her socioeconomic status. However, Keaton wasn't comfortable with the wardrobe that costumer Jeffrey Kurland chose for her because it was too colorful. Keaton claims she doesn't like a lot of color: "It's too much at once. I like to do one thing at a time" (qtd. in T. Green, "Duds" D2). She does manage to make her own fashion statement with the wide belt she wears over one jacket and the chunky pearls that accessorize a loose-fitting pants suit.

One thing that didn't bother Keaton, however, was playing a character her own age. She was 47 when she made this film and obviously comfortable playing a middle-aged woman with a son old enough to attend Brown University. As Lax points out, "Her no-nonsense histrionics and refreshingly uncosmeticized appearance augment her character's daffiness and almost childlike enthusiasm to perfection" (240). Keaton has never been afraid to look unglamorous, if the role calls for it. In one scene, for example, Carol and Larry are lying in bed when she gets a yen to do a little investigating in Mr. House's apartment. With her rumpled nightshirt, tousled hair, and no makeup, Carol looks like she just got out of bed, as a nervous Larry tries to talk her out of going. "I command you to go back to bed," he whines. "I'm forbidding you to go." She leaves as he calls after her, "Is that what you do when I forbid you?" It's a funny bit made more realistic because of her willingness to sacrifice ego and appearance for the sake of the scene.

Like all of Allen's films, *Manhattan Murder Mystery* is an amalgam of his favorite film genres. Part murder mystery, part film noir, and part screwball comedy, the film pays homage to these genres to tunes like Cole Porter's "I Happen to Like New York" and Benny Goodman's "Sing, Sing, Sing." References to *Casablanca*, *Double Indemnity*, and *Rear Window* abound. And the end of the film is a brilliant tip of the hat to Orson Welles's hall of mirrors scene in *The Lady from Shanghai*.

By this time, Carol has dragged Larry into the game, along with Ted and Marcia. Together they solve the case, but it is this murder that breathes new life into their marriage. As Larry saves a bound and gagged Carol, he cries: "I'll never say that life doesn't imitate art again!" In the final shot, we see them literally turn the corner onto their street, laughing about their adventure. Carol turns to Larry suddenly saying: "You know, I love you, Larry."

LARRY: How could you ever be jealous of Marcia? Isn't that ridiculous? Don't you know that I could only love you?
CAROL: You were jealous of Ted.
LARRY: Ted? You're kidding. Take away his elevator shoes, his fake suntan, his capped teeth, and what do you have?
CAROL: You.

They both find this exchange hilarious as they enter the doors of their apartment building arm in arm, pals in art as Keaton and Allen are in life. The upbeat film and the experience of working with Keaton again helped Allen focus on something constructive and get through his troubles, as well as demonstrate to anyone who might have forgotten why they will go down in film history as one of the great comedy duos. Keaton received yet another Golden Globe nomination for Best Actress in a Motion Picture Comedy/Musical.

Look Who's Talking Now

Amy Heckerling's 1989 romantic comedy, *Look Who's Talking*, starring John Travolta and Kirstie Alley, about a pregnant accountant looking for a suitable father for her child, spawned two sequels: *Look Who's Talking Too* (1990) and *Look Who's Talking Now* (1993). Heckerling bowed out after the first two, vacating the director's chair to Tom Ropelewski. This last installment deserves mention only because it also stars the voices of Diane Keaton and Danny DeVito as Daphne and Rocks, one a high-strung poodle and the other a wise-cracking mutt. They not only save their pathetically inept owners, they also save the movie from going directly to the video graveyard with their canine antics. Keaton delivers some of the best lines in the film as the stereotypically snooty, slightly hysterical poodle who succumbs to the pedestrian charms of DeVito's Rocks. At one point, the pampered Daphne, who drinks bottled water, calls him a "tick magnet." When he takes her out in a "leashless state," she shivers: "I hate this haircut. My butt is freezing." On the search for her master who is stuck in her car in a snowdrift, a frustrated Daphne cries: "I'm just an in-bred washout. I can't even sniff."

According to Franz Lidz, whose biography inspired Keaton's *Unstrung Heroes*, his uncle, the gentle, child-like Arthur, was smitten with Diane Keaton. He wrote her many letters, which she responded to. One day, Arthur rented *Look Who's Talking Now* because he understood that Keaton was in it. He kept asking, "Which character is Diane?" Lidz kept telling him, "The one with the tail." Lidz writes: "Uncle Arthur wagged this around in his head awhile. 'She's a pretty good actress,' he said at last. 'I thought I was watching a real dog'" ("My Nutty Uncle" 72).

Unstrung Heroes

Producers Susan Arnold and Donna Roth obtained the rights to the Franz Lidz memoirs back in the late 80s; they just couldn't seem to find the right person to bring them to the screen. When Arnold and Roth saw *Wildflower*, they knew they had their director because of her combination of "emotional depth and wild crazy sense of humor" (qtd. in Mathews, "Secure" 3). They didn't want to sentimentalize the story about a young Jewish boy who must come to terms with a dying mother, a distraught father, and a pair of eccentric uncles. Keaton's experience with comedy and drama as well as her aversion to sentimentality made her a perfect choice.

Scripted by Richard LaGravenese (*The Fisher King* and *The Bridges of Madison County*), *Unstrung Heroes* opened on Friday, September 22, 1995, to stunning reviews. Jay Boyar of *The Orlando*

Sentinel wrote: "It's as astonishing a debut as Francois Truffaut's *The Four Hundred Blows* (1959), another great movie about growing up. How Keaton maintains that delicate balance between joy and sorrow is mysterious" ("*Unstrung Heroes*" 21). Richard Schickel of *Time* said that Keaton "knows how to touch on an emotion without squeezing every last tear out of it" ("Dysfunctioning" 68). And David Ansen of *Newsweek* captured Keaton's "guiding spirit" when he wrote: "You can detect her sensibility in every detail, from the California swapmeet style of interior decoration to her understanding of the outsider Steven's struggle to find his place in the world. He triumphs, as Keaton has in her varied career, not by blending in, but by letting his true, eccentric soul blossom" ("This Boy's Oddball Life" 90). The film also received a ringing endorsement from Cannes Film Festival audiences when it premiered in May 1995.

Only Franz Lidz seemed to be unhappy with Keaton's interpretation of his family memoirs. She had moved the setting of the film from New York to Los Angeles (for budgetary reasons) and had not retained enough of the Jewish flavor for Lidz. Keaton understood his objections: "If I had written a book about my life, and somebody did it, I think I would have a lot to say in terms of 'that's not right'.... I tried to be as honorable as I could to the material and make it work" (qtd. in Barnes, "Annie Hall in Director's Chair" E1). Keaton's version is more of a coming-of-age for both a father and a son who must learn to understand each other after they lose the one woman they both adore.

Several elements of the story attracted Keaton to *Unstrung Heroes* initially: the portrait of the mother, Selma (Andie MacDowell); the relationship between Steven/Franz (Nathan Watt) and his father (John Turturro) as well as his uncles Danny (Michael Richards) and Arthur (Maury Chaykin); and the idea of documenting memories as a way of holding onto family. She said once: "It's a way to take a look at what you lost, the person who meant so much to you, and letting them be there again for you. Then you don't lose them completely" (qtd. in Pearlman E1).

In the beginning of the film, which takes place in the late fifties and early sixties, Sidney Lidz (Turturro), a somewhat intense scientist/inventor who believes that "there's nothing broken that science can't fix," is the family historian. With his 8mm camera, he records the details and progress of the lives of his wife Selma (MacDowell) and two children, Steven and Sandy (Kendra Krull), systematically labeling each precious reel. The opening black-and-white home-movie footage clearly establishes Sid's own eccentricities and his love for his wife who is the emotional center of the family.

According to Keaton, it was difficult to cast the part of Sid because he had to be a man who would totally worship his wife—whose abject devotion to her and preoccupation with her illness would threaten his relationship with his son. She wasn't sure that John Turturro, who usually plays quirky, nerdy characters, would be believable in the role until she talked to him about his own mother: "He was so great talking about his mom that I knew he was going to be OK. And he was simply adoring of Andie" (qtd. in Mowe S9).

Selma is the intermediary between the two men in her life. Though father and son are very similar, they have a hard time understanding each other. From Sid, Steven learns that documentation is key and that "science is the only heroic path." For Steven's birthday dinner, Sid invents a machine that will reflect the stars and planets on the ceiling and walls. Keaton frames the scene through the kitchen doorway as the family sits around the table watching the circling heavenly patterns of light as they listen to Sid try to answer Sandy's question "What's the highest number?" The camera slowly pulls back on this tableau and cuts to Steven and his mother, who is tucking him into bed. In a tight, medium close-up, Steven asks his mother if his dad is from another planet. "Well, he could be," she smiles. "Your dad is a genius. Just be proud of him as he is of you." The tender moment illustrates Steven's attachment to his mother as much as her attempt to bring father and son together. Steven remarks on how good her hands smell when she caresses his face, and, when Selma leaves his room, the camera lingers momentarily on Steven looking at his hands.

Keaton said that she cast Andie MacDowell because of her ability to project warmth and sincerity as a mother, the kind of mother no one would want to lose. In fact, Keaton revealed: "I think that what struck me the most was the fear of losing your mother. For me it was sort of a Valentine in a way to her. What a great mom she was. That was the first thing that got me" (personal interview).

Early in the film, we see Steven dancing with his mother in the kitchen as she makes pancakes. She is the one who tells her son that "a hero is anyone who finds his own way through this life." She is the one who listens to a nervous Steven practice his campaign speech for class president. And Selma is the one who defends Steven's decision to be bar mitzvahed against her husband's objections that heaven exists only "in the minds of morons." Selma and Steven's scenes together illustrate her importance to her son and serve to explain his decision to live with his uncles, "just until you get better" he tells her.

Well before shooting ever began on *Unstrung Heroes*, Keaton knew exactly how she wanted the sets and family to look. According to one source, she hired an assistant and "went around to all the locations with a video camera, figuring out what she needed for every scene. Then she entered all the data into her computer and created a kind of bible, which she gave to her department heads with photos attached indicating the look she wanted" (Greenberg 20). The director shopped for props herself and even used some articles from her own collection, like the clown pictures over Uncle Danny's bed. Keaton claims that she really overprepared for the film, confessing: "I think if a really big problem presents itself and I'm not prepared, I can fall apart" (qtd. in Greenberg 20).

The result of her effort is a film, rich with details layered gently one upon the other. Nothing about the acting or pacing seems forced or artificial or obvious. And the humor and pathos arise subtly and naturally from the situations and behavior. In one scene, a paranoid Uncle Danny disrupts a gathering of family and friends upon Selma's return from the hospital. Entering the house through a window, he announces: "We were followed!" After raving on about a conspiracy, he notices Selma: "Selma, you look like death. You have absolutely no color. It's frightening. Why don't you go and get some air instead of sitting around here with these phony, miserable bastards." The scene is funny, shocking, and sad at the same time. Richards keeps a tight rein on his outrageous character, who is, in a sense, just as sick as Selma.

His personality is juxtaposed to the gentle Arthur's in the quiet scene that follows, as an upset Selma goes outside to have a cigarette. Arthur follows her, where they sit on a bench together under the rose trellis. He's brought Selma a special remedy to get rid of her itching. She just has to rub it on the infected area.

> SELMA: I don't have any itching, Arthur.
> ARTHUR: Danny had mentioned that something was irritating you.
> SELMA: Something is irritating me. If I rub it on Danny, will he go away?
> ARTHUR: I'm not sure. You'll have to read the label under "Other Uses."

The Lidz brothers, as Michael Richards explains, represent the mind (Sid), the spirit (Danny), and the heart (Arthur) (Mathews, "Secure" 3). All three eccentrics, they are bound by the idea of documentation. Sid uses scientific rigor to document the events that shape their daily lives. Danny lives in a world of newspapers, stacks and stacks of them, that detail shady government dealings and conspiracies against the Jewish people. Arthur documents what the world has lost in collecting what it casts off, the trash that nobody wants. Keaton says that she was drawn to the collector uncle the most "because I really understand that" (personal interview).

Steven is a composite of all three men. Lost and frightened, Steven enters another world when he opens the door of his uncles' apartment—a world where difference is accepted and celebrated. Keaton shoots him walking through hallways, made narrow by rows and rows of newspapers, to a room filled from floor to ceiling with family photographs. He opens another door, and hundreds of balls come tumbling out on him. When Uncle Arthur shows him his collection, Steven finds Arthur's dream book. "Dreams are like memories," Arthur tells him. "They're easy to lose."

It is Danny who first recognizes Steven's intelligence and potential and gives him confidence in himself, telling him "You're the one. You're the one to watch." It is also Danny who gives Steven a more fitting name, Franz, but the good and simple Arthur—the collector—empathizes with Steven's pain of losing his mother. Arthur still decorates his own mother's grave with trinkets and gifts. He gives Franz a special box to put things in. "Not Cracker Jacks or music," he says. "They've already got boxes for themselves. It's for more important things that you don't want to disappear." When Franz opens the box, it contains a photo of his parents on their wedding day, and thus begins Franz's own life of documentation.

He uses the box to collect memories of his mother.

Franz's escapades with his uncles provide a distraction from his troubles and allow his own eccentric soul to bloom. He helps Danny and Arthur foil a cigar-smoking Landlord Lindquist who wants the fire marshal to have them evicted. Franz comes up with a clever plan which he writes down with crayon in a notebook. While his uncles sleep, Franz takes out his flashlight and works on his scheme. He goes about it systematically, making two columns: Possible Ideas and Available Materials under the heading, The Lindquist Solution. His father would be proud of him.

To the delight of his uncles, the plan works, and Franz becomes one of them—something that is not lost on Selma when she receives a box of pancakes that Franz has sent her to show her how well they turned out. He rigs a basketball net to help Uncle Arthur catch the balls that flush down the sewer pipes. And he refuses to say the "Pledge" in school, singing "The Internationale" instead. "It's against my beliefs," he tells his teacher, who asks, "What does that mean?" In an echo of Uncle Danny's favorite phrase, he tells her: "It means what it means. How can I pledge my allegiance to a country that suffers fools, mediocrity, not to mention crucifying the Rosenbergs?"

Franz leaves his uncles a different person, returning home before his mother's death. In one of the film's most beautiful, sensitive scenes, mother and son finally talk about her death while sitting at the kitchen table after his bar mitzvah (an event his father refuses to document). Franz happens upon her sitting alone, with the light filtering through the window across her face. He runs to get the camera to record the moment. He tells her that she's beautiful, and she tells him that she's proud of him. "Do me a favor," she asks. "Try to love your dad. It's not easy being from another planet." Franz asks, "Mom, are you dying?" "Yes I am, Franz. I'm so sorry." He buries his head in her hands. In this brief, simple scene, Keaton elicits touching yet unsentimental performances from her actors, lending a realism to the moment that is almost unbearably heartbreaking.

After her death, Sid throws his reels of film in the garbage cans. Franz promptly retrieves them. The family finds him after the funeral projecting the collected images of his mother on the wall above her coffin. "It's not right to throw memories away," Arthur tells an angry Sid. "He just needs to say good-bye." In the end, it is these images that unite father and son and allow the family to grieve together. The theme of documentation is carefully threaded throughout the narrative, never intrusive but always present. "This theme moved me enormously and made me want to tell this story," Keaton says. "That and people who are unsung heroes, not Unstrung Heroes, but unsung heroes who get a chance to be seen and appreciated in some real way" (qtd. in "Greek Goddess" G1).

Today Keaton claims that she would like to direct more but has a long way to go.

> I think I need to learn a lot more. I don't think I'm ready for anything real big. Funny. Maybe funny. I do like funny. And I think I love behavior, and if the funniness is coming out of behavior, I think I could maybe handle something like that. But I don't want to stretch beyond what I'm comfortable with. It's a huge undertaking to direct a movie [personal interview].

She also has no intention of giving up acting: "I'd like to participate in both for as long as I can. It's really a privilege to be able to express yourself in some fashion" (qtd. in Bobbin 5). On December 14, 1995, three months after *Unstrung Heroes* was released, Keaton received a Muse Award from New York Women in Film and Television for her ability to express herself.

The annual award is for outstanding vision and achievement.

Keaton surprised most critics and audiences with *Unstrung Heroes*. Not many people even knew that she had been building up a portfolio of work behind the camera since the critical failure of *Heaven* because she did it so quietly, without making a fuss. Writers and interviewers alike began to play up the intelligent, artistic, courageous characteristics of her persona and downplay the neurotic and shy. Critics talked about her natural talent for directing, but Keaton knew better. She had worked hard, educated herself, prepared, observed other directors, and drew on her knowledge of still photography. In the second half of the nineties, she had more work than she knew what to do with, both as an actress and a director. She was also taking on a new challenge, a new role: motherhood.

CHAPTER 8

1996–1999

The Artist and the Icon

I'm just glad to be in the movies. I'm amazed I'm still working. Sometimes, I'm just amazed I can take care of myself.
—Diane Keaton (*Star Tribune*, Sept. 20, 1996)

Diane Keaton's career gained momentum in the mid-nineties. By the time the century wound to a close, she had made seven films: *The First Wives Club* (1996), *Marvin's Room* (1996), *Northern Lights* (1997), *The Only Thrill* (1998), *The Other Sister* (1999), *Hanging Up* (2000), and *Town and Country* (2001). She directed and starred in *Hanging Up*. Her fourth photography collection, *Local News*, was published in the fall of 1999. Keaton also took on a new challenge in her personal life. Shortly after finishing *Unstrung Heroes*, Diane Keaton, who had played a mother in 11 of her films, adopted a baby girl, Dexter.

Keaton's old friends Woody Allen, Warren Beatty, and Al Pacino had all adopted or fathered children late in their lives.

We were all late developers. You know, we postponed life in a way. We wanted to act and be involved with things, but postponed our own participation in it. And I'm happy for them because I think that it's like putting your foot in life and say-

ing there's more than just the success of it [qtd. in Dowd, "Old Pals Act" 6].

Daughter Dexter brought a welcome change in Keaton's life. "It's turning my life upside down, which is good. It needs it," she says (qtd. in Westbrook, "Keaton Says" 9). Keaton joined the ranks of stars like Michelle Pfeiffer, Rosie O'Donnell, Jamie Leigh Curtis, George Lucas, Linda Ronstadt, and Nicole Kidman and Tom Cruise who also adopted children in the recent past. When she's working, she simply packs up Dexter and her nanny and takes them on location with her. "I don't have a choice," she says. "I have to make money" (qtd. in Westbrook, "Keaton Says" 9).

Keaton sold her Lloyd Wright home in the Hollywood Hills after becoming a first-time mother and moved to Beverly Hills. She bought a 1926 Spanish Colonial Revival, designed by Wallace Neff, that was in danger of being leveled. Keaton, who enjoys the whole buying and restoring process, worked with friend and interior designer Stephen Shadley, completely renovating the home, inside and out, and retaining its authentic California architecture and landscape. Trolling antique shops and swapmeets, Keaton found just the right pieces of vintage Monterey furniture and period art for her hacienda. The July 1999 layout in *Architectural Digest* reveals the home's open, clean, uncluttered style, filled with light. She says that the family spends most of the time in the kitchen and the pool. "This house is all about indoor-outdoor living," Keaton states. "It's that whole California lifestyle that I love because this is where I grew up" (qtd. in Collins, "*Architectural Digest* Visits Diane Keaton" 88).

From the bleached cement floors to the front yard covered with lavender and olive trees, the house stands out from the stately homes nearby. It is as distinctive and original as Keaton herself. Even her choice of homes reflects a person sensitive to the castoffs and the unwanted in society, as her remarks to Nancy Collins indicate. Bemoaning the fate of Jimmy Stewart's nearby Tudor, which was destroyed after his death, Keaton said of her own: "I saved this house, and I'm glad I did. I hope that, someday, when I leave, somebody doesn't tear it down. They shouldn't be allowed to do that" (qtd. in Collins, "*Architectural Digest* Visits Diane Keaton" 172).

Hollywood history is filled with stories about stars who have sacrificed family for career, but Keaton seems to have found a balance. Yet her lifestyle is far from conventional. Resigned to the fact that she may always be a single parent, Keaton vigorously points to society's waning prejudice against spinsterhood as a step in the right direction.

I think in the past women picked men first, or they didn't have a choice. You know, I always think about the issue of being an old maid. I remember when I was a little girl thinking "My God, it's just like a tragedy to be an old maid."

That's what's been handed down to you is the old maid, and, technically, I'm an old maid. I mean, I realize now that I've never been married, and I'm just the old maid. Of course now my feeling about what the old maid is is just like "What does that mean?" Of course, that's ridiculous. You can't label somebody as the old maid anymore and, certainly, I don't find it a pitiable situation. It's sort of a bad label. Those gross generalizations probably now don't even come up. You can spend your life and not be married, and people don't go, "Oh, she's an old maid" [personal interview].

Keaton seems content with her personal life and her career today. She may not make *Entertainment Weekly's* list of the top 25 most powerful stars in Hollywood, but, by anyone's standards, Diane Keaton is a success. She has learned how to navigate fame through a high-profile service industry, keeping a clear distance between her private and professional life. If she has sacrificed romance and marriage for fame and privilege, she doesn't seem at all bitter or regretful. In her typical no-nonsense way, she simply says "no one gets everything"—and moves on.

First Wives Club

In the early nineties, Keaton thought she was "finished" as a leading actress. Ironically, *Unstrung Heroes* changed all that. Her success as a first-time feature film director thrust her back into the spotlight, reminding other directors that the actress was still around. Keaton tends to keep such a low profile that Hollywood forgets she's there.

In 1996, she made two important films in her career: *The First Wives Club*, a financial success, and *Marvin's Room*, a critical success. *The First Wives Club*, directed by Hugh Wilson, is a comedy that spoke to millions of divorced women in America. It became a catharsis and call-to-action for women of a certain age whose husbands had cheated, lied, and dumped them for younger women. *Marvin's Room*, directed by Jerry Zaks, is a drama about a single, middle-aged caregiver who discovers she is dying of cancer. The role won Keaton her third Academy Award nomination, as well as Golden Globe and Screen Actors Guild nominations, for Best Actress. On the whole, 1996 seemed like a replay of 1977, the year Keaton made two entirely different films, *Annie Hall* and *Looking for Mr. Goodbar*, back-to-back.

Perhaps even more interesting, *The First Wives Club* and *Marvin's Room* illustrated the current development of American movie-making. As Louis Giannetti and Scott Eyman have observed in *Flashback: A Brief History of Film*, "movies of the 1990s have tended to develop in two directions: vast, expensive bread-and-circus entertainments for the mass audience, and small, personal films with critical approval and specialized audiences" (536–37). Not many actors have the opportunity to cross back and forth between the blockbuster and the independent film. Not many actors want to take the risk. Those who do, like Nick Nolte, for example, are noted for their versatility as well as their commitment to their art. In short, they do not take on a role for money or exposure alone. They look for substantive parts that not only expand their range but also prevent acting ennui. Keaton has been fortunate enough to experience both: "I feel like I had a terrific opportunity to play two very different parts in one year.... As an actress, that's all you can hope for" (qtd. in Baldwin 44).

The First Wives Club, adapted for the screen by Robert Harling from Olivia Goldsmith's bestselling novel of the same title, kicked off the London Film Festival in 1996. Released in September, it dominated U. S. boxoffice receipts in its first few weeks and hit the $100 million mark in its 64th day ("*First Wives*," St. Petersburg Times B2). It was an instant hit. Women threw preview parties. Some even arrived at theaters in limos and in evening wear (Gleick 80). According to one source, the film became "a favourite subject of discussion at Manhattan dinner parties, where details of New York's most expensive divorces are followed as closely as the latest fashions from Paris or Milan" (Katz, "Screen Revenge" 11).

The First Wives Club received an enormous amount of press coverage. Along with her two costars, Goldie Hawn and Bette Midler, Keaton was featured on the cover of *Time*. Collectively and separately, they granted interviews for virtually every major magazine, newspaper, and television talk show in America. The film also spawned a slew of sidebar articles about real-life first wives and their travails. In short, *The First Wives Club* struck a chord with female audiences, many of whom were fast becoming an all-too familiar statistic.

Keaton confesses that she has no idea why this particular film created such a stir with audiences.

> I really don't know about audiences. I really don't understand any of it at all. For example, why was *The First Wives Club* such a big hit, which hadn't happened to me for years and years and years and years and years? And why was something like *Baby Boom* not? I don't get it. I mean within its own terms, I don't even understand why something works, why something doesn't work, why something just hits a button, and really just goes berserk or not. I mean, I don't know. I don't know. Maybe in *Baby Boom*, it's just me, and we didn't have Goldie Hawn and Bette Midler. I don't even know [personal interview].

The note of self-doubt and modesty has a way of creeping into a Keaton comment. She is her own toughest critic. *Baby Boom* did eventually find its audience on video and has become an enduring classic. But while it is true that the Keaton-Hawn-Midler dynamic might have had something to do with *The First Wives Club*'s instant success, there were other contributing factors.

Producer Lynda Obst noted that the film's phenomenal success was part of an entire "year in which women audiences became a factor in the marketing and production of movies" (qtd. in Waxman B7). Sharon Waxman added:

> The key to the shift, most seem to agree, is the growing number of female executives at the studios where movies are conceived, financed and carried out. Market researchers have long considered women to be important decision-makers in moviegoing, but it is only very recently that Hollywood started to make movies primarily to attract them [B7].

According to a 1997 survey on women in film conducted by *Premiere* magazine, 50% of New Line Cinema's vice-presidents and above were women, with Sara Risher as chairman. Women accounted for 60% of New Line's other creative executives. Paramount Pictures, headed by Sherry Lansing, came in second with women holding 44% of the vice-presidencies and above and 50% of the other creative executives slots ("Creative Executives" 51).

Since *Premiere*'s first survey in 1993, many studios have shown similar increases in the numbers of women employed in all facets of the movie-making business. Monica Johnson, long-time comedy writer and coauthor of Albert Brooks' *Mother*, starring a 64-year-old Debbie Reynolds, said in 1997: "All the development people are women now.... I don't think I had a meeting with a man all last year" (qtd. in Peterson E2). Keaton herself says, "They're really making huge steps for women. There are just more and more women directors, more and more producers in every walk of movie making and that's good. That's incredible. I'm proud of that" (personal interview). And as *Premiere* Editor-in-Chief James B. Meigs explained in the 1999 Women in Hollywood issue,

It's growing harder to remember that when *Premiere* published its first Women in Hollywood issue back in 1993, women were scarce in the upper ranks of the movie business, and movies that openly addressed female concerns were scarcer still. Today, the situation couldn't be more different ["Editor's Letter" 14].

What does it all mean? More movies for, by, and about women. Hollywood is finally noticing the huge baby boom female demographic sitting in the audience.

Produced by Scott Rudin, *The First Wives Club* is about four college friends who go their separate ways after graduation—and get traded in for younger models by their selfish, scheming husbands. Cynthia (Stockard Channing) marries a Wall Street tycoon, who leaves her for a blond trophy wife played by Heather Locklear. Elise Eliot Atchison (Goldie Hawn) becomes a movie star who is all too aware of the three ages in Hollywood: "Babe, District Attorney, and Driving Miss Daisy." But no amount of "freshening up" can buy her youthful parts or hold her conniving husband who has ridden to fame and fortune on her coattails and who has left her for a younger version of herself. Annie MacDuggan Paradis (Keaton) marries advertising hot shot Aaron (Stephen Collins). Separated after 25 years, he seduces her one night and asks for a divorce the next morning so he can marry their marriage counselor, Dr. Leslie Rosen (Marcia Gay Harden). Brenda Morelli Cushman (Bette Midler) is a housewife still in love with Morty (Dan Hedaya), her appliance-king husband who is living with a social-climbing, gold-digging ditz named Shelly (Sarah Jessica Parker). The friends reunite after the discarded and depressed Cynthia takes a leap off her penthouse balcony and discover what can happen when they join forces and get tough. Like the female characters in *9 to 5* or *Girls Town* or *The Color Purple*, they find strength together. Elise tells Annie and Brenda in one scene: "All we need is us. Three women who aren't afraid to fight, to stand up for our dignity, our self-esteem—and then we'll let them have it!"

Goldsmith—who has also written *Flavor of the Month*, *The Bestseller*, *Marrying Mom*, and *Switcheroo*—says: "In the Olivian universe ... everybody gets what they deserve. My books have been described as revenge novels, but I think what is really at their center is compassion" (qtd. in Bargreen E1). Keaton agrees: "The real core of the movie is affection. There's life beyond the grave of a dead marriage" (qtd. in Westbrook, "Keaton Says" 9). The friends not only exact revenge on their ex-husbands but also help each other through difficult times and ultimately channel their anger into something more constructive by opening The Cynthia Swann Griffin Crisis Center for Women.

The film also exposes the myth of the ideal American family, the bill of goods sold to women that said if they just stuck to the script and remembered their place all would be well. The opening credit sequence immediately underscores this conflict in the film. Dionne Warwick sings "Wives Must Always Be Lovers Too" as characters right out of fifties and sixties romance comic books roll by with the credits. Annie, Elise, Brenda, and Cynthia are mired in the mentality of an era when a man was the center of a woman's universe.

Twenty-five years later, they are disillusioned to discover that the center won't hold. The song reinforces everything they've been told, like "Don't send him off with your hair still in curlers—you may not see him again." They bought into the idea that a woman's place was right behind her man, right or wrong. Brenda kept the books for Morty during the lean years. Elise pushed her husband up the corporate ladder. And Annie gave Aaron a daughter and starched his shorts. By the end of the film, they have a new anthem: Lesley Gore's 1963 hit "You Don't Own Me," written and composed by John Madara and David White. Shoulder to shoulder, they sing an up-tempo version of the song and dance off triumphantly into the night, empowered by their friendship.

John Anderson of *Newsday* argues that the movie works because Hawn, Keaton, and Midler are "actresses with gravity. With star power. With well-defined personae that are permanently projected in the very private screening room of the mass American psyche" ("The EX Files" 10). The daffy blond, the wise-cracking redhead, and the neurotic brunette clicked on screen. They were an ensemble casting director's dream: different enough in physical appearance and demeanor to be interesting, yet alike enough in professional behavior and sensitivity to submerge their egos for the sake of each others' performances. Goldie Hawn said: "There is a level of respect we have for each other that transcends any level of competition of who's better" (qtd. in Schappell 48). Keaton added, "We are all exactly the same age—50, and so it felt really familiar, like I was back in high school" (qtd. in Schappell 46). Those expecting cat fights on the set were disappointed.

Keaton's Annie is the linchpin of the trio, the peacemaker. Most of the time she is framed between Elise and Brenda, two strong-willed, sharp-tongued characters. Though affectionate towards each other, Elise and Brenda hurl verbal zingers at each other while the insecure, often verbally inept Annie gets caught in the crossfire. Keaton says there is no mystery to why she got the part of Annie: "*Insecure, insecure*. I don't have to guess why I got the part. I *know* why I got the part" (qtd. in Wloszczyna, "*Wives*" D1).

Keaton projects Annie's insecurity in her every move and gesture. For example, after Cynthia's funeral, the three friends gather for lunch and drinks at a restaurant. Though the camera cuts back and forth between the women, Annie is in the center. She is in denial about her relationship

The First Wives Club (Paramount, 1996). Keaton gravitates to female ensemble films like *The First Wives Club*, in which she acts opposite two other screen icons—Goldie Hawn and Bette Midler. In what became a call-to-action film for dumped and divorced first wives and a renaissance of sorts for middle-aged actresses, Keaton plays the insecure and neurotic Annie Paradis, a housewife who has devoted her life to raising her daughter and supporting her ad-executive husband (Stephen Collins). He seduces her one night and asks for a divorce the next morning. Annie's college friends, Elise (Hawn) and Brenda (Midler), have suffered similar fates, but together they get mad and get even. Annie, the mediator, is often positioned between the more outspoken, often bickering, Elise and Brenda. Female audiences cheered them on and made the film one of the year's biggest box office hits.

with Aaron. As the drinks flow, they discuss Cynthia and their own situations. But while Elise and Brenda lay their problems right on the table, Annie refuses to admit that her own marriage is in trouble and that her daughter is a lesbian until it all comes tumbling out sideways in this confession:

> Everything is just fine, really. I mean, Aaron is just so terrific, and, well, let's think. Ah, we've been ... for, ah, 25 years. Click, click, click. Yep. And, uh, Chris is just perfect. I mean, lesbians are great nowadays. And, ah, well, the marriage is just ... it's just going to be really fine. Aaron and I are, well, just, we're, um, temporarily, sort of, we're just a little bit—we're separated.

Few, if any, actresses can deliver this kind of dialogue. The combination of *what* Keaton says with *how* she delivers the lines elicits the humor. This entire speech, for example, begins by fits and starts as she hems and haws, goes one way and then another, until the last two words—which come out loud, fast, and clear. Keaton is also a very physical actress, punctuating a phrase or underscoring a word with a head movement or finger waving in the air, imbuing her characters with what sometimes seems an astonishing array of mannerisms. Keaton's style is not easily duplicated, as Bette Midler found out on the set of *The First Wives Club*: "I always thought she was a consummate performer, and I never knew *how* she did *what* she did. And then I spent three months watching her, and I *still* couldn't figure it out!" (qtd. in Gerosa, "Girl Talk" 135).

In another scene, the inhibited Annie is lying on the couch talking to her therapist, Dr. Leslie Rosen, author of *Get What You Want ... And Look Beautiful Doing It*. She tells Annie to repeat after her: "Work from love. Grow from love. Screw the world." But Annie, with her WASPish bob, wire-rimmed glasses, and starched, tailored ensembles is too ladylike and shy. She can't say those last three words. Dr. Rosen tells her she has a problem with unexpressed anger, so she has Annie take out her anger toward Aaron on her. Uncomfortable and reluctant at first, Annie taps Rosen with a foam rubber club and then builds to a wild frenzy as she pummels the stunned doctor. Annie surprises herself, too, and immediately says, "Oh, I'm so sorry. Please don't tell Aaron." One critic described Keaton's style as "cerebral zaniness" (Delmont SF 39). Another wrote: "Keaton, who can spin from disciplined and delicate social portraiture to gibbering hysteria to head-spinning silliness without pausing for breath, is an unmitigated joy to watch" (Campbell, "Light and Lively" LAG 29).

Two scenes in particular illustrate Keaton's range. When Aaron calls to arrange a dinner meeting with Annie, she thinks he wants to get back together. She tells her mother: "I bet it means that he has reprioritized. He's worked through all his relationship phobias. His fear of intimacy. His thing about my, you know, my poisoning his food, and is ready to recommit." Annie wears a smashing long, black dress and looks so good that Aaron seduces her. The next morning as she is getting dressed, Annie tells him, "We should get therapy gold stars." Aaron has other plans. He wants a divorce. "But we just made love!" Annie screams.

AARON: I asked you out to tell you, but you looked so great. It was so romantic. I thought, gee, one last time. Don't be childish. You know how you manipulate me.
ANNIE: Manipulate? What!? Oh, my God, is there someone else?

Just then, Dr. Rosen walks in and all hell breaks loose. Annie is flying around Aaron's apartment, gathering up her things while Rosen is telling Aaron that Annie is allowed to be angry and apologizing to Annie at the same time. Finally, Annie's unexpressed anger bubbles to the surface and spews out in a voice that escalates to a high-pitched wail:

So am I! I am sorry that I ever met you. And I am sorry that I allowed myself to love you all those years. I'm sorry that I did nothing but be there for you every minute of every day and support you in your every move.

All the while she is edging for the door where she turns and shouts "I'm sorry!" at the top of her voice as she storms out and slams the door on their astonished faces. Keaton is funny and touching all at the same time. The last shot in the scene is Annie crying as she waits for the elevator. Keaton says she had a great time doing the scene: "When I was much younger, the words I used most in my life were, 'I don't know' and 'I'm sorry.' And to actually be able to say, 'I'm sorry,' meaning 'Go f__ yourself,' was the most fun I ever had" (qtd. in Wloszczyna, "*Wives*" D1).

In the second scene, Keaton uses slapstick to convey her character's fear of being caught at something illegal as well as her fear of heights. When the three devise a plan to get into Morty and Shelly's apartment and steal some papers that may incriminate Morty, they almost get caught. What happens next is like an escapade from a Three Stooges comedy. They are trapped in Morty's office when Annie becomes hysterical. Out of control, she blubbers and gibbers, her arms and body and head moving wildly in different directions, as she starts to slide down the wall, Brenda and Elise catch her. They pull her out onto the balcony and push her, still screaming, onto a conveniently available window-washing scaffold. The remote gets stuck, however, and they end up flying down about 40 stories at top speed. Annie, hair standing on end, grabs the remote from Brenda and finally stops the runaway scaffold just in time.

While Keaton loved doing the physical humor in the film, she is probably best known as one of Hollywood's great reactors. Anyone starring opposite talent like Hawn and Midler must be able to react, or register the impact of what they are saying or doing. Much of Keaton's humor comes from her ability to register sincerity and gullibility in the face of the absurd. In one scene, Annie goes with Brenda to her son's bar mitzvah only to discover that Morty has brought his mistress, the brazen Shelly, wearing a red dress and a fur coat. Brenda is devastated: "He brought her to my son's bar mitzvah," she whispers to Annie who nods in sympathy and innocently asks, "Is she a gift?"

In Annie's revenge scene, Keaton gleefully reacts to Stephen Collins's Aaron as he goes from incredulous to outraged to pleading. With Elise's help, she has bought Aaron's ad agency. Sitting at the conference table, Annie is wearing a pinstripe power suit and a superior smile as she watches the arrogant Aaron get his comeuppance. As she gets up to leave, a desperate Aaron follows her to the door:

> AARON: Is that all you can do is think of yourself, yourself, yourself? If you go through with this, I'll have nothing. No one's going to want me. I'm 45 years old. I'd have to start from scratch.
> ANNIE: (Feigning a sympathetic nod) I know just how you feel. (Pause) Oh, Aaron. (Gives him one of Dr. Rosen's cards) Grow from love.

The First Wives Club, was like a shot of adrenaline for Keaton's career, and perhaps for the careers of other 40-plus actresses. The success of the film and the popularity of its three stars led to talk of a sequel, *Avon Ladies of the Amazon*, inspired by a *People* magazine article that revealed the Amazon jungle as the fastest-growing market for Avon products ("*First Wives*," *Chicago Sun-Times* 20). To date, the reteaming of the three queens of comedy remains just talk.

Marvin's Room

Marvin's Room, directed by Jerry Zaks, was adapted for the screen by Scott McPherson just before he died of AIDS in 1992. The movie was based on McPherson's play of the same title which was first produced at the Goodman Theatre in 1990. The vivid characters are drawn from his life and the compelling themes from his personal experiences with dying. McPherson and his lover, who also had AIDS, found a kind of spiritual fulfillment in taking care of each other, and therein lies the uplifting but deceptively simplistic message of the film, best summed up by the words of "The End," the Beatles' tune, which goes "in the end, the love you take is equal to the love you make."

Keaton told Larry King that *Marvin's Room* is more than just a sweet little film. "It deals with delicate issues. It deals with family matters, young people growing up, all the things that we all have to deal with. There is humor in it. It's also touching." In the wrong hands, such films tend to devolve into melodramatic tearjerkers, but *Marvin's Room* is poignant and compelling, without being sentimental, mostly because of the honest, natural performances of the film's incredible ensemble cast which includes Robert De Niro (co-producer) as Dr. Wally; Meryl Streep (Lee); Leonardo DiCaprio (Hank); Marvin (Hume Cronyn); Aunt Ruth (Gwen Verdon); Dan Hedaya (Bob, doctor Wally's brother); Hal Scardino (Charlie); and Diane Keaton as Bessie.

The title of the film refers to McPherson's grandfather, the bedridden Marvin, who suffered from Parkinson's disease. McPherson's elderly, ailing, and slightly daffy Aunt Ruth lived with Marvin in Florida while Aunt Bessie devoted her life to caring for them both (Guthmann, "This Is a 'Room' Full" D3). In the film, when the middle-aged Bessie learns she's dying of leukemia and her only chance for life is a bone-marrow transplant, she must contact her estranged sister Lee and Lee's two sons, the young Charlie and the troubled teenager Hank, who travel to Florida to be tested. In the end, none of them are suitable donors, and Bessie faces her death the same way she has faced life: with grace and pluck. Her foremost concern is that no one will care for her elderly relatives when she's gone, and her humanity eventually reconciles a suffering, angry, divided family. The key to Bessie is that she sees caregiving as a privilege.

Keaton said of Bessie: "I've never seen a more heroic character come my way" (qtd. in Baldwin, 44). "She's a brave, courageous, warm, loving person, and I've never really played anybody like that," she told another reporter (qtd. in Sumner, "Blooming" C1). The comments offer a rare glimpse into Keaton's perception of herself, and, while perhaps she hasn't played characters as saintly as Bessie, Keaton does have a long history of enacting characters whose lives are not typically chronicled in movies.

Marvin's Room was actually shot in the fall of 1995 before *The First Wives Club*, though both films were released virtually back to back. *Wives* came out first in September of 1996 while *Marvin's Room* debuted in December of the same year. In fact, it was Keaton's work in *Marvin's Room* that led to her role in *The First Wives Club*. When the producer of both films, Scott Rudin, saw her work in *Marvin's Room*, he gave her the script for *Wives*.

Keaton's role as Bessie, however, was not as easily won. The story goes that Harvey Weinstein, head of Miramax, refused to consider Keaton, until Meryl Streep stepped in. It was Streep who insisted Keaton play the part of Bessie. According to one source, Streep threatened to walk if Keaton wasn't her costar. Streep said: "If there's anything good about being old, it's that you get a say about who gets to be in (the film) with you" (qtd. in Karen Thomas, "Keaton's Age of Anxiety" D1). Director Zaks, who also supported Keaton, said: "Because they would be playing sisters, the idea that Diane was someone Meryl really wanted to work with seemed an important element" (qtd. in Pickle E1).

Streep was a long-time fan of Keaton's. They had both starred in Woody Allen's *Manhattan*, but had no scenes together. When *Marvin's Room* came along, Streep knew Keaton was the best choice for Bessie:

> She has no cover on her emotions.... And because her work always contains an element of sadness—even the comedies— I thought Diane had the right sensibility to play Bessie. She's just incapable of doing anything phony [qtd. in Guthmann, "Keaton Gets" E1].

Originally cast as Bessie, Streep ultimately opted to play the angry, tough, controlling, self-absorbed Lee who throws herself into the rigors of beauty school because she can't deal with her difficult son, Hank. With *Marvin's Room*, Streep wanted to play someone vastly different from her own personal experiences. "In my life, I am the good daughter, the responsible one. I wanted to be that bad daughter" she confessed (qtd. in Steffan F1). Streep won a Golden Globe Nomination for Best Actress in a Drama for her role as Lee, but Keaton received the Academy Award nomination for Best Actress plus a Screen Actors Guild nomination for Best Actress in 1996.

Keaton has nothing but the highest praise for her costar.

> To me, Meryl is from another planet. She's incredible. She's a brilliant technician, but then she's also a radiant, brilliant woman. She's a beautiful woman. She's a great heroine, and I don't think there's anybody like her at all. I think she's an amazing creature [personal interview].

Together, along with Leonardo DiCaprio, they defy cliché and lift their characters and the story to that plane of absolute believability, though their acting styles are very different. As Eleanor Ringel wrote in her review of *Marvin's Room*, they play off of each other beautifully and "their performances are a study in contrasting styles—intuitive naturalism vs. expertly filtered technique" (P1). DiCaprio, Keaton says, is a combination of both. She explains:

> I don't do accents like Meryl Streep. I come from another place. I come from, you know, a spontaneous moment really and how I'm connecting with my acting partner. So it's totally different, and, as far as Leonardo goes, he is an actor who is brilliantly inventive. And he also is a mime. You know, she's a mime. I mean they're mimics. They can copy anybody. Both of them. And he is a genius at just imitating other people's behavior instantly. And that's like, you know, how impressionists do famous people. Well Leonardo can do anyone—the DP on the set, the cinematographer, and do him better than anybody's ever done him. I just think we haven't seen what he can do. I think he's unbelievable. He's right up there with her [personal interview].

Elaborating on her own acting style, Keaton says:

> I was always in these classes. I was always able to take off of other people's behavior. I was always able to respond to whatever was given to me, but I was very general. I remember that this was my big problem, and he [Sandy Meisner] was constantly harping on me about that. In

other words, I didn't really work hard enough on what it was—my objective in a scene or what it was I was trying to say—and he used to really bang on me for that, and, of course, we all lived in total terror of him. I mean he was a great man, and we were just students and would we be asked back next year. I mean that's all the first-year was about was would we be asked back. I knew that I had just sort of good spontaneous behavior. I knew I could do that, but shaping a part and thinking what I really wanted to say with it and what I wanted to do with it—I wasn't good at. No [personal interview].

It was a lesson that Keaton learned over the years, and with Bessie she finally felt like she was the author of her own work.

She credits Streep, however, for talking her into doing a scene that she felt was just too emotional and "corny." Lee and Bessie are in the kitchen talking when Bessie receives a call from Dr. Wally, dashing her last hope for a successful transplant. Hank's bone marrow is not a match. She tries to act brave, but Lee, sensing the fear and disappointment underneath, grabs Bessie in a hug while upsetting a tray of pills onto the floor. As they both bend down to pick them up, Lee is crying and Bessie tries to comfort her.

> BESSIE: (Smiling) Oh, Lee. I've been so lucky. I've been so lucky to have Dad and Ruth. I've had such love in my life. You know, I look back, and I've had such love. Such love.
> LEE: They love you very much.
> BESSIE: No, that's not what I mean. No. No. I mean that I've loved them. I've been so lucky to have been able to love someone so much.

Keaton refused to say the lines, arguing that they were too sentimental and unbelievable. Streep tracked Keaton down in her trailer and convinced her that the lines were important and that she could pull them off.

In several interviews, Keaton has confessed that Streep and Zaks were right. It worked so well that the scene became Miramax's publicity clip for the film. When Oprah Winfrey replayed the scene during her interview with the Oscar nominee, Keaton couldn't watch herself: "The material is stronger than my own aversion to myself," she told her host. "I don't like to look at myself on film." She admitted that Meryl had been right and she had been wrong about saying those lines. She also told Larry King that in order to work up the necessary tears and emotional level for the scene, she listened to Whitney Houston's "I Will Always Love You" over and over again on her headset. It was music that helped her through the tough scene, just as it had many years ago in *Looking for Mr. Goodbar.*

The portrait of Bessie rings true because Keaton was willing to take an artistic risk. There is no makeup or soft-focus lens here to hide the lines in Keaton's face. The close-ups are unforgiving. She looks exhausted and worn and worried and ~~~~~~ Her ensembles are dowdy, not

a simple, old-fashioned ~~~~ knows exactly who she is and what her responsibilities are" ("Actors" B3).

For example, Bessie is reluctant to call Lee after twenty years, but she has no choice if she wants to live, a desire driven

Marvin's Room (Miramax, 1996). The old double standard still exists in Hollywood. In order to be taken seriously in the business, beautiful and brainy *and* talented actresses often look for roles that downplay their attractiveness. They "de-glam," taking off the makeup and eye-catching costumes, in an effort to draw attention to the character and performance. Farrah Fawcett, golden-haired member of *Charlie's Angels* and pin-up goddess of the '70s, gained overnight respect for her raw, gritty portrayal of a rape victim who exacts her revenge in the Broadway play *Extremities.* The usually stunning Susan Sarandon won a Best Actress Oscar for playing a nun who tries to save the soul of a convicted killer in the film *Dead Man Walking.* Keaton, perhaps like Bette Davis before her, has never been known as a glamorous actress and will do whatever it takes to make the part authentic. In most of her roles, she wears little makeup and prefers more natural hairstyles. As Bessie, the middle-aged caregiver dying of cancer, however, she lets all the wrinkles show. Her wig is simple and easy to care for while her clothing is functional and nondescript. Bessie is a woman with little time to spend on herself, as her whole appearance suggests. Keaton's ability to capture the inner soul of this woman, her goodness and selflessness, evident in this shot, won her an Academy Award nomination for Best Actress.

by her concern for her elderly relatives. She is filled with resentment for Lee who, as Bessie sees it, has abdicated her familial responsibilities. When they meet again, the anger, fear, and resentment reignite—on both sides. Ever conscious of her looks, Lee spends extra time preparing for the moment, practicing what she's going to say in front of a mirror while she applies her makeup and a hair extension. Bessie, however, has spent no time on herself and greets Lee with an armful of soiled laundry from Marvin's room.

At this point, Bessie is surprised and relieved to see Lee, but too many hard feelings stand between them. Her greeting ends up hitting Lee exactly where it will hurt: "Oh, goodness. Oh, my goodness. Oh, look at you. Are you that old? ... 'Cause how old does that make me then?" She dismisses Lee's offers to help care for Marvin or Ruth with comments couched in resentment, like "Oh, no. I've been doing it this long." She offhandedly rejects Lee's gift of cookies for Marvin and Ruth, saying: "Oh, Dad and Aunt Ruth can't eat them, and I am trying to stay away from sugar now ... but this is just a lovely canister."

Meanwhile Hank and Charlie are still outside, sitting in the car listening to loud music. Lee explains that Hank is just trying to get attention and that he hasn't agreed to be tested, another ploy to get attention. He will, though, because she will make him. Bessie quickly responds: "How are you going to make him, Lee? You can't make him come in from the car." Bessie's meeting with her nephew is funny and sweet, which only serves to underscore the tension of her reunion with Lee as well as the animosity between Lee and her son. Bessie goes out to the car and knocks on the window. Hank immediately turns off the radio. As Bessie smiles at him, she says: "I'm your Aunt Bessie who you've never laid eyes on, and I don't care how grown up you are I expect a big fat hug."

Bessie is able to reach out to Hank because they have no past wounds to heal, and he responds to her innate warmth and compassion. In one scene, Hank takes Bessie on a ride through the surf. Bessie squeals with delight, and the two return soaking wet, still laughing. Keaton and DiCaprio also had a great on- and off-screen chemistry. Keaton has said that she couldn't wait to see him every day, while DiCaprio, who also rarely gives interviews, admitted his feelings about Keaton on the *Oprah Winfrey Show*:

> I never felt more funny in my life. She cracked up at everything. She has the greatest laugh in the world, and I had a crush on her. I'm sure everyone else in the world does too. She's a fantastic lady and one of America's greatest actresses.

Their scenes together show Lee what her relationship with her son might be, and it is only through Bessie and their concern for her that mother and son finally reconnect and begin to understand each other.

Bessie's credo is "You're supposed to take care of family!" which she screams at Lee in frustration. Lee sees Bessie's life as wasted. She wants no part of caring for Dad or Ruth. "I'm finally getting my life together," she tells Bessie. "Nobody's going to take it away from me." But even Lee begins to respond to Bessie's example, and, as the defenses drop, the sisters begin to reach out to each other.

Much has been written about the "I've had such love" scene; however, the two actresses share what is perhaps a more privileged on-screen moment when, sitting at Bessie's dressing table, Lee offers to fix Bessie's wig and Bessie tells Lee about Clarence, a carnival worker and the love of her life. The two are seated in medium close-up, with Bessie occupying the left of the frame and Lee the right. They are facing each other, and, as Bessie begins to tell the story, the camera moves in to a tight shot of her face.

Marvin's Room (Miramax, 1996). Though these two icons of American cinema both starred in Woody Allen's *Manhattan*, they had no shared scenes. Seventeen years later, their mutual dream of working together finally materialized when Streep insisted that Keaton play good sister Bessie to her bad sister Lee in Scott McPherson's drama about family and responsibility. Bessie's credo, "You take care of family," is in direct conflict with Lee's: "I'm not going to waste my life." Their opposing viewpoints are reflected even in their physical demeanor. Although Bessie considers caring for her ailing father and aunt a privilege, her hunched posture suggests that she has shouldered the responsibility over the years. Worry over who will take care of them when she's gone has deepened the lines around her mouth and eyes. The self-absorbed, almost flippant Lee sits smoking in the doctor's waiting room, oblivious to how her actions might affect others around her. She has made something of her life, and she has the cosmetology degree to prove it. She deals with family issues by not dealing with them. As Lee tells one of her clients, "There's no reason to be nervous—ever—as long as you have a positive mental attitude." Lee's mantra, however, is as empty as her smile until Bessie shows her what courage and family really mean.

BESSIE: He was only around during the summer. He mostly ran the ferris wheel. He had the funniest laugh. He would open his mouth real wide and no sound would come out. (Keaton imitates Clarence's ape-like appearance and wide-mouthed laugh.)

LEE: What happened?

BESSIE: Well, you know how they used to have that last picnic down by the river? Well, Clarence goes swimming, and he knows everybody's watching him and everybody's there—his family and friends ... and me. And he's laughing. He's making that monkey face. (Keaton makes the face.) That. And, you know, and he gets all of us laughing. And so then he dunks under the water and laughs, up again and he's laughing even harder, and then he dives under again. And then he doesn't come up, and he doesn't come up, and he ... doesn't come up.

LEE: (Stops laughing) What?

BESSIE: (Laughing and crying at the same time) Oh, God. We were just standing there watching.

LEE: Oh, my God. You should have told me.

BESSIE: We were never that close.

LEE: We weren't?

BESSIE: No.

In this moment of shared intimacy, the sisters find the closeness they never had growing up. The scene is beautifully acted on both parts. Keaton peels away the layers of Bessie's personality revealing a woman who finds humor in the absurd but whose emotional intensity and sense of tragic loss save Clarence from an undignified death. Her expression reveals her grief as well as the realization that her own death cannot be far off. In a symbolic gesture of trust, Bessie then takes off her wig, the last layer of defense, and hands it to Lee. In doing so, she exposes the grotesque side effects of her chemotherapy and finally allows Lee to see her vulnerable and weak. Lee's defenses also crumble at the image of Bessie sitting there, her remaining tufts of hair straw-like and matted. Streep's reaction is perfectly believable as Lee pretends not to notice and then makes up an excuse to leave the room just so that she can catch her breath. At that moment, they both realize and acknowledge that Bessie has just transferred the mantle of caregiver to Lee.

In the end, *Marvin's Room* is more life-affirming than depressing. The pathos is laced with wonderful, humorous lines as when Bessie tells Dr. Wally about Marvin and Aunt Ruth:

> Dad's dying. He's been doing it real slow, so I don't miss a thing. Aunt Ruth suffers from crippling back pain, but she has an anesthetizer now. Any time she uses it, our garage door goes up, but that's a small price to pay, don't you think?

The absent-minded Dr. Wally, played by De Niro, and his bumbling brother Bob (Hedaya) also provide bits of low-key humor, understated enough so that they don't seem tacky or intrusive; otherwise, the comedy might trivialize the serious issues.

Indeed, the film never trivializes the lives or concerns of these characters. It's more likely that the subject matter hit close to home for many people sitting in the audience. *Marvin's Room* is a rare and realistic portrait of two women, two sisters, who give each other strength, courage, and hope. In the face of sickness and family quarrels, anger and sibling rivalries, Bessie teaches Lee what family means and Lee actually finds herself in helping someone else. The final tableau shows a family united through the courage of both sisters. Keaton calls her work in *Marvin's Room* one of the great experiences in her life and her character one of the most heroic.

Northern Lights

Written by John Hoffman and Kevin Kane and based on Hoffman's one-man stage play, *Northern Lights* was a script without a future, until Diane Keaton got involved. Like many screenplays, it had been kicking around Hollywood for a long time. "Nobody, nobody, nobody wanted it," Keaton said. "Too small, too small, too small" (personal interview). But once she read it, she was relentless in her efforts to bring it to the screen because the material meant so much to her. Keaton and her business partner, Bill Robinson, along with Meg Ryan's partner, Nina Sedowski, who owned the rights to the material, shopped it around town, but, again, "nobody would buy it," Keaton said (personal interview). Finally the Disney Channel offered to do it in hopes that Keaton herself would direct, but she chose the executive producer's seat and a starring role instead.

> We thought, hey, we want to do this, so let's do it—and we did. We did it for not much money. We went up to Vancouver, and we just sort of did it. And I don't think anybody saw it, but at least we got to do it. I'm really proud of the fact that we did [personal interview].

Keaton brought in Linda Yellen (*Playing for Time, Liberace: Behind the Music*) to direct the film which premiered on the Disney Channel on August 23, 1997.

The story is actually set in Bright River Junction, a small town in Vermont filled with an assortment of oddballs, most of whom hang out at the King Edward Hotel. There's the desk clerk who keeps ringing the bell after every sentence because he likes its tone; a rat-faced bellhop who hides his face behind stacks of towels or food trays; a comatose old man who sits in an upstairs hallway soaking his feet; a hairlip (Hoffman) who must repeat everything twice; and Daphne, an ethereal romantic who can't carry a tune. "I've always been drawn to outsiders," Keaton explained. "I was in love with the uncles in *Unstrung Heroes*. In this one, I'm in love with the town" (qtd. in Appelo 114).

Bright River Junction is the Valhalla of the unwanted. When one of their own, the kind-hearted Frank who owns the local junk shop, dies while trying to rescue Sassy the Cat, the whole town rallies around Frank's bereft nine-year-old son, Jack (Joseph Cross), a child consumed by guilt that his father should die while trying to rescue his cat.

In carrying out his will, they send for Frank's sister, Roberta Blumstein (Keaton), and his best friend, Ben Rubadue (Maury Chaykin). It seems Frank has appointed them the boy's guardians, without their prior knowledge, and they strenuously resist their new role as caregivers. Not that Jack isn't a sweet and wonderful child. He is sensitive and wise for his years. Scared, yet trying to make the best of the situation, Jack tries to make conversation with Roberta and Ben, only to be ignored or rebuffed. He takes refuge on the roof of the hotel contemplating phenomena like the northern lights, or aurora borealis, those luminous, mystical bands of electrically-charged light that show up in the northern skies—in their own time.

Frank knew what he was doing in bringing Roberta and Ben to Bright River Junction. They are oddniks and lost souls in need of home and family. The high angle shot of their arrival is shrouded in darkness and mist and confusion as they wait at the station for a ride to the hotel. But their world and life changes once they walk through the gates of the King Edward, and they are bathed in the glow of a thousand twinkling lights. The town works its magic on them, and, like the northern lights, Ben and Roberta show their true spirit in their own time.

Rotund and gentle, Ben's pain stems from his divorce. His wife left him six years ago, and his children are all grown up. Since the only thing he was ever good at was "being a father," his life now seems empty and meaningless. Ben is working at a boring, thankless job in a grocery store in Florida when he gets the call about Frank's death and heads north. He keeps leaving pathetic messages on his ex-wife's answering machine about what he should do or wear until Daphne sets her cap for him and literally draws him back into the world of the living.

Keaton says of her costar: "He was a genius in *Northern Lights*. He was a romantic in there. I think he's a great actor" (personal interview). The innocent, child-like quality that we saw in Chaykin's Uncle Arthur of *Unstrung Heroes* serves him well in his portrayal of Ben, whose kindness and fatherly instincts blossom in Bright River to the point that he decides to stay with Jack. In one charming scene, the two sit on a pair of swings, talking and bonding, when suddenly they turn upside down, feet flying in the air, laughing at the trick Frank taught them both.

Roberta, on the other hand, is in many ways unlike any character Keaton has ever played. With her platinum blond, bobbed wig, dark-rimmed glasses, and brassy, faux Chanel suits cut way above the knee, Roberta certainly *looks* unlike any of Keaton's former characters—and her behavior is as outrageous as her appearance. Roberta is a bitchy, prickly,

cynical klutz—or, "an asshole," in Keaton's
words. Unrestrained, Roberta puts her
mouth and body in high gear before thinking about the impact of her words or actions on the people around her. For the
part, Keaton combines her genius for slapstick and her facility with fast-paced,
crackling dialogue to create the kind of
over-the-top, "total idiot" that she has
always wanted to play. Costar and writer
John Hoffman noted: "Diane's taking
risks she hasn't before.... We're talking
hard-edged" (qtd. in Appelo 114).

The tough, chain-smoking Roberta
works as a Manhattan telephone operator fielding ridiculous questions from
ignorant callers about Broadway plays
with cynicism and disdain. Roberta's
outward behavior, however, masks a
wound caused by a rift she had twenty
years earlier with her brother Frank,
whom she raised after their parents died.
Together they developed a successful cabaret act until Frank decided to quit the
show because the demanding lifestyle left
him feeling empty and unfulfilled. It gave
the simple, sweet-natured Frank little
time to contemplate the wonders of the
universe, like why a robin's egg is the perfect shade of blue. When Roberta receives
the call about Frank's death, all the suppressed memories and feelings about her
brother and the future that could have
been begin to surface in ways that she
can't control once she arrives in Bright
River Junction.

Roberta's defense system collides with
the openness and naiveté of the town's residents. That she feels superior to them is
evident from the beginning. "Doesn't all
of this seem a little like that show Rod Ser-
ling used to host?" she asks Ben on the
way to their rooms. In another scene, she
snickers and giggles when Daphne leads a
choir of whistlers at Frank's memorial service. When the will is read in an elementary school classroom, Roberta sits on a
child's chair and falls over backwards,
bruising her leg and running her nylons

and prompting the following diatribe before the attorney and Ben.

ROBERTA: Oh, my God! This is ludicrous.
Okay?
BEN: We can't lose sight of the fact that
there is an orphaned boy here.
ROBERTA: Well then, okay, fine. You take
him. Where do I sign? I came up here
thinking that my brother had left me
some of mother's china or a gravy
boat ... but a son! I mean what does
that mean anyway in the scheme of
things? All right? By the way, it's impossible to give custody of a child to
a person without their prior consent.
So I am going to call my lawyer in
New York City, and he's going to take
care of this, believe you me. I'm not
staying in this godforsaken town any
longer than I have to.

The monologue is bitchy enough, but
Roberta's next comment to her nephew is
downright mean. Jack, sitting on the steps
of the schoolhouse when Roberta haugh-
tily exits, simply asks: "Do you know your
way back?" She responds over her shoulder: "I happen to be from New York City,
darling. I can figure it out."

At every turn, however, Roberta's
snootiness is punctured by some bit of
slapstick that peels away the layers of
pretense. There's a real heart beating underneath all the caustic comments and superior airs. Keaton has never played a
character who is a total asshole, and in
this film it's the comedy that humanizes
Roberta. Keaton explained in one interview:

People spill things on her.... She's constantly falling down and being hurt. She
gets trapped in an elevator. She ends up
a mess. It's wonderful. What she held so
dear—like her rip-off Chanel suit—just
isn't important at all [qtd. in Solomon
42].

The elevator scene is particularly funny
as Roberta, stuck between floors, is shot
from the waist down. We see only her legs
in their ripped stockings flailing around

the elevator while she screams for help. At one point she drops her "one-of-a-kind scarf from Bloomingdale's" into the elevator shaft. Jack finally comes to her rescue. In another scene, she loses one of her heels in a swinging bridge and shows up at a memorial picnic for Frank in black high top sneakers and her Chanel suit with food stains all over it. But the more contact Roberta has with Jack, as well as the townspeople, the more her defenses break down.

She is not simply a cartoon. Keaton, who often plays characters with conflicting traits, gives us the flip side, the emotionally confused but caring woman underneath, in several touching scenes. While Roberta dines with Ben in the King Edward Hotel's lounge, for instance, Daphne coerces her to get up and sing, something she hasn't done since her cabaret days with Frank. Keaton's voice is lovely, deeper, more mature than in her earlier films. But part way through "What'll I Do," Roberta bursts into tears and runs out of the lounge and into the solarium, tripping over a tray on the way, with Ben and Daphne in pursuit. "Do you know, I haven't sung that song in years," she tells them. "I haven't even thought about that song.... I'm sure you think I'm a cold person for not just opening up my arms to my nephew ... and, I just can't!" she screams. Jack, who has been listening to her sing from the rooftop, cries too.

At the picnic, Roberta finally reveals her feelings toward her brother to Jack when he asks why she was so angry with his father. As the two sit on a bench in the garden, Roberta begins: "I guess I've been hurt and angry for so long. I guess I got used to feeling that way. But, Jack, I loved your dad so much. We made a good team once, too. The truth is, I didn't want him to leave." She puts her arms around Jack, but when he asks if she will stay, she says, "No, you don't understand." Jack runs from her, saying: "Yes I do. You still want to make my dad feel as bad as you did."

It takes an accident to jolt Roberta back into the world of the living. That evening, just as Roberta is about to catch a train back to New York, Jack tumbles from the roof of the hotel and hangs precariously by a piece of falling spouting. Ben and Roberta run toward him immediately. Frank's faith in the two has not been misplaced. While Ben runs to the roof, Roberta calms Jack and gets the residents to lock arms and catch him, surely a symbolic gesture that suggests their solidarity in raising Frank's child. Roberta sweeps Jack up into a tight embrace, rocking him, as they simultaneously mourn a father and brother and find each other.

The final scene is literally a celebration of life. Roberta has a costume party for Jack's birthday, documenting the occasion (much like Sid Lidz does in *Unstrung Heroes*) by videotaping their cadre of friends wishing him well as the northern lights make their magical appearance in the night sky. A bit corny, the film is nevertheless great family fare, teaching children important lessons like respecting and appreciating the things that make us different from each other and forgiving those who are closest to us. *Northern Lights* also represents Keaton's passion for family themes and her belief that good material and good roles aren't necessarily the domain of the big screen. She once said: "There are lots of them [acting jobs] out there ... and it doesn't matter where you play them" (qtd. in Gardella, "Few Complaints" 44).

The Only Thrill

Despite its premiere as a feature film in February, 1998, *The Only Thrill*, directed by Peter Masterson (*The Trip to Bountiful*), seemed destined for the small screen. It caused little critical stir and, after a limited run in the theaters, shot straight to the video stores where it isn't exactly in high demand. Those stores that do carry it are few. The film had a seasoned director and an excellent cast, including Diane Keaton (Carol Fritzsimmons), Sam Shepard (Reece McHenry), Diane Lane (Katherine Fritzsimmons) and Robert Patrick (Tom McHenry). Adapted for the screen by Larry Ketron from his play *The Trading Post*, the film also had an intriguing story within a story. It should have worked, but, as Keaton has pointed out, it just didn't (personal interview). What went wrong?

Several factors worked against the success of *The Only Thrill*, which Keaton calls "a very small movie with a very adult theme" (personal interview). First, it is a downbeat story, ponderously long and depressing. The film spans 30 years in the life of a couple who can never really be a couple. Reece McHenry is a land developer and vintage clothing shop owner whose wife has been in a coma for years. He meets the local seamstress, Carol Fritzsimmons, and the two carry on a long-term love affair until she moves to Canada to take care of her sister who is ill. They meet sporadically over the years, but, essentially, Reece won't leave his wife. He can't commit to a full, loving relationship with Carol and realizes too late what the theme song keeps telling us: "Time is a stealer. You learn if you're lucky never waste a day. Love is the thing you don't save for a rainy day."

In the film's opening sequence, Masterson makes the point visually that these characters can't connect. In a series of medium, long, and extreme long shots, we see Reece in his white convertible and Carol in her blue Volkswagen beetle pass each other briefly as they drive along the same road but in opposite directions. Their lives intersect over the next three decades, but, inevitably, they end up going their separate ways.

His son Tom and her daughter Katherine fall in love at one intersecting point, and their story begins to run parallel to that of Reece and Carol's. It looks like they are traveling down the same metaphorical road as their parents; however, in the younger generation, it's Katherine who can't commit to the relationship until years later when she realizes what her mother and Reece have lost. With Reece's help, Katherine and Tom are saved, but, by this time, we are so worn down by the plodding events of their lives that we barely notice the ever-so-slightly uplifting ending.

As Linda Seger points out in *The Art of Adaptation: Turning Fact and Fiction into Film*, when a movie covers a long expanse of time, the drama and focus tend to dissipate. "When too much time has elapsed in a story, it becomes difficult to bridge events. Transitions from one year to another are essentially nondramatic, and usually consist of words across the screen such as FIVE YEARS LATER. If we're seeing only events that are far apart in time," Seger argues, "we begin to lose their relationship and the story becomes episodic, rather than developmental" (55). This is exactly what happens in *The Only Thrill* which opens in 1966, fast-forwards to 1978 and then jumps to 1990 and finally 1996. Instead of one dramatic incident in the lives of these characters, we have a series of vignettes that tend to lose their intensity over time. Not even Reece's outburst of anger and remorse over time wasted or his crazy effort to bring Tom and Katherine together can revive the film's waning energy.

The aging process of the characters also poses an inherent problem in a narrative of this breadth. In this case, it is doubly problematic. Keaton and Shepard were both in their fifties at the time the film was made. Their characters meet in their early forties and must age thirty years. Masterson solves both problems with varying degrees of success. When Carol and Reece first meet, for example, he keeps the characters in full- to long-shot or with their backs to the camera. There are no close-ups, especially of

Keaton, to reveal the facial lines. We never get a close-up of Carol's face in the opening sequence, and, when she strides into Reece's store to ask for work, her back is mainly to the camera. Her long, straight hair with bangs and her dark glasses cover most of her face in the profile shots as she speaks with Reece, standing behind the counter.

Most of the scene is played out in a high angle shot, far enough away to preserve the believability of a couple approximately 12 years younger than the stars themselves. When the characters must face the camera, Masterson uses a soft focus lens in the medium shots. The overall effect of these de-aging techniques is to distance the audience from these characters. We never get in close enough to connect emotionally with them until later in the movie. The characters are much more believable in their later years, however, largely due to expert makeup work. Keaton and Shepard spent two hours a day in makeup for some of these scenes.

Another problem stems from the focus of *The Only Thrill*. Most successful Hollywood scripts involve a hero who wants something tangible, a visible goal, which he or she reaches by overcoming some obstacle, opposition, or conflict. The actions build toward a climax in which hero and antagonist confront each other. The hero risks everything, puts it all on the line, overcomes the inner doubts and fears, and finds the courage to reach for the goal. Sometimes he/she succeeds, sometimes not, but, in most cases, the conflict is visible, giving the audience something to root for. *The Only Thrill* is about internal landscapes, the inner feelings and motivations of these characters, which can be difficult to convey. There is no real action because the conflicts are internal.

There are also no discernible heroes in the film, so it's hard for the audience to know who to cheer for. Seger cautions: "Be careful of material where your main subject is his or her own worst enemy. If the subject causes his or her own problems, we may lose sympathy" (56). Reece McHenry is such a character. On the one hand, his refusal to abandon his comatose wife can be seen as honorable, but as his mistress and best friend's wife tells him: "If somebody starts getting too close, you have got the perfect excuse, the perfect responsibility, just lying up there in that hospital bed." Stoic and stubborn, he begins his relationship with Carol by stating "I'm still married," a status that she accepts for 12 years until she tests his feelings for him by moving to Canada to take care of her sister.

They have spent years in harmonious bliss, the perfect companions, obvious soul mates, yet Reece doesn't see the irony in his reaction to Carol's announcement that she won't turn her back on her sister. "She can't ask you to change your whole life," he says incredulously. Carol's situation mirrors his own. He has changed his whole life for a woman who will never wake up. (At this point, the audience wonders if Masterson misses an opportunity in not making the issue of euthanasia the focus of the film.) On his one trip to Canada to visit Carol, Reece complains, "You knew you were breaking us up," with no thought to how his own situation has affected the woman he really loves, or his own life for that matter. After Carol leaves, he becomes virtually comatose himself, sitting amid the ruins of a once prosperous clothing shop, doing nothing but staring into space or watching videos.

When Carol moves back to Texas after her sister's death, a spark of life returns when they meet and he helps her hunt for an apartment. Reece extinguishes the spark himself, however, when in a heated argument about their past Carol asks him, "Who was the love of your life?" They are standing in front of a giant, sliding-glass door. Beyond them is a patio surrounded by a brick wall, a symbol of where their relationship has come to. Reece knows what Carol wants him to say.

He also knows that his response couldn't be more untrue, yet he says the words that destroy them anyway: "My wife." Six years later, when it's much too late, he finally clings to her, crying: "You're the love of my life. You are." By this time, anger and frustration replace any sympathy we might have for Reece, a blind and foolish man. He is a passive hero whose one good deed is to keep his son from making the same mistake he did.

Carol is certainly a more likable character and somewhat more sympathetic. Like Bessie in *Marvin's Room*, and like Keaton herself, she believes in taking care of family. She has the maturity and self-confidence of a woman who experienced the nightmare of an abusive marriage and survived. Her personal misfortunes have not made her bitter; instead, Carol seems determined to make the most of her life and supports herself and her daughter as a seamstress. She is no one's fool. After their first afternoon together, Reece shows up at her door that evening, unannounced, and is upset that Carol is entertaining someone else. When he voices his displeasure, Carol matter-of-factly tells him: "We had sex on the bathroom floor. You barely said a word to me. You left. I had no idea you were coming over here tonight ... and I have a guest. Excuse me. Goodbye." That high, sweet, unsure, child-like voice that marks so many of Keaton's characters has been replaced by a lower, deeper, surer register, as Carol shuts the door in his face.

The next day, when a sullen Reece thinks they've had a fight, Carol sets him straight:

A fight is when you and your husband exchange blows. When the house is destroyed. When the horrible words you scream at each other echo years and years later. When he gets into a car and drives it off into the night to burn to death on some highway. And when your only daughter forever has screaming nightmares, Reece. That's what a fight is.... We had a few ... words.

This is one of the strongest characters Keaton has ever played, but the softness and the beautiful smile that she is noted for surface as Carol and Reece's love affair blossoms. She gets him to *do* things like go to the movies in the middle of the afternoon, take a week-end trip to his cabin that he hasn't visited in years, or let her take his photograph. They play movie trivia games, walk along the street arm in arm, and talk over drinks. Masterson often shoots them in the same frame, at an intimate distance, suggesting their compatibility and closeness. Keaton infuses her character with an enthusiasm for life which, for a time, gives Reece a reason to live.

In one scene, for example, Carol and Reece reconnect after she returns to Texas at their favorite bar, at their favorite table. They sit in the same positions, but nothing is the same between them. Still vital and vibrant, Carol enjoys keeping busy and is trying her hand at writing mystery novels while Reece does "hardly anything." He has moved into his store, the only place he likes to be because she was there.

Always a brilliant reactor, Keaton expresses conflicting emotions of love, pain, regret, anger, and sympathy simultaneously as she realizes what a wasted existence Reece leads. With her long hair streaked with gray and gathered in a braid to one side and wearing a hip but tasteful leather jacket, Carol makes no pretense about her disappointment in him: "Oh boy, Reece. When I first met you, you were driving a Cadillac." The only response Reece can make is a petty recrimination: "Your sister hung on a long time," to which Carol quickly responds: "Well, not as long as some." Reece still doesn't get it. He still doesn't see the hypocrisy in his comments like "You gave up a lot for her." The audience identifies with Carol's frustration over how any man can be so slow-witted.

Keaton and Shepard—two actors

known for their offbeat, intelligent performances, for their tendency to choose projects that challenge them as actors regardless of monetary rewards, and for their closely guarded private lives outside mainstream Hollywood—work beautifully together in their third teaming. Neither are known for their superstar egos, but rather for being there for their acting partners. They project sincerity and naturalness in a broad range of emotions for the other to respond to. And, though they do not possess the god-like beauty of a Cary Grant or Grace Kelly, they photograph well. Their interesting, expressive faces command our attention. They look comfortable together, they fit, and their timing is impeccable. Shepard, in fact, says working with Keaton again was a dream (Westbrook, "Made in Texas" Houston 1). "We've got a great working relationship.... She's just a thrill to work with—no pun intended" (qtd. in Westbrook, "For the Love of a 'Thrill'" 19). Unfortunately, in this case, they transcend their material. As Emanuel Levy wrote in *Variety*, "The most interesting aspect of *The Only Thrill* is the unresolvable tension between the rather dazzling screen personae of its stars and the colorless, dreary roles they are asked to play" (Rev. *The Only Thrill* 55).

With a 25-day shooting schedule and a total budget of under $4 million, the stars worked fast and for less, largely because they believed in the project. Shepard, a playwright himself, was drawn to Ketron's play and his script because "genuine love stories without sentimentality and gushing are difficult to find," he said (qtd. in Westbrook, "Made in Texas" Houston 1). However, as Keaton has pointed out, the subject matter may be "interesting" and "wonderful"—"but, you know, it didn't work" (personal interview).

The Other Sister

Keaton's next film, *The Other Sister*, did work, not that the box office receipts were any indication. Released in February, 1999, the movie made a mere $27.8 million in theaters before its rather successful debut at number 11 on the video rental charts in September, a short seven months later. It would seem that, like *Baby Boom*, *The Other Sister* found its audience on video. One thing that might have kept people away from the theaters was the film's confusing tag line: "A love story for the romantically challenged." Part romantic comedy and part family drama, nobody knew what to expect. The film doesn't fit into any specific category or genre, and, with ticket prices on the increase, audiences today are less likely to plunk down their money unless they're sure of a good thing. A few dollars on an unknown video doesn't seem as wasteful or risky.

Directed by Garry Marshall, the man responsible for two of the highest grossing romantic comedies of all time (*Pretty Woman* and *The Runaway Bride*), and cowritten by Marshall and Bob Brunner, *The Other Sister* is a story about the joys and frustrations of human relationships, family relationships—exactly the kind of story Keaton would be drawn to. The external conflict is between mother and daughter, and the inner struggle is for human dignity, independence, and understanding. True to Marshall's style, he treats these serious issues and situations with heavy doses of humor. Here's how Keaton describes the film:

> It was kind of a serious but sweet, with funny elements to it, look at this family, but basically it's about Juliette Lewis, my daughter. It's about her. She's a slightly retarded, or mentally challenged, young girl, and it's about how she finds love with this other boy. The obstacle in the movie is me. I'm like a mean mother [personal interview].

She says this almost gleefully because the role presented another challenge, another risk for Keaton in that for most of the film, she plays an essentially cold, critical, dogmatic woman. The warmth and vulnerability that characterize so many of her performances surface only fleetingly at the end of the film.

Many critics shared Keaton's assessment of her character, Elizabeth Tate, describing her as a snobbish, overprotective, manipulating bitch. On closer look, it's not so easy to judge Elizabeth Tate. Like most good writers, Marshall has a tendency to put two diametrically opposed people in the same room and make them both right. Elizabeth may be an overprotective, controlling socialite, but she does care about the welfare of her family, especially Carla (Juliette Lewis), the other sister, who is slightly mentally challenged but stubborn and defiant. Like her character Roberta Blumstein in *Northern Lights*, Elizabeth has an essentially good heart; circumstances have just hardened it a bit over the years.

Elizabeth moves among the rich and famous of San Francisco. She has a wealthy husband, Radley Tate (Tom Skerritt), a successful dentist whose father built the country club; a beautiful home in the San Francisco hills; and three daughters: Caroline (Poppy Montgomery), Heather (Sarah Paulson), and Carla. She also has impeccable taste. Her tailored, designer suits in shades of brown from cinnamon to taupe reek of money and refinement. Her hair, always under control, is often pulled back into a chic chignon. Keaton has never looked this elegant in a film. The family housekeeper, Winnie (Juliet Mills), keeps the home immaculate while Elizabeth keeps up on the latest news in the art world and supports all the right causes, from AIDS to animal rights.

Elizabeth gauges her success by how many plaques the city has given her. The problem is that Elizabeth's philanthropic work doesn't necessarily extend to her family. Engaged daughter Caroline finds nobility in being an elementary school teacher, but Elizabeth asks her: "Isn't it just as noble to be a college professor and earn four times the money?" Beautiful daughter Heather is a lesbian and wants to bring her partner Michele to her sister's wedding. Mom doesn't want to hear it. "I know what being gay is, okay. I give to gay causes. I support gay parades. They even gave me a plaque," Elizabeth says. "So why support them and not me?" Heather asks. "Because I'm not their mother," Elizabeth shoots back.

Later in the film we learn that Elizabeth started out as a dental hygienist who married her boss. And while the kind, easygoing Radley, born into this society, seems comfortable in his own skin, his wife is unyielding and edgy and obsessed with the social strictures of the upper class. In one scene, Elizabeth and Radley are out on their sailboat. Dressed perfectly appropriately for the occasion in white slacks and shirt with a white bowler hat (a nice Keaton touch), Elizabeth confesses: "I feel like I'm the mother of a dedicated underachiever, a gay workaholic, and Carla, who thinks she can conquer this whole terrifying world." Radley tries to reassure her: "Honey, they're doing fine. They're not drug addicts. They're not axe murderers. They're not democrats." Not good enough for Elizabeth. She's still worried. "It's not fair," she whines. "First you're judged as a person, and then you're not just judged as a person, but by how well your children are doing—not who they are, not what they think, but how well they're doing."

Elizabeth desperately wants to fit in this world, but she also has a wound, a source of pain that, according to screenwriter Michael Hague, underlies a character's outer motivations. In a flashback early in the film, Elizabeth forces Radley to sign the papers admitting Carla to an expensive private school for the mentally challenged. Her decision is prompted by an incident in which a young Carla pushes a boy down a flight of stairs because he teased her about her disabilities. Carla hates to be laughed at. Marshall's low key lighting in this scene gives Keaton and Skerritt an illusion of youth. Shadows fall across their faces as Elizabeth argues that Carla could really hurt someone next time, or burn the house down. A distraught Radley signs the papers, sending his daughter to Roselake School and then retreats into a world of alcohol for a time.

Consumed by guilt, Elizabeth throws herself into her charitable work until Carla returns eight years later. Elizabeth can assuage her conscience by "making it up" to her daughter. However, the things that all well-bred young women study—tennis, chess, bridge, art, the art of shopping— don't interest Carla. She wants to attend Bay Area Polytech, a vocational school, and eventually become a veterinarian. Mom has other plans. In fact, the tension between these two characters is established as soon as Carla walks in the front door. Elizabeth tries to take her coat, and the first word Carla says to her is "NO!" Yet she hugs Winnie and tells her she missed her.

It gets worse. Elizabeth has redecorated Carla's room, pitching the "little girl things" like her daughter's tea party table. Carla is not happy. She wants her old room back. "I really think that you should live with these things for awhile," Elizabeth tells her. "I'm sure that you will grow to like them very much." When Elizabeth takes Carla along on one of her recognition luncheons for the Animal Rescue Shelter, chaos ensues. Carla pants and barks at the dogs. "Elizabeth, your daughter is barking," one woman caustically observes as Carla turns a pen full of yowling strays loose on the group of incredulous socialites.

Elizabeth has no allies in her family. They all rally behind Carla. Even Carla's doctor tells Elizabeth that she is smothering her daughter. "I give her love, I protect her, I teach her and suddenly that's smothering?" Elizabeth returns. But the doctor explains that Carla doesn't want to do any of the things Elizabeth wants her to do. "They don't work for her," he says.

> ELIZABETH: Maybe she doesn't know what works for her.
> DOCTOR: And you do?
> ELIZABETH: I think so. I'm her mother.
> DOCTOR: This is a girl who is determined to push the edge of the envelope. I for one like the fact that she never quits. She wants to attend Bay Area Polytech…. Independence can give Carla something that you and I will never be able to give her—dignity.

Elizabeth may be the nemesis character in this film, but she is not altogether wrong when it comes to Carla nor is she a totally unsympathetic character. Carla does keep pushing the envelope. She gets her way and goes to Polytech. She meets Danny, a young man who is also mentally challenged, perhaps a bit more severely than Carla, and who loves marching bands. They fall in love. Then Carla wants her own apartment. Her father and her sisters think she's ready to be on her own. They want to vote on it, but Elizabeth steps in. "This is not a political referendum," she scolds. "This is a child's life, and this is my child's life." Her concern for her daughter is genuine; it's the way she expresses it that Carla and the rest of the family object to.

After a huge row, Elizabeth finally caves in to their wishes. Sitting alone at the dinner table, Elizabeth watches them come in one by one, wearing the necklaces Carla has made for them. Carla hangs back. "Oh, come on. I'm going to try to see it your way," Elizabeth tells her. A joyous Carla practically knocks her out of her chair with a hug and kiss and a "You can help me pick out my apartment, Mom." With a reserved smile, Elizabeth folds her hands and says: "Okay, maybe we will. Maybe I could do that. Is everybody happy?"

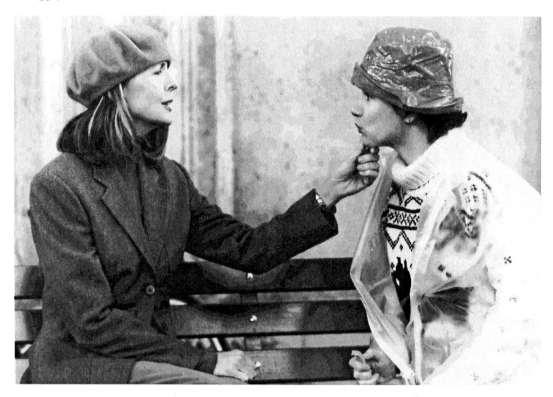

The Other Sister (Touchstone Pictures, 1999). Keaton has never been afraid to play unlikable characters. The aloof Renata (*Interiors*), the selfish Mary Wilke (*Manhattan*), the driven Louise Bryant (*Reds*), the misguided Charlie (*Little Drummer Girl*), and the bitchy Roberta Blumstein (*Northern Lights*) come quickly to mind. In most cases, we're never totally alienated from these women because their basic decency and flicker of warmth keep us pulling for them. In *The Other Sister*, she plays Elizabeth Tate, a social-climbing control freak whose obsession with appearances is in direct conflict with her genuine concern for her mentally challenged daughter, Carla (Juliette Lewis), who wants to live on her own. Here, Elizabeth tries to quiet Carla who loudly and proudly proclaims the meaning of coitus. Elizabeth's maternal instinct manifests itself in smothering, manipulating, and dominating her daughter, as well as the rest of the family. When they all rebel, she accepts defeat with humor and good grace. Keaton, who usually plays middle-class women, looks stunning in one of her few ventures into the upper class.

Keaton is marvelous here in portraying a mother torn between wanting what's best for her daughter and wanting her family's good will. Although she frequently plays a naturally warm and affectionate mother to her on-screen children, this time Keaton delivers a finely controlled performance where the affection is almost warped by her character's obsessive worry over her daughter's safety and well-being.

Elizabeth tries to do the right thing. Afraid that men may take advantage of Carla, Elizabeth initiates a "sex talk" with Carla while sitting on a park bench. Wear-ing an elegantly tailored, cinnamon-colored pants suit with a matching coat and beret, Elizabeth attempts to find out if Carla actually knows what "doing it" really means. Carla, looking all of 12 years old in her red plastic rain hat, assures her mother that indeed she does, as she explains loudly and in very clinical terms what coitus involves. Elizabeth looks around, embarrassed, and then comically says: "Okay, Carla, we've got it. Fifty billion sperm in one shot. No, you know all about it. I understand that." At the end of the conversation, Carla runs down to the lake to play with the ducks, and Elizabeth collapses in a heap on the bench. But as the scene shifts, we hear Elizabeth's voice: "No! Carla, get away from the water!"

Keaton and Lewis interact quite believably as mother and daughter whose relationship is fraught with both tension and love. When Elizabeth teaches an exuberant Carla to dance, they laugh and twirl and fall into a happy embrace. But Elizabeth's instructions are punctuated with tips like "Just keep it calm down there," "You don't want to get too close," and "When they start to play a slow dance, you and your partner should immediately go get yourself a soda."

The friction between Carla's need for independence and Elizabeth's need to control becomes increasingly worse until the conflict finally ignites at Caroline's wedding when Danny interrupts the service to propose to Carla. By the time Carla provokes Elizabeth into an ill-timed discussion about her own wedding plans at Caroline's reception, we almost feel sorry for Elizabeth. Their heated conversation on the golf course divides our sympathy. Both are right. Both are wrong.

> ELIZABETH: It's not that I don't like Danny. It has nothing to do with whether I like Danny or not.
> CARLA: What's wrong with him?
> ELIZABETH: Nothing. He's fine. He's perfectly fine. I'm just asking for you to wait. Danny's the first boy you've met, and I think you can do better.
> CARLA: I can't do better 'cause I'm not better.
> ELIZABETH: You're better. You're better.
> CARLA: Can't you see me? You never look at me. And no matter how long I wait, I can't be a painter, and I can't play tennis, and I'm not an artist. I know how to do some things. And I can love. And I love Danny, and he loves me very much.
> ELIZABETH: Yes, but Carla I just don't think that he can take care of you. He can barely take care of himself.
> CARLA: We can take care of each other. We don't need you, mother. Don't

worry. You don't have to come to my wedding. I'll do my own wedding. I hate everything you did for Caroline's wedding. I hated this dumb hat and these dumb shoes and the big ugly centerpieces. The only think I like is the dress. This is pretty. I'm going to keep it.

As in many of Keaton's comedies, a bit of humor or slapstick interrupts the intensity of the drama. In this scene, the sprinkler system suddenly comes on, drenching both mother and daughter, which serves to lift the mood as well as stop the conversation before any more words that can't be taken back get spoken.

Instead of the sprinkler, Elizabeth's hat serves to lighten the atmosphere at the end of the film. It's Carla and Danny's wedding day. Elizabeth isn't going; however, as Carla and Danny walk down the aisle after the ceremony, Carla sees Elizabeth standing in the back of the church. She's wearing a smart, red suit with a wide-brimmed red hat. As she reaches out once more in reconciliation with her family, people keep bumping into her hat, knocking it all askew. She hugs Danny, welcoming him to the family, and greets Heather's partner with a genuine warmth.

The title of the film is almost deceiving, as *The Other Sister* becomes a coming-of-age for Elizabeth. Carla is really the same person from beginning to end. Elizabeth grows, and, like Roberta Blumstein, she learns that nothing is more important than family.

After her role as Elizabeth Tate, Keaton said:

> I realized that I would really love to play a very, very flamboyant bad person in a funny movie. An evil witch. I would just love to do it, and in a really wild way. Just go way overboard. Just once. Or, I would like to play in a comedy a much more physical comedy where I really take a lot of falls because that part of *The First Wives Club* was really fun for me. And that was also fun in *Northern Lights*. Every time I would have to fall. I would

just love to do something really, wildly physical [personal interview].

"Flamboyant," at least, adequately describes her next role.

Hanging Up

In *Hanging Up*, released in February 2000, Keaton again plays the eldest of three sisters who can't seem to resolve their differences until their divisive father (played by Walter Matthau) dies. The important thing about *Hanging Up*, costarring Meg Ryan and Lisa Kudrow, is that Keaton not only stars in but directs the film. When Nora Ephron, who cowrote the screenplay with her sister Delia, left the project to direct *You've Got Mail*, she gave her director's chair to Keaton.

The thought terrified her, Keaton admitted to *Entertainment Weekly*. "I panicked and said absolutely no, no way, too scary.... Then the reality of the fact that somebody would have to play the part dawned on me. I knew I was going to be terrified, so why not just double-wham it?" (qtd. in "Fall Movie Preview" 77). According to the article, Keaton had once again prepared carefully. "When Kudrow and Ryan showed up for the first day of filming, they discovered that Keaton had already videotaped the entire movie, shot by shot, using stand in actors" (77). As for saying she would never direct herself, Keaton says: "I'm so full of shit, as always" (qtd. in "Book 'Em" 58).

The phrase aptly describes her character, Georgia, the outrageously egotistical dynamo who heads up her own magazine, called *Georgia*. She leaves no doubt as to who's in charge as she strides down hallways barking orders or flies off to meetings in her exquisitely cut black suits, strands of pearls, and perfectly coifed hair. Her ever-present entourage swarms around her like drones to a queen bee. She is condescending to them and patronizing

to her sisters, Eve (Meg Ryan) and Maddy (Lisa Kudrow). Imagine J. C. Wiatt without any of the warmth. Totally self-absorbed, Georgia largely ignores youngest sister Maddy, a second-rate soap actress, and publishes Eve's stuffing recipe under her own name in the *New York Times*. Eve tells her: "If anything happens that is not about you, you are bored witless." In her one moment of self-reflection, Georgia responds: "That is true.... God help anyone who needs me." She finally admits to Eve: "I have never been jealous of anyone in my life, but, I am just the tiniest bit jealous of your heart."

Eve is the heart and soul of this dysfunctional family that communicates mainly by telephone. She's trying to get her event-planning business off the ground while caring for her husband and son, Maddy's ailing Saint Bernard, and her father, a retired screenwriter and "uproar man," played to the hilt by Matthau in his last screen appearance. As one character tells Eve, "He's never happy unless everyone is upset all the time." His screenwriting partner and wife (Cloris Leachman) abandoned him and the girls years earlier, so he spends most of his time drinking, chasing women, reminiscing about John Wayne, and driving his "little Evie" crazy.

We learn about Eve's relationship with her family, especially her father, through a series of flashbacks. Situations or conversations in the present trigger memories that provide the missing pieces of the family puzzle. At first, the flashbacks seem too frequent and disruptive. Too many interruptions to the main story line invite confusion. And then we realize that this story is really about one woman, Eve, who is trying to make some sense of her present life, by looking for clues in the past. Watching the film is like sitting down with a photo album and watching the history and complex dynamics of a family unfold.

Eve clearly adores her father, but, in

Hanging Up (Columbia Pictures, 2000). Family dynamics once again take center stage in Keaton's *Hanging Up*, adapted by sisters Delia and Nora Ephron from Delia's semiautobiographical novel. Georgia (Keaton), Eve (Ryan), and Maddy (Kudrow) are three sisters distanced by their busy schedules, connected mostly by the telephone, until their "nightmare" of a father (Walter Matthau), a former screenwriter, decides to die. When Nora Ephron vacated the director's chair to shoot *You've Got Mail*, Keaton took her place. It was the first time she directed herself in a movie, but she made the film her own. The subject matter naturally appealed to her. Keaton has always maintained that "family is everything." Georgia is the character that she's always wanted to play: larger-than-life and overwhelmingly egotistical. And the artistic style is decidedly Keaton's with a collage of beautifully framed images and lyrical moving camera.

one scene, she admits: "He's a nightmare. He's never going to clean up his act. He's never going to give me wisdom or comfort." Now he's dying, and it seems his care and feeding have been left to Eve who is operating on sensory overload and headed for a breakdown—until she backs her car into Dr. Omar's in the hospital parking lot. It's his mother who gives Eve the wisdom and comfort she needs. "What should I do?" cries Eve. "Press end," the doctor's mother advises. "Sometimes it is necessary to disconnect." She pulls the plug on her communication devices and confronts her sisters face-to-face. They reconnect after their father's funeral, and the final snapshot is a playful scene of the sisters making Eve's stuffing recipe in her kitchen.

Though the screenplay for *Hanging Up* is based on the experiences of the Ephron sisters, the look of the film clearly reflects Keaton's artistic sensibilities, from the photo collage in the exposition to set pieces like the Visit the Zoo poster. Technically, the film is much more sophisticated than *Unstrung Heroes,* with its sweeping crane shots, lyrical camera movement, use of slow motion, and careful *mise-en-scène.*

Keaton's latest film, *Town and Country,* directed by Peter Chelsom, is scheduled for release in the spring of 2001. After 20 years, she costars again with Warren Beatty, playing his society wife. The film also reteams Keaton with Andie MacDowell (*Unstrung Heroes*) and Goldie Hawn (*First Wives Club*). But if her work on *Hanging Up* is any indication, Keaton may well be spending more and more time behind the camera. With a new home, a daughter, and a cadre of family and friends who encourage her, Diane Keaton is still taking risks. As the German magazine *Bunte* ("Jung durch Denk-Training") so succinctly puts it: Keaton "is constantly exercising her powers of creating thinking.... It proves that whoever exercises his/her brain stays young, even into old age" (80). Talent, persistence, and a strong work ethic are the hallmarks of her enduring star image. After a 30-year career, she still surprises her audiences—and herself—with what she can do. As Keaton says of her life: "'It's just been so much more interesting and amazing and dramatic and full of astonishing things than what I expected.... I thought it would be much duller'" (Dowd, "The Old Pals Act" 6).

Conclusion

The Sum of Her Parts

I remember Woody calling me one day and saying he's just watched the rough film [Annie Hall] and discovered that whenever he cut away from Annie, it lost something. That's the way a lot of us feel about Diane.
　　　　　　　—Tony Roberts (*Los Angeles Times*, Oct. 4, 1992)

It would be difficult to find another star today who inspires the kind of loyalty and affection that Diane Keaton has over the last three decades. Dominick Dunne is fond of saying that she's "almost too good to be true, for a movie star." He tells the story of a New York playwright who sent her a copy of a play that he had written in hopes that she might be interested in a part. She turned him down, but the letter she wrote to him was one of the nicest he had ever received. According to Dunne, it was so nice that he sent her a thank you note, "saying that her letter was better than his play" (40).

The articles and interviews about the star over the years may prove Dunne right. Family, friends, fans, ex-lovers, costars, directors, critics—the overwhelming majority are captivated by this centered, down-to-earth woman who seems totally unaffected by fame, wealth, or power. One reporter said: "After a few minutes of talking to Diane Keaton, you begin to think she'd be a great person to have a beer with.... Nothing about her seems rehearsed" (Denerstein, "At 51" D6). Woody Allen says: "She brings out the best in everybody. She has the kind of personality that lights up the whole project. She's such a positive personality" (qtd. in Bjorkman 257). Perhaps one of Keaton's own remarks best reveals her attitude toward stardom and explains her charismatic persona. Sitting at that New York café table in 1977, she told Rex Reed, "I hope life never gets so complicated that I don't do my own dishes" (qtd. in Reed 7). She has always believed that movie stars are just working people.

Keaton is most comfortable *not* being the center of attention. She keeps such a low profile in Hollywood that we almost forget she's there—until we see her on the screen. And that screen persona is potent. In the course of Diane Keaton's star history, she has created images so vivid that they seem permanently imprinted on the public consciousness. Her face at the end of *The Godfather*, as she watches her husband become the new don, captured the single moment when innocence and trust are lost forever. In *Annie Hall*, with her bowler hat, layered masculine ensembles, stammering la-de-da-isms, she does a fidgety courtship dance with Woody Allen that captivated a country and showed audiences that neurotic and charming were not mutually exclusive. As the doomed Terry Dunn in *Looking for Mr. Goodbar*, she saunters down a seedy street pulsating with flashing neon and a disco beat. Glancing back over her shoulder for her next pick up, she became a symbol for the dark side of the sexual revolution. In *Reds*, we remember her tortured Louise Bryant hunched on the edge of the bed telling Jack Reed: "I'm just living in your margins." The scene epitomized the angst of a woman desperate to rise above her own mediocre talent as a writer and escape the shadow of her famous lover.

There are many other vivid reminders of Keaton's powerful screen persona: Faith Dunlap lying in the bathtub smoking a joint and singing "If I Fell" in *Shoot the Moon*; Kate sitting in her prison cell at the end of *Mrs. Soffel*; J. C. Wiatt striding down the corporate hallways in her Armani suit in *Baby Boom*; and Bessie describing the drowning of her boyfriend Clarence to her sister in *Marvin's Room*. As Woody Allen once noted, Keaton is difficult to ignore on the screen. She gravitates to ensemble acting because she likes the experience of playing off of other actors, but, even in these films, it is Keaton's performance we are drawn to. She pulls us into her characters' lives, though we may not always like them, with her natural, honest style of acting. Committed to finding the truth of a character, whether in comedy or drama, she conveys sincerity, not sentimentality.

There is no ego or worrying about which side to present to the camera in a Keaton performance. She has never objected to doing whatever is necessary to make the part believable, even if it means taking off the makeup and showing a few wrinkles or falling over backwards and ungracefully in a chair to get a laugh. Because she believes in her characters, audiences tend to believe in them also. Critic Eleanor Ringel wondered once whether Keaton could be the Cary Grant of her generation because she makes it all look so easy (Rev. *Marvin's Room* P1).

Keaton has breathed life into characters very few others would be interested in or care about. She likes "small films about unexplored people" (qtd. in Romano and Welch, "Reliable Source" D3). In her dramas, the women she plays are often outsiders, people who live in the margins. With a few exceptions like Louise Bryant, Kate Soffel, and Amelia Earhart, her characters are not famous people, or infamous as in the case of Kate Soffel. They are a complex, flawed assortment of oddniks imbued with many of the same conflicting traits associated with her own personality. They tend to be intelligent and a bit eccentric, vulnerable but tough enough to stand up for themselves or others they care about.

Keaton's comedic characters harken back to the days of slapstick and screwball comedies. Her facility for comic timing, fast-paced dialogue, and physical humor is partly innate and partly a result of her years of practice in Woody Allen's early comedies. Their stars crossed at the right time, in the right place, changing and influencing both their lives. Allen's portrait of Keaton as the free-spirited but self-doubting modern woman in *Annie Hall* made her an icon. To this day, she says: "*Annie Hall* had the biggest impact of any movie I've ever been in. Career-wise. Every-wise. If I hadn't done that movie, there would have been nothing" (qtd. in Denerstein, "At 51" D6).

But it was her own talent and drive and determination that took her beyond his sphere, though she has remained a faithful friend to Allen. Because of Keaton, he confesses that his portraits of women are more sensitive. He relies on her good judgment as well as her artistic vision, which come across in everything from her directing to her photography to her layered style of dressing. Allen paid Keaton the highest compliment when he told Stig Bjorkman: "Once I make a film, if *she* likes it, then I feel I have accomplished my goal and it becomes utterly irrelevant to me whether anybody else in the world does" (qtd. in Bjorkman 54). Keaton's most recent films, like *The First Wives Club* and *Northern Lights*, suggest a return to the broad, physical comedy she and Allen did so well together.

With the exception of Sonja in *Love and Death*, Allen's spoof of Russian literature, all of Keaton's characters are modern American women. Her films deal with the issues and concerns of contemporary women, like balancing a career and a family. Her few period pieces—*Harry and Walter Go to New York, Reds, Mrs. Soffel,* and *Amelia Earhart*—are set for the most part in early 20th-century America and, in each case, she plays an unconventional, forward-thinking woman for that time period. Her physical movements and mannerisms are too modern for traditional Jane Austen adaptations. Nor will you see Keaton anytime soon in a Merchant-Ivory film. Unlike Meryl Streep, she doesn't do dialects because, by her own admission, her speech patterns don't fit them. In short, she is an actress for her generation, and her star trajectory parallels the course of intelligent, talented American women who have been slowly but steadily building successful careers by working hard and putting in the time.

Keaton hasn't always made popular choices or chosen mainstream Hollywood vehicles. Some of her movies, like *The Only Thrill,* are made on a small scale with limited distribution. Without a big studio behind them, spending a fortune on promotion, most of these small films are released one month, only to disappear quickly and reappear several months later in video. Some of Keaton's movies, like *Baby Boom,* don't even find their audience until they get to video. She has no regrets about her choices, however, and says: "In my case, it wasn't that I made the wrong moves as much as I probably didn't make enough moves" (qtd. in Willens, *TV Times* 4). She explained in one interview: "When I was first a movie star, when *Annie Hall* happened (in '77), I was scared. And careful. Careful because I wanted to do the 'right thing' as an actress. I was cautious. Now I feel totally different" (qtd. in Schaefer 33).

Today, though Keaton still goes about her work quietly and with little fanfare, shunning the spotlight, she takes more risks—like directing herself in *Hanging Up.* As an actress, director, producer, and photographer, she chooses to work with material that moves her, regardless of the monetary rewards. Allen refers to her multi-dimensional persona as "a phenomenal gift—every activity she does is full of feeling so they all ignite audiences" (personal interview). But the important thing for Keaton is the work itself, the process and the challenge. By all accounts, she has a rich, full professional and family life. But ever the realist, Keaton likes to say that no one can have it all. Happiness is elusive at best. All we can do is "try and make a little reasonable place in the chaos" (qtd. in Hirschberg 42). In retrospect, it seems a fitting description for the enduring, evolving Keaton canon.

Filmography

(Principal characters are listed in alphabetical order.)

Lovers and Other Strangers
Released 1970

PRODUCER: David Susskind for ABC Pictures; DIRECTOR: Cy Howard; SCREENWRITERS: Joseph Bologna, David Goodman, and Renée Taylor; CINEMATOGRAPHER: Andrew Laszlo; EDITORS: David Bretherton and Sidney Katz; PRODUCTION DESIGNER: Ben Edwards; SET DESIGNER: Alan Hicks; COSTUME DESIGNER: Albert Wolsky; MUSIC: Fred Karlin; AWARDS: AA for Best Song: "For All We Know" (Karlin with lyricists Robb Royer and James Griffin); RUNNING TIME: 104 minutes.

CAST: Bea Arthur (Bea Vecchio), Bonnie Bedelia (Susan Henderson), Michael Brandon (Mike Vecchio), Richard Castellano (Frank Vecchio), Bob Dishy (Jerry), Harry Guardino (Johnny), Marian Hailey (Brenda), Joseph Hindy (Richie Vecchio), Anthony Holland (Donaldson), Anne Jackson (Cathy), Diane Keaton (Joan Vecchio), Cloris Leachman (Bernice Henderson), Mort Marshall (Father Gregory), Anne Meara (Wilma), Gig Young (Hal Henderson)

The Godfather
Released 1972

PRODUCER: Albert S. Ruddy for Paramount; DIRECTOR: Francis Ford Coppola; SCREENWRITERS: Francis Ford Coppola and Mario Puzo (adapted from Puzo's novel of the same title); CINEMATOGRAPHER: Gordon Willis; EDITORS: William Reynolds and Peter Zinner; PRODUCTION DESIGNER: Dean Tavoularis; SET DESIGNER: Philip Smith; COSTUME DESIGNER: Anna Hill Johnstone; MUSIC: Nino Rota; AWARDS: AA for Best Picture (Albert Ruddy), Adapted Screenplay (Coppola and Puzo), and Best Actor (Marlon Brando); British Academy Award for Music (Rota); Golden Globe Awards for Best Director (Coppola), Best Motion Picture (Drama), Best Actor in a Drama (Brando), Best Original Score (Rota), and Best Screenplay (Coppola and Puzo); Grammy Award for Best Original Score for a Motion Picture (Rota); Directors Guild of America (Coppola); Writers Guild of America Award for Best Adapted Drama; New York Film Critics Award for Best Supporting Actor (Robert Duvall); National Society of Film Critics Award for Best Actor (Al Pacino); RUNNING TIME: 175 minutes.

CAST: Marlon Brando (Vito Corleone), James Caan (Sonny Corleone), Richard Castellano (Peter Clemenza), John Cazale (Fredo Corleone), Richard Conte (Barzini), Robert Duvall (Tom Hagen), Corrado Gaipa (Don Tommasino), Tony Giorgio (Bruno Tattaglia), Sterling Hayden (McCluskey), Diane Keaton (Kay Adams), Morgana King (Mrs. Vito [Mama] Corleone), Al Lettieri

(Sollozzo), Al Martino (Johnny Fontane), John Martino (Paulie Gatto), Lenny Montana (Luca Brasi), Al Pacino (Michael Corleone), Alex Rocco (Moe Greene), Victor Rendina (Phillip Tattaglia), Talia Shire (Connie Corleone), Simonetta Stefanelli (Apollonia)

Play It Again, Sam
Released 1972

PRODUCERS: Charles H. Joffe and Arthur P. Jacobs for Paramount; DIRECTOR: Herbert Ross; SCREENWRITER: Woody Allen (adapted from his play of the same title); CINEMATOGRAPHER: Owen Roizman; EDITOR: Marion Rothman; PRODUCTION DESIGNER: Ed Wittstein; SET DESIGNER: Doug von Koss; COSTUME DESIGNER: Anna Hill Johnstone; MUSIC: Billy Goldenberg; RUNNING TIME: 85 minutes.

CAST: Woody Allen (Allan Felix), Susan Anspach (Nancy), Diane Keaton (Linda Christie), Jerry Lacy (Bogart), Tony Roberts (Dick Christie)

Sleeper
Released 1973

PRODUCERS: Charles H. Joffe and Jack Grossberg for MGM/UA; DIRECTOR: Woody Allen; SCREENWRITERS: Woody Allen and Marshall Brickman; CINEMATOGRAPHER: David Walsh; EDITOR: Ralph Rosenblum; PRODUCTION DESIGNER: Dale Hennesy; SET DESIGNER: Gary Moreno; COSTUME DESIGNER: Joel Schumacher; MUSIC: Woody Allen with the Preservation Hall Jazz Band; AWARDS: Hugo Award and Nebula Award for Best Dramatic Presentation (Allen); RUNNING TIME: 88 minutes.

CAST: Woody Allen (Miles Monroe), Brian Avery (Herald Cohen), John Beck (Erno Windt), Chris Forbes (Rainer Krebs), Mary Gregory (Dr. Melik), Peter Hobbs (Dr. Dean), Diane Keaton (Luna Schlosser), Don Keefer (Dr. Tryon), John McLiam (Dr. Agon), Susan Miller (Ellen Pogrebin), Bartlett Robinson (Dr. Orva), Mews Small (Dr. Nero)

The Godfather: Part II
Released 1974

PRODUCER: Francis Ford Coppola for Paramount; DIRECTOR: Francis Ford Coppola;

SCREENWRITERS: Francis Ford Coppola and Mario Puzo; CINEMATOGRAPHER: Gordon Willis; EDITORS: Peter Zinner, Barry Malkin, and Richard Marks; PRODUCTION DESIGNER: Dean Tavoularis; SET DESIGNER: George Nelson; COSTUME DESIGNER: Theadora Van Runkle; MUSIC: Nino Rota; AWARDS: AA for Best Picture (Coppola and co-producers Gray Frederickson and Fred Roos), Director (Coppola), Supporting Actor (Robert De Niro), Adapted Screenplay (Coppola and Puzo), Original Music: Score (Rota with Carmine Coppola), and Set Decoration (Tavoularis, Nelson, and Angelo Graham); British Academy Award for Best Actor (Al Pacino); Directors Guild of America Award (Coppola); Writers Guild of America Award for Best Adapted Drama (Coppola and Puzo); National Society of Film Critics Award for Best Cinematography (Willis) and Best Director (Coppola); RUNNING TIME: 200 minutes.

CAST: Danny Aiello (Tony Rosato), Oreste Baldini (Vito Corleone as a boy [née Andolini]), Richard Bright (Al Neri), James Caan (Sonny Corleone), Maria Carta (Vito's mother), John Cazale (Fredo Corleone), Mario Cotone (Don Tommasino), Robert De Niro (Vito as a young man), Francesca DeSapio (Mama Corleone as a young woman), Troy Donahue (Merle Johnson), Robert Duvall (Tom Hagen), Michael Gazzo (Frankie Pentangeli), James Gounaris (Anthony Corleone), Diane Keaton (Kay Adams Corleone), Morgana King (Mrs. Vito [Mama] Corleone), Gastone Moschin (Fanucci), Al Pacino (Michael Corleone), Tom Rosqui (Rocco Lampone), Gianni Russo (Carlo Rizzi), Talia Shire (Connie Corleone), Giuseppe Sillato (Don Francesco), G. D. Spradlin (Senator Pat Geary), Lee Strasberg (Hyman Roth), Abe Vigoda (Sal Tessio)

Love and Death
Released 1975

PRODUCERS: Charles H. Joffe and Martin Poll for MGM/UA; DIRECTOR: Woody Allen; SCREENWRITER: Woody Allen; CINEMATOGRAPHER: Ghislain Cloquet; EDITORS: Ralph Rosenblum and Ron Kalish; PRODUCTION DESIGNER: Willy Holt; COSTUME DESIGNER: Gladys de Segonzac; MUSIC: Sergei Prokofiev; AWARDS: Berlin International Film Festival UNICRIT Award (Allen); RUNNING TIME: 82 minutes.

CAST: Woody Allen (Boris Grushenko), Lloyd Battista (Don Francisco), Brian Coburn

(Dimitri), Henry Czarniak (Ivan Grushenko), Olga Georges-Picot (Countess Alexandrovna), Harold Gould (Count Anton Ivanovitch), Harry Hankin (Uncle Sasha), Jessica Harper (Natasha Petrovna), Diane Keaton (Sonja), Jack Lenoir (Krapotkin), Leib Lensky (Father Andre), Alfred Lutter III (Young Boris)

I Will, I Will ... for Now
Released 1976

PRODUCER: George Barrie for 20th Century–Fox; DIRECTOR: Norman Panama; SCREENWRITERS: Norman Panama and Albert Lewin; CINEMATOGRAPHER: John Alonzo; EDITOR: Robert Lawrence; COSTUME DESIGNER: PRODUCTION DESIGNER: Fernando Carrere; MUSIC: George Barrie, Sammy Cahn, and Bob Larimer; RUNNING TIME: 96 minutes.

CAST: Robert Alda (Dr. Magnus), Warren Berlinger (Steve Martin), Candy Clark (Sally Bingham), Elliott Gould (Les Bingham), Diane Keaton (Katie Bingham), Victoria Principal (Jackie Martin), Madge Sinclair (Dr. Williams), Paul Sorvino (Lou Springer)

Harry and Walter Go to New York
Released 1976

PRODUCERS: Tony Bill, Don Devlin, and Harry Gittes for Columbia; DIRECTOR: Mark Rydell; SCREENWRITERS: John Byrum, Don Devlin, and Robert Kaufman; CINEMATOGRAPHER: László Kovács; EDITORS: David Bretherton and Don Guidice; PRODUCTION DESIGNER: Harry Horner; SET DESIGNER: Ruby Levitt; COSTUME DESIGNER: Theoni Aldredge; MUSIC: Alan Bergman, Marilyn Bergman, and David Shire; RUNNING TIME: 123 minutes.

CAST: Val Avery (Chatsworth), James Caan (Harry Dighby), Michael Caine (Adam Worth), Michael Conrad (Billy Gallagher), Dennis Dugan (Lewis), Charles Durning (Rufus T. Crisp), Jack Gilford (Mischa), Elliott Gould (Walter Hill), Kathryn Grody (Barbara), Carol Kane (Florence), Diane Keaton (Lissa Chestnut), David Proval (Ben), Lesley Ann Warren (Gloria Fontaine)

Annie Hall
Released 1977

PRODUCER: Charles H. Joffe for MGM/UA; DIRECTOR: Woody Allen; SCREENWRITERS: Woody Allen and Marshall Brickman; CINEMATOGRAPHER: Gordon Willis; EDITORS: Ralph Rosenblum and Wendy Greene Bricmont; PRODUCTION DESIGNER: Mel Bourne; SET DESIGNERS: Robert Drumheller and Justin Scoppa, Jr.; COSTUME DESIGNERS: Ruth Morley and Ralph Lauren; AWARDS: AA for Best Picture (Joffe), Best Director (Allen), Best Actress (Keaton), Best Original Screenplay (Allen and Brickman); British Academy Awards for Best Film, Best Director, Best Actress, Best Screenplay, and Best Editing (Rosenblum and Bricmont); Golden Globe Award for Best Actress; Directors Guild of America Award (Allen); New York Film Critics Award for Best Film, Best Director, Best Actress and Best Screenplay; Los Angeles Film Critics Award for Best Screenplay; National Board of Review Award for Best Supporting Actress (Keaton); National Society of Film Critics Award for Best Film, Best Actress, and Best Screenplay; Writers Guild of America Award for Best Comedy (Allen and Brickman); RUNNING TIME: 99 minutes.

CAST: Woody Allen (Alvy Singer), Colleen Dewhurst (Mrs. Hall), Shelley Duvall (Pam), Jeff Goldblum (Man on telephone), Shelley Hack (Woman on the street interviewee), Carol Kane (Allison), Diane Keaton (Annie Hall), Helen Ludlam (Grammy Hall), Janet Margolin (Robin), Marshall McLuhan (Himself), Jonathan Munk (Young Alvy), Tony Roberts (Rob), Paul Simon (Tony Lacey), Donald Symington (Mr. Hall), Christopher Walken (Duane Hall), Sigourney Weaver (Alvy's date)

Looking for Mr. Goodbar
Released 1977

PRODUCER: Freddie Fields for Paramount; DIRECTOR: Richard Brooks; SCREENWRITER: Richard Brooks (adapted from Judith Rossner's novel of the same title); CINEMATOGRAPHER: William Fraker; EDITOR: George Grenville; ART DIRECTOR: Edward Carfagno; SET DESIGNER: Ruby Levitt; COSTUME DESIGNER: Jodie Lynn Tillen; MUSIC: Artie Kane; RUNNING TIME: 136 minutes.

CAST: William Atherton (James), Tom Berenger (Gary), Richard Bright (George), LeVar Burton (Cap Jackson), Marilyn Coleman (Mrs. Jackson), Alan Feinstein (Martin), Richard Gere (Tony), Diane Keaton* (Theresa Dunn), Richard Kiley (Mr. Dunn), Priscilla Pointer (Mrs. Dunn), Tuesday Weld (Katherine Dunn).

Keaton received a Golden Globe nomination for Best Motion Picture Actress in a Drama.

Interiors
Released 1978

PRODUCER: Jack Rollins, Charles H. Joffe, and Robert Greenhut for MGM/UA; DIRECTOR: Woody Allen; SCREENWRITER: Woody Allen; CINEMATOGRAPHER: Gordon Willis; EDITOR: Ralph Rosenblum; PRODUCTION DESIGNER: Mel Bourne; SET DESIGNER: Mario Mazzola; COSTUME DESIGNER: Joel Schumacher; AWARDS: British Academy Award for Best Supporting Actress (Page); New York and Los Angeles Film Critics Award for Best Supporting Actress (Maureen Stapleton); RUNNING TIME: 92 minutes.

CAST: Kristin Griffith (Flyn), Mary Beth Hurt (Joey), Richard Jordan (Frederick), Diane Keaton (Renata), E. G. Marshall (Arthur), Geraldine Page (Eve), Maureen Stapleton (Pearl), Sam Waterston (Mike)

Manhattan
Released 1979 in B&W

PRODUCERS: Jack Rollins, Charles H. Joffe, and Robert Greenhut for MGM/UA; DIRECTOR: Woody Allen; SCREENWRITERS: Woody Allen and Marshall Brickman; CINEMATOGRAPHER: Gordon Willis; EDITOR: Susan Morse; PRODUCTION DESIGNER: Mel Bourne; SET DESIGNER: Robert Drumheller; COSTUME DESIGNER: Albert Wolsky; MUSIC: George Gershwin; AWARDS: British Academy Adward for Best Film and Best Screenplay; New York Film Critics Award for Best Director; National Society of Film Critics Award for Best Director and Best Supporting Actress (Streep); National Board of Review Award for Best English Language Picture and Best Supporting Actress (Streep); Los Angeles Film Critics Award for Best Supporting Actress (Streep); César Award for Best Foreign Language Film (Allen); Italian National Syndicate of Film Journalists Silver Ribbon Award for Best Director; RUNNING TIME: 96 minutes.

CAST: Woody Allen (Isaac Davis), Anne Byrne (Emily), Mariel Hemingway (Tracy), Diane Keaton* (Mary Wilke), Michael Murphy (Yale), Meryl Streep (Jill)

Keaton received a British Academy Award nomination for Best Actress.

Reds
Released 1981

PRODUCERS: Warren Beatty and Simon Relph for Paramount; DIRECTOR: Warren Beatty; SCREENWRITERS: Warren Beatty and Trevor Griffiths; CINEMATOGRAPHER: Vittorio Storaro; EDITORS: Dede Allen and Craig McKay; ART DIRECTOR: Simon Holland; PRODUCTION DESIGNERS: Michael Seirton and Richard Sylbert; COSTUME DESIGNER: Shirley Russell; MUSIC: Stephen Sondheim; AWARDS: AA for Best Director, Best Cinematography, Best Supporting Actress (Maureen Stapleton); British Academy Award for Best Supporting Actor (Jack Nicholson) and Best Supporting Actress (Maureen Stapleton); Directors Guild of America Award (Beatty); Golden Globe Award for Best Director; New York Film Critics Award for Best Film; National Society of Film Critics Award for Best Supporting Actress (Maureen Stapleton); Writers Guild of America Award for Best Drama Written Directly for the Screen (Beatty and Griffiths); Los Angeles Film Critics Award for Best Cinematography, Best Director, and Best Supporting Actress (Maureen Stapleton); National Board of Review Award for Best Picture, Best Director, and Best Supporting Actor (Jack Nicholson); RUNNING TIME: 194 minutes.

CAST: Warren Beatty (Jack Reed), Norman Chancer (Barney), Nicolas Coster (Paul Trullinger), Leigh Curran (Isa Ruth), Brenda Currin (Marjorie Jones), Harry Ditson (Maurice Becker), MacIntyre Dixon (Carl Walters), Nancy Duiguid (Jane Heap), Kathryn Grody (Crystal Eastman), Gene Hackman (Pete Van Wherry), Edward Herrmann (Max Eastman), Diane Keaton* (Louise Bryant), Oleg Kerensky (Kerensky), Jerzy Kosinski (Grigory Zinoviev), Bessie Love (Mrs. Partlow), Jack Nicholson (Eugene O'Neill), George Plimpton (Horace Whigham), Stuart Richman (Trotsky), Roger Sloman (Lenin), Paul Sorvino (Louis Fraina), Maureen Stapleton (Emma Goldman), Pat Starr (Helen Walters), Dolph Sweet (Big Bill Haywood), Eleanor Wilson (Mrs. Reed), Ian Wolfe (Mr. Partlow), Max Wright (Floyd Dell). Witnesses include: Jacob Bailin, Roger Baldwin, John Ballato, Harry Carlisle, Kenneth Chamberlain, Andrew Dasburg, Tess Davis, Will Durant, Blanche Hays Fagen, Hamilton Fish, Dorothy Frooks, Hugo Gellert, Emmanuel Herbert, Isaac Levine, Arthur Meyer, Adele Nathan, Scott Nearing, Dora Russell, George Seldes, Art Shields, Jessica Smith, Arne Swabeck, Bernadine Szold-Fritz, Galina von Meck, Heaton Vorse, Will

Weinstone, Rebecca West, and Lucita Williams. Appearing but not listed in credits are George Jessel and Adela Rogers St. Johns.

Keaton received Academy Award and British Adademy Award nominations for Best Actress and a Golden Globe nomination for Best Motion Picture Actress in a Drama.

Shoot the Moon
Released 1982

PRODUCERS: Edgar Scherick, Stuart Miller, and Alan Marshall for MGM/UA; DIRECTOR: Alan Parker; SCREENWRITER: Bo Goldman; CINEMATOGRAPHER: Michael Seresin; EDITOR: Gerry Hambling; PRODUCTION DESIGNER: Geoffrey Kirkland; SET DESIGNERS: Robert Nelson and Doug von Koss; COSTUME DESIGNER: Kristi Zea; RUNNING TIME: 125 minutes.

CAST: Karen Allen (Sandy), Viveka Davis (Jill Dunlap), Albert Finney (George Dunlap), Tracey Gold (Marianne Dunlap), Dana Hill (Sherry Dunlap), Diane Keaton* (Faith Dunlap), Peter Weller (Frank Henderson), Tina Yothers (Molly Dunlap).

Keaton received a Golden Globe nomination for Best Motion Picture Actress in a Drama.

Little Drummer Girl
Released 1984

PRODUCERS: Patrick Kelley and Robert Crawford for Warner Brothers; DIRECTOR: George Roy Hill; SCREENWRITER: Loring Mandel (adapted from John Le Carré's novel of the same title); CINEMATOGRAPHER: Wolfgang Treu; EDITOR: William Reynolds; PRODUCTION DESIGNER: Henry Bumstead; SET DESIGNER: Heidi Ludi; COSTUME DESIGNER: Ille Sievers; MUSIC: Dave Grusin; RUNNING TIME: 130 minutes.

CAST: Smadar Brener (Toby), Michael Cristofer (Tayeh), Eli Danker (Litvak), Sabi Dorr (Ben), Sami Frey (Khalil), Shlomit Hagoel (Rose), Diane Keaton (Charlie), Klaus Kinski (Kurtz), Ben Levine (Dimitri), Juliano Mer (Julio), Doron Nesher (David), Danni Roth (Oded), Jonathan Sagall (Teddy), David Suchet (Mesterbein), Yorgo Voyagis (Joseph)

Mrs. Soffel
Released 1984

PRODUCERS: Edgar Scherick, Scott Rudin, and David Nicksay for MGM/UA; DIRECTOR: Gillian Armstrong; SCREENWRITER: Ron Nyswaner; CINEMATOGRAPHER: Russell Boyd; EDITOR: Nicholas Beauman; PRODUCTION DESIGNER: Luciana Arrighi; SET DESIGNERS: Jacques Bradette, Dan Conley, and Hilton Rosemarin; COSTUME DESIGNER: Shay Cunliffe; MUSIC: Mark Isham; RUNNING TIME: 113 minutes.

CAST: Trini Alvarado (Irene Soffel), Maury Chaykin (Reynolds), Danny Corkill (Eddie Soffel), Harley Cross (Clarence Soffel), Jennie Dundas (Margaret Soffel), Joyce Ebert (Matron Garvey), Mel Gibson (Ed Biddle), Edward Herrmann (Peter Soffel), Diane Keaton* (Kate Soffel), Matthew Modine (Jack Biddle), Terry O'Quinn (Buck McGovern), Pippa Pearthree (Maggie), Wayne Robson (Halliday), Les Rubie (Mr. Stevenson), Paula Trueman (Mrs. Stevenson), William Youmans (Koslow), Dana Wheeler-Nicholson (Jessie Bodyne)

Keaton received a Golden Globe nomination for Best Motion Picture Actress in a Drama.

Crimes of the Heart
Released 1986

PRODUCERS: Burt Sugarman and Freddie Fields for DeLaurentiis Entertainment Group; DIRECTOR: Bruce Beresford; SCREENWRITER: Beth Henley (adapted from her play of the same title); CINEMATOGRAPHER: Dante Spinotti; EDITOR: Anne Goursaud; PRODUCTION DESIGNER: Ken Adams; SET DESIGNER: Garrett Lewis; COSTUME DESIGNER: Albert Wolsky; MUSIC: Georges Delerue; AWARDS: Golden Globe Award for Best Actress in a Comedy/Musical (Sissy Spacek); and New York Film Critics Award for Best Actress (Sissy Spacek); RUNNING TIME: 105 minutes.

CAST: David Carpenter (Barnette Lloyd), Beeson Carroll (Zackery Botrelle), Tess Harper (Chick Boyle), Hurd Hatfield (Granddaddy), Diane Keaton (Lenny MaGrath), Jessica Lange (Meg MaGrath), Sam Shepard (Doc Porter), Sissy Spacek (Babe MaGrath Botrelle), Greg Travis (Willie Jay)

Radio Days
Released 1987

PRODUCERS: Charles H. Joffe, Jack Rollins,

and Robert Greenhut for Orion; DIRECTOR: Woody Allen; SCREENWRITER: Woody Allen; CINEMATOGRAPHER: Carlo Di Palma; EDITOR: Susan Morse; PRODUCTION DESIGNER: Santo Loquasto; SET DESIGNERS: Leslie Bloom, George DeTitta, Jr., and Carol Joffe; COSTUME DESIGNER: Jeffrey Kurland; AWARDS: British Academy Awards for Costume (Kurland) and Production (Loquasto) Design; RUNNING TIME: 85 minutes.

CAST: Danny Aiello (Rocco), Woody Allen (Narrator), Hy Anzell (Mr. Waldbaum), Jeff Daniels (Biff Baxter), Mia Farrow (Sally White), Seth Green (Joe), Julie Kavner (Tess), Diane Keaton (Monica Charles [cameo role]), Julie Kurnitz (Irene), Judith Malina (Mrs. Waldbaum), Tony Roberts (Silver Dollar MC), Wallace Shawn (Masked Avenger), Michael Tucker (Martin), David Warrilow (Roger), Diane Wiest (Bea)

Heaven (directed only)
Released 1987

PRODUCERS: Tom Kuhn, Charles Mitchell, Arnold Holland, Arlyne Rothberg, and Joe Kelly for Lightyear; DIRECTOR: Diane Keaton; SCREENWRITER: Diane Keaton; CINEMATOGRAPHERS: Frederick Elmes and Joe Kelly; EDITOR: Paul Barnes; PRODUCTION DESIGNER: Barbara Ling; MUSIC: Howard Shore; RUNNING TIME: 88 minutes.

CAST: None listed

Baby Boom
Released 1987

PRODUCERS: Bruce Block and Nancy Meyers for MGM/UA; DIRECTOR: Charles Shyer; SCREENWRITERS: Charles Shyer and Nancy Meyers; CINEMATOGRAPHER: William Fraker; EDITOR: Lynzee Klingman; PRODUCTION DESIGNER: Jeffrey Howard; SET DESIGNER: Lisa Fischer; Costumer Designer Susan Becker; MUSIC: Bill Conti; RUNNING TIME: 103 minutes.

CAST: Pat Hingle (Hughes Larabee), Diane Keaton* (J. C. Wiatt), Kristina Kennedy (Elizabeth Wiatt), Michelle Kennedy (Elizabeth Wiatt), George Petrie (Everett Sloane), Harold Ramis (Steven Bochner), Sam Shepard (Jeff Cooper), James Spader (Ken Arrenberg), Sam Wanamaker (Fritz Curtis)

Keaton received a Golden Globe nomination for Best Motion Picture Actress in a Comedy/Musical.

The Good Mother
Released 1988

PRODUCER: Arnold Glimcher for Touchstone; DIRECTOR: Leonard Nimoy; SCREENWRITER: Michael Bortman (adapted from Sue Miller's novel of the same title); CINEMATOGRAPHER: David Watkin; EDITOR: Peter Berger; PRODUCTION DESIGNER: Stan Jolley; SET DESIGNER: Anthony Greco; COSTUME DESIGNER: Susan Becker; MUSIC: Elmer Bernstein; RUNNING TIME: 104 minutes.

CAST: Margaret Bard (Aunt Rain), Nancy Beatty (Anna's Mother), Barry Belchamber (Anna's Father), Ralph Bellamy (Grandfather), David Gardner (Judge), Diane Keaton (Anna Dunlap), Joe Morton (Frank Williams), James Naughton (Brian), Liam Neeson (Leo Cutter), Jason Robards (Muth), Katey Sagal (Ursula), Asia Vieira (Molly), Teresa Wright (Grandmother)

The Lemon Sisters
Released 1990

PRODUCERS: Diane Keaton, Arne Holland, Joe Kelly, Tom Kuhn, and Charles Mitchell for Miramax; DIRECTOR: Joyce Chopra; SCREENWRITER: Jeremy Pikser; CINEMATOGRAPHER: Bobby Byrne; EDITORS: Michael Miller and Joe Weintraub; PRODUCTION DESIGNER: Patrizia von Brandenstein; SET DESIGNER: Elaine O'Donnell; COSTUME DESIGNER: Susan Becker; MUSIC: Dick Hyman and Howard Shore; RUNNING TIME: 93 minutes.

CAST: Rachel Aviva (Franki as a young girl), Ruben Blades (C. W.), Kourtney Donohue (Eloise as a young girl), Elliott Gould (Fred Frank), Kathryn Grody (Nola Frank), Rachel Hillman (Nola as a young girl), Carol Kane (Franki D'Angelo), Diane Keaton (Eloise Hamer), Aidan Quinn (Frankie McGuiness)

The Godfather: Part III
Released 1990

PRODUCERS: Francis Ford Coppola, Fred

Fuchs, and Nicholas Gage for Paramount; DI-RECTOR: Francis Ford Coppola; SCREENWRIT-ERS: Francis Ford Coppola and Mario Puzo; CINEMATOGRAPHER: Gordon Willis; EDITORS: Barry Malkin, Lisa Fruchtman, and Walter Murch; PRODUCTION DESIGNER: Dean Tavoularis; SET DESIGNER: Gary Fettis; COSTUME DESIGNER: Milena Canonero; MUSIC: Nino Rota and Carmine Coppola; RUNNING TIME: 200 minutes.

CAST: Helmut Berger (Frederick Kelmszig), Richard Bright (Al Neri), Robert Cicchini (Lou Pennino), Franco Citti (Calo), Sofia Coppola (Mary Corleone), Franc D'Ambrosio (Anthony Corleone), Mario Donatone (Mosca), Donal Donnelly (Archbishop Gliday), Vittorio Duse (Don Tommasino), Bridget Fonda (Grace Hamilton), Andy Garcia (Vincent Mancini), George Hamilton (B. J. Harrison), Diane Keaton (Kay Adams Corleone), Joe Mantegna (Joey Zasa), Al Martino (Johnny Fontane), Don Novello (Dominic Abbandando), Al Pacino (Michael Corleone), Enzo Robutti (Lucchesi), Michele Russo (Spara), John Savage (Andrew Hagen), Talia Shire (Connie Corleone), Raf Vallone (Cardinal Lamberto), Eli Wallach (Don Altobello)

Wildflower (television movie, directed only)
Released 1991

PRODUCERS: Richard Freed, Ira Laufer, and Judith Polone for Lifetime; DIRECTOR: Diane Keaton; SCREENWRITER: Sara Flanigan (adapted from her novel, Alice); CINEMATOGRAPHER: Janusz Kaminski; EDITOR: Stephen Rivkin; PRODUCTION DESIGNER: Garreth Stover; COSTUME DESIGNER: Deena Appel; MUSIC: Kenny Edwards and Jon Gilutin; AWARDS: Human Family Educational & Cultural Institute Humanitas Prize (Sara Flanigan); RUNNING TIME: 120 minutes.

CAST: Patricia Arquette (Alice Guthrie), Susan Blakely (Ada Guthrie), Beau Bridges (Jack Perkins), Norman Maxwell (Ormand Guthrie), William McNamara (Sammy Perkins), Reese Witherspoon (Ellie Perkins)

Father of the Bride
Released 1991

PRODUCERS: Sandy Gallin, James Orr, and Jim Cruickshank for Touchstone; DIRECTOR:

Charles Shyer; SCREENWRITERS: Frances Goodrich and Albert Hackett (1950 screenplay); Charles Shyer and Nancy Meyers (1991 screenplay); CINEMATOGRAPHER: John Lindley; EDITOR: Richard Marks; PRODUCTION DESIGNER: Sandy Veneziano; SET DESIGNER: Cynthia McCormac; COSTUME DESIGNERS: Susan Becker, Rosemarie Fall, and Dennis Schoonderwoerd; MUSIC: Alan Silvestri; RUNNING TIME: 105 minutes.

CAST: Kieran Culkin (Matty Banks), Peter Michael Goetz (John MacKenzie), Diane Keaton (Nina Banks), Steve Martin (George Banks), Kate McGregor-Stewart (Joanna MacKenzie), George Newbern (Bryan MacKenzie), Martin Short (Franck Eggelhoffer), Kimberly Williams (Annie Banks), B. D. Wong (Howard Weinstein)

Running Mates (television movie)
Released 1992

PRODUCERS: James Brubaker and Marvin Worth for HBO; DIRECTOR: Michael Lindsay-Hogg; SCREENWRITER: A. L. Appling; CINEMATOGRAPHER: Jeff Jur; EDITOR: Claudia Finkle; PRODUCTION DESIGNER: Glenda Ganis; SET DESIGNER: Ross Silverman; COSTUME DESIGNERS: Sandy Davidson and Jolie Anna Jimenez; MUSIC: Peter Rodgers Melnick; RUNNING TIME: 110 minutes.

CAST: Ed Begley, Jr. (Chapman Snow), Robert Harper (Gordy Faust), Ed Harris (Hugh Hathaway), Diane Keaton (Aggie Snow), Brandon Maggart (Jack Delaney), Ben Masters (Mel Fletcher), Edgar Small (Senator Seaton), Russ Tamblyn (Frank Usher)

Look Who's Talking Now
Released 1993

PRODUCERS: Leslie Dixon for Columbia Tristar; DIRECTOR: Tom Ropelewski; SCREENWRITERS: Leslie Dixon and Tom Ropelewski; CINEMATOGRAPHER: Oliver Stapleton; EDITORS: Harry Hitner and Michael Stevenson; PRODUCTION DESIGNER: Michael Bolton; SET DESIGNER: Jim Erickson; COSTUME DESIGNERS: Molly Maginnis and Mary McLeod; MUSIC: William Ross; RUNNING TIME: 96 minutes.

CAST: Kirstie Alley (Mollie Ubriacco),

Lysette Anthony (Samantha), Danny DeVito (Rocks [voice]), Olympia Dukakis (Rosie), David Gallagher (Mikey Ubriacco), Diane Keaton (Daphne [voice]), Tabitha Lupien (Julie Ubriacco), George Segal (Albert), John Travolta (James Ubriacco)

Ruth Last (Lillian's Sister), Melanie Norris (Helen Moss), Marge Redmond (Mrs. Dalton), Ron Rifkin (Sy)

Keaton received a Golden Globe nomination for Best Actress in a Motion Picture Comedy/Musical.

Amelia Earhart: The Final Flight (television movie)

Released 1994

PRODUCER: Randy Robinson for TNT; DIRECTOR: Yves Simoneau; SCREENWRITERS: Anna Sandor (adapted from Doris Rich's book, *Amelia Earhart: A Biography*); CINEMATOGRAPHER: Lauro Escorel; EDITOR: Michael Ornstein; PRODUCTION DESIGNER: Bill Malley; COSTUME DESIGNER: Jill Ohanneson; MUSIC: George Clinton.

CAST: Denis Arndt (Joseph Laughlin), Diana Bellamy (Mrs. Atkinson), Don Bloomfield (Sid Smith), David Carpenter (Harry Kanning), Bruce Dern (George Putnam), Paul Guilfoyle (Paul Mantz), Rutger Hauer (Fred Noonan), Diane Keaton* (Amelia Earhart)

Keaton received an Emmy nomination for Outstanding Actress in a Miniseries or Special; a Golden Globe nomination for Best Actress in a Miniseries or Motion Picture Made for TV; and a Screen Actors Guild nomination for Outstanding Performance by a Female Actor in a TV Movie or Miniseries.

Manhattan Murder Mystery

Released 1993

PRODUCERS: Charles H. Joffe, Jack Rollins, and Robert Greenhut for Columbia Tristar; DIRECTOR: Woody Allen; SCREENWRITERS: Woody Allen and Marshall Brickman; CINEMATOGRAPHER: Carlo Di Palma; EDITOR: Susan Morse; PRODUCTION DESIGNER: Santo Loquasto; SET DESIGNER: Susan Bode; COSTUME DESIGNER: Jeffrey Kurland; RUNNING TIME: 108 minutes.

CAST: Alan Alda (Ted), Jerry Alder (Paul House), Woody Allen (Larry Lipton), Joy Behar (Marilyn), Zach Braff (Nick Lipton), Lynn Cohen (Lillian House), Anjelica Huston (Marcia Fox), Diane Keaton* (Carol Lipton),

Father of the Bride: Part II

Released 1995

PRODUCERS: Sandy Gallin, Carol Baum, and Nancy Meyers for Touchstone; DIRECTOR: Charles Shyer; SCREENWRITERS: Frances Goodrich and Albert Hackett (1951 screenplay, *Father's Little Dividend*); Charles Shyer and Nancy Meyers (1995 screenplay, *Father of the Bride: Part II*); CINEMATOGRAPHERS: William Fraker and Elliot Davis; EDITORS: Adam Bernardi and Stephen Rotter; PRODUCTION DESIGNER: Linda DeScenna; SET DESIGNER: Ric McElvin; COSTUME DESIGNER: Enid Harris; MUSIC: Alan Silvestri; RUNNING TIME: 106 minutes.

CAST: Jane Adams (Dr. Megan Eisenberg), Kieran Culkin (Matty Banks), Peter Michael Goetz (John MacKenzie), Diane Keaton (Nina Banks), Steve Martin (George Banks), Kate McGregor-Stewart (Joanna MacKenzie), George Newbern (Bryan MacKenzie), Martin Short (Franck Eggelhoffer), Kimberly Williams (Annie Banks-MacKenzie), B. D. Wong (Howard Weinstein)

Unstrung Heroes (directed only)

Released 1995

PRODUCERS: Susan Arnold, Donna Roth, and Bill Badalato for Hollywood Pictures; DIRECTOR: Diane Keaton; SCREENWRITER: Richard LaGravenese (adapted from Franz Lidz's autobiography); CINEMATOGRAPHER: Phedon Papamichael; EDITOR: Lisa Churgin; PRODUCTION DESIGNER: Garreth Stover; SET DESIGNER: Larry Dias; COSTUME DESIGNER: Jill Ohanneson; MUSIC: Thomas Newman; RUNNING TIME: 93 minutes.

CAST: Maury Chaykin (Arthur Lidz), Kendra Krull (Sandy Lidz), Andie MacDowell (Selma Lidz), Michael Richards (Danny Lidz), John Turturro (Sid Lidz), Nathan Watt (Steven/Franz Lidz)

The First Wives Club
Released 1996

PRODUCERS: Scott Rudin, Adam Schroeder, and Ezra Swerdlow for Paramount; DIRECTOR: Hugh Wilson; SCREENWRITERS: Robert Harling (adapted from Olivia Goldsmith's novel of the same title); CINEMATOGRAPHER: Donald Thorin; EDITOR: John Bloom; PRODUCTION DESIGNER: Peter Larkin; SET DESIGNER: Leslie Rollins; COSTUME DESIGNER: Theoni Aldredge; MUSIC: Marc Shaiman; AWARDS: ASCAP Award (Shaiman); RUNNING TIME: 104 minutes.

Cast: Philip Bosco (Uncle Carmine), Stockard Channing (Cynthia Swann Griffin), Stephen Collins (Aaron Paradis), Jennifer Dundas (Chris Paradis), Victor Garber (Bill Atchison), Marcia Gay Harden (Dr. Leslie Rosen), Goldie Hawn (Elise Eliot Atchison), Dan Hedaya (Morton Cushman), Diane Keaton (Annie MacDuggan Paradis), Bette Midler (Brenda Morelli Cushman), Sarah Jessica Parker (Shelly Stewart), Bronson Pinchot (Duarto Feliz), Maggie Smith (Gunila Garson Goldberg)

Marvin's Room
Released 1996

PRODUCERS: Tod Scott Brody, Lori Steinberg, Scott Rudin, Jane Rosenthal, and Robert De Niro for Miramax; DIRECTOR: Jerry Zaks; SCREENWRITER: Scott McPherson (adapted from his play of the same title); CINEMATOGRAPHER: Piotr Sobocinski; EDITOR: Jim Clark; PRODUCTION DESIGNER: David Gropman; SET DESIGNER: Tracey Doyle; COSTUME DESIGNER: Julie Weiss; MUSIC: Rachel Portman; RUNNING TIME: 98 minutes.

CAST: Hume Cronyn (Marvin), Robert De Niro (Dr. Wally), Leonardo DiCaprio (Hank), Dan Hedaya (Bob), Diane Keaton* (Bessie), Hal Scardino (Charlie), Meryl Streep (Lee), Gwen Verdon (Ruth)

*Keaton received an Academy Award nomination for Best Actress, a Golden Globe nomination for Best Actress in a Motion Picture Drama, and a Screen Actors Guild nomination for Outstanding Performance by a Female Actor in a Leading Role.

Northern Lights
(television movie)
Released 1997

PRODUCERS: Diane Keaton, Warren Carr, Laurie Pozmantier, Bill Robinson, Meg Ryan, and Nina Sadowsky for Disney; DIRECTOR: Linda Yellen; SCREENWRITER: John Hoffman (adapted from his play of the same title); CINEMATOGRAPHER: Joseph Yacoe; EDITOR: Jan Northrop; PRODUCTION DESIGNER: Brent Thomas; SET DESIGNER: Lesley Beale; COSTUME DESIGNER: Tish Monaghan; MUSIC: Patrick Seymour; RUNNING TIME: 90 minutes.

CAST: Thomas Cavanagh (Frank), Maury Chaykin (Ben Rubadue), Joseph Cross (Jack), John Hoffman (Joe Scarlotti), Diane Keaton (Roberta Blumstein), Kathleen York (Daphne)

The Only Thrill
Released 1998

PRODUCERS: Carol Baum, Erin Gorman, Gabriel Grunfeld, James Holt, Peter Masterson, Ernst Stroh, and Yael Stroh for Moonstone; DIRECTOR: Peter Masterson; SCREENWRITER: Larry Ketron (adapted from his play, The Trading Post); CINEMATOGRAPHER: Don Fauntleroy; EDITOR: Jeff Freeman; PRODUCTION DESIGNER: John Frick; SET DESIGNER: Gabriella Villarreal; COSTUME DESIGNER: Jean-Pierre Dorléac; MUSIC: Peter Rodgers Melnick; RUNNING TIME: 107 minutes.

CAST: Tate Donovan (Eddie), Diane Keaton (Carol Fritzsimmons), Diane Lane (Katherine Fritzsimmons); Sharon Lawrence (Joleen Quillet), Robert Patrick (Tom McHenry), Sam Shepard (Reece McHenry), Stacey Travis (Lola Jennings)

The Other Sister
Released 1999

PRODUCERS: David Hoberman, Mario Iscovich, and Alexandra Rose for Touchstone; DIRECTOR: Garry Marshall; SCREENWRITERS: Alexandra Rose, Blair Richwood, Garry Marshall, and Bob Brunner; CINEMATOGRAPHER: Dante Spinotti; EDITOR: Bruce Green; PRODUCTION DESIGNER: Stephen Lineweaver; SET DESIGNER: Jay Hart; COSTUME DESIGNER: Gary Jones; MUSIC: Rachel Portman; RUNNING TIME: 130 minutes.

CAST: Hector Elizondo (Ernie), Diane Keaton (Elizabeth Tate), Juliette Lewis (Carla Tate), Juliet Mills (Winnie), Poppy Montgomery (Caroline Tate), Sarah Paulson (Heather Tate), Tracy Reiner (Michelle), Giovanni Ribisi (Danny), Tom Skerritt (Radley Tate)

Hanging Up
(directed and starred)
Released 2000

PRODUCERS: Delia Ephron, Nora Ephron, Laurence Mark, and Bill Robinson for Columbia; DIRECTOR: Diane Keaton; SCREENWRITERS: Nora and Delia Ephron (adapted from Delia Ephron's book); CINEMATOGRAPHER: Howard Atherton; EDITOR: Julie Monroe; PRODUCTION DESIGNER: Waldemar Kalinowski; SET DESIGNER: Florence Fellman; COSTUME DESIGNER: Bobbie Read; MUSIC: David Hirschfelder; RUNNING TIME: 94 minutes.

CAST: Adam Arkin (Joe), Ann Bortolotti (Ogmed Kunundar), Jesse James (Jesse), Diane Keaton (Georgia), Lisa Kudrow (Maddy), Cloris Leachman (Pat), Walter Matthau (Lou), Duke Moosekian (Dr. Omar Kunundar), Meg Ryan (Eve)

Bibliography

Abramovitch, Ingrid. "The Bankses' Pretty Baubles." Rev. of *Father of the Bride: Part II*, dir. Charles Shyer. *Sun-Sentinel* 8 Dec. 1995, sec. E: 3.

"Allen and Keaton Star Again." *South China Morning Post* 18 Aug. 1993, sec. News: 15.

Amelia Earhart: The Final Flight. Dir. Yves Simoneau. With Diane Keaton and Rutger Hauer. TNT, 12 Jun. 1994.

Anderson, John. "The EX Files." *Newsday* 25 Feb. 1996, sec. Fanfare: 10.

____. "The Father of All Old Baby Jokes." Rev. of *Father of the Bride: Part II*, dir. Charles Shyer. *Newsday* 8 Dec. 1995, sec. B: 7.

____. "Lovable Lunatics: Two Eccentric Uncles Transform a Troubled Boy." Rev. of *Unstrung Heroes*, dir. Diane Keaton. *Newsday* 15 Sep. 1995, sec. B: 3.

Andrews, Nigel. "Cheering on the Revolution." Rev. of *Reds*, dir. Warren Beatty. *Financial Times* (London) 26 Feb. 1982, sec. I: 17.

Angel, Ralph. "*Interiors*." *Magill's Survey of Cinema*. Ed. Frank Magill. Vol. II. Englewood Cliffs, N.J.: Salem Press, 1980, 844–47.

Annie Hall. Dir. Woody Allen. With Diane Keaton. United Artists, 1977.

Ansen, David. "Are There Diets in Heaven?" *Newsweek* 27 Apr. 1987: 79.

____. "The Best Revenge." *Newsweek* 23 Sep. 1996: 74.

____. "Man, Money and Motherhood." *Newsweek* 12 Oct. 1987: 84.

____. "Marital Blitz." Rev. of *Shoot the Moon*, dir. Alan Parker. *Newsweek* 25 Jan. 1982: 75.

____. "Romance on the Run." Rev. of *Mrs. Soffel*, dir. Gillian Armstrong. *Newsweek* 14 Jan. 1985: 52.

____. "This Boy's Oddball Life." Rev. of *Unstrung Heroes*, dir. Diane Keaton. *Newsweek* 25 Sep. 1995: 90.

____. "When the Bough Breaks." Rev. of *The Good Mother*, dir. Leonard Nimoy. *Newsweek* 7 Nov. 1988: 116.

Appelo, Tim. "Unstrung Heroine: Diane Keaton Lets Her Hair Down as Star and Executive Producer of *Northern Lights*." *Entertainment Weekly* 22 Aug. 1997: 114.

Armatage, Kay. "Women in Film." *Take One* 6.8 (1978): 36, 38.

Arnold, Gary. "Allen's *Annie Hall*: Bittersweet Romance." *Washington Post* 27 Apr. 1977, sec. C: 1.

____. "*Annie Hall* Dominates the Film Critics' Awards." *Washington Post* 20 Dec. 1977, sec. B: 5.

____. "*Lemon Sisters* Is Apt Title for This Weak, Seedy Film." *Washington Times* 3 Sep. 1990, sec. E: 3.

____. "Love's Bitter Season: Keaton and Finney in a Stellar *Shoot the Moon*." *Washington Post* 19 Feb. 1982, sec. D: 1.

____. "*Reds*: The Passions of John Reed." *Washington Post* 4 Dec. 1981, sec. D: 1.

____. "Woody Allen on Woody Allen." *Washington Post* 17 Apr. 1977, sec. N: 1.

"Arts: The Perils of Fame." *Atlanta Journal and Constitution* 2 Jan. 1991, sec. D: 3.

Ascher-Walsh, Rebecca, et al. Rev. of *Father of the Bride: Part II*, dir. Charles Shyer. *Entertainment Weekly* 1 Sep. 1995: 82.

____. Rev. of *First Wives Club*, dir. Hugh Wilson. *Entertainment Weekly* 23 Aug. 1996: 28+.

Attanasio, Paul. "*Crimes* Doesn't Play." *Washington Post* 12 Dec. 1986, sec. C: 11.

____. "Daring *Drummer*." *Washington Post* 19 Oct. 1984, sec. B: 1.

Baby Boom. Dir. Charles Shyer. With Diane Keaton and Sam Shepard. MGM/UA, 1987.

"*Baby Boom*." *People* 28 Dec. 1987: 27.

Baldwin, Kristen. "Diane Keaton: Twenty Years After *Annie Hall*, There's Always Room for One More Oscar." *Entertainment Weekly* (Special Collector's Issue/Academy Awards Extra) Mar. 1997: 44.

Baltake, Joe. "Small *Heroes* Has a Big Heart." *Sacramento Bee* 22 Sep. 1995, sec. TK: 22.

Bargreen, Melinda. "She'll Stick to Fiction, Thanks." *Seattle Times* 7 May 1998, sec. E: 1.

Barnes, Harper. "Annie Hall in Director's Chair: Diane Keaton Makes Switch from Acting." *St. Louis Post-Dispatch* 22 Sep. 1995, sec. E: 1.

____. "Diane Keaton's Nuanced Study: Slow but Worth It." Rev. of *Unstrung Heroes*. *St. Louis Post-Dispatch* 22 Sep. 1995, sec. E: 3.

____. "Script Squeezes Little Wit Out of 3 Women Buddies *The Lemon Sisters*." *St. Louis Post-Dispatch* 7 Sep. 1990, sec. F: 3.

____. "Streep and Keaton: Chemistry." *St. Louis Post-Dispatch* 28 Feb. 1997, sec. E: 3.

Barnett, Sheryl A. "From Hollywood: The '80s Woman." *New York Newsday* 7 Oct. 1987: 9.

Baron, David. "*Heroes* Goes into Trenches of Family Pain." *Times-Picayune* (New Orleans) 22 Sep. 1995, sec. L: 30.

____. "*Lemon Sisters* a Rambling Tale of Friendship." *Times-Picayune* (New Orleans) 6 Sep. 1990, sec. E: 14.

____. "*Marvin's Room* Needs a Good Straightening Up." *Times-Picayune* (New Orleans) 28 Feb. 1997, sec. L: 28.

____. "*Murder Mystery* a Killer Comedy." *Times-Picayune* (New Orleans) 17 Sep. 1993, sec. L: 26.

Bash, Alan. "Keaton's 'Flight' into life of Earhart." *USA Today* 9 June 1994, sec. D: 3.

Beck, Marilyn. "Carol Kane Leaves 'Frankie' for a Gig with Her 'Sisters.'" *Orange County Register* 17 Jun. 1988, sec. P: 33.

____. "Diane Keaton Says She, Steve Martin Only 'Good Friends.'" *Rocky Mountain News* 12 Dec. 1995, sec. D: 8.

____. "Diane, Warren Go House Hunting in N.Y." *Star-Ledger* 28 Sep. 1978: 44.

____. "*The Good Mother* May Fare Better Overseas, Nimoy Says." *Courier-Journal* (Louisville) 6 Feb. 1989, sec. C: 3.

____. "Keaton Wants Pacino in 'Man of the Hour.'" *Courier-Journal* (Louisville) 24 Jan. 1990, sec. C: 3.

____. "Leonard Nimoy Sees No Oscar in *The Good Mother's* Future." *Orange County Register* (California) 6 Feb. 1989, sec. F: 4.

____. "Richards Has to Wait for *Heroes*." *Sacramento Bee* 17 Apr. 1995, sec. C: 3.

Beddow, Reid. Rev. of *Friend and Lover: The Life of Louise Bryant* by Virginia Gardner. *Washington Post* 13 Feb. 1983, sec. Book World: 10.

Bekey, Michelle. "The Rocky Road to Launching a Business." *Working Woman* 14.6 (1989): 41.

Berger, Jerry. "Stardust Column." *St. Louis Post-Dispatch* 30 Aug. 1989, *You* Magazine: 1.

Berlin, Joey. "Another Mother." *New York Post* 3 Nov. 1988: 41.

Berman, Janice. "Diane Keaton's Women." *Newsday* 3 Nov. 1988, Part II, Interview: 3.

Bernard, Jami. "*First Wives Club*: Ex Makes the Spot." *Daily News* 20 Sep. 1996, sec. New York Now: 44.

____. "Love and Death and Diane." *New York Daily News* 25 May 1995: 57.

Berry, Robert. Rev. of *Diane Keaton: The Story of the Real Annie Hall* by Jonathan Moor. *Atlanta Journal Constitution* 22 Oct. 1989, sec. L: 10.

Berson, Misha. "*Marvin's Room* Faces Terrors of Dependency." *Seattle Times* 10 Jan. 1997, sec. F: 4.

Bilson, Anne. Rev. of *Manhattan Murder Mystery*, dir. Woody Allen. *Sunday Telegraph* 23 Jan. 1994: 6.

Birnie, Peter. "First Wives Exact Revenge on Callous Ex-Husbands." *Gazette* (Montreal) 20 Sep. 1996, sec. C: 4.

Bjorkman, Stig. *Woody Allen on Woody Allen*. New York: Grove Press, 1993.

Blades, K. Sweeney. "Picture of Self-Doubts." *Sacramento Bee* 21 May 1995, sec. A: 2.

Blake, Kimberly. "Life as Hollywood Lived

It." Rev. of *Still Life* by Diane Keaton. *New York Daily News* 4 Nov. 1983: 15.

Blake, Richard A. Rev. of *Manhattan Murder Mystery*, dir. Woody Allen. *America* 169.16 (1993): 22.

Blau, Douglas. "Manhattan." *Magill's Survey of Cinema*. Ed. Frank Magill. Vol. II. Englewood Cliffs, N.J.: Salem Press, 1980, 1067–69.

Blowen, Michael. "Diane Keaton Lost at Center Stage." *Boston Globe* 27 Nov. 1988, sec. B: 6.

____. "*Lemon Sisters*, Other Lemons." *Boston Globe* 4 Jan. 1991, sec. P: 50.

Bobbin, Jay. "Keaton's TV-Film Acting Debut." Rev. of *Running Mates*, dir. Michael Lindsay-Hogg. *Star Tribune* 4 Oct. 1992, sec. TV Week: 5.

Boggs, Joseph M. and Dennis W. Petrie. *The Art of Watching Films*. 5th ed. Mountain View, CA: Mayfield, 2000.

"Book 'Em." *Premiere*. Fall Movie Preview. Sep. 1999: 58.

Booth, Michael. "Musical Score Mars Room." *Denver Post* 10 Jan. 1997, sec. F: 4.

"Box-Office Charts." *The Independent* (London) 10 Oct. 1996, sec. Film Reviews: 7.

Boyar, Jay. "*Godfather III*: Crime Lord Tries to Change His Ways." *Orlando Sentinel Tribune* 11 Oct. 1991, sec. Calendar: 30.

____. "Keaton Used Life's Lessons in Directing Film." *Orlando Sentinel* 22 Sep. 1995, sec. Calendar: 23.

____. "Stars Are Fine but Film Is Not." Rev. of *Marvin's Room*, dir. Jerry Zaks. *Orlando Sentinel* 28 Feb. 1997, sec. Calendar: 20.

____. "*Unstrung Heroes* Is an Instant Classic." *Orlando Sentinel* 22 Sep. 1995, sec. Calendar: 21.

____. "Woody Allen Had Impact on Keaton: *Unstrung* Director Credits Her Mentor." *Arizona Republic* 21 Sep. 1995, sec. E: 3.

Boyum, Joy Gould. Rev. of *The Good Mother*, dir. Leonard Nimoy. *Glamour* 87.1 (1989): 103.

Britton, Bonnie. "Diane Keaton's Film Values Family." Rev. of *Unstrung Heroes*. *Indianapolis Star* 22 Sep. 1995, sec. G: 5.

____. "Sisters Cope with Present, Past in Drama." *Indianapolis Star* 28 Feb. 1997, sec. F: 1.

____. "*Wives* Succeeds with Humor, but Falters on Reality." *Indianapolis Star* 20 Sep. 1996, sec. E: 1.

Bromwich, David. Rev. of *Manhattan Murder Mystery*, dir. Woody Allen. *The New Leader* 76.12 (1993): 21.

Brownstein, Bill. "Cheap Sentiment Not Enough to Make Us Care About Bride." Rev. of *Father of the Bride*, dir. Charles Shyer. *The Gazette* 21 Dec. 1991, sec. E: 4.

Brownstone, David M. "Diane Keaton." *People in the News*. New York: MacMillan Pub. Co., 1991. 172–73.

Buck, Joan Juliet. "Inside Diane Keaton." *Vanity Fair* Mar. 1987: 105–07+.

Buehrer, Beverley Bare. "*Marvin's Room*." *Magill's Cinema Annual 1997*. Ed. Beth A. Fhaner. 16th ed. Detroit: Gale, 1998. 189–90.

Bunce, Alan. "Worth Noting on TV." *Christian Science Monitor* 10 Jun. 1994, sec. Television: 12.

Burkett, Michael. "Diane Keaton's Directorial Debut Is a Smug, Self-Righteous Semi-Documentary." Rev. of *Heaven*, dir. Diane Keaton. *Orange County Register* (California) 17 Apr. 1987, sec. P: 5.

Butler, Jeremy. "The Star System and Hollywood." *The Oxford Guide to Film Studies*. Eds. John Hill and Pamela Church Gibson. New York: Oxford UP, 1998. 342–53.

Butler, Robert W. "Stringing Together Quirks and Warmth: *Unstrung Heroes* Is Director Diane Keaton's Finest Film Thus Far." *Kansas City Star* 22 Sep. 1995, sec. Preview: 5.

Campbell, Bob. "Light and Lively *Wives* Perfect Recipe for Laughs." *Times-Picayune* (New Orleans) 27 Sep. 1996, sec. LAG: 29.

____. "They're Older, Wiser—and at Peace." Rev. of *The First Wives Club*, dir. Hugh Wilson. *Star Tribune* (Casper, WY) 20 Sep. 1996, sec. E: 13.

Canby, Vincent. "Critics' Choices." *New York Times* 24 Jun. 1984, sec. A: 2.

____. "Film: A Documentary, Diane Keaton's *Heaven*." *New York Times* 17 Apr. 1987, sec. C: 8.

____. "Film: Finney and Miss Keaton in *Shoot the Moon*." *New York Times* 22 Jan. 1982, sec. C: 13.

____. "Film: *Love and Death* Is Grand Woody Allen." *New York Times* 11 Jun. 1975, sec. L: 48.

____. "Film View: Two New Triumphs Cap a Fine Year for Actresses." Rev. of *Shoot the Moon*, dir. Alan Parker. *New York Times* 12 Dec. 1982, sec. 2: 21.

____. "*Little Drummer Girl*, Based on La

Carré Novel." *New York Times* 19 Oct. 1984, sec. C: 18.

____. "Love, Death, God, Sex, Suicide and Woody Allen." *New York Times* 22 Jun. 1975, sec. 2: 1, 19.

____. "Much Ado About Clint, Sly, Woody and Emma." *New York Times* 26 Dec. 1993, sec. 2: 9.

____. "Screen: Beatty's *Reds*, with Diane Keaton." *New York Times* 4 Dec. 1981, sec. C: 8.

____. "Screen: Diane Keaton Portrays *Mrs. Soffel*." *New York Times* 26 Dec. 1984, sec. C: 15.

____. "Screen: Woody Allen's *Manhattan*." *New York Times* 25 Apr. 1979, sec. 3: 17.

____. "Woody Allen: Risking It Without Laughs." Rev. of *Interiors*. *New York Times* 6 Aug. 1978, sec. 2: 1.

Carman, John. "HBO's Timely *Running Mates*." *San Francisco Chronicle* 2 Oct. 1992, sec. C: 1.

____. "*Lemon Sisters* Leaves Sour Taste." *Houston Post* 3 Sep. 1990, sec. B: 1.

____. "*Wildflower* Is Tale of Innocence." *San Francisco Chronicle* 3 Dec. 1991, sec. E: 1.

Carmody, John. "The TV Column." *Washington Post* 15 Dec. 1995, sec. F: 8.

Carr, Jay. "Allen's *Mystery*: The Old Comic Magic Is Back." *Boston Globe* 20 Aug. 1993, sec. Living: 41.

____. "Diane Keaton: 'Not a Nice, Neat Package.'" *Boston Globe* 1 Nov. 1988, sec. Living: 23.

____. "Diane Keaton Put Her Fears Aside for *The Good Mother*." *Chicago Tribune* 4 Nov. 1988, sec. CN: L.

____. "Diane Keaton Rejoins the Club." *Boston Globe* 15 Sep. 1996, sec. N: 1.

____. "An Exhausted *Godfather III*." *Boston Globe* 24 Dec. 1990, sec. P: 31.

____. "*First Wives* Whip Up Juicy Just Deserts." *Boston Globe* 20 Sep. 1996, sec. D: 1.

____. "Keaton's *Heroes* Excels Through Restraint." *Boston Globe* 11 Sep. 1995, sec. Arts & Film: 31.

____. "Keaton, Streep Act in Perfect Sync." *Boston Globe* 10 Jan. 1997, sec. C: 5.

____. Rev. of *The Good Mother*, dir. Leonard Nimoy. *Boston Globe* 4 Nov. 1988, sec. Living: 47.

Carroll, Tim. *Woody and His Women*. London: Little, Brown and Co., 1993.

Castro, Peter, et al. "Family Reunion: On the 25th Anniversary of *The Godfather*, Cast Members Look Back on Life with the Don and Reveal What Came Afterward." *People* 24 Mar. 1997: 48+.

Cedrone, Lou. "Elliott Gould Ranks with the Survivors." *St. Petersburg Times* 18 Sep. 1990, sec. D: 3.

Champlin, Charles. "The Attention Intimidates the *Annie Hall* Girl." *New York Post* 31 Jan. 1978: 36.

____. "Bringing Up *Baby*: Diane Keaton Plays Annie Hall in an Apron for New Film." *Los Angeles Times* 4 Oct. 1987, sec. Calendar: 29.

Chang, Yahlin. "A Light Touch with Tough Stuff." *Newsweek* 25 Sep. 1995: 90.

"Cinema: Murders and Merry Mayhem." Rev. of *Manhattan Murder Mystery*, dir. Woody Allen. *The Observer* 23 Jan. 1994, sec. Review: 11.

Clark, John. "All in the Family." *Premiere* 5.5 (1992): 26–28.

Clark, Mike. "*Unstrung Heroes* a Tangle of Misfits." *USA Today* 15 Sep. 1995, sec. D: 4.

____. "Wily Women Bring *Club* to Raucous Life." *USA Today* 20 Sep. 1996, sec. D: 1.

Clements, Marcelle. "On the Keaton Track." *Lear's* 6.7 (1993): 80–84, 103–04.

Cobb, Chris. "Despite Its Title, This Flick Isn't Gender Exclusive." Rev. of *First Wives Club*, dir. Hugh Wilson. *Ottawa Citizen* 20 Sep. 1996, sec. E: 4.

Coe, Jonathan. "Amusing Things." Rev. of *Diane Keaton: The Story of the Real Annie Hall* by Jonathan Moor. *Guardian* (Manchester) 19 Apr. 1990, sec. 23: 5.

____. Rev. of *First Wives Club*, dir. Hugh Wilson. *New Statesman* 125 (1996): 40.

Cohn, Al. "A Current Couple's Similar Pasts." *Newsday* 18 Sep. 1989, sec. News: 8.

____. "Diane Keaton: All-Business Actress." *Newsday* 14 Jan. 1988, sec. News: 9.

Collins, Nancy. "Annie Hall Doesn't Live Here Anymore." *Vanity Fair* Nov. 1995: 92–98.

____. "*Architectural Digest* Visits Diane Keaton." *Architectural Digest* Jul. 1999: 87–94+.

Cook, Catherine. "Fall Fashion: *Annie Hall* Returns." *St. Louis Post-Dispatch* 13 Jul. 1989, sec. Style West: 11.

Conant, Jennet. "Krizia's Executive Class." *Newsweek* 26 Oct. 1987: 70.

Coppola, Francis Ford. Interview. *A Look Back*. The Godfather Video Collection. Paramount, 1997.

Corliss, Richard. "Art, War, Death and Sex: Big Issues in Four 'Small' Independent

Films." Rev. of *Heaven*, dir. Diane Keaton. *Time* 27 Apr. 1987: 79.

____. "The Ladies Who Lunge." *Time* 7 Oct. 1996: 86–87.

____. "Pulp from the Woodpile." Rev. of *Woody Allen* by Eric Lax. *Time* 10 Jun. 1991: 68.

Cowie, Peter. *Annie Hall*. London: British Film Institute, 1996.

Cox, Yvonne. "People." *Maclean's* 2 Nov. 1987: 48.

Coyle, Mary. "*Baby Boom*." *Video* 12.3 (1988): 83.

"Creative Executives at the Studios." *Premiere*. Women in Hollywood Special Issue. 1997: 51.

Crimes of the Heart. Dir. Bruce Beresford. With Diane Keaton and Jessica Lange. DeLaurentiis Entertainment Group, 1986.

Cunningham, Kim. "Pros and Icons." *People Weekly* 47 (1997): 212.

Curtis, Quentin. "The Arts: The Family Epic to End All Family Epics." *Daily Telegraph* (London) 26 Jul. 1996: 16.

D'Angelo, Vince. Rev. of *Running Mates*, starring Diane Keaton. *People* 38.14 (1992): 13+.

Davenport, Hugo. "Mr. Neurosis Is Back in Town." Rev. of *Manhattan Murder Mystery*, dir. Woody Allen. *Daily Telegraph* (London) 21 Jan. 1994: 16.

____. "Tears at the Heart." Rev. of *Unstrung Heroes*, dir. Diane Keaton. *Daily Telegraph* (London) 8 Dec. 1995: 26.

Davis, Daphne. *Stars!* New York: Stewart, Tabori & Chang Pubs., 1983.

Davis, Douglas. "Photographs by Annie Hall." *Newsweek* 17 Mar. 1980: 96.

Dawson, Greg. "*Running Mates*: She'd Be Far-Fetched First Lady." *Orlando Sentinel Tribune* 4 Oct. 1992, sec. F: 1.

Dearborn, Mary. *Queen of Bohemia, the Life of Louise Bryant*, Replica Books, 2001.

deCordova, Richard. *Picture Personalities: The Emergence of the Star System in America*. Chicago: U. of Illinois P., 1990.

Decurtis, Anthony. "Woody Allen: The Rolling Stone Interview." *Rolling Stone* 16 Sep. 1993: 45+.

Delean, Paul. "You Can't Dislike These Heroes." Rev. of *Unstrung Heroes*, dir. Diane Keaton. *The Gazette* (Montreal) 22 Sep. 1995, sec. D: 5.

Delmont, Jim. "Revenge Not Sweet in *Wives*." *Omaha World Herald* 20 Sep. 1996, sec. SF: 39.

Demaris, Ovid. "Diane Keaton at Forty-Two:

Older, Warmer, Stronger." *Parade* 17 Jan. 1988: 4–6.

Denby, David. "Getting Even." Rev. of *First Wives Club*, dir. Hugh Wilson. *New York* 29.39 (1996): 46–47.

____. "Paying the Price for Pleasure." Rev. of *The Good Mother*, dir. Leonard Nimoy. *Premiere* 2.7 (1989): 30.

Denerstein, Robert. "At 51, Keaton's Happy to Act Her Age." *Rocky Mountain News* (Denver) 12 Jan. 1997, sec. D: 6.

____. "*Bride* Gives Birth to Sappy Sequel." *Rocky Mountain News* (Denver) 8 Dec. 1995, sec. D: 6.

____. "Showy *Wives Club* Is Fluffy, but Fun Affair." *Rocky Mountain News* (Denver) 20 Sep. 1996, sec. D: 8.

____. "*Unstrung Heroes* Sweet as Well as Quirky." *Rocky Mountain News* (Denver) 22 Sep. 1995, sec. D: 6.

Denton, Herbert H. "Hollywood North." *Washington Post* 24 Apr. 1988, sec. F: 1.

DeRosa, Robin. "*First Wives* Joins Club of Box-Office Biggies." *USA Today* 23 Sep. 1996, sec. D: 1.

"Diane Keaton." *Almanac of Famous People*. Lexis-Nexis: Biographical Sources (1998: Sixth Edition).

"Diane Keaton." *Contemporary Theatre, Film and Television*: Vol. 13. Lexis-Nexis: Biographical Sources (10 Jul. 1995).

"Diane Keaton." *Marquis Who's Who*. Lexis-Nexis: Biographical Sources (19 Aug. 1997).

"Diane Keaton." *Movie People*. Hollywood OnLine (1998).

"Diane Keaton." *Newsmakers 1997*: Issue 4. Lexis-Nexis: Biographical Sources (6 Jan. 1998).

"Diane Keaton Is Signed for *Mr. Goodbar*." *New York Times* 22 Sep. 1976: 28.

"Diane Keaton Is Well, Uh, You Know ... Don't You?" *The Orlando Sentinel Tribune* 7 Jun. 1994, sec. A: 2.

"Diane Keaton: J. C. Wiatt." UA Press Release, circa 1987.

"Diane Keaton, Kay in *The Godfather: Part II*, Lets Her Hair Down About Taking Her Clothes Off." Paramount Pictures Press Release, circa 1974.

"Diane Keaton Not Great with Goodbyes." *USA Today* 23 Dec. 1991, sec. D: 2.

"Diane Keaton: The Story of the Real Annie Hall." Rev. of Jonathan Moor biography. *Variety* 336.2 (26 July 1989): 95.

Dodd, Johnny, et al. "Second Wives: Real Life First Wives Claim Revenge Is Sweet, but

That Starting Over Can Be Even Better." *People* 14 Oct. 1996: 114+.

Dominguez, Robert. "In *The Godfather* We Trust: As the Definitive Crime Saga Turns 25, A Salute to an American Classic." *Daily News* (New York) 16 Mar. 1997, sec. Spotlight: 16.

Dowd, Maureen. "Diane and Woody, Still a Fun Couple." *New York Times* 15 Aug. 1993, sec. 2: 1, 16.

____. "The Old Pals Act." *The Guardian* (London) 25 Sep. 1993, sec. Weekend Page: 6.

____. "The Return of an Older, Wiser Keaton." *Dallas Morning News* 20 Aug. 1993, sec. C: 2.

Dreher, Rod. "*Heroes* Goes Far on Emotional Ride." *Sun-Sentinel* 22 Sep. 1995, sec. Showtime: 5.

Dudek, Duane. "*Unstrung Heroes* Brings Little to a Familiar, Traumatic Theme." *Milwaukee Journal Sentinel* 22 Sep. 1995, sec. Cue: 5.

____. "*Unstrung Heroes* Her Debut in New Role." *Milwaukee Journal Sentinel* 24 Sep. 1995, sec. Cue: 1.

Dunkley, Robert. "Departure Points: On Location—The Place: '21 Club. The Film: *Manhattan Murder Mystery*." *Sunday Telegraph* (London) 6 Feb. 1994: 24.

Dunne, Dominick. "Hide-and-Seek with Diane Keaton." *Vanity Fair* Feb. 1985: 35–42, 96.

Dutka, Elaine. "'Avon Ladies' Calling: After the Success of *First Wives*, the Stars Are Talking About Reuniting—But for a Rival Studio." *Los Angeles Times* 9 Jan. 1997, sec. F: 1.

Dwyer, Michael. "Diane and Andie." *Irish Times* 9 Dec. 1995, sec. Weekend: 12.

____. "Woody Allen's Private Life Becomes Very Public." *Irish Times* 19 Aug. 1992, sec. News Features: 8.

Dwyer, Michael, et al. "Wives, Witches and H. G. Wells." *Irish Times* 15 Nov. 1996, sec. Cinema: 15.

Dyer, Richard. "Four Films of Lana Turner." *Star Texts: Image and Performance in Film and Television.* Ed. Jeremy G. Butler. Detroit: Wayne State UP, 1991. 214–39.

____. *Heavenly Bodies: Film Stars and Society.* London: MacMillan Press Ltd., 1986.

____. "Introduction to Film Studies." *The Oxford Guide to Film Studies.* Eds. John Hill and Pamela Church Gibson. New York: Oxford UP, 1998. 3–10.

____. *Stars.* London: BFI Publishing, 1979.

Easton, Nina J. "Coppola to Reshoot Portions of *Godfather: Part III*." *Los Angeles Times* 7 Aug. 1990, sec. D: 2.

Ebert, Roger. "Here Comes the Sequel: *Bride II* Gives Birth to 'Surrogate Happiness.'" *Chicago Sun-Times* 8 Dec. 1995, sec. NC: 27.

____. "Murder, He Wrote." Rev. of *Manhattan Murder Mystery*, dir. Woody Allen. *Chicago Sun-Times* 20 Aug. 1993, sec. Weekend Plus: 45.

____. "Old Wives' Tale: Dumped Spouses Bond in Forgettable Revenge Comedy." *Chicago Sun-Times* 20 Sep. 1996, sec. NC: 31.

____. "Our Heroes: Eccentric Characters Accent Dramedy." *Chicago Sun-Times* 15 Sep. 1995, sec. NC: 37.

____. Rev. of *The Good Mother*, dir. Leonard Nimoy. *San Diego Union-Tribune* 17 Feb. 1989, sec. C: 2.

____. "'Room' to Grow: Anatomy of a Reunion." *Chicago Sun-Times* 10 Jan. 1997, sec. NC: 25.

____. "'Unstrung,' Not Hamstrung: Diane Keaton Limits Her Role." *Chicago Sun-Times* 17 Sep. 1995, sec. NC: 5.

Edelstein, David. "Knockin' on Heaven's Door." *Rolling Stone* 7 May 1987: 23–24+.

Egerton, Judith. "*Unstrung Heroes* Performances." *Courier-Journal* (Louisville) 23 Sep. 1995, sec. S: 23.

"8 Funny Movies You Can Rent—*Sleeper* Starring Woody Allen and Diane Keaton." *Good Housekeeping* 221.3 (1995): 144.

Elber, Lynn. "Keaton Feels Free and Fine Over 50." *Toronto Sun*, 23 Aug. 1997, sec. Entertainment: 36.

Elder, Sean. "Keaton's Comeback." *Vogue* 183.9 (1993): 316–20.

Elliott, David. "*Baby Boom* Goes Bust in a Hurry." *San Diego Union-Tribune* 7 Oct. 1987, sec. D: 5.

____. "Diane's Heroes." Rev. of *Unstrung Heroes*, dir. Diane Keaton. *San Diego Union-Tribune* 21 Sep. 1995, sec. Entertainment: 17.

____. "*Good Mother* Hits Home with Serious Message." *San Diego Union-Tribune* 4 Nov. 1988, sec. D: 1.

____. "*Heaven* Isn't That Rewarding." *San Diego Union-Tribune* 29 Apr. 1987, sec. E: 7.

____. "Movie Moms." *San Diego Union-Tribune* 20 Nov. 1988, sec. E: 1.

____. "Not Much Mystery, but Plenty of Pleasure." Rev. of *Manhattan Murder Mystery*, dir. Woody Allen. *San Diego Union-Tribune* 19 Aug. 1993, sec. Entertainment: 17.

____. Rev. of *First Wives Club*, dir. Hugh Wilson. *San Diego Union-Tribune* 19 Sep. 1996, sec. Entertainment: 7.

Emerson, Jim. "Diane Keaton Babies Her Expanding Career." *The Orange County Register* 7 Oct. 1987, sec. L: 1.

"Emmy Nominees." *Washington Post* 10 Sep. 1995, sec. Y: 4.

Endrst, James. "Keaton, HBO Dusting Off *Running Mates*." *Hartford Courant* 13 Jul. 1992, sec. C: 1.

____. "Mystery Lifts TNT's Earhart Drama." *Hartford Courant* 6 Jun. 1994, sec. B: 1.

Everett, Todd. "*Running Mates*." *Variety* 348.11 (1992): 66.

"Fall Movie Preview." *Entertainment Weekly,* 20/27 Aug. 1999: 77.

"Fanfare: The Keaton Complex, *Newsday* 17 Sept. 1995: 12.

Father of the Bride. Dir. Charles Shyer. With Diane Keaton and Steve Martin. Touchstone, 1991.

Father of the Bride: Part II. Dir. Charles Shyer. With Diane Keaton and Steve Martin. Touchstone, 1995.

Fenster, Bob. "Men from Uncle to the Rescue." Rev. of *Unstrung Heroes*, dir. Diane Keaton. *Arizona Republic* 22 Sep. 1995, sec. E: 4.

Fink, Mitchell. "A Deal He Can't Refuse?" *People* 15 Jan. 1990: 27.

____. "Progress Report." *People* 5 Feb. 1990: 29.

First Wives Club. Dir. Hugh Wilson. With Diane Keaton, Goldie Hawn, and Bette Midler. Paramount, 1996.

"*First Wives Club* Is First to $100-Million." *St. Petersburg Times* 26 Nov. 1996, sec. B: 2.

"*First Wives* Stars May Do New Movie." *Chicago Sun-Times* 7 Jan. 1997, sec. FTR: 20.

Flatley, Guy. "The Applause You Hear Is for Diane Keaton." *Los Angeles Times* 12 May 1974, sec. Calendar: 25+.

____. "*The Good Mother*: Movie Reviews." *Cosmopolitan* 206.1 (1989): 26.

____. "Woody Allen Is Not Playing His Next One for Laughs." *New York Times* 21 Oct. 1977, sec. C: 8.

Fong-Torres, Ben. "The Life and Lurves of Diane Keaton." *Rolling Stone* 30 Jun. 1977: 71–77.

Fox, Julian. *Woody: Movies from Manhattan.* New York: The Overlook Press, 1996.

Freeman, John. "Like the Missing Earhart, Movie About Pilot's Flight a Lost Cause." *San Diego Union-Tribune* 12 Jun. 1994, sec. Entertainment: 8.

Freeman, Paul. "*Father of the Bride* Quirks Work in a Big Way for Short." *San Francisco Chronicle* 15 Dec. 1991, sec. Sunday Datebook: 23.

Friedman, Roger D. "Annie Hall Grows Up in New *Manhattan*." *Chicago Sun-Times* 3 Sep. 1993, sec. NC: 27.

Friendly, David T. "*Godfather III*: The Movie Waiting to Happen." *Los Angeles Times* 24 Nov. 1985, sec. Calendar: 22.

Froelich, Janis D. "*Boom* Goes Bust as TV Series." *St. Petersburg Times* 10 Sep. 1988, sec. D: 1.

____. "*Running Mates* a Shallow Tale." *St. Petersburg Times* 2 Oct. 1992, sec. Weekend: 19.

Fuller, Graham. Rev. of *Marvin's Room*, dir. Jerry Zaks. *Interview* 26.12 (1996): 62–63.

Futterman, Ellen. "Martin and Remake Successful Marriage." *St. Louis Post Dispatch* 20 Dec. 1991, sec. G: 3.

____. "The Revenge of Three Jilted Wives." *St. Louis Post-Dispatch* 20 Sep. 1996, sec. E: 3.

____. "Sequel to a Remake? The Laughs Are Diluted." Rev. of *Father of the Bride: Part II*, dir. Charles Shyer. *St. Louis Post-Dispatch* 8 Dec. 1995, sec. E: 3.

Gabrenya, Frank. "Last Laughs." Rev. of *First Wives Club*, dir. Hugh Wilson. *Columbus Dispatch* 20 Sep. 1996, sec. E: 12.

____. "Mystery Loves Company in Allen's Latest." Rev. of *Manhattan Murder Mystery*, dir. Woody Allen. *Columbus Dispatch* 2 Sep. 1993, sec. Features: 4.

Gage, Joan. "'Woody Was as Scared of Me as I Was of Him.'" *New York Times* 28 May 1972: 9, 14.

Gallagher, Maggie. "*First Wives* Reminds Us About Fault." *Dallas Morning News* 1 Oct. 1996, sec. A: 19.

Gamson, Joshua. *Claims to Fame: Celebrity in Contemporary America.* Los Angeles: U of California P, 1994.

Gardella, Kay. "Diane Keaton Heads a Winning Ticket of Love and Politics." *Atlanta Constitution* 2 Oct. 1992, sec. F: 4.

____. "Keaton Has Few Complaints About Direction of Her Career." *Orange County Register* (California) 2 Oct. 1992, sec. P: 44.

Garis, Leslie. "Keaton's Single Spirit." *The Times* (London) 8 Dec. 1990, sec. Features.

Garner, Jack. "Stars Buoy Middling Look at Middle Age." Rev. of *First Wives Club*, dir. Hugh Wilson. *Courier-Journal* (Louisville) 20 Sep. 1996, sec. C: 1.

Gehr, Richard. "Drama." Rev. of *The Good*

Mother, starring Diane Keaton. *Video* 13.1 (1989): 60.

Gelmis, Joseph. "The Allure of the Underworld Is Paying Quite Well as Hollywood Rediscovers the Gangster Movie." *Newsday* 21 Oct. 1990, sec. Part II: 4.

____. "A New Film Genre That Isn't Just Kids' Stuff." *Newsday* 13 Apr. 1990, sec. Weekend: 21.

Gerosa, Melina. "Girl Talk." *Ladies' Home Journal* 113.9 (1996): 134–37+.

Gerosa, Melina, and Rob Medich. "Autumn Sonatas: The Best of Early Fall." Rev. of *The Lemon Sisters*, dir. Joyce Chopra. *Premiere* 3.2 (1989): 66–72.

Gerstel, Judy. "Cast, Keaton Combine for Zesty Family Comedy." Rev. of *Unstrung Heroes*, dir. Diane Keaton. *Toronto Star* 16 Sep. 1995, sec. C: 3.

Giannetti, Louis. *Understanding Movies*. 8th ed. Englewood Cliffs, N.J.: Prentice Hall, 1999.

Giannetti, Louis, and Scott Eyman. *Flashback: A Brief History of Film*. 3rd ed. Englewood Cliffs, N.J.: Prentice Hall, 1996.

Gibson, Pamela Church. "Film Costume." *The Oxford Guide to Film Studies*. Eds. John Hill and Pamela Church Gibson. New York: Oxford UP, 1998. 36–42.

Gilbert, Matthew. "This *Father* Tampers with Perfection." Rev. of *Father of the Bride*, dir. Charles Shyer. *Boston Globe* 20 Dec. 1991, sec. Arts & Film: 54.

____. "Woody & Mia." *Toronto Star* 23 Jun. 1991, sec. D: 1.

____. "Woody in Wonderland." *Boston Globe* 8 Feb. 1991, sec. P: 39.

Gilby, Ryan. "That Turturro Feeling." *The Independent* (London) 10 Apr. 1997, sec. Film: 4.

Gillette, Jennifer. "*Marvin's* Characters Powerful." *Sun-Sentinel* (Fort Lauderdale) 14 Mar. 1997, sec. Showtime: 66.

Gilliatt, Penelope. "Profiles: Her Own Best Disputant." *New Yorker* 25 Dec. 1978: 38–43.

Girgus, Sam B. *The Films of Woody Allen*. New York: Cambridge UP, 1993.

Gittelson, Natalie. "The Faces of Diane Keaton." *McCall's* Nov. 1978: 26+.

Gleiberman, Owen. "Ms.-Guided Effort." Rev. of *First Wives Club*, dir. Hugh Wilson. *Entertainment Weekly* 27 Sep. 1996: 53.

____. "Strained Relations." Rev. of *Unstrung Heroes*, dir. Diane Keaton. *Entertainment Weekly* 22 Sep. 1995: 57.

Gleick, Elizabeth. "Hell Hath No Fury." *Time* 148.17 (1996): 80–85.

Gliatto, Tom. Rev. of *The First Wives Club*, dir. Hugh Wilson. *People* 46.13: 19.

____. Rev. of *Unstrung Heroes*, dir. Diane Keaton. *People* 44.13 (1995): 21.

Gliatto, Tom, and Ralph Novak. Rev. of *Manhattan Murder Mystery*, starring Diane Keaton. *People* 23 Aug. 1993: 13.

Glicksman, Marlaine. "Hotel *Heaven*." *Film Comment* 23.2 (March 1987): 32–37.

The Godfather. Dir. Francis Ford Coppola. With Marlon Brando and Al Pacino. Paramount, 1972.

The Godfather: Part II. Dir. Francis Ford Coppola. With Al Pacino and Diane Keaton. Paramount, 1974.

The Godfather: Part III. Dir. Francis Ford Coppola. With Al Pacino and Diane Keaton. Paramount, 1990.

Gold, Sylviane. Interview with Diane Keaton. *New York Post* 16 Apr. 1977: 31, 40.

Goldman, Debra. "Indie Top Six: *The Lemon Sisters* Directed by Joyce Chopra and Starring Diane Keaton, Carol Kane and Kathryn Grody." *Premiere* 2.10 (1989): 81.

Golightly, Bill. "Committing Crimes." *Horizon* 29.9 (1986): 33–35.

The Good Mother. Dir. Leonard Nimoy. With Diane Keaton and Liam Neeson. Touchstone, 1988.

Gottlieb, Sidney. "*The Godfather: Part III*." *Magill's Cinema Annual*. Ed. Frank Magill. Englewood Cliffs, N.J.: Salem Press, 1991, 121–25.

Graham, Jefferson. "Keaton Still Prefers the Offbeat Path." *USA Today* 22 Aug. 1997, sec. D: 3.

Grahnke, Lon. "HBO's *Mates* Wins: Comedy Tackles Politics and Love." *Chicago Sun-Times* 1 Oct. 1992, sec. 2: 49.

Grant, Hugh. *The Today Show*. Interview. May 2000.

"Greek Goddess Don't Let Her Ditziness Fool You: Diane Keaton's Talent Goes Sky-High." *Buffalo News* 24 Sep. 1995, sec. G: 1.

Green, Michelle, and David Wallace. "The Dish from Down Under." *People* 4 Feb. 1985: 70.

Green, Tom. "Diane's 'Mystery' Duds Strictly Out of Character." *USA Today* 26 Aug. 1993, sec. D: 2.

____. "There's no 'Mystery' to Keaton's relation to Woody." *USA Today* 24 Aug. 1993, sec. D: 1.

Greenberg, James. "Not at All Unstrung, and Calling the Shots." *New York Times* 3 Sept. 1995, sec. H: 6, 20.

Griffiths, John, and Terry Kelleher. Rev. of

Northern Lights, dir. Linda Yellen. *People* 25 Aug. 1997: 17.

Gristwood, Sarah. "Keaton but Uncowed." *The Guardian* (London) 10 Nov. 1995, sec. T: 6.

Guarino, Ann. "Off Camera." Interview with Diane Keaton. *New York Daily News* 24 Mar. 1974, sec. Leisure: 17.

Guthmann, Edward. "Keaton as Director Has the Right Touch." *San Francisco Chronicle* 15 Sep. 1995, sec. C: 3.

____. "Keaton Gets Room to Grow." *San Francisco Chronicle* 9 Jan. 1997, sec. E: 1.

____. "A Revival That We Can't Refuse." *San Francisco Chronicle* 21 Mar. 1997, sec. C: 3.

____. "This Is a 'Room' Full of Acting Treasures." Rev. of *Marvin's Room*, dir. Jerry Zaks. *San Francisco Chronicle* 10 Jan. 1997, sec. D: 3.

____. "*Wives* Get Even and Even More." *San Francisco Chronicle* 20 Sep. 1996, sec. C: 1.

Hagen, Bill. "*Crimes* Intelligent, Exquisitely Cast and Very Funny." *San Diego Union-Tribune* 15 Dec. 1986, sec. E: 9.

____. "Keaton Explodes Fast-Track, Rat-Race Myth in *Baby Boom*." *San Diego Union-Tribune* 6 Oct. 1987, sec. D: 8.

____. "Tedious *Lemon Sisters* Lives Up to Name." *San Diego Union-Tribune* 4 Sep. 1990, sec. C: 6.

Hall, Carla. "Director Parker, Master Manipulator." *Washington Post* 9 Dec. 1988, sec. C: 1.

Haller, Scot. "*Mrs. Soffel*." *People* 28 Jan. 1985: 10.

Hamill, Denis. "A Movie Fan Who's Calling the Shots." *Daily News* 27 Apr. 1997, sec. Spotlight: 5.

Hanging Up. Dir. Diane Keaton. With Walter Matthau and Meg Ryan. Columbia, 2000.

"*Hanging Up*." *Entertainment Weekly*. Fall Movie Preview. 20/27 Aug. 1999: 77.

Harrop, David, et al. "Who Makes What $." *People* 25 Mar. 1985: 97.

Harry and Walter Go to New York. Dir. Mark Rydell. With Diane Keaton and Elliott Gould. 1976.

Hartl, John. "*First Wives Club* Could Have Made a Great Short." *Seattle Times* 20 Sep. 1996, sec. F: 1.

____. "Gloom with a View—Masochism Is Star of *The Only Thrill*." *Seattle Times* 3 Apr. 1998, sec. G: 8.

____. "*Godfather 3*: The Story Never Ends." *Seattle Times* 25 Dec. 1990, sec. F: 1.

____. "This Time Around, *Father* Is One Sad Sitcom." *Seattle Times* 8 Dec. 1995, sec. G: 3.

Haskell, Molly. *Biography*. "Susan Hayward." Arts and Entertainment Network. 6 Oct. 1999.

____. *From Reverence to Rape*. Chicago: U of Chicago P, 1973.

____. "Venus Substitutes." *Vogue* 178.1 (1988): 38+.

Haun, Harry. "'I Didn't Know If Diane Could Do It.'" Interview with Richard Brooks. *New York Daily News* 16 Oct. 1977, sec. L: 7.

Havis, Richard James. "Actresses Wreak a Delicious Revenge." Rev. of *First Wives Club*, dir. Hugh Wilson. *South China Morning Post* 17 Nov. 1996: 5.

Hawkins, Robert J. "Producer, Director Talking About Oscars." *San Diego Union-Tribune* 4 Nov. 1988, sec. C: 1.

Hearty, Kitty Bowe. "Air Amelia." *Premiere* June 1994: 31.

Heaven. Dir. Diane Keaton. Lightyear Entertainment, 1987.

"*Heaven*." Rev. of *Heaven*, dir. Diane Keaton. *People* 11 May 1987: 10.

Helligar, Jeremy. "Passages." *People* 17 Feb. 1997: 87.

"Hello, Diane Keaton." *Toronto Star* 11 Jun. 1995, sec. F: 2.

"Her Gamble on *Goodbar* Put Woody Allen's Flaky Foil in the Hollywood Catbird Seat." *People* 26 Dec. 1978: 34–35.

Hettrick, Scott. "Depression Tale's Powerful Idea Lost in Botched Direction." Rev. of *Wildflower*, dir. Diane Keaton. *Sun-Sentinel* (Fort Lauderdale) 1 Jan. 1993, sec. Showtime: 18.

____. "*Mystery* Is Step Back; Allen Fans Should Cheer." *Sun-Sentinel* (Fort Lauderdale) 18 Mar. 1994, sec. Showtime: 15.

Hibben, Sally. Rev. of *Mrs. Soffel*, dir. by Gillian Armstrong. *Film Dope* 29 (1984): 39.

____. "Star Profile: Diane Keaton." *Film Dope* 29 (1984): 4–5.

Hickman, Christie. "Hooray for Hollywood, but Not at Any Price." *The Times* 18 Feb. 1993, Features.

Hill, John and Pamela Church Gibson, eds. *The Oxford Guide to Film Studies*. New York: Oxford UP, 1998.

Hinman, Catherine. "Actresses to Become Floridians During 3-Week Filming of Movie." *Orlando Sentinel* 10 Oct. 1995, sec. A: 2.

____. "Theme Park Visitors Ignore Streep,

Keaton." *Orlando Sentinel* 26 Oct. 1995, sec. A: 2.

Hinson, Hal. "*Bride II*: Duddy Daddy." *Washington Post* 8 Dec. 1995, sec. F: 1.

____. "*The Good Mother* and the Far Better Keaton." *Washington Post* 4 Nov. 1988, sec. B: 1.

____. "New on Tape." Rev. of *The Good Mother*, dir. Leonard Nimoy. *Washington Post* 9 Feb. 1989, sec. C: 7.

Hirschberg, Lynn. "Keaton Talks Funny." *Premiere* Oct. 1987: 40–44.

Hiscock, John. "Woody Allen in Custody Battle with Mia Farrow." *Daily Telegraph* 15 Aug. 1992: 3.

Hoffman, Adina. "Play It Again: Warmed-Over Woody." Rev. of *Manhattan Murder Mystery*, dir. Woody Allen. *Jerusalem Post* 5 Nov. 1993, sec. Arts: 5.

____. "Sister Act." Rev. of *Marvin's Room*, dir. Jerry Zaks. *Jerusalem Post* 2 May 1997, sec. Arts: 5.

Horton, Marc. "Diane Keaton Considers Directing an Excuse to Explore Lives of Others." *Ottawa Citizen* 15 Sep. 1995, sec. C: 8.

Horwitz, Jane. "Martin's Double-Duty *Father*." Rev. of *Father of the Bride: Part II*, dir. Charles Shyer. *Buffalo News* 14 Dec. 1995, sec. D: 2.

Howe, Desson. "Earhart Film's Early Arrival." *Washington Post* 3 Jun. 1994, sec. N: 45.

____. "*Godfather*: Offer Accepted." *Washington Post* 21 Mar. 1997, sec. N: 49.

____. "Keaton Meets 'Baby' Boom." *Washington Post* 9 Oct. 1987, sec. N: 31.

Hoyle, Martin. Rev. of *Unstrung Heroes*, dir. Diane Keaton. *Financial Times* (London) 7 Dec. 1995, sec. Arts: 23.

Hunter, Stephen. "First Wives, Last Laughs." *Baltimore Sun* 20 Sep. 1996, sec. E: 1.

Hyde, Nina S. "Fashion Notes." *Washington Post* 17 Jul. 1977, sec. G: 3.

____. "Fashion Notes." *Washington Post* 30 Jul. 1978, sec. K: 7.

Iachetta, Michael. "Diane, Through Tears." *New York Daily News* 29 May, 1974: 64.

Inman, David. "Movie Review: *Father of the Bride*." *Courier-Journal* (Louisville) 21 Dec. 1991, sec. S: 27.

Insdorf, Annette. "Play It Again, Woody: The Filmmaker Resurrects His Comic Style in *Manhattan Murder Mystery*." *Chicago Sun-Times* 15 Aug. 1993, sec. NC: 1.

____. "Woody Moves On: Director Ignores Private Woes, Opens *Manhattan Murder Mystery*." *San Francisco Chronicle* 15 Aug. 1993, sec. Sunday Datebook: 21.

Interiors. Dir. Woody Allen. With Diane Keaton and Geraldine Page. MGM-UA, 1978.

I Will, I Will...For Now. Dir. Norman Panama. With Diane Keaton and Elliott Gould. 1976.

Janos, Leo. "The Vivid (Very Private) World of Diane Keaton." *Cosmopolitan* 207.4 (1989): 230–33, 251.

Janusonis, Michael. "A Little Marital Teamwork Produces *Baby Boom*." *Orange County Register* 25 Oct. 1987, sec. L: 12.

Jeffords, Susan. *Hard Bodies: Hollywood Masculinity in the Reagan Era*. New Brunswick, N.J.: Rutgers UP, 1994.

Jerome, Jim. "Diane Keaton Booms Back into Comedy." *St. Petersburg Times* 25 Oct. 1987, sec. F: 4.

Johnson, Beth. "*Mr. Goodbar* Unwrapped: The 1977 Film Embodied the Dark Side of the Sexual Revolution." *Entertainment Weekly* 25 Oct. 1996: 134.

Johnson, Brian D. "A Family Affair." *Maclean's* 14 Nov. 1988: 58–59.

Johnson, Malcolm. "Disjointed Directing by Keaton: *Unstrung Heroes* Has Rich Characters, Fragmented Story." *Hartford Courant* 22 Sep. 1995, sec. E: 5.

____. "Revenge Is Tart in Witty Farce, *The First Wives Club*." *Hartford Courant* 20 Sep. 1996, sec. E: 1.

Johnson, Timothy W. "*Annie Hall*." *Magill's Survey of Cinema*. Ed. Frank Magill. Vol. I. Englewood Cliffs: N.J.: Salem Press, 1980, 86–89.

Johnston, Sheila. "Good Things in Soft Packages." Rev. of *Unstrung Heroes*, dir. Diane Keaton. *The Independent* (London) 7 Dec. 1995, sec. Features: 8.

____. "Woody Allen and His Women." *The Independent* (London) 4 Nov. 1995, sec. Arts: 5.

Jones, Bill. "*Unstrung* Is Gentle But Uneven." *Phoenix Gazette* 22 Sep. 1995, sec. E: 1.

Jones, Kenneth. "Women Scorned: Weak Script Hampers Stars of *The First Wives Club*." *Detroit News* 20 Sep. 1996, sec. D: 1.

"Julia Knight: A Bite of a Billion-Dollar Market." *Business Dateline* 22.6 (1991): 73.

"Jung durch Denk-Training." *Bunte*. 23 Nr. 1998: 80.

Kael, Pauline. "The Current Cinema: Trials." Rev. of *The Good Mother*, dir. Leonard Nimoy. *New Yorker* 64.41 (1988): 105–08.

____. *For Keeps: 30 Years at the Movies*. New York: Plume, 1994.

Kalfatovic, Mary. "Diane Keaton." *Newsmakers*. Ed. Sean R. Pollock. Detroit: Gale Res., 1997. 246–49.

Kalins, Dorothy. "The Design 100." *Metropolitan Home* 24.4 (1992).

Kanin, Garson. "Allen & Keaton: A Shy Love Duo." *New York Post* 27 Nov. 1981: 35, 93.

____. "She's the Real-Life Annie Hall." *New York Post* 27 Nov. 1981: 35.

Kasindorf, Martin. "The Zany Faces of Carol Kane." *Newsday* 26 Aug. 1990, sec. Part II: 15.

Katz, Ian. "Revenge Is a Dish Best Eaten with Popcorn." *Guardian* (Manchester) 23 Sep. 1996, sec. 1: 10.

____. "Screen Revenge for Scorned Wives." *Guardian* (Manchester) 20 Sep. 1996, sec. 1: 11.

Kauffmann, Stanley. "*The Godfather: Part III.*" *New Republic* 204.3 (1991): 26+.

Kaufman, Joanne. Rev. of *Father of the Bride*, dir. Charles Shyer. *People* 23 Dec. 1991: 18.

Keaton, Diane. Interview with Larry King. *Larry King Live*. CNN. Mar. 1997.

____. Interview with Oprah Winfrey. *Oprah Winfrey Show*. NBC. WFMJ, Youngstown. Mar. 1997.

____. Interview with Roseanne Barr. *Roseanne*. NBC. WFMJ, Youngstown. 9 Sep. 1999.

____. "The Mask." *Mirabella* Apr. 1993: 52–56.

____. *Mr. Salesman*. New York: Petrified Films, Inc., 1993.

____. Personal Telephone Interviews. 30 March 1998 and 1 April 1998.

____. *Reservations*. New York: Alfred A. Knopf, 1980.

____. *Still Life*. New York: Callaway, 1983.

____, ed. *Local News: Tabloid Pictures from the* Los Angeles Herald Express *1936–1961*. New York: Lookout, 1999.

"Keaton and Martin Ponder 'A New Leaf.'" *Toronto Sun* 4 Apr. 1997, sec. Entertainment: 59.

"Keaton Came on Strong in Past Year." *Milwaukee Journal Sentinel* 7 Mar. 1997, sec. Cue: 8.

"Keaton Clears the Wall at 50." *Toronto Sun* 30 Nov. 1996, sec. Entertainment: 44.

"Keaton, Diane." *Current Biography*. 57.5 (May 1996): 28–32.

"Keaton Fears Other Actors." *Rocky Mountain News* (Denver) 21 May 1995, sec. A: 130.

"Keaton, Hawn Teaming Up Again." *Toronto Sun* 7 Mar. 1997, sec. Entertainment: 72.

Keats, Carmen. "Immedia." Rev. of *Baby Boom*, starring Diane Keaton. *Melody Maker* 64.12 (1988): 48.

Kelleher, Terry, and John Griffiths. "Tube." Rev. of *Northern Lights*, starring Diane Keaton. *People* 25 Aug. 1997: 17.

Keller, Julia. "Name on 'Lights.'" *Columbus Dispatch* 21 Aug. 1997, sec. G: 8.

Kelly, Tom. "Tears and Fears, Not Birthday Toasts, as Baby Boomers Begin to Reach 50." *Sun-Sentinel* (Fort Lauderdale) 26 Jan. 1996, sec. A: 21.

Kemp, Philip. Rev. of *Manhattan Murder Mystery*, dir. Woody Allen. *Sight and Sound* 4.2 (1994): 57.

Kemply, Rita. "Allen's Carefree Caper." Rev. of *Manhattan Murder Mystery*, dir. Woody Allen. *Washington Post* 20 Aug. 1993, sec. D: 6.

____. "*Baby Boom*: Keaton's Parent Flap." *Washington Post* 7 Oct. 1987, sec. C: 1.

____. "*Lemon Sisters*: Yak to the Future." *Washington Post* 1 Sep. 1990, sec. C: 1.

____. "Twisted Sisters, High *Crimes*." *Washington Post* 12 Dec. 1986, sec. N: 39.

____. "*Unstrung*: At Loose Ends." *Washington Post* 23 Sep. 1995, sec. C: 4.

Kennedy, Dana. "In the Name of the Father: The Star and Author of *Heroes*." *Entertainment Weekly* 22 Sep. 1995: 58.

Kidder, Gayle. "Has Success Been Good to Miller?" *San Diego Union-Tribune* 7 Jun. 1990, sec. D: 1.

King, Barry. "Articulating Stardom." *Stardom: Industry of Desire*. Ed. Christine Gledhill. London: Routledge, 1991: 167–82.

Kirkland, Bruce. "Cannes Keen on Keaton." *Toronto Sun* 22 May 1995, sec. Entertainment: 29.

____. "Heroes' Welcome." *Toronto Sun* 10 Sep. 1995, sec. Entertainment: 46.

____. "Medal of Honor for Heroes: Keaton Director's Debut Conquers New Ground." *Toronto Sun* 15 Sep. 1995, sec. Entertainment: 6.

____. "Michael Richards Can't Lose Cosmo Kramer." *Toronto Sun* 22 May 1995, sec. Entertainment: 32.

____. "There's No Crisis in Diane's Mid-Life." *Toronto Sun* 6 Dec. 1995, sec. Entertainment: 67.

____. "This Club Not Worth Joining." Rev. of *The First Wives Club*, dir. Hugh Wilson. *Toronto Sun* 20 Sep. 1996, sec. Entertainment: 67.

Klady, Leonard. Rev. of *The First Wives Club*, dir. Hugh Wilson. *Variety* 364.7 (1996): 63, 65.

Klemesrud, Judy. "Diane Keaton: From Mr. Allen to *Mr. Goodbar*." *New York Times* 17 Apr. 1977, sec. 2: 1+.

Koch, John. "Choosing Icons, Not Actors." *Boston Globe* 20 Feb. 1991, sec. Living: 67.

____. "An Offbeat, Lighthearted *Northern Lights*." *Boston Globe* 22 Aug. 1997, sec. F: 2.

Koenig, Rhoda. "Holy Ghost." Rev. of *Heaven*, dir. Diane Keaton. *New York* 5 May 1986: 31.

Koltnow, Barry. "The Man Behind Kramer Stays True to His Art." *Sacramento Bee* 21 Sep. 1995, sec. F: 1.

Kowal, Patricia. "*Marvin's Room*." *Magill's Cinema Annual 1997*. Ed. Beth A. Fhaner. 16th ed. Detroit: Gale, 1998, 347–48.

Kroll, Jack. "The Best and the Worst." *Newsweek* 9 Jan. 1978: 58.

____. "In the Theater of the Real." Rev. of *Little Drummer Girl*, dir. George Roy Hill. *Newsweek* 15 Oct. 1984: 118.

Kroll, Jack, et al. "Thoroughly Modern Diane." *Newsweek* 15 Feb. 1982: 54+.

____. "Woody Funny, but He's Serious." *Newsweek* 24 Apr. 1978: 62+.

Lane, Anthony. "Charmed by the Muses of the Movies." *The Independent* (London) 7 Jul. 1991, sec. Sunday Review: 16.

____. Rev. of *Marvin's Room*, dir. Jerry Zaks. *New Yorker* 72.43 (1997): 99.

Lansden, Pamela. "Take One." *People* 16 Mar. 1987: 23.

LaSalle, Mick. "It's a *Godfather* You Can't Refuse." *San Francisco Chronicle* 25 Dec. 1990, sec. E: 1.

____. "*Lemon Sisters* Strike a Sour Note." *San Francisco Chronicle* 1 Sep. 1990, sec. C: 3.

____. "This *Bride's* Father Is a Sap." *San Francisco Chronicle* 20 Dec. 1991, sec. C: 1.

Latimer, Joanne. "Pro or Cannes?" *Ms.* 6.2 (1995): 87.

Lau, Joan. "Definitely Male-Bashing at Its Most Gleeful." Rev. of *The First Wives Club*, dir. Hugh Wilson. *New Straits Times* (Malaysia) 29 Mar. 1997, sec. Arts Cinema: 4.

Lawson, Mark. "Television: Life After Father Ted." *The Guardian* (London) 18 May 1996, sec. Features: 30.

Lawson, Terry. "For Actresses of a 'Certain Age,' the Season Is Sweet." *Pittsburgh Post-Gazette* 1 Oct. 1996, sec. D: 1.

Lax, Eric. "Off the Screen: Out of the Woody (Allen) Work Emerges a Classically Insecure Comedienne, Diane Keaton." *People* 18 Aug. 1975: 41, 43–45.

____. *Woody Allen: A Biography*. New York: Vintage Books, 1991.

Lebo, Harlan. *The Godfather Legacy*. New York: Fireside, 1997.

L'Ecuyer, Gerald. "Diane Keaton: Crime Does Pay." *Interview* Dec. 1986: 34–40.

____. "Her Film *Heaven* Stretches Her Talents into the Great Beyond." *Orange County Register* 1 Mar. 1987, sec. J: 1.

Lee, Jeff. "Bringing Up Some of Life's Pertinent Questions." Rev. of *Marvin's Room*, dir. Jerry Zaks. *New Straits Times* (Malaysia) 10 Jan. 1998, sec. Arts Cinema: 4.

The Lemon Sisters. Dir. Joyce Chopra. With Diane Keaton and Carol Kane. Miramax, 1990.

Leonard, Elizabeth. "Familiarity Breeds Content." Rev. of *Northern Lights*, starring Diane Keaton. *People* 48.7 (18 Aug. 1997).

Leonard, John. "Fly Girl." *New York* 27.24 (1994): 74–75.

____. "Tidings of Comfort and Joy." Rev. of *Wildflower*, dir. Diane Keaton. *New York* 24.48 (1991): 78–79.

Lepage, Mark. "Woody-Diane Show Keeps Mystery Moving." *The Gazette* (Montreal) 20 Aug. 1993, sec. C: 3.

Levy, Emanuel. Rev. of *The Only Thrill*, dir. Peter Masterson. *Variety* 367.5 (1997): 55.

Liberatore, Karen. "A Touch of Hollywood in Nicasio." *San Francisco Chronicle* 2 Sep. 1992, sec. Z7: 4.

Lidz, Franz. "My Nutty Uncle Goes to Hollywood." *Life* 18.11 (September 1995): 68–74.

"Like, You Know, Well, Stick to the Script." *Phoenix Gazette* 6 Jun. 1994, sec. A: 2.

Lim, Rebecca. "Quite a Scream After Build-Up." Rev. of *Manhattan Murder Mystery*, dir. Woody Allen. *Straights Times* (Singapore) 18 Sep. 1994, sec. Entertainment: 11.

Lindgren, Kristina. "Civil Engineer Jack Newton Hall Dies." *Los Angeles Times* 4 Sep. 1990, sec. B: 6.

Linet, Beverly. "Looking for Diane Keaton: The Fantasies, the Fears, the Funkiness of Filmdom's Newest Darling." *M P* (circa 1977), 10–12, 48+.

Lipper, Hal. "Sour Story Can't Squeeze By." Rev. of *The Lemon Sisters*, dir. Joyce Chopra. *St. Petersburg Times* 3 Sep. 1990, sec. D: 3.

Little Drummer Girl. Dir. George Roy Hill. With Diane Keaton and Klaus Kinski. Warner Bros., 1984.

"Lloyd Wright Recast." *Architectural Record* 179.9 (1991): 126–33.

Looking for Mr. Goodbar. Dir. Richard Brooks. With Diane Keaton and Richard Gere. Paramount, 1977.

Look Who's Talking Now. Dir. Tom Ropelewski. With John Travolta and Kirstie Alley. 1993.

Lorando, Mark. "Back in the 'Running.'" *Times-Picayune* (New Orleans) 1 Aug. 1992, sec. E: 1.

____. "Keaton's Debut Film Is a Masterwork." *Times-Picayune* (New Orleans) 5 Dec. 1991, sec. E: 1.

Love and Death. Dir. Woody Allen. With Diane Keaton. MGM-UA, 1975.

Lovers and Other Strangers. Dir. Cy Howard. With Diane Keaton and Bea Arthur. Anchor Bay, 1970.

Luscombe, Belinda. "No Cattiness Here, Please. We're Actresses." *Time* 15 Jan. 1996: 75.

Lynch, Lorrie. "Who's News." *USA Weekend* 28 Sep. 1997: 2.

Macinnis, Craig. "Woody Allen at His Best." Rev. of *Manhattan Murder Mystery.* *Toronto Star* 20 Aug. 1993, sec. B: 1.

Macnah, Geoffrey. Rev. of *Unstrung Heroes,* dir. Diane Keaton. *Sight and Sound* 5.12 (1995): 53–54.

Malcolm, Derek. "Feelgood Disaster." Rev. of *First Wives Club,* dir. Hugh Wilson. *Guardian* (Manchester) 15 Nov. 1996, sec. 3: 6.

____. "Mad About the Girls." *Guardian* (London) 8 Apr. 1996, sec. Features: 4.

____. "Warm Soak in Deep Water." Rev. of *Manhattan Murder Mystery,* dir. Woody Allen. *Guardian* (London) 20 Jan. 1994, sec. Features: 5.

Malkin, Marc. S. Rev. of *Unstrung Heroes,* dir. Diane Keaton. *Premiere* 9.9 (1996): 98.

Maltin, Leonard. *Leonard Maltin's 1997 Movie & Video Guide.* New York: Plume, 1996.

____. Rev. of *The First Wives Club.* *Modern Maturity* 40.4 (1997): 28.

Mammie, Cherilyn. "Diane Keaton: 'Movie Stars Aren't Important Anymore!'" (journal title missing, Circa 1977) 14–15, 66.

Mandell, Jonathan. "3 Lemons Miss the Jackpot." *Newsday* 5 Sep. 1990, sec. Part II: 12.

Manhattan. Dir. Woody Allen. With Diane Keaton and Mariel Hemmingway. MGM-UA, 1979.

Manhattan Murder Mystery. Dir. Woody Allen. With Diane Keaton. TriStar, 1993.

"*Manhattan Murder Mystery.*" Rev. *Irish Times* 21 Jan. 1994, sec. Cinema: 15.

Mansfield, Stephanie. "Diane Keaton, Up from *Heaven.*" *Washington Post* 22 Apr. 1987, sec. C: 1.

____. "When Life Imitates Heart: Marshall Brickman." *Washington Post* 14 Mar. 1983, sec. B: 1.

"Marquee Values—*Manhattan Murder Mystery* starring Diane Keaton and Woody Allen. *Billboard* 106.6 (1994): 74.

"Marquee Values—*Running Mates* starring Diane Keaton and Ed Harris. *Billboard* 105.8 (1993): 66.

Marshall, P. David. *Celebrity and Power: Fame in Contemporary Culture.* Minneapolis: U. of Minnesota P., 1997.

Mars-Jones, Adam. "The Comfort of Strangers." Rev. of *Manhattan Murder Mystery,* dir. Woody Allen. *The Independent* (London) 21 Jan. 1994, sec. Film: 23.

____. "Sisterhood, Hollywood Style." Rev. of *The First Wives Club,* dir. Hugh Wilson. *The Independent* (London) 14 Nov. 1996, sec. Film: 6.

Marvin's Room. Dir. Jerry Zaks. With Diane Keaton and Meryl Streep. Miramax, 1996.

Maslin, Janet. "Allen and Keaton Together Again and Dizzy as Ever." *New York Times* 18 Aug. 1993, sec. C: 13.

____. "*Baby Boom.*" *New York Times* 7 Oct. 1987, sec. C: 24.

____. "Bittersweet Lessons as a Family Reunites." Rev. of *Marvin's Room,* dir. Jerry Zaks. *New York Times* 18 Dec. 1996, sec. C: 15.

____. "Love's Revenge, or, Spite Is a Many-Splendored Thing." Rev. of *The First Wives Club.* *New York Times* 20 Sep. 1996, sec. C: 21.

____. "*Marvin's Room*: Powerhouse Casting." *New York Times* 18 Dec. 1996.

____. "Now, Mother-Daughter Pregnancies." Rev. of *Father of the Bride II,* starring Diane Keaton. *New York Times* 8 Dec. 1995, sec. C:3.

____. "Nuttiness as Solace in a Son's Moment of Grief." *New York Times* 15 Sep. 1995, sec. C: 5.

____. "Passion vs. Parenthood in *The Good Mother.*" *New York Times* 4 Nov. 1988, sec. C: 15.

____. "Pre-Wedding Jitters, Mostly Dad's." *New York Times* 20 Dec. 1991, sec. C: 17.

____. Rev. of *Father of the Bride,* dir. Charles Shyer. *New York Times* 20 Dec. 1991.

____. Rev. of *Manhattan,* dir. Woody Allen. *New York Times* 24 Mar. 1985, sec. 2: 30.

____. "TV: Offbeat Votes Made Oscar Night a Winner." *New York Times* 31 Mar. 1982, sec. C: 23.

____. "Woody's New Winner." Rev. of *Annie Hall*. *Newsweek* 2 May 1977: 78.

Masters, Kim. "Hollywood's Best Revenge." *Time* 7 Oct. 1996: 84.

Mathews, Jack. "Actors Crowd *Marvin's Room*: Streep, Keaton and DiCaprio Outshine Script." *Newsday* 18 Dec. 1996, sec. B: 3.

____. "*Father* Is as Cheap as Ever." Rev. of *Father of the Bride*, dir. Charles Shyer. *Newsday* 20 Dec. 1991, sec. Weekend: 78.

____. "Movies: Secure About Her Insecurity." *Los Angeles Times* 10 Sep. 1995, Calendar: 3.

____. "Woody Allen's Latest: A Nick and Nora Wannabe." Rev. of *Manhattan Murder Mystery*, dir. Woody Allen. *Newsday* 18 Aug. 1993, sec. Part II: 52.

Mazey, Steven. "Film Finds the Joy in Sorrow: Streep, Keaton Bring Best Aspects of Original Play to the Big Screen." *Ottawa Citizen* 6 May 1997, sec. B: 8.

____. "Hawn, Midler, Keaton Keep Spinning to Movie Comedy Magic." *Ottawa Citizen* 20 Sep. 1996, sec. E: 3.

McAleavey, Andrew. "*Unstrung Heroes* Is Moving, Magnificent." *Sun-Sentinel* (Fort Lauderdale) 13 Oct. 1995, sec. Showtime: 54.

McCabe, Bruce. "Keaton Gets Her Goodbar from Hasty Pudding Club." *Boston Globe* 13 Feb. 1991, sec. Arts & Film: 59.

McClure, Holly. "*First Wives* Comedy Is Fun for Adults." *Orange County Register* (California) 27 Sep. 1996, sec. F: 28.

McCormick, Patrick. "Death Becomes Us: Motion Picture *Marvin's Room* Depicts Spiritual Side of Death." *U.S. Catholic* 11.62 (1997): 45+.

McDonald, Paul. "Film Acting." *The Oxford Guide to Film Studies*. Eds. John Hill and Pamela Church Gibson. New York: Oxford UP, 1998. 30–35.

____. "Star Studies." *Approaches to Popular Film*. Eds. Joanne Hollows and Mark Jancovich. Manchester, England: Manchester UP, 1995. 79–97.

McGrady, Mike. "A Mother's Expectations, and Reality." Rev. of *The Good Mother*, dir. Leonard Nimoy. *Newsday* 4 Nov. 1988, sec. Weekend: 3.

McKerrow, Steve. "Remembering the Ladies of Laughter." *Baltimore Sun* 29 Jun. 1995, sec. E: 8.

McLellan, Joseph. Rev. of *Crimes of the Heart*, dir. Bruce Beresford. *Washington Post* 2 Jul. 1987, sec. C: 7.

McNally, Owen. "A Return to the Good Old Neurotic Days with Allen, Keaton in *Mystery*." *Hartford Courant* 20 Aug. 1993, sec. D: 3.

McWilliams, Michael. "25 Years of Oscar Favorites." *Detroit News* 21 Mar. 1997, sec. E: 2.

____. "Wonder Women: After Decades of Great Actors, Three Actresses Come into Their Own." *Detroit News* 21 Mar. 1997, sec. E: 1.

Medhurst, Andy. Rev. of *First Wives Club*, dir. Hugh Wilson. *Sight and Sound* 6.12 (1996): 45.

Meigs, James B. "Editor's Letter: Women in Hollywood." *Premiere*. Women in Hollywood Special Issue. 1999: 14.

Mendoza, Manuel. "*Amelia Earhart* Never Takes Off." *Dallas Morning News* 12 Jun. 1994, sec. C: 10.

Meyers, Nancy and Charles Shyer. "Feminist Heroines." Letter. *New York Times* 13 Aug. 1989, sec. 2: 3.

Michener, Charles. "The Way We Were." Rev. of *Still Life*, by Diane Keaton. *The Movies* 1.5 (1983): 23–29.

Millar, Jeff. "*Marvin's Room*: A Heartfelt Tale of Loving and Being Loved." *Houston Chronicle* 10 Jan. 1977, sec. Weekend Preview: 1.

____. "Performers Have Fun with *Wives*." *Houston Chronicle* 20 Sep. 1996, sec. F: 1.

____. "*Unstrung Heroes*: Film Earns Our Laughter, Tears, Cheers." *Houston Chronicle* 22 Sep. 1995, sec. Weekend Preview: 1.

Mink, Eric. "Diane Keaton Lights Up Dim Disney Film." Rev. of *Northern Lights*, dir. Linda Yellen. *Daily News* 22 Aug. 1997, sec. Television: 127.

Mitchell, W.J.T. *Iconology: Image, Text, Ideology*. Chicago: U of Chicago P, 1986.

Monaco, James. *American Film Now*. New York: Oxford UP, 1979.

____. "Looking for Diane Keaton." *Take One* 5.12 (1977): 26–28.

Moor, Jonathan. *Diane Keaton: The Story of the Real Annie Hall*. New York: St. Martin's Press, 1989.

Moorhead, Joanna. "Looking After Number One." *The Guardian* (London) 7 Nov. 1996, sec. T: 4.

Mordue, Mark. "Homeward Bound." *Sight and Sound* 58.4 (1989): 270–72.

Morgenstern, Joe. "Film: A Boy Among Eccentrics." *Wall Street Journal* 15 Sep. 1995, sec. A: 12.

____. "Notable New Movies." Rev. of *Marvin's Room*, dir. Jerry Zaks. *Wall Street Journal* 7 Jan. 1997, sec. A: 14.

Morice, Laura. "Diane Keaton." *Us* 227 (1996): 77–80.

Morley, Sheridan. Rev. of *Diane Keaton: The Story of the Real Annie Hall* by Jonathan Moor. *Sunday Times* (London) 6 May 1990, sec. Features.

Morrison, Benjamin. "Something About Amelia." *Times-Picayune* (New Orleans) 12 Jun. 1994, sec. TV: 4.

"The Movie She Directed Was a Hit at Cannes—But Surely She Shouldn't Get the Credit." *Newsday* 17 Sep. 1995, sec. Fanfare: 12.

"Movies—*Unstrung Heroes* directed by Diane Keaton." Rev. of *Unstrung Heroes. Rolling Stone* 21 Sep. 1995.

Movshovitz, Howie. "*First Wives Club* Takes Formula Stab at Funny." *Denver Post* 20 Sep. 1996, sec. G: 3.

____. "*Godfather III* Worthy Successor." *Denver Post* 25 Dec. 1990, sec. E: 1.

Mowe, Richard. "Hall Marked." *Scotland on Sunday* 28 Mar. 1995, sec. S: 9.

Moya, Eric W. "*Lemon Sisters* Would Be Sweeter if It Had a Plot." *Orlando Sentinel Tribune* 7 Sep. 1990, sec. Calendar: 13.

Mrs. Soffel. Dir. Gillian Armstrong. With Diane Keaton and Mel Gibson. MGM-UA, 1984.

Munshower, Susan. "Diane Keaton: From Woody to Warren." *Cue New York* 17 Aug. 1979: 18–21, 96.

____. *The Diane Keaton Scrapbook.* New York: Grosset & Dunlap, 1979.

____. *Warren Beatty: His Life, His Loves, His Work.* New York: St. Martin's Press, 1983.

Murray, Angus Wolfe. "The Ex Files." Rev. of *The First Wives Club*, dir. Hugh Wilson. *The Scotsman* 14 Nov. 1996: 18.

Murry, Steve. "Diane Keaton." *Atlanta Journal and Constitution* 16 Jan. 1997, sec. G: 5.

____. "Top Cast at Home in *Marvin's Room*." *Atlanta Journal and Constitution* 12 Jun. 1997, sec. E: 7.

Myers, Marc. "The Story of *Reds* and the Reed House." *New York Times* 3 Jan. 1982, sec. 11: 1.

Natale, Richard. "Night Life." *Women's Wear Daily* 30 May 1974: 24.

Nechak, Paula. "Keaton's *Heroes* a Quirky Winner." *Seattle Times* 22 Sep. 1995, sec. E: 3.

Nelson, Sharon. "First Wives Share Pain, Not Venom." *New Straits Times* (Malaysia) 12 Apr. 1997: 1.

"New Heroines." *Newsweek* 10 Oct. 1977: 7.

Newman, Janis Cooke. "This Club Has a Special Password." *Denver Post* 7 Dec. 1997, sec. H: 4.

Newmark, Judith. "Parents Helping Parents: Everybody Benefits." Rev. of *Father of the Bride: Part II*, dir. Charles Shyer. *St. Louis Post-Dispatch* 17 Sep. 1997, sec. E: 4.

____. "Why Neatness Counts." *St. Louis Post-Dispatch* 31 Jul. 1994, sec. PD Magazine: 10.

Northern Lights. Dir. Linda Yellen. With Diane Keaton. Disney Channel. 23 Aug. 1997.

Novak, Ralph. "Picks & Pans." Rev. of *Baby Boom*, dir. Charles Shyer. *People* 19 Oct. 1987: 15.

____. "Picks & Pans." Rev. of *The Lemon Sisters*, dir. Joyce Chopra. *People* 17 Sep. 1990: 13.

O'Connor, Anne Marie. "Sibling Rivals." Rev. of *Marvin's Room*, dir. Jerry Zaks. *Mademoiselle* 103.1 (1997): 68.

O'Connor, John. "True Love vs. Politics in an HBO Comedy." Rev. of *Running Mates*, starring Diane Keaton. *New York Times* 7 October 1992, sec. C:20.

O'Connor, Kyrie. "*First Wives Club* Does Disservice to Angry Women Everywhere." *Hartford Courant* 2 Jan. 1997, sec. Calendar: 19.

O'Hare, Kate. "Keaton Gets to Fly High in Earhart Biography." *Orange County Register* (California) 12 Jun. 1994, sec. TV Mag.: 6.

The Only Thrill. Dir. Peter Masterson. With Diane Keaton and Sam Shepard. Moonstone Entertainment, 1997.

The Other Sister. Dir. Garry Marshall. With Diane Keaton and Tom Skerritt. Touchstone, 1999.

O'Toole, Lawrence. "Passionate Partners in Love and Crime." Rev. of *Mrs. Soffel*, dir. Gillian Armstrong. *Maclean's* 11 Feb. 1985: 51.

Pacheco, Patrick. "Diane in La-La Land." *Connoisseur* 222.960 (1992): 46–51+.

Pandya, Nick. "Juggle That's Worth All the Struggle." *Guardian* (London) 16 May 1998, sec. Money Page: 22.

Parish, James Robert and Don Stanke. *Hollywood Baby Boomers*. New York: Garland, 1992.

Parker, John. *Warren Beatty: The Last Great Lover of Hollywood*. New York: Carroll & Graf, 1994.

Parks, Louis B. "Strong & Sensitive Streep." *Houston Chronicle* 16 Jan. 1997, sec. D: 1.

____. "*Unstrung* Director a Richards Hero." *Houston Chronicle* 24 Sep. 1995, sec. Zest: 12.

Patteson, Jean. "Keaton's Flight of Fashion." *Orlando Sentinel* 10 Jun. 1994, sec. E: 3.

Pearlman, Cindy. "Quirky Diane Keaton, A Long Way from *Annie Hall*." *Buffalo News* 15 Sep. 1996, sec. E: 1.

Peerman, Dean. Rev. of *Heaven*, dir. Diane Keaton. *Christian Century* 104.20 (1987): 600.

Penfold, Phil. "Diane, Unstrung Heroine." *The Herald* (Glasgow) 4 Nov. 1995: 2.

Pennington, Gail. "Delta Burke, Diane Keaton, Ann Miller Fill Small Screen." Rev. of *Northern Lights*, dir. Linda Yellen. *St. Louis Post-Dispatch* 20 Aug. 1997, sec. E: 8.

____. "Earhart Bio Doesn't Find Route to Insight." *St. Louis Post-Dispatch* 12 Jun. 1994, sec. C: 14.

"People." *Dallas Morning News* 5 Mar. 1997, sec. A: 2.

Pergament, Alan. "Amelia Earhart Film Sputters." *Buffalo News* 9 Jun. 1994, sec. Television: 6.

Peters, Linda. "Singular and Satisfied." *New Woman* 19.5 (1989): 86–87.

Peterson, Deborah. "The Silver Screen: Older Women Are Finally Getting Meaty Parts in the Movies." *St. Louis Post-Dispatch* 24 Jan. 1997, sec. E: 2.

Picker, Deborah. "*Manhattan Murder Mystery*." *Magill's Cinema Annual 1993*. Ed. Frank Magill. Englewood Cliffs, N.J.: Salem Press, 1994, 218–20.

Pickle, Betsy. "Diane Keaton: 'I Thought I Was Finished.'" *Star Tribune* (Minneapolis) 8 Mar. 1997, sec. E: 1.

Play It Again, Sam. Dir. Herbert Ross. With Woody Allen and Diane Keaton. Paramount, 1972.

Podhoretz, John. "Diary of a Moviegoer." Rev. of *Marvin's Room*, dir. Jerry Zaks. *Weekly Standard* 2.18 (1997): 37–39.

Pogel, Nancy. *Woody Allen*. Boston: Twayne Publishers, 1987.

Pollack, Joe. "Old-Fashioned Woody Allen— for a Change." Rev. of *Manhattan Murder Mystery*. *St. Louis Post-Dispatch* 3 Sep. 1993, sec. EV: 3.

Pollitt, Katha. "*First Wives*, Last Laugh." *The Nation* 263.12 (1996): 9.

Pope, John. "Queen B." *Times-Picayune* (New Orleans) 3 Mar. 1996, sec. E: 7.

Potts, Jackie. "'Witches of Upper East Side' Get Slapstick Revenge." *Miami Herald* 20 Sep. 1996, sec. G: 5.

"Power Dessert." Interview with Jessica Lange. *Premiere*. Women in Hollywood: Special Issue 1993: 60.

Powers, John. "People Are Talking About Movies." Rev. of *Marvin's Room*, dir. Jerry Zaks. *Vogue* 187.1 (1997): 78.

Pye, Michael. "Lightweight Woody Is Fighting Back." *Daily Telegraph* 19 Aug. 1993: 13.

Radio Days. Dir. Woody Allen. With Diane Keaton and Mia Farrow. Orion, 1987.

Rafferty, Diane. "The Way They Wore." *Mademoiselle* 98.7 (1992): 137.

"Ramis Balances Acting with Writing." *Orange County Register* (California) 30 Oct. 1987, sec. P: 13.

Reds. Dir. Warren Beatty. With Diane Keaton and Maureen Stapleton. Paramount, 1981.

Reed, Rex. "Diane Keaton: Shy Girl in Stardom's Shadow." *New York Daily News* 15 May 1977, sec. Leisure: 7.

"Relationship of the Week." *Sacramento Bee* 9 Jan. 1998, sec. SC: 2.

"Re-Visionism: *The Godfather I* Starring Al Pacino and Diane Keaton." *Ms.* Sep.-Oct. 1990: 24.

Rev. of *The Girl with the Crazy Brother*, dir. Diane Keaton. *Variety* 7 Feb. 1990: 158.

Rich, Chuck. Rev. of *Unstrung Heroes*, dir. Diane Keaton. *Washingtonian* 31.1 (1995): 47.

____. "Two Bits a Movie." Rev. of *Father of the Bride II*, dir. Charles Shyer. *Washingtonian* 31.4 (1996): 39.

Richards, David. "A Door Left Ajar in *Marvin's Room*." *Washington Post* 5 Jan. 1997, sec. G: 1.

Ringel, Eleanor. "*Father of the Bride* Is a Marry Update." *Atlanta Journal and Constitution* 20 Dec. 1991, sec. D: 5.

____. "On Film: Ford, Pacino, Keaton as Luminous as Ever." *Atlanta Journal Constitution* 13 Apr. 1997, sec. L: 2.

____. "Hollywood's Age Bias Hardest on Actresses." *Star Tribune* (Minneapolis) 25 Sep. 1996, sec. E: 10.

____. Rev. of *First Wives Club*, dir. Hugh Wilson. *Atlanta Journal and Constitution* 20 Sep. 1996, sec. P: 17.

____. Rev. of *Marvin's Room*, dir. Jerry Zaks. *Atlanta Journal and Constitution* 10 Jan. 1997, sec. P: 1.

____. Rev. of *Unstrung Heroes*, dir. Diane Keaton. *Atlanta Journal and Constitution* 22 Sep. 1995, sec. P: 9.

____. "Will *First Wives* Be Their Last Stand?" *Dallas Morning News* 6 Oct. 1996, sec. C: 1.

Rizzo, Frank. "Steve Martin, Diane Keaton Together Again." *Hartford Courant* 6 Jul. 1997, sec. G: 9.

Robbins, Tom. "Diane Keaton" in "Women We Love." *Esquire* 107.6 (1987): 154–68.

Robinson, David. "Folly, Fantasy, Fiction and Fact." *The Times* (London) 10 Sep. 1994, sec. Features.

Rochlin, Margy. "Tender Crimes." *American Film* 12.4 (January 1987): 36–40+.

Rodriguez, Rene. "Diane Keaton's New Direction." *Miami Herald* 23 Sep. 1995, sec. G: 1.

____. "*Marvin's Room* Explores Guilty Fears, Slow Death." *Miami Herald* 28 Feb. 1997, sec. G: 6.

Roeper, Richard. "Woody's Latest Drama Casts Him in New Light." *Chicago Sun-Times* 20 Aug. 1992, sec. News: 11.

Romano, Lois. "Ed Harris, on the Power Trail." *Washington Post* 28 Sep. 1992, sec. B: 3.

Romano, Lois, and Mary Alma Welch. "The Reliable Source." *Washington Post* 2 Jun. 1995, sec. D: 3.

Romney, Jonathon. "Turn of the Screwball." Rev. of *Unstrung Heroes*, dir. Diane Keaton. *The Guardian* (London) 10 Nov. 1995, sec. T: 6.

Rosenbaum, Ron. "Al Pacino: Out of the Shadows." *Vanity Fair* 52.10 (1989): 180–86+.

____. "Unnatural actresses." *Mademoiselle* 95.1 (1989): 46, 48–49.

Rosenthal, Donna. "Oh, Diane!" *New York Daily News* 4 Oct. 1987: 3.

Roush, Matt. "*Amelia* Barely Takes Off." *USA Today* 10 June 1994, sec. D: 3.

____. "Keaton, Delany Ignite Brilliance of *Beach*." *USA Today* 2 November 1990, sec. D: 1.

____. "*Northern Lights* Casts a Soft Glow." *USA Today* 22 Aug. 1997, sec. D: 3.

____. "*Running Mates*: A Frisky Ticket." *USA Today* 2 Oct. 1992, sec. D: 3.

____. "*Wildflower* Thrives in Keaton's Care." *USA Today* 3 December 1991, sec. D: 3.

Rozen, Leah. "Screen." Rev. of *Father of the Bride: Part II*. *People* 44.25 (1995): 18–19.

____. "Screen." Rev. of *Marvin's Room*, dir. Jerry Zaks. *People* 46.26 (1996): 17.

Rubin, Rich. "New York Stories." *Boston Globe* 28 Sep. 1997, sec. M: 1.

Running Mates. Dir. Michael Lindsay-Hogg. With Diane Keaton and Ed Harris. HBO, 4 Oct. 1992.

"Rushes: *Mrs. Soffel*." *Time* 14 Jan. 1985: 66.

Russell, Candice. "Allen and Keaton Make Mystery-Comedy to Die For." Rev. of *Manhattan Murder Mystery*, dir. Woody Allen. *Sun-Sentinel* (Fort Lauderdale) 20 Aug. 1993, sec. Showtime: 5.

Ryan, Ann. "Life Imitates ... the Movies." *Business Dateline* 3.2 (1992): 69.

Ryan, Desmond. "Keaton Directs Sheen Clan." *Toronto Star* 9 Apr. 1991, sec. D: 7.

Ryon, Ruth. "Hot Property: A New Home for Baby." *Los Angeles Times* 22 Sep. 1996, sec. K: 1.

Salem, Rob. "Filmmaking Just Like 'Shopping' for the Right Bits, says Keaton." *Toronto Star* 8 Sep. 1995, sec. D: 1.

Sarris, Andrew. "The Divine Diane." *Village Voice* 17 Oct. 1977: 49.

____. Rev. of *Heaven*, dir. Diane Keaton. *Video Reviews* 8.13 (1988): 76–77.

Sauer, Mark. "Hollywood History Is Alive and Well and Living at the Chateau Marmont." *Orange County Register* (California) 9 Jan. 1988, sec. E: 10.

Schaefer, Stephen. "Keaton Directs Her Career Back on Track with *Heroes*." *Boston Herald* 14 Sep. 1995, sec. Features: 33.

Schappell, Elissa. "We Are Not Men! We Are Divas!" *Premiere* September 1996: 45–49.

Schickel, Richard. "Dysfunctioning Just Fine: Family Values Are Out of Kilter, but the Eccentricity Is Essential in Diane Keaton's Flaky, Charming *Unstrung Heroes*." *Time* 25 Sep. 1995: 68.

____. "Love, Rage and the Quotidian." Rev. of *Shoot the Moon*, dir. Alan Parker. *Time* 1 Feb. 1982: 79.

Schnedler, Jack. "*Godfather*: Italy's Luster Shines Through Dark Doings." *Orange County Register* (California) 24 Mar. 1991, sec. E: 3.

Schneller, Johanna. "Woody Allen." *Us* 229 (1997): 46–48+.

"Schulman, Sandra. "Literati Glow Under Moon, Stars." *Sun-Sentinel* 5 Jul. 1996, sec. Showtime: 34.

Schwarzbaum, Lisa. "First You Cry, Then You Laugh: Keaton, Streep, and DiCaprio Relate in *Marvin's Room*." *Entertainment Weekly* 20 Dec. 1996: 56.

Segrave, Kerry, and Linda Martin. *The Post-Feminist Hollywood Actress*. Jefferson, N.C.: McFarland & Company, Inc., 1990.

Seger, Linda. *The Art of Adaptation: Turning Fact and Fiction into Film*. New York: Henry Holt, 1992.

____. *When Women Call the Shots: The Developing Power and Influence of Women in Television and Film*. New York: Henry Holt, 1996.

Shakespeare, William. *Richard III*. Ed. E. A. J. Honigmann. London: Penguin Books, 1968.

Shales, Tom. "*Annie Hall* and *Star Wars* Are Top Oscar Winners." *Washington Post* 5 Apr. 1978, sec. B: 3.

____. "The Oscars." *Washington Post* 30 Mar. 1982, sec. B: 1.

____. "*Wildflower*: Keaton's Bloom." *Washington Post* 3 Dec. 1991, sec. B: 1.

Shalit, Gene. "What's Happening?" Interview with Diane Keaton. *Ladies Home Journal*, circa 1977, 12, 20.

Shannon, Jeff. "Allen *Mystery* Offers Comic Relief." *Seattle Times* 20 Aug. 1993, sec. D: 14.

Sheehan, Henry. "Allen Wisely Returns to Silliness." Rev. of *Manhattan Murder Mystery*, dir. Woody Allen. *Orange County Register* 20 Aug. 1993, sec. P: 13.

____. "*First Wives* Blends, Warmth, Revenge." *Orange County Register* 20 Sep. 1996, sec. F: 10.

____. "Lowering the Boomers on Hollywood Wives' Tale." *Orange County Register* 1 Oct. 1996, sec. F: 2.

____. "Stars Shine Bright in *Marvin's Room*." *Orange County Register* 10 Jan. 1997, sec. F: 12.

Sherman, Betsy. "These *Lemons* Are Just Too Sweet." Rev. of *The Lemon Sisters*, dir. Joyce Chopra. *Boston Globe* 31 Aug. 1990, sec. 59: 1.

Sherman, Jean. "Opening Credits." *Public Relations Journal* Nov. 1987: 26.

Shilling, Jane. "Girl Talk." *Punch* 336.2 (1990): 36–37.

Shinkle, Florence. "Mother Knows Best." *St. Louis Post-Dispatch* 12 Apr. 1990, sec. E: 1.

Shoot the Moon. Dir. Alan Parker. With Diane Keaton and Albert Finney. MGM-UA, 1982.

Siegel, Sol Louis. Rev. of *Unstrung Heroes*, dir. Diane Keaton. *Video* 20.1 (1996): 78.

Silverberg, Larry. *The Sanford Meisner Approach: An Actor's Workbook*. Lyme, N.H.: Smith and Kraus, 1994.

Silverman, Stephen M. "Having It All." *New York Post* 6 Oct. 1987: 27.

____. "Working with Woody—It's Been a While." *New York Post* 6 Oct. 1987: 27.

Simon, Jeff. "Oscar's Blind Eye: Are the Academy Awards About to Shut Out the Best Movie of the Year?" Rev. of *Marvin's Room*, dir. Jerry Zaks. *Buffalo News* 9 Feb. 1997, sec. F: 1.

____. "A Sampling of Big-Screen Delicacies." Rev. of *Unstrung Heroes*, dir. Diane Keaton. *Buffalo News* 12 Sep. 1995, sec. D: 1.

____. "A Walk on the Woody Side." *Buffalo News* 9 Nov. 1995, sec. D: 1.

Simon, John. Rev. of *Manhattan Murder Mystery*, dir. Woody Allen. *National Review* 45.18 (1993): 76.

Siskel, Gene. "*The Good Mother* a Good Character Film for Keaton." *Chicago Tribune* 4 Nov. 1988, sec. A: CN.

____. "Inept *Lemon Sisters* an Aptly Named Failure." *Chicago Tribune* 7 Sep. 1990, sec. C: CN.

____. "Keaton's *Heaven* Is Offbeat, but Fun." *Chicago Tribune* 17 Apr. 1987, sec. A: C.

____. "Low-Brow *First Wives* Missed Chance for Biting Social Humor." *Chicago Tribune* 20 Sep. 1996, sec. 2: CN.

____. "*Manhattan* Returns to an Earlier Woody Allen." Rev. of Manhattan Murder Mystery. *Chicago Tribune* 20 Aug. 1993, sec. C: CN.

____. "Michael's Story." *Chicago Tribune* 23 Dec. 1990, sec. 16: C.

____. Rev. of *Baby Boom*, dir. Charles Shyer. *Chicago Tribune* 9 Oct. 1987, sec. A: N.

____. "Steve Martin Delivers in *Father of the Bride* Sequel." *Chicago Tribune* 8 Dec. 1995, sec. 7: D.

____. "Woody Allen at 50: A Happier Man ... Considering." *Chicago Tribune* 26 Jan. 1986, sec. 3: C.

Skow, John, with Janice Castro. "Love, Death and La-De-Dah." *Time* 26 Sep. 1977: 68–72, 77.

Sleeper. Dir. Woody Allen. With Diane Keaton. MGM-UA, 1973.

Smith, Peter. "Guilt Triumphs Over Love." Rev. of *The Good Mother*, dir. Leonard Nimoy. *St. Petersburg Times* 4 Nov. 1988, sec. Weekend: 6.

Smith, Steven Cole. "Review: HBO Chooses a Losing Ticket with *Running Mates*." *Orange County Register* 2 Oct. 1992, sec. P: 44.

"Snippets." Rev. of Music in *First Wives Club*, dir. Hugh Wilson. *Houston Chronicle* 7 Oct. 1996, sec. Houston: 2.

Solomon, Harvey. "Television: Keaton Sees Warmth in *Northern Lights*." *Boston Herald* 20 Aug. 1997, sec. Features: 42.

"Songs of Empowerment from *First Wives Club*." *Plain Dealer* 24 Sep. 1996, sec. E: 3.

Soter, Tom. Rev. of *Marvin's Room*, dir. Jerry Zaks. *Video* 21.4 (1997): 75.

Spignesi, Stephen J. *The Woody Allen Companion*. Kansas City: Andrews and Mc-Meel, 1992.

Sragow, Michael. "Super Keaton, Fine Finney *Shoot the Moon*." *Rolling Stone* 18 Feb. 1982: 27.

Stack, Peter. "*Father of the Bride* Married to a Formula." *San Francisco Chronicle* 8 Dec. 1995, sec. C: 1.

Stanbrook, Alan. "Film Choice: A 'Transplendent' Comedy." *Sunday Telegraph* 19 Jul. 1992: 123.

Stark, John. "*Heaven* Can Wait." *People* 4 Mar. 1985: 122.

Stark, Susan. "Heart-Felt Drama Clings to Its Family Roots." Rev. of *Unstrung Heroes*, dir. Diane Keaton. *Detroit News* 22 Sep. 1995, sec. Screens.

____. "Plain and Simple, Keaton and Streep Can Still Light Up *Marvin's Room*." *Detroit News* 28 Feb. 1997, sec. D: 1.

____. "*Wives* Offers More Interest in How Its Stars Duke It Out." *Detroit News* 4 Oct. 1996, sec. E: 1.

Steffan, Janine Dallas. "Star Watcher." *Seattle Times* 24 Jan. 1997, sec. F: 1.

Stein, Joe. Rev. of *Wildflower*, dir. Diane Keaton. *San Diego Union-Tribune* 3 Dec. 1991, sec. D: 6.

Stein, Ruthe. "'Annie Hall' Goes Behind the Camera." *San Francisco Chronicle* 12 Sep. 1995, sec. E: 1.

Sterritt, David. "Actress Tess Harper Welcomes Today's Meatier Roles for Women." *Christian Science Monitor* 28 Jan. 1987, sec. Arts and Leisure: 22.

____. "The Americans Make a Return to High Profile at Cannes." *Christian Science Monitor* 26 May 1995, sec. 10: 2.

____. "Freeze Frames." Rev. of *Crimes of the Heart*, dir. Bruce Beresford. *Christian Science Monitor* 12 Dec. 1986, sec. Arts and Leisure: 35.

____. *Good Mother*: The Film Is as Controversial as the Book." *Christian Science Monitor* 4 Nov. 1988, sec. Arts and Leisure: 23.

____. "Woody Allen's Evocative *Radio Days*." *Christian Science Monitor* 30 Jan. 1987, sec. Arts and Leisure: 23.

Stesin, Nancy. "Baby Boom, Part Two." *Working Woman* 19.1 (1994): 60.

Stewart, Susan. "Script Sends *Amelia Earhart* into a Tailspin." *Detroit News & Free Press* 12 Jun. 1994, sec. G: 3.

Steyn, Mark. "Fading Stars." Rev. of *The First Wives Club*, dir. Hugh Wilson. *The Spectator* 277.878 (1996): 62–63.

Stiller, Ben. "She's the One." *Premiere*: Special Issue 1997: 76.

Stone, Jay. "*Father of the Bride: Part II* Delivers Babies, but Few Laughs." *Ottawa Citizen* 8 Dec. 1995, sec. C: 14.

____. "Return of the *Godfather*: Re-released Classic Shines as a Cinematic Touchstone." *Ottawa Citizen* 31 Jul. 1997, sec. F: 1.

____. "These Odd Heroes Can Unstring Audience." *Ottawa Citizen* 22 Sep. 1995, sec. B: 10.

Streisand, Barbra. "We Are the Girlz in the Hood." *Premiere*. Women in Hollywood: Special Issue. 1993: 27.

Strickler, Jeff. "*Marvin's Room* Rare Look at Real Love." *Star Tribune* (Minneapolis) 10 Jan. 1997, sec. E: 10.

____. "Movie Novice Kimberly Williams Discovers Hollywood Stars Can Put Their Egos Aside." *The Gazette* (Montreal) 2 Jan. 1992, sec. E: 2.

____. "'Unstrung Heroes' Director, Stars Shine." *Star Tribune* (Minneapolis) 22 Sep, 1995, sec. E: 4.

Stuart, Jan. "The Inexorable Corleone Whirlpool." *Newsday* 24 Dec. 1990, sec. Part II: 39.

"Style Setters 1974–1994." *People* 41.9 (1994): 236–39.

Sumner, Jane. "Keaton Keeps on Blooming." *Dallas Morning News* 12 Jan. 1997, sec. C: 1.

____. "*Marvin's Room*: Stars Cast Warm Light Over Dark Subject." *Dallas Morning News* 10 Jan. 1997, sec. C: 1.

____. Rev. of *First Wives Club*, dir. Hugh Wilson. *Dallas Morning News* 20 Sep. 1996, sec. Guide: 50.

Sunila, Joyce. "Disappointing in Love." Rev. of *Mrs. Soffel*, dir. Gillian Armstrong. *Los Angeles Times* 3 Mar. 1985, sec. Calendar: 34.

Taubman, Leslie. "*The Godfather*." *Magill's Survey of Cinema*. Ed. Frank Magill. Vol. II. Englewood Cliffs: N.J.: Salem Press, 1980, 638–43.

____. "*The Godfather: Part II*." *Magill's Survey of Cinema*. Ed. Frank Magill. Vol. II. Englewood Cliffs: N.J.: Salem Press, 1980, 644–47.

"10 Worst Dressed: Diane Keaton." *Time* 40.17 (1993): 96.

Thomas, Bob. "Diane Keaton Moves Closer to Top Roles." *Courier Journal & Times* 4 Jan. 1976, sec. H: 6.

Thomas, Karen. "Keaton's Age of Anxiety." *USA Today* 18 Dec. 1996, sec. D: 1.

Thomas, Kevin. "HBO's *Running Mates* Funny but Serious, Too." *Los Angeles Times* 3 Oct. 1992, sec. F: 12.

____. "Satire That Lowers the *Baby Boom.*" *Los Angeles Times* 7 Oct. 1987, sec. Calendar: 1.

____. "A Sentimental *Bride II*: Jolly Respite for Holidays." *Los Angeles Times* 8 Dec. 1995, sec. F: 1.

____. "*Thrill* Contemplates Love, Life's Lost Chances." *Los Angeles Times* 6 Mar. 1998, sec. F: 18.

Thompson, Anne. "Diane Keaton Babies Her Expanding Career." *Orange County Register* (California) 7 Oct. 1987, sec. L: 1.

Thompson, David. *Warren Beatty and Desert Eyes: A Life and a Story.* New York: Doubleday, 1987.

Thompson, Frank. "When Actors Take the Chair." *American Film* 15.12 (1990): 52–54.

"Top Five." *Washington Post* 29 Sep. 1983, sec. D: 7.

Travers, Peter. "Annie Small." Rev. of *Manhattan Murder Mystery*, dir. Woody Allen. *Rolling Stone* 2 Sep. 1993: 68–69.

____. "Men Behaving Badly." Rev. of *The First Wives Club*, dir. Hugh Wilson. *Rolling Stone* 3 Oct. 1996: 77–78.

____. Rev. of *Crimes of the Heart*, dir. Bruce Beresford. *People* 15 Dec. 1986: 12.

____. Rev. of *The Good Mother*, dir. Leonard Nimoy. *People* 30.19 (1988): 18.

____. Rev. of *The Little Drummer Girl*, dir. George Roy Hill. *People* 22 Oct. 1984: 10.

Trebbe, Ann. "Keaton on Pacino: 'Bittersweet' End." *USA Today* 18 Dec. 1990, sec. D: 2.

Tryster, Hillel. "*Father of the Bride*, Spencer Tracy He Ain't." *Jerusalem Post* 6 Oct. 1992, sec. Arts.

Tucker, Ken. "A Brood Awakening: Paternity Suits Steve Martin in *Father of the Bride: Part II.*" *Entertainment Weekly* 15 Dec. 1995: 50.

Tulloch, Lee. "Gillian's Island: Director Gillian Armstrong." *Harper's Bazaar* 3375 (1993): 102.

Turan, Kenneth. "Dependence Day." Rev. of *Marvin's Room*, dir. Jerry Zaks. *Los Angeles Times* 18 Dec. 1996, sec. F: 1.

____. "Keaton's Sure Hand Guides *Heroes.*" *Los Angeles Times* 15 Sep. 1995, sec. F: 1.

____. "Lights, Action, Keaton." *Los Angeles Times* 22 May 1995, sec. F: 1.

____. "No Fury Like 3 Ex-Wives Getting Even." *Newsday* 20 Sep. 1996, sec. B: 2.

Turgenev, Ivan. *Fathers and Sons.* Trans. George Reavey. New York: Signet, 1862.

Ueghing, Mark D. "Annie Hall as Yuppie with Kid." *Newsweek* 26 Jan. 1987: 84.

Upchurch, Michael. "*The Lemon Sisters* Definitely Leaves a Sour Taste." *Seattle Times* 1 Sep. 1990, sec. C: 5.

____. "There Goes the *Bride.*" Rev. of *Father of the Bride*, dir. Charles Shyer. *Seattle Times* 20 Dec. 1991, sec. Tempo: 24.

Unstrung Heroes. Dir. Diane Keaton. With Andie McDowell and John Turturro. Hollywood Pictures, 1995.

Vancheri, Barbara. "Doggie Chatter." Rev. of *Look Who's Talking Now*, dir. Tom Ropelewski. *Pittsburgh Post-Gazette* 5 Nov. 1993, sec. Entertainment: 5.

____. "The Lighter Side of Woody." Rev. of *Manhattan Murder Mystery*, dir. Woody Allen. *Pittsburgh Post-Gazette* 3 Sep. 1993, sec. Entertainment: 4.

Vaughan, Bonnie. "Time to Put Gender on the Agenda." *Guardian* (Manchester) 12 Mar. 1992, sec. 31: 2.

Verniere, James. "Movies: Comic Pablum." Rev. of *Father of the Bride: Part II*, dir. Charles Shyer. *Boston Herald* 8 Dec. 1995, sec. S: 3.

____. "Movies: *Unstrung Heroes* Takes Its Disarmingly Simple Direction from Keaton." *Boston Herald* 15 Sep. 1995, sec. S: 1.

Warick, C. "Reviews." Rev. of *The Good Mother*, starring Diane Keaton. *Us* 3.90 (1985): 66.

"Warren Beatty Film May Co-Star Ex-Lover Diane Keaton." *Arizona Republic*, 12 Feb. 1998: 32.

Waxman, Sharon. "Role Reversal: Women Become More of a Force in Film." *Washington Post* 4 Mar. 1997, sec. B: 7.

"The Way We Were." *The Movies.* Nov. 1983: 23.

"Weekend Birthdays." *The Guardian* (London) 4 Jan. 1997, sec. Features: 17.

Weis, Susan L. "Mother & Lover." Rev. of *The Good Mother*, dir. Leonard Nimoy. *Jerusalem Post* 28 Feb. 1989, sec. Entertainment.

Welsh, James M. Rev. of *Manhattan Murder Mystery*, dir. Woody Allen. *Films in Review* 44.11–12 (1993): 413–14.

Werts, Diane. "Cable Runs Its Own Slates." Rev. of *Running Mates*, dir. Michael Lindsay-Hogg. *Newsday* 29 Sep. 1992, sec. Part II: 53.

Westbrook, Bruce. "For the Love of a *Thrill*." Rev. of *The Only Thrill*, dir. Peter Masterson. *Houston Chronicle* 8 Feb. 1998, sec. Z: 7.

____. "Keaton Says *Wives* Fun, Not Spiteful." *Houston Chronicle* 15 Sep. 1996, sec. Zest: 9.

____. "Made in Texas." Rev. of *The Only Thrill*, dir. Peter Masterson. *Houston Chronicle* 10 Dec. 1996, sec. Houston: 1.

Wheeler, Drew. Rev. of *Heaven*, dir. Diane Keaton. *Video Magazine* 12.7 (1988): 76.

____. Rev. of *Manhattan Murder Mystery*, dir. Woody Allen. *Billboard* 5 Feb. 1994: 74.

White, Diane. "For Actresses, It's an Old Story." *Boston Globe* 6 Sep. 1993, sec. Living: 37.

Wildflower. Dir. Diane Keaton. With Patricia Arquette. The Lifetime Channel, 3 Dec. 1991.

Wilkens, John. "Out of Control: When Sex Becomes an Addiction, It's Time to Take the Twelve Steps." *San Diego Union-Tribune* 24 Feb. 1998, sec. E: 1.

Willens, Michele. "Cover Story: A Different Diane." Rev. of *Running Mates*, dir. Michael Lindsay-Hogg. *Los Angeles Times* 4 Oct. 1992, sec. TV Times: 4.

Williams, Christian. "*Reds*: Warren Beatty's Mysterious Movies Is Hollywood's Best Kept Secret." *Washington Post* 30 Nov. 1981, sec. B: 1.

Williams, Jeannie. "Subbing for Mia: Keaton at Work with Woody." *USA Today* 15 Sep. 1992, sec. D: 2.

Williamson, Bruce. Rev. of *Heaven*, dir. Diane Keaton. *Playboy* 34 (1987): 17.

____. Rev. of *Mrs. Soffel*, dir. Gillian Armstrong. *Playboy* 32 (1985): 32.

____. Rev. of *The Lemon Sisters*, dir. Joyce Chopra. *Playboy* 37.11 (1990): 24.

____. Rev. of *The Little Drummer Girl*, dir. George Roy Hill. *Playboy* 32 (1985): 42.

____. Rev. of *Unstrung Heroes*, dir. Diane Keaton. *Playboy* 42.11 (1995): 22.

Willman, Chris. "Keaton's Touching *Wildflower* on Lifetime." *Los Angeles Times* 3 Dec. 1991, sec. F: 7.

Wilmer, Norman. "Francis Ford Coppola." *Toronto Star* 5 Oct 1991, sec. S: 12.

Wilmington, Michael. "*The Lemon Sisters* Sinks Despite Its Able Cast." *Los Angeles Times* 31 Aug. 1990, sec. F: 6.

____. "More Gal Pals." Rev. of *First Wives Club*, dir. Hugh Wilson. *Chicago Tribune* 20 Sep. 1996, sec. CN: C.

____. "Pop Psychology: *Father Part II* Bounces Pointlessly Around the Boomers' Generation Gap." *Chicago Tribune* 8 Dec. 1995, sec. CN: C.

____. "Wedding Bell Blues for Martin." Rev. of *Father of the Bride*, dir. Charles Shyer. *Los Angeles Times* 20 Dec. 1991, sec. F: 16.

Wilson, Earl. "Diane: 'Woody? We're Just Film-Mates.'" *New York Post* 21 Jun. 1975: 18.

Winslow, Harriet. "Keaton Takes a Spin as Amelia Earhart." *The Washington Post* 12 Jun. 1994, sec. Y: 7.

Wloszczyna, Susan. "A Little Twist of *Lemon* Is Plenty." *USA Today* 5 Sep. 1990, sec. D: 2.

____. "*Robo 3*: Out on a Limp: Third *Look Who's Talking* Lacks Voice." *USA Today* 5 Nov. 1993.

____. "Winningly Weary Performance Illuminates *Marvin's Room*." *USA Today* 18 Dec. 1996, sec. D: 1.

____. "*Wives*: Feisty Femmes." *USA Today* 20 Sep. 1996, sec. D: 1.

Wolff, Isabel. "Was Amelia a Flying Spy?" *The Daily Telegraph* (London) 4 Aug. 1997, sec. Features: 11.

"Women in Hollywood: A Timeline." *Premiere*. Women in Hollywood: Special Issue, 1993: 52–57.

Worth, Larry. "Diane: 50 and Loving It." *New York Post* 14 Dec. 1996: 23.

Wrightson, Jane. "Slice-of-Life Look at Divided Family." Rev. of *Marvin's Room*, dir. Jerry Zaks. *Evening Post* (Wellington) 17 Jul. 1997, sec. Features: 18.

Wuntch, Philip. "*Godfather* Can Still Exert Its Vito Power." *Dallas Morning News* 21 Mar. 1997, sec. C: 2.

____. "Maverick Filmmaker Richard Brooks Makes Movies with Mind of His Own." *Chicago Tribune* 16 Feb. 1986, sec. C: 18.

____. Rev. of *Unstrung Heroes*. *Dallas Morning News* 22 Sep. 1995, sec. Guide: 46.

____. "*Unstrung Heroes*: Tightly Wound Direction Tames Emotional Plot." *Dallas Morning News* 22 Sep. 1995, sec. C: 1.

____. "Wuntch's Classics." Rev. of *Looking for Mr. Goodbar*, dir. Richard Brooks. *Dallas Morning News* 8 May 1994, sec. TV Magazine: 46.

Zaslow, Jeffrey. "Diane Keaton: 'Realize You Can't Have Everything.'" *USA Weekend* 10 Dec. 1995: 18.

Index